HISTORY AND RELATED DISCIPLINES
SELECT BIBLIOGRAPHIES
GENERAL EDITOR: R. C. RICHARDSON

BRITISH WOMEN'S HISTORY

This wide-ranging bibliography provides the only up-to-date guide to the burgeoning work on the history of women in Britain from c. 500 AD to the present day.

The new approaches of feminist and women's history are covered in an extensive methodological section dealing with concepts, problems, historiography and sources. Traditional concerns such as women and family; women and education; women, politics and power; women and religion; feminism and all aspects of women's work are well represented. In addition, attention is paid to more recent developments in women's history, such as women's sexuality, women and crime, prostitution, women's biography and autobiography and women's involvement with the wider world as travellers and emigrants.

June Hannam is Principal Lecturer in History at the University of the West of England, Bristol, Ann Hughes is Professor of Early Modern History at the University of Keele and Pauline Stafford is Professor of History at the University of Huddersfield.

HISTORY AND RELATED DISCIPLINES
SELECT BIBLIOGRAPHIES
GENERAL EDITOR: R. C. RICHARDSON

Bibliographical guides designed to meet the needs of under-graduates, postgraduates and their teachers in universities and colleges of higher education. All volumes in the series share a number of common characteristics. They are selective, manageable in size, and include those books and articles which are most important and useful. All volumes are edited by practising teachers of the subject and are based on their experience of the needs of students. The arrangement combines chronological with thematic divisions. Many of the items listed receive some descriptive comment.

Already published in the series:

EUROPEAN ECONOMIC AND SOCIAL HISTORY

THE STUDY OF HISTORY

SOCIETY AND ECONOMY IN EARLY MODERN EUROPE

BRITISH AND IRISH ARCHAEOLOGY

AFRICA, ASIA AND SOUTH AMERICA SINCE 1800

WESTERN POLITICAL THOUGHT: POST-WAR RESEARCH

ANCIENT GREECE AND ROME

BRITISH ECONOMIC AND SOCIAL HISTORY

UNITED STATES HISTORY

JAPANESE STUDIES

BRITISH WOMEN'S HISTORY
A BIBLIOGRAPHICAL GUIDE

COMPILED BY

JUNE HANNAM, ANN HUGHES
AND PAULINE STAFFORD

MANCHESTER UNIVERSITY PRESS
Manchester and New York

Distributed exclusively in the USA and Canada by St. Martin's Press

Copyright © June Hannam, Ann Hughes and Pauline Stafford 1996

Published by
MANCHESTER UNIVERSITY PRESS
Oxford Road, Manchester M13 9NR, UK
and Room 400, 175 Fifth Avenue, New York
NY 10010, USA
Distributed exclusively in the USA and Canada by
St. Martin's Press, Inc., 175 Fifth Avenue, New York
NY 10010, USA

British Library Cataloguing-in-Publication Data
A catalogue record for this book is available from the
British Library

Library of Congress Cataloging-in-Publication Data
Hannam, June, 1947–
    British women's history : a bibliographical guide / compiled by
June Hannam, Ann Hughes, and Pauline Stafford.
        p.   cm. — (History and related disciplines select
bibliographies)
    Includes index.
    ISBN 0-7190-4652-1
    1. Women—Great Britain—History—Bibliography.   I. Hughes, Ann,
1951– . II. Stafford, Pauline. III. Title IV. Series.
Z7964.G7H36   1996
[HQ1593]
016.3054′0941—dc20
                                                                              95-1038
                                                                              CIP

ISBN 0 7190 4652 1 *hardback*

Photoset in Linotron Plantin
by Northern Phototypesetting Co. Ltd, Bolton

Printed in Great Britain
by Cromwell Press Ltd, Broughton Gifford

CONTENTS

CONTENTS

GENERAL EDITOR'S PREFACE

History, to an even greater extent than most other academic disciplines, has developed at a prodigious pace in the twentieth century. Its scope has extended and diversified, its methodologies have been revolutionised, its philosophy has changed, and its relations with other disciplines have been transformed. The number of students and teachers of the subject in the different branches of higher education has vastly increased, and there is an ever-growing army of amateurs, many of them taking adult education courses. Academic and commercial publishers have produced a swelling stream of publications – both specialist and general – to cater for this large and expanding audience. Scholarly journals have proliferated. It is no easy matter even for specialists to keep abreast of the flow of publications in their particular field. For those with more general academic interests the task of finding what has been written on different subject areas can be time-consuming, perplexing, and often frustrating.

It is primarily to meet the needs of undergraduates, postgraduates and their teachers in universities and colleges of higher education, that this series of bibliographies is designed. It will be a no less valuable resource, however, to the reference collection of any public library, school or college.

Though common sense demands that each volume will be structured in the way which is most appropriate for the particular field in question, nonetheless all volumes in the series share a number of important common characteristics. First – quite deliberately – all are *select* bibliographies, manageable in size, and include those books and articles which in the editor's judgement are most important and useful. To attempt an uncritically comprehensive listing would needlessly dictate the inclusion of items which were frankly ephemeral, antiquarian, or discredited and result only in the production of a bulky and unwieldy volume. Like any select bibliography, however, volumes in this series will direct the reader where appropriate to other, more specialised and detailed sources of bibliographical information. That would be one of their functions. Second, all the volumes are edited not simply by specialists in the different fields but by practising teachers of the subject, and are based on their experience of the needs of students in higher education. Third, there are common features of arrangement and presentation. All volumes begin with listings of general works of a methodological or historiographical nature, and proceed within broad chronological divisions to arrange their material thematically. Most items will receive some descriptive comment. Each volume, for ease of reference, has an index of authors and editors.

R. C. RICHARDSON

PREFACE

This bibliography covers the history of British women from the Middle Ages to the present day. Its geographical focus is Britain, including Ireland. Where appropriate, reference has been made to work whose geographical focus is wider, particularly where this provides insights into areas not yet covered in British-centred work, or in areas such as the history of ideas where geographical boundaries do not always seem appropriate. It is confined almost exclusively to work written in English, and all works are published in Britain unless otherwise indicated. Pauline Stafford was responsible for the medieval section, Ann Hughes for the early modern and June Hannam for the modern; all three editors contributed to the general and methodological sections.

No attempt has been made at comprehensiveness. Instead, the editors have used a number of criteria for selection: to ensure breadth of coverage; to be up-to-date but not at the expense of important and still relevant earlier work, and to give a guide to the concerns of the current burgeoning work of women's historians. The aim is to provide a bibliography which will be useful firstly to those wishing to produce courses in women's history, or to bring women's history into existing courses at further and higher education level, secondly to students seeking bibliographical guidance for theses, projects and similar work, and thirdly to those with an amateur interest in women's history. It

cannot pretend to be a detailed guide for those at more advanced stages of research in women's history, though it is hoped that these too will benefit from its wide range and methodological concerns.

The bibliography covers material published before the end of 1992. Although some work published in 1993 or 1994 has been included, the work for this bibliography was essentially completed by autumn 1993; given the delay in publication of many journals, this means that no claim is made for complete coverage of items appearing in 1993.

The material has been organised into three broad chronological periods: $c. 500–c. 1500; c. 1500–c. 1800; c. 1800$ to the present. The boundaries of these periods are permeable, and users should be ready to cross them, especially if their interests lie at their margins. Users are strongly encouraged to use the general and methodological sections at the beginning whatever their specific period of interest. No attempt has been made to divide these works among the three periods, on the grounds that knowledge of the theoretical approaches is now essential for all historians working on women's history in whatever period. Each period begins with a General section. This includes general surveys, and other work covering more than one aspect of the period. The "General" works are not necessarily cross-referenced under subsequent subject headings, and users are encouraged to consult the General section.

The same major subject divisions have been maintained across the three periods. This is designed to facilitate use by those interested in a long overview of a particular topic, in the belief that certain major themes are important in all periods of women's history. It has also encouraged the editors, and hopefully will encourage users, to draw inspiration from thematisations not always familiar to their own period. At the same time subdivisions have been changed from period to period to reflect the different concerns of historians and the varying experiences of women. The large number of divisions and subdivisions is designed to facilitate use. It has thus not been felt necessary to annotate all entries, since in most cases their categorisation plus title should enable the user to determine their content and utility. Debates and seminal items have, however, been flagged.

Cross-references have been made, but cannot be exhaustive. In the Modern section, for example, there is much on midwifery in the section on childbirth and motherhood not all of which has been cross-referenced to "Professions". Users are encouraged to browse widely.

Major collections of printed sources are indicated in the "Methodology" section or cross-referenced there. Many other useful printed sources are included within specific sections.

No attempt has been made to include all the important work on women's writing which has recently been produced by literary scholars. Editors have attempted to give some guidance to major recent work here, particularly where it has a historical slant. However, as practising historians they are aware of a degree of arbitrariness in the choice of items in this area.

The editors are aware that the use of the term "feminism" as a subject heading for the sixteenth and seventeenth century is contentious and that many of the works here cited might be challenged for conceptual confusion. It was nonetheless decided to retain it, not least on the grounds that users should have the opportunity of deciding for themselves.

Finally we would like to thank Norma Peel without whose efforts as an editorial assistant this work would have been much delayed; the University of Huddersfield for providing financial assistance for this editorial work and for the patience of its library and inter-library loan staff in chasing up references; and Dirk Wilkinson who caught the final ones which almost got away.

ABBREVIATIONS

Agric. H. R.   Agricultural History Review
Am. H. R.   American Historical Review
Am. J. Comp. Law   American Journal of Comparative Law
Am. J. Legal Hist.   American Journal of Legal History
Am. J. Soc.   American Journal of Sociology
Ampleforth J.   Ampleforth Journal
Anglican and Ecumenical Hist.   Anglican and Ecumenical History
Annals Am. Acad. Pol. Soc. Sci.   Annals of the American Academy of Political and Social Science
Antiquaries J.   Antiquaries Journal
Arch. J.   Archaeological Journal
Art Hist.   Art History
Australian Ec. H. R.   Australian Economic History Review
Australian Fem. Studs.   Australian Feminist Studies
Auto/Biog. Studs.   AB – Auto/Biographical Studies
B. A. R.   British Archaeological Reports
B. J. Ed. Studs.   British Journal of Educational Studies
Baptist Q.   Baptist Quarterly
Brit. J. Hist. Sc.   British Journal for the History of Science
Brit. J. Sociol.   British Journal of Sociology
Brit. J. Sports Hist.   British Journal of Sports History
Brit. Lib. J.   British Library Journal

Brit. ser.   British series
Brontë Scy. Trans.   Brontë Society Transactions
Bull. Bd. Celt. Studs.   Bulletin of the Board of Celtic Studies
Bull.   Bulletin
Bull. Hist. Ed. Scy.   Bulletin of the History of Education Society
Bull. Hist. Medicine   Bulletin of the History of Medicine
Bull. Inst. Hist. Res.   Bulletin of the Institute of Historical Research
Bull. J. Ryl. Lib.   Bulletin of the John Rylands Library
Bull. N. W. Labour Hist. Scy.   Bulletin of the North West Labour History Society
Bull. Soc. Hist. Medicine   Bulletin of the Social History of Medicine
Bus. Ec. Hist.   Business and Economic History
Business Hist.   Business History
Cambridge Hist. J.   Cambridge Historical Journal
Cambridge J. Ec.   Cambridge Journal of Economics
Cambridge Law J.   Cambridge Law Journal
Camden Scy.   Camden Society
Can. J. Hist.   Canadian Journal of History
Catholic H. R.   Catholic Historical Review
Chaucer Rev.   Chaucer Review
Church Hist.   Church History
Colby Q.   Colby Quarterly

Comp. Studs. Soc. and Hist.   Comparative Studies in Society and History
Contemporary R.   Contemporary Review
Cont. and Change   Continuity and Change
Crim. Justice Hist.   Criminal Justice History
Crim. Law R.   Criminal Law Review
Dev. and Change   Development and Change
Downside R.   Downside Review
Dublin Hist. Rec.   Dublin Historical Record
Dumfriesshire and Galloway Nat. Hist. Antiq. Scy. Trans.   Dumfriesshire and Galloway Natural History and Antiquarian Society Transactions
Ec. Pol. Weekly   Economic and Political Weekly
Economic H. R.   Economic History Review
Ec. J.   Economic Journal
Edn.   Edition
Eighteenth Cent. Life   Eighteenth Century Life
Eighteenth Cent. Studs.   Eighteenth Century Studies
Eng. H. R.   English Historical Review
Eng. Lang. Notes   English Language Notes
Eng. Lit. Hist.   English Literary History
Eng. Lit. in Trans.   English Literature in Transition
Eng. Lit. Ren.   English Literary Renaissance
Eng. Studs. English Studies
Essex Arch. Scy. Trans.   Essex Archaeological Society Transactions
Fam. Hist.   Family History
Fem. R.   Feminist Review
Fem. Studs.   Feminist Studies
Folk. For.   Folklore Forum
Gend. and Ed.   Gender and Education
Gend. and Hist.   Gender and History
Geographical J.   Geographical Journal
Govern. and Opp.   Government and Opposition
Harvard Law R.   Harvard Law Review
Harvard Lib. Bull.   Harvard Library Bulletin
Haskins Soc. J.   Haskins Society Journal
Hist. and Theory   History and Theory
Hist. Child. Q.   History of Childhood Quarterly
Hist. Ed.   History of Education

Hist. Ed. Q.   History of Eucation Quarterly
Hist. Ed. R.   History of Education Review
Hist. Ed. Scy. Bull   History of Education Society Bulletin
Hist. European Ideas   History of European Ideas
Hist.   History
Hist. J.   Historical Journal
Hist. Meths.   Historical Methods
Hist. Pol. Thought   History of Political Thought
Hist. Res.   Historical Research
Hist. Studs.   Historical Studies
Hist. Today   History Today
Hist. Universities   History of the Universities
Hist. Workshop J.   History Workshop Journal
Hon. Scy. Cymmrodorion Trans.   Honourable Society of Cymmrodorion Transactions
Hum. Biol.   Human Biology
Hunt. Lib. Q.   Huntington Library Quarterly
Int. H. R.   International History Review
Int. J. Hist. Sport   International Journal of the History of Sport
Int. J. Women's Studs.   International Journal of Women's Studies
Int. Labor and Working-Class Hist.   International Labor and Working-Class History
Int. Migration R.   International Migration Review
Int. R. Soc. Hist.   International Review of Social History
Intro.   Introduction
Irish Ec. Soc. Hist. J.   Irish Economic and Social History Journal
Irish Ed. Studs.   Irish Educational Studies
Irish Hist. Studs.   Irish Historical Studies
Irish Hist. Workshop   Irish History Workshop
Irish Jurist   The Irish Jurist
J. African Hist.   Journal of African History
J. Am. Hist.   Journal of American History
J. Australasian Univ. Lang. and Lit. Assoc.   Journal of the Australasian Universities Language and Literature

Association

J. Brit. Studs. Journal of British Studies

J. Contemp. Hist. Journal of Contemporary History

J. Decorative and Propaganda Arts Journal of Decorative and Propaganda Arts

J. Ec. Hist. Journal of Economic History

J. Ecc. Hist. Journal of Ecclesiastical History

J. Ed. Am. and Hist. Journal of Educational Administration and History

J. European Ec. Hist. Journal of European Economic History

J. European Hist. Journal of European History

J. Fam. Hist. Journal of Family History

J. Friends Hist. Scy. Journal of the Friends Historical Society

J. Hist. Biol. Journal of the History of Biology

J. Hist. Ideas Journal of the History of Ideas

J. Hist. Medicine Journal of the History of Medicine

J. Hist. Sexuality Journal of the History of Sexuality

J. Hist. Sociol. Journal of Historical Sociology

J. Imp. Commonwealth Hist. Journal of Imperial and Commonwealth History

J. Interdis. Hist. Journal of Interdisciplinary History

J. Irish Labour Hist. Scy. Journal of the Irish Labour History Society

J. Journal

J. Legal Hist. Journal of Legal History

J. Marr. and Fam. Journal of Marriage and the Family

J. Med. and Ren. Studs. Journal of Medieval and Renaissance Studies

J. Med. Hist. Journal of Medieval History

J. Mod. Hist. Journal of Modern History

J. Pacific Hist. Journal of Pacific History

J. Pop. Cult. Journal of Popular Culture

J. Psychohist. Journal of Psychohistory

J. Reg. Local Studs. Journal of Regional and Local Studies

J. Religion Journal of Religion

J. Religious Hist. Journal of Religious History

J. Rocky Mountain Med. and Ren. Assoc. Journal of the Rocky Mountain Medieval and Renaissance Association

J. Royal Soc. Antiq. Ireland Journal of the Royal Society of Antiquaries of Ireland

J. Scot. Labour Hist. Scy. Journal of the Scottish Labour History Society

J. Soc. Hist. Journal of Social History

J. Soc. Pol. Journal of Social Policy

J. South African Studs. Journal of South African Studies

J. Sports Hist. Journal of Sports History

J. Women's Hist. Journal of Women's History

Jewish Q. Jewish Quarterly

Labor Hist. Labor History

Law H. R. Law and History Review

Law Q. R. Law Quarterly Review

Leic. Arch. and Local Hist. Scy. Trans. Leicestershire Archaeological and Local Historical Society Transactions

Lincs. Hist. Arch. Lincolnshire History and Archaeology

Lit. and Hist. Literature and History

Local Histn. Local Historian

Local Pop. Studs. Local Population Studies

London Arch. London Archaeologist

London J. The London Journal

McMaster Uty. Assoc. for Eighteenth Century Studs. McMaster University Association for Eighteenth Century Studies

Med. et Hum. Medievalia et Humanistica

Med. Fem. News. Medieval Feminist Newsletter

Med. Hist. Medieval History

Med. Prosopog. Medieval Prosopography

Med. Scandinavia Medieval Scandinavia

Med. Studs. Medieval Studies

Medical Biol. Illus. Medical and Biological Illustrations

Medical Hist. Medical History

Mid. Hist. Midland History

Mod. Lit. Q. Modern Literature Quarterly

N. E. Gp. Study Labour Hist. North East Group for the Study of Labour History

N. Staffs. J. Field Studs. North

Staffordshire Journal of Field Studies

N. W. Gp. Study Labour Hist. North West Group for the Study of Labour History

Nat. Lib. Wales J. National Library of Wales Journal

New Left R. New Left Review

New ser. New series

North. Hist. Northern History

Northamptonshire P. P. Northamptonshire Past and Present

Nottingham Med. Studs. Nottingham Medieval Studies

Old ser. Old series

Ontario Hist. Ontario History

Oral H. R. Oral History Review

Oral Hist. Oral History

Orig. ser. Original series

Ox. R. Ed. Oxford Review of Education

P. P. Past and Present

Pacific H. R. Pacific History Review

Papers in Ling. Papers in Linguistics

Papers on Lang. and Lit. Papers on Language and Literature

Parl. Hist. Parliamentary History

Pcdgs. Am. Philos. Scy. Proceedings of the American Philosophical Society

Pcdgs. Brit. Acad. Proceedings of the British Academy

Pcdgs. Proceedings

Pcdgs. Royal Soc. Medicine Proceedings of the Royal Society of Medicine

Pcdgs. Wesley Hist. Scy. Proceedings of the Wesley Historical Society

Peasant Studs. Peasant Studies

Philos. Philosophy

Pol. and Soc. Politics and Society

Pol. Studs. Political Studies

Political Q. Political Quarterly

Pop. Dev. Rev. Population and Development Review

Pop. Studs. Population Studies

Prose Studs. Prose Studies

Publications Mod. Lang. Assoc. Publications of the Modern Language Association

Publishing Hist. Publishing History

Q. Quarterly

Quaker Hist. Quaker History

R. Rad. Pol. Ec. Review of Radical Political Economy

R. Review

Radical H. R. Radical History Review

Recusant Hist. Recusant History

Ren. and Ref. Renaissance and Reformation

Renaissance Q. Renaissance Quarterly

Rev. Edn. Revised edition

Ricardian The Ricardian

Royal Arch. Inst. G.B. and Ireland Royal Archaeological Institute of Great Britain and Ireland

Rural Hist. Rural History

Science and Soc. Science and Society

Scot. Ec. Soc. Hist. Scottish Economic and Social History

Scot. Gaelic Studies Scottish Gaelic Studies

Scot. H. R. Scottish Historical Review

Scy. Study Labour Hist. Society for the Study of Labour History

Sec. ser. Second series

Ser. Series

Seventeenth Cent. The Seventeenth Century

Shakespeare Q. Shakespeare Quarterly

Sixteenth Cent. Bib. Sixteenth Century Bibliography

Sixteenth Cent. J. Sixteenth Century Journal

Soc. Hist. Medicine Social History of Medicine

Soc. Hist. Social History

Soc. Sc. Hist. Social Science History

Soc. Sc. Q. Social Science Quarterly

Sociolog. R. Sociological Review

South. Hist. Southern History

Studs in Ren. Studies in the Renaissance

Studs. Eighteenth Cent. Cult. Studies in Eighteenth Century Culture

Studs. in Eng. Studies in English

Studs. Med. Cult. Studies in Medieval Culture

Studs. Phil. Studies in Philology

Studs. Studies

Suffolk R. Suffolk Review

Sussex Arch. Colls. Sussex Archaeological Collections

T. R. H. S. Transactions of the Royal

Historical Society

Textile Hist. Textile History

Theatre R. Theatre Review

Trans. Arch. Scy. Worcs. Transactions of the Archaeological Society of Worcestershire

Trans. Cumb. West. Antiq. Arch. Soc. Transactions of the Cumberland and Westmorland Antiquarian and Archaeological Society

Trans. East Riding Antiq. Soc. Transactions of the East Riding Antiquarian Society

Trans. Hist. Scy. Lancs. Ches. Transactions of the Historical Society of Lancashire and Cheshire

Trans. Hunter Arch. Scy. Transactions of the Hunter Archaeological Society

Ulster J. Arch. Ulster Journal of Archaeology

Univ. Edinburgh J. University of Edinburgh Journal

Urban Hist. Yearbk. Urban History Yearbook

Vict. News. Victorian Newsletter

Vict. Period. R. Victorian Periodicals Review

Vict. Studs. News. Victorian Studies Newsletter

Vict. Studs. Victorian Studies

Welsh H. R. Welsh History Review

Western Pol. Q. Western Political Quarterly

Westminster Studs. Ed. Westminster Studies in Education

Wm. and Mary Q. William and Mary Quarterly

Women and Lit. Women and Literature

Women's Art. J. Women's Art Journal

Women's H. R. Women's History Review

Women's Studs. Int. For. Women's Studies International Forum

Women's Studs. Int. Q. Women's Studies International Quarterly

Women's Studs. Q. Women's Studies Quarterly

Women's Studs. Women's Studies

Yale R. Yale Review

Yorks. Arch. J. Yorkshire Archaeological Journal

1

GENERAL SURVEYS

1.1 **Anderson**, B. S. and **Zinsser**, J. P., *A History of Their Own: Women in Europe from Prehistory to the Present*, 2 vols. (1990). Wide-ranging comparative study.

1.2 **Bridenthal**, R., **Koonz**, C., **Stuard**, S., eds., *Becoming Visible: Women in European History*, completely rev. sec. edn. (Boston, Mass., 1987). First edn. (Boston, Mass., 1977), eds. Bridenthal and Koonz. Essays on varied aspects of women's social, political and economic activities in selected European countries, from the earliest times to the twentieth century. Significant changes in the sec. edn.

1.3 **Crawford**, P., ed., *Exploring Women's Past. Essays in Social History* (1983). Essays on Britain and Australia from the early modern period onwards.

1.4 **Devine**, T. M. and **Mitchison**, R., eds., *People and Society in Scotland*, (1988).

1.5 **Leggett**, J., *Local Heroines: a women's history gazetteer of Scotland, England and Wales* (1988). Useful for field trips.

1.6 **Lerner**, G., *The Creation of Feminist Consciousness: from the middle ages to 1870*, Women and History, vol. II (1993).

1.7 **Levin**, C. and **Watson**, J., eds., *Ambiguous Realities: women in the Middle Ages and Renaissance* (Detroit, Michigan, 1987).

1.8 **MacCurtain**, M. and **O'Corráin**, D. O., eds., *Women in Irish Society. The Historical Dimension* (Dublin, 1978). Essays on women in Irish society from the earliest times.

1.9 **Marshall**, R. K., *Virgins and Viragos. A History of Women in Scotland from 1080–1980* (1983).

1.10 **Mitchell**, J. and **Oakley**, A., eds., *The Rights and Wrongs of Women* (1976). Collection of essays exploring the rights of women over time.

1.11 **Rowbotham**, S., *Hidden From History: 300 Years of Women's Oppression and the Fight Against It* (1974). Pioneering study of women's history which has become a classic.

1.12 **Stenton**, D. M., *The English Woman in History* (1957, reprinted 1977).

1.13 **Utley**, F. L., *The Crooked Rib: an analytical index to the argument about women in English and Scots literature to the end of the year 1568* (Ohio, 1944, reprinted New York, 1970). An excellent introduction to the debate about women in the Middle Ages and early sixteenth century, followed by an index and analysis of MSS and printed versions of the texts.

1.14 **Vallance**, E., *Europa Biographical Dictionary of British Women* (1983).

See also: 2.61; 2.77.

1

2

METHODOLOGY

(a) HISTORIOGRAPHY AND CHANGING APPROACHES

2.1 **Allan**, J., 'Evidence and silence: feminism and the limits of history', in C. and E. Gross, eds., *Feminist Challenges* (1986), 173–89.

2.2 **Angerman**, A., et al, eds., *Current Issues in Women's History* (1987).

2.3 **Anthias**, F. and **Davis**, Y., 'Contextualising feminism – gender, ethnic and class divisions', *Fem. R.*, 15 (1983), 62–75.

2.4 **Armitage**, S., 'Making the personal political: women's history and oral history', *Oral H. R.*, 17, Fall (1989), 154–64.

2.5 **Auchmuty**, R., **Jeffreys**, S. and **Miller**, E., 'Lesbian history and gay studies: keeping a feminist perspective', *Women's H. R.*, 1.1 (1992), 89–108.

2.6 **Beddoe**, D., 'Towards a Welsh women's history', *Llafur*, 3.2 (1981), 32–8.

2.7 **Bennett**, J. M., ' "History that stands still": women's work in the European past', *Fem. Studs.*, 14.2 (1988), 269–83. Argues that women's work in pre-industrial society was not a rosy picture.

2.8 — 'Women's History: a study in continuity and change', *Women's H. R.*, 2 (1993), 173–184. A reply to Hill 2.52 below; a radical feminist position defended against Hill's socialist–feminist approach.

2.9 — 'Medieval women, modern women: across the great divide', in D. Aers, ed., *Culture and History, 1350–1600; essays on English communities, identities and writing*, (1992), 147–75.

2.10 — 'Comment on Tilly: who asks the questions for women's history?', *Soc. Sc. Hist.*, 13.4 (1989), 471–8.

2.11 — 'Feminism and history', *Gend. and Hist.*, 1.3 (1989), 251–72.

2.12 **Bock**, G., 'Women's history and gender history: aspects of an international debate', *Gend. and Hist.*, 1.1 (1989), 7–30. Excellent survey of recent approaches to women's history, and a significant contribution to the debate about the differences between women's and gender history.

2.13 **Bowles**, G. and **Duelli Klein**, R., *Theories of Women's Studies* (1983).

2.14 **Burton**, A., ' "History is now": feminist theory and the production of historical feminisms', *Women's H. R.*, 1.1 (1992), 25–38.

2.15 **Cant**, B. and **Hemmings**, S., eds., *Radical Records. Thirty Years of Lesbian and Gay History* (1988).

2.16 **Carroll**, B. A., ed., *Liberating Women's History* (Urbana, Illinois, 1976). A collection of articles exploring the theory and practice of women's history in Britain and America.

2.17 **Casey**, K., 'The Cheshire Cat: reconstructing the experience of medieval woman', in B. A. Carroll, ed., *Liberating women's history* (Urbana, Illinois, 1976), 224–49.

2.18 — and **Erickson**, C., 'Women in the middle ages: a working bibliography', *Med. Studs.*, 38 (1976), 340–59.

2.19 **Chandler**, V., 'Gundrada de Warenne and the Victorian gentlemen-scholars', *Southern History*, 12 (1990), 68–81. Nineteenth-century historiography of an eleventh-century woman.

2.20 **Colls**, R., *Feminism and Women's History* (1988).

2.21 **Crosby**, C., *The Ends of History: Victorians and the 'Woman Question'* (1991). Challenges the orthodoxies of the Victorian historical perspective by a reading of selected texts and discusses their significance for writers of women's history.

2.22 **Cullen**, M., 'Women's history in Ireland', in K. Offen, R. R. Pierson and J. Rendall, eds., *Writing Women's History: International Perspectives* (1991), 429–41.

2.23 **Daniels**, K., 'Feminism and social history', *Australian Fem. Studs.*, 1 (1985), 27–40.

2.24 **Davidoff**, L., ' "Adam spoke first and named the orders of the world": masculine and feminine domains in history and sociology', in H. Corr and L. Mamieson, eds., *The Politics of Every Day: Continuity and Change in Work, Labour and the Family* (1990), 229–55.

2.25 **Davin**, A., 'Feminism and labour history', in R. Samuels, ed., *People's History, Socialist Theory* (1981), 176–81. Argues for labour history to include the insights of feminist history.

2.26 — 'Redressing the balance or transforming the art? The British experience' in J. Kleinberg, ed., *Retrieving Women's History* (1988), 60–78.

2.27 — 'Standing on Virginia Woolf's doorstep', *Hist. Workshop J.*, 31 (1991), 73–83.

2.28 — 'Women and history' in M. Wandor, compiled, *The Body Politic: Women's Liberation in Britain, 1969–72* (1972), 215–24. An early attempt to examine the nature and importance of women's history.

2.29 **Davis**, N. Z., 'Women's history in transition: the European case', *Fem. Studs.*, 3 (1975–6), 83–103.

2.30 — 'Women's history as women's education' in N. Z. Davis and J. W. Scott, eds., *Women's History as Women's Education* (Northampton, Mass., 1985).

2.31 **Degler**, C., *Is There a History of Women?* (1975).

2.32 **Doughan**, D., 'The end of women's history? A view from the Fawcett Library', *Women's H. R.*, 1.1 (1992), 131–9.

2.33 **Duberman**, M. B., **Vicinus**, M. and **Chauncy**, G., eds., *Hidden from History: Reclaiming the Gay and Lesbian Past* (1991). Collection of articles, most of which have already been published elsewhere. Covers several continents and a long time period.

2.34 **Echols**, A. and **Williams**, M., eds., *Women in Medieval Times: an annotated bibliography* (Princeton, New Jersey, 1991).

2.35 **Evans**, R. J., 'The history of European women: a critical survey of recent research,' *J. Mod. Hist.*, 52.4 (1980), 656–75.

2.36 — 'Women's history: the limits of reclamation', *Soc. Hist.*, 5.2 (1980), 273–81.

2.37 **Feinson**, M. C., 'Where are the women in the history of aging?', *Soc. Sc. Hist.*, 9.4 (1985), 429–52.

2.38 **Ferris**, I., 'From trope to code: the novel and the rhetoric of gender in nineteenth-century critical discourse', in L. M. Shires, ed., *Rewriting the Victorians: Theory, History and the Politics of Gender* (1992), 18–30.

2.39 **Fitzpatrick**, D., 'Review article: women, gender and the writing of Irish History', *Irish Hist. Studs.*, 27 (1991), 267–73.

2.40 **Fox-Genovese**, E., 'Placing women's history in history', *New Left R.*, 133 (May/June, 1982), 5–29.

2.41 **Frantzen**, A. J., 'When women aren't enough', *Speculum*, 68 (1993), 445–71. On gender and medieval studies.

2.42 **Geiger**, S., 'What's so feminist about doing women's oral history?', *J. Women's Hist.*, 2, Spring (1990), 169–82.

2.43 **Gluck**, S. and **Patai**, D., eds., *Women's Words: The Feminist Practice of Oral History* (1991). Articles by US feminists which are self-critical about the practice of oral history.

2.44 **Gordon**, A. D., **Buhle**, M. J. and **Dye**, N. S., 'The problem of women's history', in B. A. Carroll, ed., *Liberating Women's History* (Urbana, Illinois, 1976), 75–92.

2.45 **Gullickson**, G. L., 'Comment on Tilly: women's history, social history and deconstruction', *Soc. Sc. Hist.*, 13.4 (1989), 463–70.

2.46 **Hall**, C., *White, Male and Middle Class: Explorations in Feminism and History* (1992). Key study of gender and race in the nineteenth century.

2.47 **Hammerton**, A. J., 'New trends in the history of working women in Britain', *Labor Hist.*, 31 (1976), 53–60. Discusses recent studies and changing attitudes to the history of working women.

2.48 **Hanawalt**, B., 'Golden ages for the history of medieval English women', in S. Mosher Stuard, ed., *Women in Medieval History and Historiography* (Philadelphia, 1987), 1–24.

2.49 **Harrison**, B., 'Class and gender in modern British labour history', *P. P.*, 124 (1989), 121–58. Long review essay which argues that the social partnership of working-class men and women was reflected politically. Critical of feminist historians who look for divisions between socialism and feminism.

2.50 — and **McMillan**, J., 'Some feminist betrayals of women's history', *Hist. J.*, 26.2 (1983), 375–89.

2.51 **Hartman**, M. and **Banner**, L. W., eds., *Clio's Consciousness Raised: New Perspectives on the History of Women* (1974). Articles on diverse topics in women's history in Britain and America.

2.52 **Hill**, B., 'Women's History: a study in change, continuity or standing still', *Women's H. R.*, 2 (1993), 5–22. A critique of Bennett; see nos. 2.7 and 2.8.

2.53 **History Today**, 'What is Women's History?', *Hist. Today*, 35.6 (1985). Contains responses to this question from a number of historians.

2.54 **Horne**, G., 'The liberation of British and American women's history: a bibliographical essay', *Scy. Study Labour Hist.*, Bull. 26 (1973), 28–39.

2.55 **Howell**, M. C., 'A feminist historian looks at the new historicism: what's so historical about it', *Women's Studs.*, 19.2 (1991), 139–47.

2.56 **Hufton**, O., 'What is women's history?', *Hist.Today*, 35 (June 1985), 38–48.

2.57 — 'Women in History: Early Modern Europe', *P.P.*, 101 (1983), pp. 125–41.

2.58 **Humphries**, J., ' "Lurking in the wings". Women in the historiography of the Industrial Revolution', *Bus. Ec. Hist.*, 20 (1991), 32–44.

2.59 **Johansson**, S. R., ' "Herstory" as history: a new field or another fad?', in B. A. Carroll, ed., *Liberating Women's History* (Urbana, Illinois, 1976), 400–30.

2.60 **Kamester**, M. and **Vellacott**, J., eds., *Militarism vs Feminism. Writings on Women and War* (1987).

2.61 **Kanner**, B., ed., *The Women of England From Anglo-Saxon Times to the Present: Interpretive Bibliographical Essays* (Hamden, Connecticut, 1979 and London, 1980). Examines the methodology of women's history.

2.62 **Kelly-Gadol**, J., 'Did women have a Renaissance', in R. Bridenthal and C. Koonz, eds., *Becoming Visible: Women in European History* (Boston, 1977), 137–64. Europe-wide but a seminal article on the challenge of women's history to traditional periodisations.

2.63 — 'The social relations of the sexes: methodological implications of women's history', *Signs*, 1.4 (1976), 809–24.

2.64 **Kerber**, L. K., 'Separate spheres, female worlds, woman's place: the rhetoric of women's history', *J.Am. Hist.*, 75.1 (1988), 9–39.

2.65 **Kessler Harris**, A., 'Ideologies and innovation: gender dimensions of business history', *Bus. Ec. Hist.*, 20 (1991), 45–51.

2.66 **Kleinberg**, S. J., ed., *Retrieving Women's History. Changing Perceptions of the Role of Women in Politics and Society* (1988). Articles investigating the role of women in ancient and more recent history in both European and non-European countries.

2.67 **Lambertz**, J., 'Feminist history in Britain', *Radical H. R.*, 19, Winter (1978/9), 137–42.

2.68 **Laslett**, B., 'Gender in/and social science history', *Soc. Sc. Hist.*, 16.2 (1992), 177–95.

2.69 **Lerner**, G., *The Majority Finds its Past: Placing Women in History* (1979). An influential contribution to the debate over the relationship of women's history to history.

2.70 — 'Placing women in history: definitions and challenges', *Fem. Studs.*, 3 (1975), 5–14. Revised and reprinted under title, 'Placing women in history: a 1975 perspective', in B. A. Carroll, ed., *Liberating Women's History: Theoretical and Critical Essays* (Urbana, Illinois, 1976), 357–68.

2.71 **Lesbian History Group**, *Not a Passing Phase: Reclaiming Lesbians in History, 1840–1985* (1989).

2.72 **Lewis**, J., 'Women lost and found: the impact of feminism on history', in D. Spender, ed., *Men's Studies Modified: The Impact of Women on the Academic Disciplines* (1981), 55–72.

2.73 **MacCurtain**, M., **O'Dowd**, M., and **Luddy**, M., 'An agenda for women's history in Ireland, 1500–1900', *Irish Hist. Studs.*, 28 (1992), 1–37.

2.74 **Macey**, B., 'Social dynamics of oral history making: women's experiences of wartime',

Oral Hist., 19.2 (1991), 42–8.

2.75 **Mack**, P., 'The history of women in early modern Britain', *Comp. Studs. Soc. and Hist.*, 28 (1986), 715–22.

2.76 **Newton**, J., 'Engendering history for the middle class: sex and political economy in the *Edinburgh Review*', in L. M. Shires, ed., *Rewriting the Victorians: Theory, History and the Politics of Gender* (1992), 1–17.

2.77 **O'Faolain**, J. and **Martines**, L., eds., *Not in God's Image: Women in History* (1973, reprinted 1979). Collection of extracts from contemporary writers on the position of women in European society throughout history.

2.78 **Offen**, K., **Pierson**, R. R. and **Rendall**, J., eds., *Writing Women's History: International Perspectives* (1992). Articles reviewing the 'state of the art' in women's history in a variety of countries.

2.79 **Perrot**, M., ed., trans. Pheasant, F., *A History of Women* (1992). A French perspective on the writing of women's history.

2.80 **Pollock**, G., *Vision and Difference: Femininity, Feminism and Histories of Art* (1988).

2.81 **Purvis**, J., 'Using primary sources when researching women's history from a feminist perspective', *Women's H. R.*, 1.2 (1992), 273–306. Examines methodological problems through a study of different categories of primary sources drawn from Victorian and Edwardian England.

2.82 **Roe**, J., 'Modernisation and sexism: recent writings on Victorian women', *Vict. Studs.*, 20.2 (1977), 179–92.

2.83 **Scott**, J. W., *Gender and the Politics of History* (New York, 1988).

2.84 — 'Women in history: the modern period', *P. P.*, 101 (1983), 141–57. Useful bibliographical guide which explores changes in the writing of women's history.

2.85 **Shires**, L. M., ed., *Rewriting the Victorians: Theory, History and the Politics of Gender* (1992).

2.86 **Smith**, B. G., 'The contribution of women to modern historiography in Great Britain, France and the United States, 1750–1940', *Am. H. R.*, 89.3 (1984), 709–32.

2.87 **Smith**, H., 'Feminism and the methodology of women's history', in B. A. Carroll, ed., *Liberating Women's History* (Urbana, Illinois, 1976), 369–84. Argues for a feminist approach to women's history and emphasises that women have a unique past.

2.88 **Spender**, D., ed., *Men's Studies Modified: The Impact of Feminism on the Academic Disciplines* (1981).

2.89 **Stanley**, L., 'British feminist histories: an introduction', *Women's Studs. Int. For.*, 13, 1/2 (1990), 3–7. Introduction to a special issue of articles by sociologists using historical material.

2.90 **Stuard**, S. M., 'The chase after theory: considering medieval women', *Gend. and Hist.*, 4 (1992), 135–46.

2.91 **Swindells**, J., 'Hanging up on mum or questions of everyday life in the writing of history', *Gend. and Hist.*, 2.1 (1990), 68–78.

2.92 **Thom**, D., 'A lop-sided view: feminist history or the history of women', in K. Campbell, ed., *Critical Feminism: Argument in the Disciplines* (1992).

2.93 **Tilly**, L.A. 'Gender, women's history and social history', *Soc. Sc. Hist.*, 13.4 (1989), 439–62.

2.94 — 'Women's history and family history: fruitful collaboration or missed connection?', *J. Fam. Hist.*, 12 (1987), 303–15.

2.95 **Tomaselli**, S., 'Reflections on the history of the science of woman', *Hist. of Science*, 29.2 (1991), 185–205.

2.96 **Vickery**, A. J., 'Golden Age to Separate Spheres? A review of the categories and chronology of English women's History', *Hist. J.*, 36 (1993), 383–414. An important challenge to the traditional periodisation of women's history.

2.97 — 'The neglected century: writing the history of eighteenth century women', *Gend. and Hist.*, 3 (1991), 211–19.

2.98 **Vogel**, L., 'Telling tales: historians of our own lives', *J. Women's Hist.*, 2, Winter (1991), 89–101.

2.99 **Walkowitz**, J., **Jehlen**, M. and **Chevigny**, M. and B., 'Patrolling the borders: feminist historiography and the new historicism', *Radical H. R.*, 43 (1989), 23–44.

2.100 **Ward**, M., *The Missing Sex: Putting Women into Irish History* (Dublin, 1991).

2.101 **Ware**, V., 'The good, the bad and the foolhardy: moving the frontiers of British women's history', in F. Rogilds, ed., *Every Cloud Has a Silver Lining: Lectures on Everyday Life, Cultural Production and*

Race (Copenhagen, 1990).

2.102 **Weinstein**, M. F., 'Reconstructing our Past: reflections on Tudor women', *Int. J. Women's Studs.*, 1 (1978), 133–40.

2.103 **Williams**, J. C., 'Domesticity as the dangerous supplement of liberalism', *J. Women's Hist.*, 2, Winter (1991), 69–88.

See also: 2.107; 2.132; 2.165; 3.343; 3.354; 3.471; 3.589; 5.111; 5.113; 5.123; 5.127; 5.762; 5.1393.

(b) SOURCES AND PROBLEMS

2.104 **Alexander**, S., ed., *Women's Fabian Tracts* (1988). Collection of pamphlets by Fabian women with an introduction which assesses the importance of women in the Fabian Society and their different perspectives.

2.105 **Barrow**, M., *Women, 1870–1928: A Select Guide to Printed and Archival Sources in the U.K.* (1981). Mainly covers biographies and issues of suffrage and education.

2.106 **Bauer**, C. and **Ritt**, L., *Free and Ennobled: Source Readings in the Development of Victorian Feminism* (1989).

2.107 **Beddoe**, D., *Discovering Women's History: A Manual* (1983). Excellent introduction for anyone embarking on research in women's history.

2.108 **Bennett**, J. M., 'Spouses, siblings and surnames: reconstructing families from medieval village court rolls', *J. Brit. Studs.*, 23.1 (1983), 26–46.

2.109 **Birkett**, D. and **Wheelwright**, J., ' "How could she?": Unpalatable facts and feminist heroines', *Gend. and Hist.*, 2 (1990), 49–58.

2.110 **Bornat**, J., 'Women's history and oral history: an outline bibliography', *Oral Hist.*, 5.2 (1977), 124–35.

2.111 **Bridge**, E., 'Women's employment: problems of research', *Scy. Study Labour Hist. Bull.*, 26 (1973), 5–7. Summary of a conference paper.

2.112 **Davis**, G., *Personal Writings of Women to 1900: A Bibliography of American and British Writers* (1988).

2.113 **Davis**, N. Z., and **Conway**, J. K., *Society and the Sexes: A Bibliography of Women's History in Early Modern Europe, Colonial America and the United States* (New York, 1981).

2.114 **Doughan**, D., 'Periodicals by, for and about women in Britain', *Women's Studs. Int. For.*, 10.3 (1987), 261–73. Discusses periodicals held in the Fawcett Library.

2.115 — and **Sanchez**, D., *Feminist Periodicals, 1855–1984: An Annotated Bibliography of British, Irish, Commonwealth and International Titles* (1987).

2.116 **Druker**, J., 'Women's history and trade union records', *Scy. Study Labour Hist. Bull.*, 36 (1978), 28–35.

2.117 **Evans**, M. and **Morgan**, D., *Work on Women: A Guide to the Literature* (1979). Useful starting point for further reading.

2.118 **Evans**, N., 'Inheritance, women, religion and education in early modern society as revealed by wills', in P. Riden, ed., *Probate Records and the Local Community* (1985), 53–70.

2.119 **Frey**, L., **Frey**, M., and **Schneider**, J., *Women in Western European History: A Select Chronological, Geographical and Topical Bibliography from Antiquity to the French Revolution* (Brighton, 1982).

2.120 **Goldberg**, J., 'Women in later medieval English archives', *J. of the Society of Archivists*, 15.1 (1994), 59–71.

2.121 **Hamilton**, P. and **Gothard**, J., ' "The other half": sources of British female emigration at the Fawcett Library with special reference to Australia', *Women's Studs. Int. For.* 10.3 (1987), 305–9.

2.122 **Hellerstein**, E., **Hume**, L. P. and **Offen**, K., eds., *Victorian Women: A Documentary Account of Women's Lives in Nineteenth-Century England, France and the United States* (1981). Document extracts.

2.123 **Henderson**, J., 'Pagan Saxon cemeteries: a study of the problems of sexing by grave goods and bones', in C. A. Roberts, F. Lee and J. Bintcliffe, eds., *Burial Archaeology: Current Research, Methods and Developments* B.A.R. Brit. ser., 211 (1989), 77–83.

2.124 **Hill**, B., *Eighteenth Century Women: An Anthology* (1984). A wide-ranging collection.

2.125 **Hollis**, P., *Women in Public: The Women's Movement, 1850–1900* (1979). Collection of documents largely written by members of the women's movement.

2.126 **Hunter**, F., 'The Bessie Rayner Parkes collection at Girton College Cambridge', *Vict. Period. R.*, 16.1 (1983), 32–3.

Collection of a prominent nineteenth-century women's rights campaigner.

2.127 **Ireland**, C. M., 'Highlights from the treasures in the Fawcett Library', *Women's Studs. Int. For.*, 10.3 (1987), 241–59. On old and rare books illustrating the social position of women.

2.128 **Jalland**, P. and **Hooper**, J., *Women from Birth to Death: The Female Life Cycle in Britain, 1830–1914* (1986). Contains extracts from contemporary writings, including medical textbooks, journals, letters and diaries, concerning women's biological nature/purpose, with critical commentaries.

2.129 **James**, M., *The Emancipation of Women in Great Britain* (1972). Extracts from contemporary documents with an introduction.

2.130 **John**, A. V., 'What to read on modern British women's history', *Local Histn.*, 17.3 (1986), 150–8.

2.131 **Johnson**, D. A., *Women in English Religion, 1700–1925* (New York, 1983). Documentary collection.

2.132 **Kanner**, B., *Autobiographical Writings. Women in English Social History: A Guide to Research*, Vol. III (New York, 1987). Lists and briefly describes 600 personal writings published by women from varied classes, regions and occupations who were born between the late eighteeenth century and the early twentieth century.

2.133 — 'The women of England in a century of social change, 1815–1914: a select bibliography', in M. Vicinus, ed., *Suffer and Be Still: Women in the Victorian Age* (Bloomington, Indiana, 1972), 173–206.

2.134 — 'The women of England in a century of social change, 1815–1914: a select bibliography, part II', in M. Vicinus, ed., *Widening Sphere: Changing Roles of Victorian Women* (Bloomington, Indiana, 1977), 199–270.

2.135 **Lacey**, C. A., *Barbara Leigh Smith Bodichon and the Langham Place Group* (1987). Collection of pamphlets and other papers.

2.136 **Lewis**, J., ed., *Before the Vote Was Won: Arguments For and Against Women's Suffrage, 1864–1896* (1987). Collection of pamphlets and papers, usually reprinted in full. Interesting introduction.

2.137 **Manchester Women's History Group**, *Resources for Women's History in Greater Manchester*, National Museum of Labour History Publications (1993).

2.138 **Marcus**, J., ed., *Suffrage and the Pankhursts* (1987). Collection of writings by the Pankhursts. Introduction urges the need to re-read the suffragette movement and its imagery.

2.139 **Masek**, R., 'Women in an Age of Transition 1485–1714', in B. Kanner, ed., *The Women of England from Anglo-Saxon Times to the Present. Interpretive Bibliographical Essays* (1980), 138–82. Includes printed sources as well as secondary material.

2.140 **McGregor**, O. R., 'The social position of women in England, 1850–1914', *Brit. J. Sociol.*, 5 (1956), 48–60. Useful survey of primary materials, focussing on the 'emancipation' question.

2.141 **McPhee**, C. and **Fitzgerald**, A., 'The Teresa Billington-Greig collection: two Californians tap into the Fawcett', *Women's Studs. Inter. For.*, 10.3 (1987), 311–15.

2.142 — and — eds., *The Non-Violent Militant: Selected Writings of Teresa Billington-Greig* (1988).

2.143 **Morris**, J., 'The Gertrude Tuckwell collection', *Hist. Workshop J.*, 5 (1978), 155–62. Collection contains reports, pamphlets, leaflets and press cuttings about women's political and economic struggles accumulated by Tuckwell when she was hon. secretary of the Women's Trade Union League, 1890–1920.

2.144 **O'Brien**, S., 'Ten thousand nuns: working in convent archives', *Catholic Archives*, 9 (1989), 26–33.

2.145 **O'Day**, R., 'The history of women and the family', *British Book News*, July (1986), 383–6. A bibliography.

2.146 **Open University**, *Women in Scotland: an annotated bibliography* (1991).

2.147 **Palmegiano**, E. M., 'Women and British periodicals, 1832–1867: a bibliography', *Vict. Studs. News.*, March (1976).

2.148 **Pankhurst**, R., 'Collection development and women's heritage: the case of the Fawcett Library', *Women's Studs. Int. For.*, 10.3 (1987), 225–39. Contains a short history of the Fawcett Society/Library and a discussion of the latter's objectives.

2.149 **Parratt**, C. M., ' "Athletic womanhood": exploring sources for female sport in Victorian and Edwardian England', *J. Sports Hist.*, 16 (1989), 140–57.

2.150 **Perkins**, V., 'The Fawcett Library picture

collection', *Women's Studs. Int. For.*, 10.3 (1987), 281–9.

2.151 **Reimer**, E. S. and **Fout**, J.C., eds., *European Women: A Documentary History, 1798–1945* (1984). Includes documents on Britain, France and the U.S.

2.152 **Ritchee**, M., *Women's Studies: A Checklist of Bibliographies* (1980).

2.153 **Rosenthal**, J. T., *Medieval Women and the Sources of Medieval History* (Athens, Georgia, 1990). Concerned with the use of medieval source material for women's history.

2.154 **Schneir**, M., ed., *Feminism: The Essential Historical Writings* (New York, 1972). Extracts from feminist texts.

2.155 **Schnorrenberg**, B. B., with **Hunter**, J. E., 'The Eighteenth Century Englishwoman', in B. Kanner, ed., *The Women of England from Anglo-Saxon Times to the Present. Interpretive Bibliographical Essays* (1980), 183–228.

2.156 **Smith**, H. L., and **Cardinale**, S., *Women and the Literature of the Seventeenth Century: an annotated bibliography based on Wing's 'Short-title Catalogue'* (1990). Lists works for, as well as by, women, 1641–1700.

2.157 **Spender**, D., 'Sadd Brown collection', *Women's Studs. Int. For.* 10.3 (1987), 303–4. Brief account of collection of Mary Sadd Brown, suffragette, held at the Fawcett Library.

2.158 — ed., *The Dora Russell Reader: 57 Years of Writing and Journalism, 1925–1982* (1983).

2.159 — ed., *The Education Papers: Women's Quest for Equality in Britain, 1850–1912* (1987). Collection of articles and papers by contemporay educationalists and reformers.

2.160 **Stearns**, B. M., 'Early English periodicals for ladies, 1700–1760', *Pubs. Mod. Lang. Assoc.*, 48 (1933), 38–60.

2.161 **Sweet**, M., 'When letters still were written', *Women's Studs. Int. For.*, 10.3 (1987), 275–80. Surveys letters kept in the Fawcett Library and lists archives available.

2.162 **Uglow**, J. S., *The Macmillan Dictionary Of Women's Biography* (1982).

2.163 **Vann**, R., 'Wills and the family in an English town: Banbury, 1550–1800', *J. Fam. Hist.*, 4 (1979), 346–67.

2.164 **Von den Steinen**, K., 'The discovery of women in eighteenth-century English political life', in B. Kanner, ed., *The Women of England from Anglo-Saxon Times to the Present. Interpretive Bibliographical Essays* (1980), 229–58.

2.165 **Weeks**, J., 'A survey of primary sources and archives for the history of early twentieth-century English women', in B. Kanner, ed., *The Women of England from Anglo-Saxon Times to the Present. Interpretive Bibliographical Essays* (1980), 388–418.

2.166 — 'Notes on sources: the women's movement', *Scy. Study Labour Hist. Bull.*, 29 (1974), 55–9.

2.167 **Wiesner**, M. E., 'Women in the sixteenth century: a bibliography', *Sixteenth Cent. Bib.*, 23 (1983), 1–65.

2.168 **Williamson**, J., *New Feminist Scholarship: A Guide to Bibliographies* (Old Westbury, New York, 1979).

2.169 **Witherow**, M., 'Ephemera', *Women's Studs. Int. For.*, 10.3 (1987), 291–7. On ephemera at the Fawcett Library.

See also: 2.18; 2.34; 2.63; 2.81; 3.62; 3.63; 3.193; 3.203; 3.265; 3.317; 3.563; 4.33; 4.45–54; 4.67; 4.74; 4.93; 4.108; 4.174–5; 4.202; 4.351; 4.416; 4.421; 4.446; 4.479; 4.483; 4.512; 4.546; 4.585; 4.588; 4.594; 4.604; 4.614; 4.618; 4.622–25; 4.629; 4.669; 4.672–3; 4.686; 4.786; 4.802; 4.808; 4.817; 4.845; 4.853; 4.862; 4.867–68; 4.883; 4.885; 4.889; 4.894; 4.899–90; 4.908; 4.911; 4.914–15; 4.917; 4.924; 4.928; 4.930; 4.934; 4.936; 4.945–69; 5.113; 5.871; 5.1330; 5.1580.

(c) CONCEPTS

2.170 **Alexander**, S. and **Taylor**, B., 'In defence of patriarchy', in R. Samuel, ed., *People's History and Socialist Theory* (1981), 370–3. In contrast to Rowbotham, the authors suggest that the concept of patriarchy is a useful tool for understanding sexual antagonism.

2.171 **Ardener**, S., *Perceiving Women* (1975). Anthropological work important for the whole question of woman and nature.

2.172 **Bennett**, J., 'Medievalism and feminism', *Speculum*, 68 (1993), 309–31.

2.173 **Chodorow**, N., *The Reproduction of Mothering. Psychoanalysis and the Sociology of Gender* (Berkeley, California, 1978). A discussion of motherhood in feminist thought.

2.174 **Cott**, N. F., 'What's in a name? The limits of "social feminism"; or, expanding the vocabulary of women's history', *J. Am. Hist.*, 76.4 (1989), 809–29.

2.175 **Dalla Costa**, M., *The Power of Women and the Subversion of the Community* (1972). A discussion of Marxist feminist analyses of the family under capitalism.

2.176 **David**, D., 'Ideologies of patriarchy, feminism and fiction in the *Odd Women*', *Fem. Studs.*, 10.1 (1984), 117–40.

2.177 **Davidoff**, L., **L'Esperance**, J. and **Newby**, H., 'Landscape with figures: home and community in English society', in A. Oakley and J. Mitchell, eds., *The Rights and Wrongs of Women* (1976), 139–75.

2.178 **Davis**, A., *Women, Race and Class* (1982).

2.179 **Elshtain**, J. B., *Public Man, Private Woman: Women in Social and Political Thought* (Princeton, New Jersey, 1981).

2.180 **Flax**, J., 'Postmodernism and gender relations in feminist theory', *Signs*, 12.4 (1987), 621–43.

2.181 **Fox-Genovese**, E., 'Property and patriarchy in classical bourgeois political theory', *Radical H. R.*, 4 (1977), 36–59.

2.182 **Hall**, C. 'Politics, post-structuralism and feminist history', *Gend. and Hist.*, 3.2 (1991), 204 10. Thematic review of Denise Riley and Joan W. Scott.

2.183 — 'Gender divisions and class formation in the Birmingham middle class, 1780–1850', in R. Samuel, ed., *People's History and Socialist Theory* (1981), 164–75.

2.184 **Hamilton**, R., *The Liberation of Women: A Study of Patriarchy and Capitalism* (1978).

2.185 **Hunt**, M., 'The de-eroticization of women's liberation: social purity movements and the revolutionary feminism of Sheila Jeffreys', *Fem. R.*, 34 (1990), 23–46.

2.186 **Kelly**, C., 'History and post-modernism', *P.P.*, 133 (1991), 209–13.

2.187 **Kelly**, J., *Women, History and Theory: the Essays of Joan Kelly*, C. R. Stimpson et al., eds. (Chicago, Illinois, 1984).

2.188 — 'The doubled vision of feminist theory', in C. R. Stimpson et al., eds., *Women, History and Theory: the Essays of Joan Kelly* (Chicago, Illinois, 1984), 51–64.

2.189 **Kessler-Harris**, A., 'The just price, the free market and the value of women', *Fem. Studs.*, 14.2 (1988), 235–50. Argues that historians should explore the past in dialogue with the present and thereby enrich an understanding of both.

2.190 **Lane**, A. J., 'Woman in society: a critique of Frederick Engels', in B. A. Carroll, ed., *Liberating Women's History* (Urbana, Illinois, 1976), 4–25.

2.191 **Lerner**, G., 'Reconceptualising differences among women', *J. Women's Hist.*, 1, Winter (1990), 106–22.

2.192 — *The Creation of Patriarchy* (1986). Readable and stimulating discussion of how to relate ideas about gender to the economic and social forces that shape history.

2.193 **Meller**, H., 'Planning theory and women's role in the city', *Urban Hist. Yearbk.*, 17 (1990), 85–98.

2.194 **Millett**, K., *Sexual Politics* (1971). Seminal text of the 1970s women's movement which sought to demonstrate the exercise of male power over women both historically and in the present.

2.195 **Mitchell**, J., *The Longest Revolution* (1984). Essays on the relationship between feminism, literature and psychoanalysis. Focuses on childhood in the nineteenth-century novel.

2.196 **Murray**, M., 'Property and "patriarchy" in English history', *J. Hist. Sociol.*, 2, December (1989), 303–27.

2.197 **Newman**, L., 'Critical theory and the history of women: what's at stake in deconstructing women's history', *J. Women's Hist.*, 2, Winter (1991), 58–68.

2.198 **Newton**, J., 'A feminist scholarship you can bring home to dad?', *J. Women's Hist.*, 2, Winter (1991), 102–8.

2.199 — 'Family fortunes: "new history" and "new historicism"', *Radical H. R.*, 43 (1989), 5–22. Discusses strengths and weaknesses of post-structuralist and deconstructionist accounts of the nineteenth century compared with other forms of feminist historical enquiry.

2.200 **Nicholson**, L. J., *Gender and History* (New York, 1986).

2.201 **Offen**, K., 'Defining feminism: A comparative historical approach', *Signs*, 14.1 (1988), 119–57.

2.202 **Partner**, N., 'No sex, no gender', *Speculum*, 68 (1993), 419–43. Particularly on medieval women's history.

2.203 **Pollock**, G. and **Parker**, R., *Old Mistresses: Women, Art and Ideology* (1981).

2.204 **Poovey**, M., *Uneven Developments: The Ideological Work of Gender in Mid-Victorian England* (Chicago, Illinois, 1988).

2.205 **Reiter**, R. R., *Towards an Anthropology of Women* (New York, 1975). Raises important cross-cultural questions for women in pre-industrial society.

2.206 **Riley**, D., *Am I That Name? Feminism and the Category of "Women" in History* (1988). Challenging discussion of whether 'women' is a natural category and the implications for feminism and women's history if it is not. Explores ambiguities of the category of 'women'.

2.207 **Rosaldo**, M. Z. and **Lamphere**, L., *Woman, Culture and Society* (Stanford, California, 1974). Important collection of anthropological essays relevant to any study of women in pre-industrial societies.

2.208 **Rowbotham**, S., 'The trouble with patriarchy', in R. Samuels, ed., *People's History and Socialist Theory* (1981), 364–9. Criticises use of 'patriarchy' for an understanding of male–female relationships historically.

2.209 **Samuel**, R., ed., *People's History and Socialist Theory* (1981). Collection of articles exploring debates among socialists about approaches to history.

2.210 **Scott**, J. W., 'Deconstructing equality-versus-difference: or the uses of post-structuralist theory for feminism', *Fem. Studs.*, 14.1 (1988), 33–50. A seminal article which forms the starting point for historians interested in this debate.

2.211 — 'Gender: a useful category of historical analysis', *Am. H.R.*, 91.4 (1986), 1053–75.

2.212 — 'On language, gender and working-class history', *Int. Labor and Working-Class Hist.*, 31, Spring (1987), 1–14.

2.213 **Shiach**, M., *Discourse On Popular Culture: Class, Gender and History in Cultural Analysis, 1730 To The Present* (1989).

2.214 **Smith**, R. L. and **Valenze**, D. M., 'Mutuality and marginality: Liberal moral theory and working-class women in nineteenth-century England', *Signs*, 13.2 (1988), 277–98.

2.215 **Stanley**, L., 'Recovering women in history from feminist deconstructionism', *Women's Studs. Int. For.*, 13, 1/2 (1990), 151–7. Provocative discussion of the need to recognise multiple fractures within the category 'women'.

2.216 — ed., *Feminist Praxis: Research, Theory and Epistemology in Feminist Sociology* (1990).

2.217 — and **Wise**, S., 'Feminist theory, feminist research and experiences of sexism', *Women's Studs. Int. Q.*, 2.3 (1979), 359–74.

2.218 **Strathern**, M., *The Gender of the Gift* (Berkeley, California, 1988). Important anthropological reassessment of key concepts for the study of women in pre-industrial society, e.g. public/private, relationships of power.

2.219 **Thomas**, J., 'Women and capitalism: oppression or emancipation? A review article', *Comp. Studs. Soc. and Hist.*, 30 (1990), 534–49.

2.220 **Todd**, J., *Feminist Literary History: A Defence* (1988).

2.221 **Walby**, S., *Women, Theory and Society: From Private to Public Patriarchy* (1991).

2.222 — 'From private to public patriarchy: the periodisation of British history', *Women's Studs. Int. For.*, 13, 1/2 (1990), 91–104. Argues for a historical periodisation linked to gender relations.

2.223 — *Theorising Patriarchy* (1990). Accessible discussion of the varied definitions and uses of the term 'patriarchy'.

See also: 2.62–3; 3.23; 4.447; 5.72; 5.109; 5.110; 5.121; 5.373; 5.376.

3

MEDIEVAL
CIRCA 500–1500

(a) GENERAL SURVEYS

3.1 **Bennett**, H. S., *Six Medieval Men and Women* (1955).

3.2 **Bennett**, J. M., 'Medieval women, modern women: across the great divide', in D. Aers, ed., *Culture and History, 1350–1600, Essays on English Communities, Identities and Writing* (1992), 147–75. Questions whether there was a dramatic change for women between 1300 and 1700.

3.3 **Coulton**, G. G., *Social Life in Britain from the Conquest to the Reformation* (1970). Chapter on women's life.

3.4 **Davies**, R. R., 'The status of women and the practice of marriage in late medieval Wales', in D. Jenkins and M. Owen, eds., *The Welsh Law of Women* (1980) 93–114.

3.5 **Davies**, W., 'Celtic women in the early middle ages', in A. Cameron and A. Kurht, eds., *Images of Women in Antiquity* (1983), 145–66.

3.6 **Echols**, A. and **Williams**, M., *An Annotated Index of Medieval Women* (Princeton, New Jersey, and Oxford, 1992), Europe-wide brief biographies.

3.7 **Ennen**, E., *The Medieval Woman* (1989). Primarily German material, but some general survey, and useful for comparison especially of urban women.

3.8 **Fell**, C., *Women in Anglo-Saxon England and the Impact of 1066* (1984). Optimistic view of Anglo-Saxon women and argument for decline of their status after 1066.

3.9 **Gies**, F. and J., *Women in the Middle Ages* (New York, 1978). Europe-wide survey.

3.10 **Goldberg**, P. J. P., 'Women in fifteenth-century town life', in J. A. F. Thompson, ed., *Towns and Townspeople in the Fifteenth century* (1988), 107–28. Wide-ranging survey, covering networks, servants, marriage and choice, brewing and prostitution. Brings out the effects of fifteenth-century recession on women.

3.11 **Hilton**, R. H., *The English Peasantry in the later Middle Ages* (1975). Chapter 6, 'Women in the village'.

3.12 **Hollis**, S., *Anglo-Saxon Women and the Church* (1992). Studies the impact of the Church on the status and views of women and looks at the establishment and suppression of double monasteries.

3.13 **Markale**, J., *Women of the Celts*, A. Mygind, C. Hauch and P. Henry, trans. (1980).

3.14 **Nicholson**, J., '*Feminae gloriosae*: women in the age of Bede', in D. Baker, ed., *Medieval Women*, Studies in Church History, Subsidia 1 (1978), 15–29.

3.15 **Page**, R. I., *Life in Anglo-Saxon England* (1970). Includes a chapter on 'A Woman's Place'.

3.16 **Power**, E., *Medieval Women*, ed. Postan, M. M. (1975).

3.17 — 'The position of women', in C. Crump and E. Jacob, eds., *Legacy of the Middle Ages* (1926), 401–33. Chiefly on late medieval women.

3.18 **Shahar**, S., *The Fourth Estate: a History of Women in the Middle Ages* (1983). Europe-wide but much on England.

3.19 **Sheehan**, M. M., 'The Wife of Bath and her four sisters, reflections on a woman's life in the age of Chaucer', *Med. et Hum.*, new ser., 13 (1985), 23–42.

3.20 **Simms**, K., 'Women in Norman Ireland', in M. MacCurtain and D. Ó'Corráin, eds., *Women in Irish Society: the Historical Dimension* (1979), 14–25.

3.21 — 'Women in Gaelic society during the age of transition', in M. MacCurtain and M. O'Dowd, eds., *Women in Early Modern Ireland* (1991), 32–42. Fifteenth to seventeenth centuries.

3.22 **Stafford**, P., *Unification and Conquest, a Political and Social History of England in the Tenth and Eleventh Centuries* (1989). Chapter on women and family.

3.23 — 'Women in Domesday', in K. Bate et al., eds., *Medieval Women in Southern England*, Reading Medieval Studies, 15 (1989), 75–94. Women in late eleventh-century England, especially as landowners.

3.24 **Stenton**, F. M., 'The historical bearing of place-name studies: the place of women in Anglo-Saxon society', *T.R.H.S.*, ser., 4, 25 (1943), 1–13. Also in D. M. Stenton, ed., *Preparatory to Anglo-Saxon England*, collected papers of F.M.Stenton (1970), 314–24, and H. Damico and A. H. Olsen, eds., *New Readings on Women in Old English Literature* (Bloomington and Indianapolis, Indiana, 1990), 79–88.

3.25 **Uitz**, E., *Women in the Medieval Town*, S. Marnie, trans. (1990). Europe-wide.

3.26 **Ward**, J., *English Noblewomen in the Later Middle Ages* (1992). Surveys marriage, household management, political involvement, piety etc.

See also: 2.9; 2.18; 2.34.

(b) VIEWS OF WOMEN

3.27 **Archibald**, E., 'Women and romance', in H. Aertson and A. A. MacDonald, eds., *Companion to Middle English Romance* (Amsterdam, 1990), 153–69.

3.28 **Ashley**, K. M., 'Medieval courtesy literature and dramatic mirrors of female conduct', in N. Armstrong and L. Tennenhouse, eds., *The Ideology of Conduct: Essays in Literature and the History of Sexuality* (1987), 25–38. Discusses the Towneley cycle in relation to conduct books.

3.29 **Bandel**, B., 'The English chroniclers' attitude towards women', *J. Hist. Ideas*, 16 (1955), 113–18. Chiefly up to twelfth century.

3.30 **Blamires**, A. et al, *Woman Defamed and Woman Defended. An anthology of medieval texts* (1992). Europe-wide, a very useful collection.

3.31 **Bloch**, H., *Medieval Misogyny and the Invention of Western Romantic Love* (Chicago, Illinois, 1991). Europe-wide, contains discussion of Christian ideas as well as courtly love ideals..

3.32 **Bornstein**, D., *The Lady in the Tower: Medieval Courtesy Literature for Women* (Hamden, Conn., 1983).

3.33 **Braswell**, M. F., 'Sin, the lady and the law. The English noblewoman in the late middle ages', *Med. et Hum.*, new ser., 14 (1986), 81–101. On penitential and other prescriptive literature.

3.34 **Breeze**, A., 'The virgin Mary, daughter of her son', *Études Celtiques*, 27 (1990), 267–83. Studies the *mater et filia topos* in the early poetry of Britain and Ireland.

3.35 **Bugge**, J., *Virginitas, an essay in the history of a medieval ideal* (The Hague, 1975). On virginity in general but with specific relevance to the ideal as expressed to women in England in twelfth and thirteenth centuries.

3.36 **Carruthers**, M., 'The wife of Bath and the painting of lions', in R. Evans and L. Johnson, eds., *Feminist Readings in Middle English Literature* (1994), 39–64. The wife of Bath read as a figure of resistance to late fourteenth-century misogynistic and anti-matrimonial literature.

3.37 **Chance**, J., *Woman as Hero in Old English Literature* (Syracuse, New York, 1986).

3.38 **Damico**, H., *Beowulf's Wealhtheow and the Valkyrie Tradition* (Madison, Wisconsin, 1984).

3.39 **Dor**, J., ed., *A Wyf ther was: essays in honour of Paule Mertens-Fonck* (Liège, 1992). Essays on images of women in medieval literature from the Anglo-Saxons to the fifteenth century.

3.40 **Erickson**, C., 'The view of women', in C. Erickson, *The Medieval Vision* (New York and Oxford, 1975), 181–212.

3.41 **Farmer**, S., 'Persuasive voices: clerical images of medieval wives', *Speculum*, 61 (1986), 517–43.

3.42 **Ferrante**, J. M., *Woman as Image in Medieval Literature from the Twelfth Century to Dante* (New York, 1975). Not specifically British but an important general survey.

3.43 **French**, K. L., 'The legend of Lady Godiva and the image of the female body', *J. of Med. Hist.*, 18 (1992), 3–19.

3.44 **Fries**, M., 'Popular images of women in medieval literature', *J. Pop. Cult.*, 14 (Summer 1980), 79–86.

3.45 **Furnivall**, F. J., ed., *The Babees Book*, Early English Text Scy., 32 (1868). Contains 'How the Good Wijf taugte hir daugtir', a didactic late fourteenth-century vernacular text.

3.46 **Hansen**, E. T., *Chaucer and the Fictions of Gender* (Berkeley, California, 1992). Important feminist reading of Chaucer.

3.47 **Herbert**, M., ' "Celtic heroine" the archaeology of the Deirdre story', in T. O'Brien Johnson and D. Cairns, eds., *Gender in Irish Writing* (1991), 13–22. An eighth- or ninth-century text.

3.48 **Hill**, J., ' "þaet wœs geomuru ides!" A female stereotype examined', in H. Damico and A. H. Olsen, eds., *New Readings on Women in Old English Literature* (Bloomington and Indianapolis, Indiana, 1991), 235–47. Representation of powerful women in early English literature.

3.49 **Huneycutt**, L. L., 'Images of high-medieval queenship', *Haskins Soc. J.* (1989), 61–71.

3.50 — 'The idea of the perfect princess: the *Life of St Margaret* and the reign of Mathilda II (1100–1118)', in M. Chibnall, ed., *Anglo-Norman Studies*, 12, 1989 (1990), 81–97. Discusses the *Life* as a mirror of princesses for a queen.

3.51 — 'Female succession and the language of power in the writings of twelfth-century churchmen', in J. C. Parsons, ed., *Medieval Queenship* (New York and Stroud, 1993), 189–201.

3.52 **Jarrett**, B., *Social Theories of the Middle Ages* (1926). Chapter on views of women still useful for its argument that not all such medieval views were anti-feminist.

3.53 **Kliman**, B., 'Women in Early English literature, "Beowulf" to the "Ancrene Wisse" ', *Nottingham Med. Studs.*, 21 (1977), 32–49.

3.54 **Lloyd**, G., *The Man of Reason, 'Male' and 'Female' in Western Philosophy* (1984).

Europe-wide but excellent on the alignment of reason and male in western thought in general.

3.55 **Maclean**, I., *The Renaissance Notion of Woman: a Study in the Fortunes of Scholasticism and Medical Science in European Intellectual Life* (1980). Europe-wide, but important.

3.56 **Maddern**, P., 'Honour among the Pastons: gender and integrity in fifteenth-century English provincial society', *J. of Med. Hist.*, 14 (1988), 357–71. The difference between male and female concepts of honour.

3.57 **Mann**, J., *Apologies to Women* (1991). Apologies made by male writers of the Middle Ages to women in their audience.

3.58 — *Geoffrey Chaucer* (1990). An important feminist reading which would provide a good introduction to his work on women.

3.59 — 'Chaucer and the "woman question" ', in E. Kooper, ed., *This Noble Craft, Proceedings of the Xth Research Symposium of the Dutch and Belgian University teachers of Old and Middle English and Historical Linguistics* (Amsterdam, 1991), 173–88.

3.60 **Marchalonis**, S., 'Above Rubies: popular views of medieval women', *J. Pop. Cult.*, 14, Summer (1980), 87–93.

3.61 **McLaughlin**, E. C., 'Equality of souls, inequality of sexes: women in medieval theology', in R. R. Ruether, ed., *Religion and Sexism, Images of Women in the Jewish and Christian Tradition* (New York, 1974). A useful overview.

3.62 **Millett**, B., ed, *Hali Meithhad*, Early English Text Society, orig. ser., 284 (1982). A Middle English treatise on female virginity.

3.63 — and **Wogan-Browne**, J., *Medieval English Prose for Women* (1990). Edits and translates a number of works of social instruction aimed at women, e.g. *Hali Meithhad*, two sections of the *Ancrene Wisse*, the *Life of St. Margaret*.

3.64 **Murtaugh**, D. M., 'Women and Geoffrey Chaucer', *Eng. Lit. Hist.*, 38 (1971), 473–92. Argues that Chaucer transcends both courtly love and anti-feminist traditions.

3.65 **Nederman**, C. J. and Lawson, E. N., 'The frivolities of courtiers follow the footprints of women: public women and the crisis of virility in John of Salisbury', in C. Levin and J. Watson, eds., *Ambiguous Realities: Women in the Middle Ages and the*

3.66 *Renaissance* (Detroit, Michigan, 1987), 82–96.

3.66 **Newman**, B., 'Flaws in the golden bowl: gender and spiritual formation in the twelfth century', *Traditio*, 45 (1990), 111–46. Literature of formation aimed at women in religious life, especially on virginity.

3.67 **O'Connor**, A., 'Images of the evil woman in Irish folklore', *Women's Studs. Int. For.*, 11.4 (1988), 281–5.

3.68 **Overbeck**, P. T., 'Chaucer's Good Women', *Chaucer R.*, 2 (1967), 75–94.

3.69 **Owst**, G. R., *Literature and the Pulpit in Medieval England, a Neglected Chapter in the History of English Letters and of the English People* (1933, rev. edn. 1961). Much on satire of women and marriage in medieval preaching.

3.70 — *Preaching in Medieval England, an Introduction to Sermon Manuscripts of the Period* c. *1350–1450* (New York, 1965). Refers to attacks on women in sermons.

3.71 **Pratt**, R. A., 'Jankyn's Book of Wikked Wyves: medieval antimatrimonial propaganda in the universities', *Annuale Medievale*, 3 (1962), 5–27.

3.72 **Randall**, L. M., *Images in the Margins of Gothic Manuscripts* (Berkeley, California, 1966). Erotic images and women in marginalia.

3.73 **Robinson**, F. C., 'The prescient woman in Old English literature', in K. Oshitari, ed., *Philologia Anglica, Essays presented to Prof. Yoshio Terasawa* (Tokyo, 1988), 241–50.

3.74 **Remley**, P. G., '*Muscipula diaboli* and medieval English antifeminism', *Eng. Studs.*, 70.1 (1989), 1–14.

3.75 **Schrader**, R. J., *God's Handiwork, Images of Women in Early Germanic Literature*, Contributions to Women's Studies, 41 (Westport, Conn, 1983).

3.76 **Stafford**, P. A., 'The portrayal of royal women in England, mid-tenth to mid-twelfth centuries', in J. C. Parsons, ed., *Medieval Queenship* (New York and Stroud, 1993), 143–67.

3.77 **Truax**, J. A,. 'From Bede to Orderic Vitalis: changing perspectives on the role of women in the Anglo-Saxon and Anglo-Norman church', *Haskins Soc. J.*, 3 (1991), 35–51. Clerical images of women.

3.78 **Tudor**, V., 'The misogyny of St Cuthbert', *Archaeologia Aeliana*, ser. 5, 12 (1984), 157–67.

3.79 **Vaughn**, S. N., 'St Anselm and women', *Haskins Soc. J.*, 2 (1990), 83–93.

3.80 **Watson**, J., 'Enid the disobedient: the *Mabinogion's Gereint and Enid*', in C. Levin and J. Watson, eds., *Ambiguous Realities: Women in the Middle Ages and the Renaissance* (Detroit, Michigan, 1987) 114–32.

3.81 **Weiss**, J., 'The wooing woman in Anglo-Norman romance', in M. Mills, J. Fellowes and C. M. Meale, eds., *Romance in Medieval England* (1991), 149–61.

3.82 **Willard**, C. C., 'A fifteenth-century view of women's role in medieval society: Christine of Pisan's *Livre des trois vertus*', in R. T. Morewedge, ed., *The Role of Woman in the Middle Ages* (1975), 90–120. Italian/French but important as a rare woman's view of woman in the Middle Ages.

3.83 **Williams**, E., 'The literary image', in C. Fell, *Women in Anglo-Saxon England and the Impact of 1066* (1984), 172–93. Survey of literary views of women in medieval England, eleventh to fifteenth centuries.

3.84 **Wogan-Browne**, J., 'The virgin's tale', in R. Evans and L. Johnson, eds., *Feminist Readings in Middle English Literature* (1994), 241–285. Discusses patterns of virginity in saints' lives, particularly with regard to authority and autonomy.

3.85 **Wright**, T., ed., *The book of the knight of La Tour-Landry, compiled for the instruction of his daughters*, Early English Text Society, old ser., 33 (1868). A fourteenth-century treatise of manners and behaviour for women.

See also: 3.12; 3.237; 3.345; 3.376; 3.404; 3.496; 3.574.

(c) WOMEN AND FAMILY

(i) General

3.86 **Altschul**, M., *A Baronial Family in Medieval England: the Clares, 1217–1314* (Baltimore, Maryland, 1965). Material on wives, widows and marriage.

3.87 **Bennett**, H. S., *The Pastons and their England* (1970). On marriage, household management etc.

3.88 **Bennett**, J. M., *Women in the Medieval English Countryside, Gender and Household in Brigstock before the Plague* (1987).

Fourteenth-century peasant women in the family and in village society.

3.89 **Biller**, P. P. A., 'Marriage patterns and women's lives: a sketch of a pastoral geography', in P. J. P. Goldberg, ed., *Woman is a Worthy Wight: Women in English Society* c. *1200–1500* (1992), 60–107. Uses pastoral manuals, i.e. manuals of directions for parish priests, to compare and contrast north-western and Mediterranean Europe on girlhood, marriage, sentiment, contraception, abortion, pregnancy, infanticide, conduct in marriage, widows, sex outside marriage, prostitution, dress.

3.90 **Britton**, E., *The Community of the Vill: a Study in the History of the Family and Village Life in Fourteenth-century England* (Toronto, 1977). Chapters on family and demography.

3.91 — 'The peasant family in fourteenth-century England', *Peasant Studs.*, 5 (1976), 2–7.

3.92 **Chandler**, V., 'Family histories: an aid in the study of the Anglo-Norman Aristocracy', *Med. Prosopog.*, 6 (1985), 1–24.

3.93 **Chibnall**, M., 'Women in Orderic Vitalis', *Haskins Soc. J.*, 2 (1990), 105–21. Argues for importance of women in family roles in eleventh- and twelfth-century England and Normandy.

3.94 **Clark**, C., 'Women's names in post-Conquest England: observations and speculations', *Speculum*, 53 (1978), 223–51. On the survival of Old English women's names after the Norman Conquest and the implications of this for intermarriage etc.

3.95 **Cokayne**, G. E., *The Complete Peerage of England, Scotland, Ireland, Great Britain and the United Kingdom*, 13 vols., V. Gibbs, ed. (1910). Contains a wealth of information on a variety of family arrangements, structures, inheritance etc.

3.96 **Du Boulay**, F. R. H., *An Age of Ambition: English Society in the Late Middle Ages* (1970). Chapters on 'Marriage and sex' and 'Household and family'.

3.97 **Faith**, R. J., 'Peasant families and inheritance customs in medieval England', *Agric. H. R.*, 14 (1966), 77–95.

3.98 **Gies**, F. and J., *Marriage and the Family in the Middle Ages* (1987). General introduction, Europe-wide.

3.99 **Goldberg**, P. J. P., 'Marriage, migration, servanthood and life-cycle in Yorkshire towns in the later middle ages: some York cause paper evidence', *Cont. and Change*, 1 (1986), 149–53.

3.100 **Hanawalt**, B., *The Ties That Bound. Peasant Families in Medieval England* (1986). High and later medieval England, chapters on women in the home, economy, inheritance, household, child-rearing, marriage, widowhood and surrogate family.

3.101 **Hill**, R., 'Marriage in seventh-century England', in M. H. King and W. M. Stevens, eds., *Saints and Scholars and Heroes, Studies in Honour of Charles W. Jones* (Minnesota, 1979), 67–75.

3.102 **Homans**, G., *English Villagers of the Thirteenth Century* (Cambridge, Mass., 1941). Still an important survey of peasant marriage, family and inheritance with much of relevance to the situation of women as wives, daughters and widows.

3.103 **Joyce**, P. W., *A Social History of Ancient Ireland* (New York, 1968). Includes a chapter on the family.

3.104 **Kirby**, J. W., 'Women in the Plumpton correspondence, fiction and reality', in I. Wood and G. A. Loud, eds., *Church and Chronicle in the Middle Ages, Essays Presented to J. Taylor* (1991), 219–32. Marriage, husband and wife relations, motherhood, widowhood.

3.105 **Kowaleski**, M., 'The history of urban families in medieval England', *J. Med. Hist.*, 14.1 (1988), 47–63.

3.106 **Macfarlane**, K. B., *The Nobility of Later Medieval England* (1973). Material on inheritance, marriage and family.

3.107 **McNamara**, J. and Wemple, S., 'The power of women through the family in medieval Europe, A.D.500–1100', in M. Hartmann and L. Banner, eds., *Clio's Consciousness Raised* (New York, 1974), 103–18. A seminal article, Europe-wide, much reprinted.

3.108 **Newman**, C. A., *The Anglo-Norman Nobility in the Reign of Henry I, the Second Generation* (Philadelphia, 1988). Contains chapters on the Anglo-Norman aristocratic family and a good deal on marriage and women in the family.

3.109 **Owen**, D. M., 'White Annays and others', in D. Baker, ed., *Medieval Women*, Studies in Church history, Subsidia 1 (1978), 331–46. A series of legal cases give insight into marriage, family life and female roles in fourteenth-century England – urban and small landholders.

3.110 **Owen**, M. E., 'Shame and reparation, women's place in the kin', in D. Jenkins and M. E. Owen, eds., *The Welsh Law of Women, Studies Presented to Prof. D. A. Binchy on his Eightieth Birthday* (1980), 40–68. On husband/wife relations, violence against women, women's sexuality and control of it.

3.111 **Painter**, S., 'The family and the feudal system in twelfth-century England', *Speculum*, 35 (1960), 1–16.

3.112 **Penelope (Stanley)**, J. and McGowan, C., '*Woman* and *wife*: social and semantic shifts in English', *Papers in Ling.*, 12 (1979), 491–502.

3.113 **Raftis**, J. A., *Tenure and Mobility: Studies in the Social History of the Medieval English Village* (Toronto, 1964). Peasant wives and widows.

3.114 **Razi**, Z., *Life, Marriage and Death in a Medieval Parish: Economy, Society and Demography in Halesowen 1270–1400* (1980). Marriage patterns, age and illegitimate children. For critique of his approach see Poos, L. R. and Smith, R. M., ' "Legal windows onto historical populations"? Recent research on demography and the manor court in England', *Law H.R.*, 2 (1984), 128–52; the debate continued in *Law H.R.*, 3 (1985), 191–200, 4 (1986), 409–29 and 5 (1987), 523–35.

3.115 — 'The myth of the immutable English family', *P.P.*, 140 (1993), 3–44. Especially fourteenth and fifteenth centuries.

3.116 **Richmond**, C., 'The Pastons revisited: marriage and the family in fifteenth-century England', *Bull. Inst. Hist. Res.*, 58 (1985), 25–36. Attitudes to love, courtship and marriage in the Paston letters.

3.117 **Rosenthal**, J. T., *Patriarchy and Families of Privilege in Fifteenth-century England* (Philadelphia, 1991).

3.118 **Sheehan**, M. L., 'The European family and canon law', *Cont. and Change*, 6 (1991), 347–60.

3.119 **Sheehan**, M. M., 'Marriage and family in English conciliar and synodal legislation', in J. R. O'Donnell, ed., *Essays in Honour of Anton Charles Pegis* (Toronto, 1974), 205–14.

3.120 **Sheingorn**, P., 'Appropriating the holy kinship. Gender and family history', in K. Ashley and P. Sheingorn, eds., *Interpreting Cultural Symbols, Saint Anne in Late Medieval Society* (Athens, Georgia, 1990), 169–98.

3.121 **Stafford**, P. A., 'Kinship and women in the world of *Maldon*: Byrhtnoth and his family', in J. Cooper, ed., *The Battle of Maldon, Fiction and Fact* (1993), 225–35. Late tenth- and eleventh-century women in a noble family.

See also: 3.10; 3.336.

(ii) Marriage, divorce, concubinage, adultery

3.122 **Barton**, J. L., 'Nullity of marriage and illegitimacy in the England of the middle ages', in D. Jenkins, ed., *Legal History Studies, Papers Presented to the Legal History Conference, Aberystwyth, 1972* (1975), 28–49.

3.123 **Bennett**, J., 'Medieval peasant marriage: an examination of marriage licence fines in the *Liber Gersumarum*', in J. Raftis, ed., *Pathways to Medieval Peasants* (Toronto, 1981), 193–246. Argues inter alia for peasant women's exercise of choice in marriage.

3.124 — 'The tie that binds: peasant marriages and peasant families in late medieval England', *J. Interdis. Hist.*, 15 (1984), 111–29.

3.125 **Brand**, P., **Hyams**, P., **Faith**, R. and **Searle**, E, 'Debate: seigneurial control of women's marriage', *P.P.*, 99 (1983), 123–60. Part of the debate begun by Scammell and Searle; *see:* 3.165; 3.166; 3.167; 3.168; 3.173.

3.126 **Brooke**, C. N. L., 'Gregorian reform in action: clerical marriage in England 1050–1200', *Camb. Hist. J.*, 12 (1956), 1–21.

3.127 — 'Marriage and society in the central middle ages', in R. B. Outhwaite, ed., *Marriage and Society: Studies in the Social History of Marriage* (1981), 17–34.

3.128 — 'The marriage of Henry II and Eleanor of Aquitaine', *Historian*, 20 (1988), 3–8.

3.129 — *The Medieval Idea of Marriage* (1989).

3.130 **Brundage**, J. A., *Law, Sex and Christian Society in Medieval Europe* (Chicago, Illinois, 1987). Europe-wide but very useful general survey of medieval canon law and its views on sex and marriage.

3.131 **Chadwick**, N. K., 'Pictish and Celtic marriage in early literary tradition', *Scot. Gaelic Studs.*, 8 (1958), 56–155.

3.132 **Clark**, E., 'The decision to marry in thirteenth and early fourteenth-century Norfolk', *Med. Studs.*, 49 (1987), 496–516.

3.133 **Cosgrove**, A., 'Marriage in medieval Ireland', in A. Cosgrove, ed., *Marriage in Ireland* (Dublin, 1985), 25–50

3.134 **Crawford**, A., 'The king's burden? The consequences of royal marriage in fifteenth-century England', in R. A. Griffiths, ed., *Patronage, the Crown and the Provinces in Later Medieval England* (1981), 33–56.

3.135 **Davies**, R. R., 'The status of women and the practice of marriage in late medieval Wales', in D. Jenkins and M. E. Owen, eds., *The Welsh Law of Women, Studies Presented to Prof. D. A. Binchy on his Eightieth Birthday* (1980), 93–114.

3.136 **DeAragon**, R. C., 'In pursuit of aristocratic women, a key to success in Norman England', *Albion*, 14 (1982), 258–66. On marriage and social mobility.

3.137 **Dockray**, K. R. D., 'Why did fifteenth-century English gentry marry? The Pastons, Plumptons and Stonors reconsidered', in M. Jones, ed., *Gentry and Lesser Nobility in Late Medieval Europe* (1986), 61–80.

3.138 **Finch**, A., 'Parental authority and the problem of clandestine marriage in the later middle ages', *Law and Hist. Rev.*, 8 (1990), 189–201.

3.139 **Fradenburg**, L. O., 'Sovereign love: the wedding of Margaret Tudor and James IV of Scotland', in L. O. Fradenburg, ed., *Women and sovereignty, Cosmos, the Yearbook of the Traditional Cosmological Society*, Vol. 7 (1992), 78–100.

3.140 **Goldberg**, P. J. P., ' "For better, for worse": marriage and economic opportunity for women in town and country', in P. J. P. Goldberg, ed., *Woman is a Worthy Wight: Women in English Society c. 1200–1500* (1992), 108–25. Argues for women's economic opportunity affecting control of marriage in late medieval towns.

3.141 — 'Marriage, migration and servanthood: the York cause paper evidence', in P. J. P. Goldberg, ed., *Woman is a Worthy Wight: Women in English Society c. 1200–1500* (1992), 1–15. Includes evidence for age at marriage.

3.142 **Habberjam**, M., 'Harrington v. Saville: a fifteenth-century divorce case', *Ricardian*, 8.101 (1988), 50–60.

3.143 **Hanham**, A., *The Celys and their World* (1985). Chapter on marriage and housekeeping.

3.144 **Haskell**, A. S., 'The Paston women on marriage in fifteenth-century England', *Viator, Medieval and Renaissance Studies*, 4 (1973), 459–71.

3.145 **Helmholz**, R. H., *Marriage Litigation in Medieval England* (1975). Includes important challenge to earlier views of instability of medieval marriage.

3.146 **Ives**, E. W., ' "Agaynst taking awaye of women": the inception and operation of the Abduction Act of 1487', in E. W. Ives, R. J. Knecht and J. J. Scarisbrick, eds., *Wealth and power in Tudor England, Essays Presented to S. T. Bindoff* (1978), 21–44.

3.147 **Kelly**, H. A., *Love and Marriage in the Age of Chaucer* (Ithaca, New York, 1975).

3.148 **Lander**, J. R., 'Marriage and politics in the fifteenth century: the Nevilles and the Wydevilles', in J. R. Lander, *Crown and Nobility, 1450–1509* (1976), 94–126.

3.149 **Lapidge**, M., 'A seventh-century Insular Latin debate poem on divorce', *Cambridge Medieval Celtic Studies*, 10 (1985), 1–23. Discusses divorce by mutual consent.

3.150 **Macfarlane**, A., *Marriage and Love in England, Modes of Reproduction 1300–1840* (1986). Controversial book arguing that individual choice in marriage, individual calculation, usually of an economic nature, and the ideal of romantic love are old in England and acted as great brakes on fertility.

3.151 **Margulies**, C. S., 'The marriage and the wealth of the Wife of Bath', *Med. Studs.*, 24 (1962), 210–16.

3.152 **Mathew**, G., 'Marriage and *Amour courtois* in late fourteenth-century England', *Essays Presented to Charles Williams* (1947), 128–35.

3.153 **Palmer**, R. C., 'The contexts of marriage in medieval England: evidence from the king's court *c.* 1300', *Speculum*, 59.1 (1984), 42–67.

3.154 **Parsons**, J. C., 'Mothers, daughters, marriage, power: some Plantagenet evidence, 1150–1500', in J. C. Parsons, ed., *Medieval Queenship* (New York and Stroud, 1993), 63–78. Royal women's role in marriage arrangement.

3.155 **Poos**, L. R., *A Rural Society after the Black Death: Essex 1350–1525* (1991). Discusses marriage, household, rural cloth industry, migration, servanthood, rural labour.

3.156 **Power**, P., *Sex and Marriage in Ancient*

Ireland (Dublin, 1976).

3.157 **Rawcliffe**, C., 'The politics of marriage in later medieval England: William lord Botreaux and the Hungerfords', *Hunt. Lib. Q.*, 51.3 (1988), 161–75.

3.158 **Richardson**, H. G., 'The marriage and coronation of Isabella of Angoulême', *Eng. H. R.*, 61 (1946), 289–314.

3.159 — 'The marriage of Isabella of Angoulême. A problem of canon law', *Studia Gratiana*, 12 (1967), 397–423.

3.160 **Rivers**, T. J., 'Adultery in early Anglo-Saxon society: Æthelberht 31 in comparison with continental Germanic law', *Anglo-Saxon England*, 20 (1991), 11–20.

3.161 **Robinson**, W. B. R., 'The marriages of knighted Welsh landowners 1485–1558', *Nat. Lib. Wales J.*, 25.4 (1988), 387–98.

3.162 **Roderick**, A. J., 'Marriage and politics in Wales, 1066–1282', *Welsh H. R.*, 4 (1968), 3–20.

3.163 **Rosenthal**, J. T., 'Aristocratic marriage and the English peerage, 1350–1500: social institution and personal bond', *J. Med. Hist.*, 10.3 (1984), 181–94.

3.164 **Ross**, M. C., 'Concubinage in Anglo-Saxon England', *P.P.*, 108 (1985), 3–34.

3.165 **Scammell**, J., 'Freedom and marriage in medieval England', *Ec. H. R.*, 27 (1974), 523–37.

3.166 — 'Wife rents and merchet', *Ec. H. R.*, 29 (1976), 487–90.

3.167 **Searle**, E., 'Freedom and marriage in medieval England: an alternative hypothesis', *Ec. H. R.*, 29 (1976), 482–90.

3.168 — 'Seigneurial control of women's marriage: the antecedents and functions of merchet in England', *P. P.*, 82 (1979), 3–43. See 3.125 and 3.173 for the culmination of the debate begun in the last four articles over peasant marriage and its control.

3.169 **Sheehan**, M. M., 'Choice of marriage partner in the middle ages: development and mode of application of a theory of marriage', in *Studies in Medieval and Renaissance History* (1978), 3–33.

3.170 — 'Marriage theory and practice in the conciliar legislation and diocesan statutes of medieval England', *Med. Studs.*, 40 (1978), 408–60.

3.171 — 'The formation and stability of marriage in fourteenth-century England: evidence of an Ely register', *Med. Studs.*, 33 (1971), 228–63.

3.172 **Sheringham**, J. G. T., 'Bullocks with horns as long as their ears', *Bull. Bd. Celt. Studs.*, 29.4 (1982), 691–708. Deals with the payment, *agweddi*, due to a woman when clandestine marriage broke up.

3.173 **Smith**, E. J., 'The medieval merchet: a late contribution to the debate', *Med. Hist.*, 2.3 (1992), 26–35. Broadens the evidence base, with material from Myntling Register of Spalding, 1253–1478 AD. See also: 3.125; 3.165; 3.166; 3.167; 3.168.

3.174 **Smith**, J. B., 'Dower in thirteenth-century Wales: a grant of the commote of Anhuniog, 1273', *Bull. Bd. Celt. Studs.*, 30, 3–4 (1983), 348–55.

3.175 **Smith**, R. M., 'Hypothèses sur la nuptualité en Angleterre au XIIe–XIVe siècles', *Annales E.S.C.*, 38 (1983), 107–36. Seminal article on the distinctiveness of the north-west European marriage regime.

3.176 — 'Geographical diversity in the resort to marriage in late medieval Europe: work, reputation and unmarried females in the household formation systems of northern and southern Europe', in P. J. P. Goldberg, ed., *Woman is a Worthy Wight: Women in English Society* c. *1200–1500* (1992), 16–59. Develops differences between north-west Europe and the Mediterranean, with stress on female employment as a critical factor.

3.177 **Walker**, S. S., 'The feudal family and the common law courts: the pleas protecting rights of wardship and marriage, c. 1225–1375', *J. Med. Hist.*, 14.1 (1988), 13–31.

3.178 **Waugh**, S. L., 'Marriage, class and royal lordship in England under Henry III', *Viator*, 16 (1985), 181–207.

3.179 **Wentersdorf**, K. P., 'The clandestine marriages of the Fair Maid of Kent', *J. Med. Hist.*, 5 (1979), 203–31.

See also: 3.4; 3.41; 3.275; 3.285; 3.311; 3.322; 3.333; 3.371.

(iii) Household structure and kinship

3.180 **Bennett**, M., 'Spiritual kinship and the baptismal name in traditional European society', in L. O. Frappell, ed., *Principalities, Powers and Estates: Studies in Medieval and Early Modern Government and Society* (Adelaide, 1979), 1–12. Wider than

Britain, but an interesting and little-studied question.

3.181 **Boyle**, A., 'Matrilineal succession in the Pictish monarchy', *Scot. H. R.*, 56 (1977), 1–10.

3.182 **Charles-Edwards**, T., *Early Irish and Welsh Kinship* (1993).

3.183 **Haas**, L., 'Social connections between parents and godparents in late medieval Yorkshire', *Med. Prosopog.*, 10.1 (1989), 1–21.

3.184 **Lancaster**, L., 'Kinship in Anglo-Saxon society', *Brit. J. Sociol.*, 9 (1938), 230–50 and 359–77.

3.185 **Loyn**, H., 'Kinship in Anglo-Saxon England', in P. Clemoes, et al., eds., *Anglo-Saxon England*, 3 (1974), 197–210.

3.186 **Nelson**, J., 'Reconstructing a royal family: reflections on Alfred, from Asser, chapter 2', in I. Wood and N. Lund, eds., *People and Places in Northern Europe, Essays in Honour of P. H. Sawyer* (1991), 47–66. On Alfred's mother and maternal ancestry.

3.187 **Patterson**, N. T., *Early Irish Kinship: the Legal Structure of the Agnatic Descent Group* (Boston, Mass., 1988).

3.188 **Philpotts**, B., *Kindred and Clan in the Middle Ages and After* (1913). Still a useful and clear survey of kindred structures.

3.189 **Smith**, L. B., 'Fosterage, adoption and god-parenthood: ritual and fictive kinship in medieval Wales', *Welsh Hist. Rev.*, 16 (1992), 1–35.

3.190 **Smith**, R. M., 'Kin and neighbours in a thirteenth-century Suffolk community', *J. Fam. Hist.*, 4 (1977), 219–56.

See also: 2.108; 3.155; 3.176.

(iv) Household management, home life, estate management, living standards

3.191 **Archer**, R. A., 'The estates and finances of Margaret of Brotherton, *c.* 1320–1399', *Hist. Res.*, 60.143 (1987), 264–80.

3.192 — ' "How ladies . . . who live on their manors ought to manage their households and estates": women as landholders and administrators in the later middle ages', in P. J. P. Goldberg, ed., *Woman is a Worthy Wight: Women in English Society c. 1200–1500* (1992), 149–81. Argues for partnership of husband and wife.

3.193 **Blackley**, D. and **Hermansen**, G., eds., *The Household Book of Queen Isabella for the Fifth Regnal Year of Edward II* (Edmonton, Alberta, 1971).

3.194 **Chambers**, W. and R., *Dame Alice de Bryene* (1977).

3.195 **Howell**, M., 'The resources of Eleanor of Provence as queen consort', *Eng. H. R.*, 102 (1987), 372–93.

3.196 **LaBarge**, M. W., *A Baronial Household of the Thirteenth Century* (1965, reprinted 1980). Chapter on the Lady of the house.

3.197 **Mate**, M., 'Profit and productivity on the estates of Isabella de Forz 1260–1292', *Ec. H. R.*, sec. ser., 33 (1980), 326–34.

3.198 **Mertes**, K., *The English Noble Household 1250–1600* (1988).

3.199 **Myers**, A. R., 'The household of Queen Elizabeth Woodville, 1466–7', *Bull. J. Ry. Lib.*, 50 (1967 and 1968), 207–35 and 443–81.

3.200 — 'The household of Queen Margaret of Anjou, 1452–3', *Bull. J. Ry. Lib.*, 40 (1957–8), 1–21.

3.201 **Owen**, G. 'Wynflaed's wardrobe', in P. Clemoes, et al., eds., *Anglo-Saxon England*, 8 (1979), 195–222. A tenth-century woman's will with details of her household effects.

3.202 **Owen-Crocker**, G. R., *Dress in Anglo-Saxon England* (1990).

3.203 **Redstone**, V. B., *The Household Book of Dame Alice de Bryene of Acton Hall, Suffolk, Sept. 1412–Sept. 1413* (1931).

3.204 **Ross**, C. D., 'The household accounts of Elizabeth Berkeley, countess of Warwick, 1420–1', *Trans. of the Bristol and Gloucestershire Archaeological Soc.*, 70 (1951), 81–105.

3.205 **Speake**, G., *A Saxon Bed Burial on Swallowcliffe Down*, English Heritage Archaeological reports, 10 (1989). A woman's grave and its grave goods, including personal and household objects.

3.206 **Underwood**, M. G., 'Politics and piety in the household of Lady Margaret Beaufort', *J. Ecc. Hist.*, 38.1 (1987), 39–52.

See also: 3.270; 3.346; 3.530.

(v) Motherhood, child/parent relations, affective and interpersonal relations

3.207 **Atkinson**, C. W., *The Oldest Vocation: Christian Motherhood in the Middle Ages* (Ithaca, New York, 1991).

3.208 **Attreed**, L. C., 'From *Pearl* maiden to

Tower princes: towards a new history of medieval childhood', *J. Med. Hist.*, 9.1 (1983), 43–58.

3.209 **Benton**, J. 'Clio and Venus, an historical view of medieval love', in F. X. Newman, ed., *The Meaning of Courtly Love* (New York, 1968). Not specifically British, but a key article in a seminal collection on courtly love.

3.210 **Demaitre**, L., 'The idea of childhood and childcare in the medical writings of the middle ages', *J. Psychohist.*, 4, Spring (1977), 461–90. Not specifically British.

3.211 **Ellis**, D. S., 'Domestic treachery in *The Clerk's tale*', in C. Levin and J. Watson, eds., *Ambiguous Realities, Women in the Middle Ages and Renaissance* (Detroit, 1987), 99–113.

3.212 **Fildes**, V., *Wet Nursing, a History from Antiquity to the Present* (1988). Europe-wide.

3.213 **Findon**, J., 'Male-female relationships in the four branches of the *Mabinogi*', *Scintilla*, 6 (1989), 1–29.

3.214 **Francois**, M. E., 'Adults and children: against evil or against each other', *Hist. Child. Q.*, 1.1 (1973–4), 164–77.

3.215 **Gransden**, A., 'Childhood and youth in medieval England', *Nottingham Med. Studs.*, 16 (1972), 3–19.

3.216 **Hanawalt**, B. A., 'Childrearing among the lower classes of late medieval England', *J. Interdis. Hist.*, 8 (1977), 1–22.

3.217 — 'Conception through infancy in medieval English historical and folklore sources', *Folk. For.*, 13 (1980), 127–57.

3.218 **Helmholz**, R. H., 'Infanticide in the province of Canterbury during the fifteenth century', *Hist. Child. Q.*, 2 (1975), 379–90.

3.219 **Kellum**, B. A., 'Infanticide in England in the later middle ages', *Hist. Child. Q.*, 1 (1974), 367–88.

3.220 **Kettle**, A. J., ' "My wife shall have it": marriage and property in the wills and testaments of later medieval England', in E. M. Craik, ed., *Marriage and Property* (1984), 89–103. Women's property rights during and after marriage and affection in marriage.

3.221 **Kueffler**, M. S., ' "A wryed existence": attitudes towards children in Anglo-Saxon England', *J. of Social History*, 24 (1991), 823–34.

3.222 **McLaughlin**, M. M., 'Survivors and surrogates: children and parents from the ninth to the thirteenth centuries', in L. deMause, ed., *History of Childhood* (New York, 1975), 101–81.

3.223 **Shahar**, S., *Childhood in the Middle Ages* (London and New York, 1990). Europe-wide.

3.224 **Smith**, R. D., 'Anglo-Saxon maternal ties', in E. Kooper, ed., *This Noble Craft*, Proceedings of the Xth Research Symposium of the Dutch and Belgian University teachers of Old and Middle English and Historical Linguistics (Amsterdam, 1991), 106–17.

3.225 **Staniland**, K., 'Royal entry into the world', in D. Williams, ed., *England in the Fifteenth Century* (1987), 297–313. Birth and baptism ceremonies for Arthur and Margaret, children of Henry VII.

3.226 **Turner**, R. V., 'Eleanor of Aquitaine and her children: an enquiry into medieval family attachment', *J. Med. Hist.*, 14.4 (1988), 321–35.

3.227 — 'The children of Anglo-Norman royalty and their upbringing', *Med. Prosopog.*, 11.2 (1990), 17–52.

3.228 **Walker**, S. S., 'The marrying of feudal wards in medieval England', *Studs. Med. Cult.*, 4.2 (1974), 209–24.

3.229 — 'Widow and ward, the feudal law of child custody in medieval England', *Fem. Studs*, 3 (1976), 104–16; also in S. M. Stuard, ed., *Women in Medieval Society* (Philadelphia, 1976), 159–72.

See also: 3.34; 3.110; 3.138; 3.147; 3.150; 3.177; 3.238; 3.535; 3,536; 3.547; 4.208.

(vi) Family size, infant mortality, family limitation, illegitimacy

3.230 **Barton**, J. L., 'Nullity of marriage and illegitimacy in the England of the Middle Ages', in D. Jenkins, ed., *Legal History Studies, Papers Presented to the Legal History Conference, Aberystwyth, 1972* (1975), 28–49.

3.231 **Biller**, P. P. A., 'Birth control in the medieval West', *P. P.*, 94 (1982), 3–26. Europe-wide.

3.232 **Helmholz**, R. H., 'Bastardy litigation in medieval England', *Am. J. Legal Hist.*, 13 (1969), 360–83.

3.233 **Hollingsworth**, T. H., 'A demographic study of the British ducal families', *Pop. Studs.*, 11 (1957–8), 4–26.

3.234 **Jones**, E. D., 'Going round in circles: some new evidence for population in the later middle ages', *J. Med. Hist.*, 15 (1989), 329–45. Evidence on villein families from Spalding Priory; particular attention given to sex ratios, rates of female marriage and child survival rates. See also a rejoinder by M. Bailey in *op. cit.*, 347–58.

3.235 **Krause**, J. T. 'The medieval household, large or small', *Ec. H. R.*, sec. ser., 9 (1956–7), 420–32. A critique of Russell.

3.236 **McLaren**, A., *A History of Contraception from Antiquity to the Present Day* (1990). Europe-wide, but a good up-to-date survey.

3.237 **Noonan**, J. T., *Contraception. A History of its Treatment by the Catholic Theologians and Canonists* (Cambridge, Mass., 1966). Europe-wide.

3.238 **Parsons**, J. C., 'The year of Eleanor of Castile's birth and her children by Edward I', *Med. Studs.*, 46 (1984), 245–65.

3.239 **Payling**, S. J., 'Social mobility, demographic change and landed society in late medieval England', *Econ. Hist. Rev.*, ser. 2, 45 (1992), 51–73. Implications of demographic change for growing numbers of female heiresses.

3.240 **Ranum**, O. and P., eds., *Popular Attitudes Toward Birth Control in Pre-industrial France and England* (1972).

3.241 **Riddle**, J. M., 'Oral contraceptives and early term abortifacients during classical Antiquity and the middle ages', *P.P.*, 132 (1991), 3–32. Europe-wide.

3.242 **Russell**, J. C., *British Medieval Population* (Albuquerque, New Mexico, 1948).

3.243 **Walker**, S. S., 'Proof of age of feudal heirs in medieval England', *Med. Studs.*, 35 (1973), 306–23.

3.244 **Warwick**, R., 'Anne Mowbray: skeletal remains of a medieval child', *London Arch.*, 5.7 (1986), 176–9.

3.245 **White**, G. H., 'Henry I's illegitimate children', in G. E. Cockayne et al., eds., *The Complete Peerage*, Vol. II (1949), Appendix D, 105–21.
See also: 3.122; 3.218; 3.219.

(vii) Widows

3.246 **Archer**, R. A., 'Rich old ladies: the problem of late medieval dowagers', in T. Pollard, ed., *Property and Politics: Essays in Later Medieval English History* (1984), 15–35.

3.247 **Bailey**, S. J., 'Countess Gundred's lands', *Camb. Law J.*, 10 (1948–50), 84–103. A

late twelfth-century widow pursues her dower.

3.248 **Brownbill**, J., 'The Countess Lucy', *Complete Peerage*, Vol. 7, Appendix J, 743–6. One of the most important noble widows of the early twelfth century.

3.249 **Clark**, E., 'The quest for security in medieval England', in M. Sheehen, ed., *Aging and the Aged in Medieval Europe*, selected papers from the annual conference of the Centre for Medieval Studies, Papers in Medieval Studies, 11 (Toronto, 1990), 189–200.

3.250 **Franklin**, P., 'Peasant widows' "liberation" and remarriage before the Black Death', *Ec. H. R.*, sec. ser., 39 (1986), 186–202. Argues for the importance and independence of widows in rural society even pre-1348.

3.251 **Fraser**, C., 'Four Cumberland widows in the fourteenth century', *Trans. Cumb. West. Antiq. Arch. Soc.*, 64 (1964), 130–7. Widows under attack and pursuing their rights.

3.252 **Griffiths**, R. A., 'Queen Katherine of Valois and a missing statute of the realm', *Law Q. R.*, 93 (1977), 248–58. Fifteenth-century regulation of the marriage of queen dowagers. Response by Hand, G., 'The king's widow and the king's widows', *Law Q. R.*, 93 (1977), 506–7.

3.253 **Hicks**, M., 'The last days of Elizabeth, countess of Oxford', *Eng. H. R.*, 100 (1988), 76–95. Discusses the dispositions the countess made of her lands and the pressure exerted on her.

3.254 **LaBarge**, M. W., 'Three medieval widows and a second career', in M. Sheehan, ed., *Aging and the Aged in Medieval Europe*, selected papers from the annual conference of the Centre for Medieval Studies, Papers in Medieval Studies, 11 (Toronto, 1990), 159–72. Loretta, countess of Leicester and Ela, countess of Salisbury.

3.255 **Minois**, G., *History of Old Age from Antiquity to the Renaissance* (1989). Europe-wide but an interesting survey of attitudes to the elderly.

3.256 **Rivers**, T. J., 'Widows' rights in Anglo-Saxon law', *Am. J. Legal Hist.*, 19 (1975), 208–15.

3.257 **Rosenthal**, J. T., 'Aristocratic widows in fifteenth-century England', in B. J. Harris and J. A. McNamara, eds., *Women in the Structure of Society, 5th Berkshire Conference on the History of Women* (Durham,

N.Carolina, 1984), 36–47 and 259–60. Insight into preoccupations and personality from wills.

3.258 — 'Other victims, peeresses as war widows, 1450–1500', *History*, 72 (1987), 213–30.

3.259 — 'Retirement and life-cycle in fifteenth-century England', in M. Sheehan, eds., *Aging and the Aged in Medieval Europe*, selected papers from the annual conference of the Centre for Medieval Studies, Papers in Medieval Studies, 11 (Toronto, 1990), 173–88.

3.260 **Sheehan**, M., 'A preliminary bibliography on aging and the aged in medieval Europe', in M. Sheehan, ed., *Aging and the Aged in Medieval Europe*, selected papers from the annual conference of the Centre for Medieval Studies, Papers in Medieval Studies, 11 (Toronto, 1990), 209–14.

3.261 **Smith**, R. M., 'The manorial court and the elderly tenant in late medieval England', in M. Pelling and R. M. Smith, eds., *Life, Death and the Elderly, Historical Perspectives* (1991), 39–61. On retirement, provision for it and enforcement of that provision.

3.262 **Walker**, S. S., 'Feudal constraint and free consent in the making of marriages in medieval England: widows in the King's Gift', *Historical papers, Communications Historiques*, Canadian Historical Association (1979), 97–110.

3.263 — 'Violence and the exercise of feudal guardianship: the action of *"ejectio custodia"* ', *Am. J. Legal Hist.*, 16 (1969), 320–33.

See also: 3.100; 3.275; 3.279.

(d) LEGAL STATUS OF WOMEN

3.264 **Archer**, R. A. and **Ferme**, B. E., 'Testamentary procedure with special reference to the executrix', in K. Bate, et al., eds., *Medieval Women in Southern England*, Reading Medieval Studies 15 (1989), 3–34. On the development of wills, executors and women's role as executors in late Middle Ages.

3.265 **Bateson**, M., *Borough Custom*, Selden Society (1904). A collection of original documents covering the statutory position of women traders, producers, control over urban property, legal relations of husband and wife.

3.266 **Buckstaff**, F., 'Married women's property in Anglo-Norman law and the origin of Common law dower', *Annals Am. Acad. Pol. Soc. Sci*, 4 (1894), 233–64.

3.267 **Charles-Edwards**, T. M., 'Nau Kynywedi teithlauc', in D. Jenkins and M. E. Owen, eds., *The Welsh Law of Women, Studies Presented to Prof. D. A. Binchy on his Eightieth birthday* (1980), 23–39. In English. Early Welsh laws on marriage, compared with Irish and Hindu.

3.268 **Collett**, K. A. S., 'Women in the laws of Hywel Dda', *Acta. Proceedings of the SUNY Regional Conferences in Medieval Studies*, 15, for 1988 (1990), 151–70.

3.269 **Crawford**, A., 'Victims of attainder: the Howard and de Vere women in the late fifteenth century', in K. Bate et al., eds., *Medieval Women in Southern England*, Reading Medieval Studies, 15 (1989), 59–74.

3.270 **Fell**, C. E., 'A *friwif locbore* revisited', in P. Clemoes et al., eds., *Anglo-Saxon England*, 13 (1984) 157–65. Argues that this term in early English law means a female householder.

3.271 **Haskins**, G. L., 'The development of common law dower', *Harvard Law R.*, 62 (1948–9), 42–55.

3.272 **Holt**, J. C., 'Feudal society and the family in early medieval England', *T.R.H.S.*, ser., 5, Vols. 32–35 (1982–5). Of particular relevance to women and their landholding is part IV, 'The Heiress and the Alien', ser. 5, Vol. 35 (1985), 1–28.

3.273 **Jenkins**, D., 'Property interests in the classic Welsh Law of Women', in D. Jenkins and M. E. Owen, eds., *The Welsh Law of Women, Studies Presented to Prof. D. A. Binchy on his Eightieth Birthday* (1980), 69–92.

3.274 — and **Charles-Edwards**, T. M., 'Texts of the tractate on the Law of Women', in D. Jenkins and M. E. Owen, eds., *The Welsh Law of Women, Studies Presented to Prof. D. A. Binchy on his Eightieth Birthday* (1980), 132–227. Text, translation and glossary.

3.275 **Jewell**, H. M., 'Women at the courts of the manor of Wakefield, 1348–1350', *North.*

Hist., 26 (1990), 59–81. Women as landholders, as creditors and debtors; on women's economic activities, crimes committed by them and against them, plus details on dower and merchet.

3.276 **Kittel**, R, 'Women under the law in medieval England, 1066–1485', in B. Kanner, ed., *The Women of England from Anglo-Saxon Times to the Present* (Hamden, Conn., 1979), 124–37.

3.277 **Klinck**, A., 'Anglo-Saxon women and the law', *J. Med. Hist.*, 8 (1982), 107–21.

3.278 **Leedom**, J. W., 'Lady Mathilda Holland, Henry of Lancaster and the manor of Melbourne', *Am. J. Legal Hist.*, 31.2 (1987), 118–25.

3.279 **Loengard**, J. S., 'Of the gift of her husband; English dower and its consequences in the year 1200', in J. Kirschner and S. F. Wemple, eds., *Women of the Medieval World* (1985), 215–55.

3.280 **McAll**, C., 'The normal paradigms of a woman's life in the Irish and Welsh texts', in D. Jenkins and M. E. Owen, eds., *The Welsh Law of Women, Studies Presented to Prof. D. A. Binchy on his Eightieth Birthday* (1980), 7–22.

3.281 **Meyer**, M. A., 'Land charters and the legal position of Anglo-Saxon women', in B. Kanner, ed., *The Women of England from Anglo-Saxon Times to the Present* (Hamden, Conn., 1979), 57–82.

3.282 **Milsom**, S. F. C., 'Inheritance by women in the twelfth and early thirteenth centuries', in M. S. Arnold et al., eds., *On the Laws and Customs of England: Essays in Honor of S. E. Thorne* (Chapel Hill, Carolina, 1981), 60–89.

3.283 **Pollock**, F. and **Maitland**, F. W., *The History of English Law*, 2 vols. (1898, reissued with intro. by S. F. C. Milsom 1968). Still an excellent starting point on family law, marriage and property, husband and wife's legal capacities etc. for the twelfth and thirteenth centuries, though substantially revised by other items in this section.

3.284 **Power**, N., 'Classes of women described in the *Senchas Mar*', in R. Thurneysen et al., eds., *Studies in Early Irish Law* (Dublin, 1936), 81–108. Still an important introduction to the legal status of early Irish women.

3.285 **Searle**, E., 'Women and the legitimation of succession at the Norman Conquest', in R. A. Brown, ed., *Proceedings of the Battle Abbey Conference 1980*, 3 (*Anglo-Norman Studies*, 3) (1981), 159–70. Argues for the role of marriage to English women in legitimating Norman succession.

3.286 **Sheehan**, M. M., 'The influence of Canon law on the property rights of married women in England', *Med. Studs.*, 25 (1963), 109–24.

3.287 **Simms**, K., 'The legal position of Irishwomen in the later middle ages', *Irish Jurist*, new ser., 9 (1975), 96–111.

3.288 **Smith**, R. M., 'Women's property rights under customary law: some developments in the thirteenth and fourteenth centuries', *Trans of Royal Hist. Soc.*, ser. 5 (1986), 165–94.

3.289 — 'Coping with uncertainty: women's tenure of customary land in England c.1370–1430', in J. Kermode, ed., *Enterprise and Individuals in Fifteenth-Century England* (1991), 43–67.

3.290 **Walters**, D. B., 'The European context of the Welsh Law of Women', in D. Jenkins and M. E. Owen, eds., *The Welsh Law of Women, Studies Presented to Prof. D. A. Binchy on his Eightieth Birthday* (1980), 115–31.

3.291 **Waugh**, S. L., 'Women's inheritance and the growth of bureaucratic monarchy in twelfth- and thirteenth-century England', *Nottingham Med. Stud.*, 34 (1990), 71–92.

See also: 2.120; 3.4; 3.95; 3.121; 3.177; 3.220; 3.229; 3.246; 3.256; 3.349; 3.354; 3.464.

(e) WOMEN AND HEALTH

3.292 **Amundsen**, D. W. and **Diers**, C. J., 'The age of menarche in medieval Europe', *Hum. Biol.*, 45 (1973), 363–8. Europe-wide, reviews the medical authorities.

3.293 — 'The age of menopause in medieval Europe', *Human Biology*, 45 (1973), 605–12. Europe-wide, reviews the medical authorities.

3.294 **Blumenfeld-Kosinski**, R., *Not of Woman Born, Representations of Caesarean Birth in Medieval and Renaissance Culture* (Ithaca, New York, and London, 1990). Europe-wide.

3.295 **Deegan**, M., 'Pregnancy and childbirth in Anglo-Saxon medical texts: a preliminary survey', in M. Deegan and D. Scragg, eds., *Medicine in Early England* (1989), 17–26.

3.296 **Grattan**, J. H. G. and **Singer**, C., *Anglo-Saxon Magic and Medicine* (1952).

3.297 **Green**, M., 'Women's medical practice and health care in medieval Europe', *Signs*, 14.2 (1989), 434–73. Europe-wide.

3.298 **Hawkes**, S. C. and Wells, C., 'An Anglo-Saxon obstetric calamity from Kingsworthy, Hampshire', *Medical Biol. Illus.*, 25 (1975), 47–51.

3.299 **Kealey**, E. J., *Medieval Medicus, a Social History of Anglo-Norman Medicine* (Baltimore, Maryland, 1981).

3.300 **Keefer**, S. L., 'A monastic echo in an Old English Charm', *Leeds Studs. in Eng.*, new ser., 21 (1990), 71–80. A charm for delayed birth.

3.301 **Murray**, J., 'On the origins and role of "wise women" in causes for annulment on the grounds of male impotence', *J. of Med. hist.*, 16 (1990), 235–49.

3.302 **Porter**, R., 'Margery Kempe and the meaning of madness', *Hist. Today*, 38.2 (1988), 39–44.

3.303 **Post**, J. B., 'Age at menopause and menarche; some medieval authorities', *Pop. Studs.*, 25 (1971), 83–7.

3.304 **Rowland**, B., 'The wife of Bath's "unlawful philtrum" ', *Neophilologus*, 56.2 (1972), 201–6.

3.305 — ed., *Medieval Woman's Guide to Health: the First English Gynecological Handbook* (Kent, Ohio, 1981) .

3.306 **Rubin**, S., *Medieval English medicine A.D. 500–1300* (New York and Newton Abbot, 1974). Ideas about and treatment of female reproductive system current in Middle Ages.

3.307 **Talbot**, C. H., *Medicine in Medieval England* (1967).

3.308 **Wood**, C. T., 'The doctors' dilemma: sin, salvation and the menstrual cycle in medieval thought', *Speculum*, 56 (1981), 710–27.

See also: 3.231; 3.532; 4.270.

(f) WOMEN'S SEXUALITY

3.309 **Bullough**, V. L., 'Transvestites in the Middle Ages', *Am. J. Soc.*, 79 (May, 1974), 1381–94.

3.310 **Campbell**, M. A., 'Redefining holy maidenhood: virginity and lesbianism in late medieval England', *Med. Fem. News.*, 13, Spring (1992), 14–15.

3.311 **Carney**, E., 'Fact and fiction in "Queen Eleanor's confession" ', *Folklore*, 95.2 (1984), 167–70. Folk memory in ballad form of Eleanor of Aquitaine's alleged adultery.

3.312 **Cotter**, J. F., 'The wife of Bath and the conjugal debt', *Eng. Lang. Notes*, 6.3 (1969), 169–72. Argues that husbands not wives owe partner sexual satisfaction.

3.313 **Davidson**, C., 'Erotic women's songs in Anglo-Saxon England', *Neophilologus*, 59 (1975), 451–62.

3.314 **Davies**, A., 'Sexual behaviour in later Anglo-Saxon England', in E. Kooper, ed., *This Noble Craft Proceedings of the Xth Research Symposium of the Dutch and Belgian University teachers of Old and Middle English and Historical Linguistics* (Amsterdam, 1991), 83–105.

3.315 **Delasanta**, R., '*Quoniam* and the wife of Bath', *Papers on Lang. and Lit.*, 8.2 (1972), 202–6. Argues that the view of sexuality here is a clerical one.

3.316 **Dinshaw**, C., 'The heterosexual subject of Chaucerian narrative', *Med. Fem. News.*, 13 (Spring 1992), 8–10. On lesbian and heterosexual identity.

3.317 **Hair**, P. E. H., *Before the Bawdy Court, Selections from the Church Court and Other Records Relating to the Correction of Moral Offences in England, Scotland and New England, 1300–1800* (1972). Material on sexual offenders.

3.318 **Jones**, E. D., 'The medieval leyrwite: a historical note on female fornication', *Eng. H. R.*, 107 (1992), 945–53. Spalding evidence on fines for female fornication, with suggestion of the operation of a brothel.

3.319 **Lemay**, H. R., 'Some thirteenth and fourteenth-century lectures on female sexuality', *Int. J. Women's Studs.*, 1 (July-August, 1978), 391–400. Europe-wide.

3.320 — 'The stars and human sexuality; some medieval scientific views', *Isis*, 71 (March, 1980), 127–37. Europe-wide.

3.321 **Meyer**, M. A., 'Early Anglo-Saxon penitentials and the position of women', *Haskins Soc. J.*, 2 (1990), 47–61. Ecclesiastical controls on women's sexuality.

3.322 **North**, T., 'Legerwite in the fourteenth

and fifteenth centuries', *P. P.* 111 (1986), 3–16.

3.323 **Partner**, N. F., 'Reading the *Book* of Margery Kempe', *Exemplaria*, 3.1 (1991), 29–66. Discusses her attitudes to marriage, sexuality and celibacy.

3.324 **Payer**, P. J., *Sex and the Penitentials* (Toronto, 1984). Concerned with the penance books of the early middle ages.

3.325 **Radcliff-Umstead**, D., ed., *Human Sexuality in the Middle Ages and Renaissance*, University of Pittsburgh Publications on the Middle Ages and Renaissance, 4 (Pittsburgh, 1978). Europe-wide.

3.326 **Schibanoff**, S., 'Chaucer's lesbians: drawing blanks', Med. Fem. News., 13, Spring (1992), 11–14.

3.327 **Spear**, L. M., 'The treatment of sexual sin in the Irish Latin penitential literature', *Dissertation Abstracts International*, A 40.11 (1980), 5963.

3.328 **Williams**, E. W., 'What's so new about the sexual revolution? Some comments on Anglo-Saxon attitudes towards sexuality in women based on four Exeter Book riddles', *Texas Q.*, 18 (1975), 46–55.

See also: 3.72; 3.89; 3.110; 3.237; 3.472; 4.313–4.

(g) WOMEN AND WORK

(i) General

3.329 **Barron**, C. M., 'The Golden age of women in medieval London', in K. Bate et al., eds., *Women in Southern England*, Reading Medieval studies, 15 (1989), 35–58. Views the late Middle Ages as a period of economic prosperity and female economic activity.

3.330 **Bennett**, J. M., 'Misogyny, popular culture and women's work', *Hist. Workshop J.*, 31, Spring (1991), 166–88.

3.331 **Charles**, L., 'Introduction' to L. Charles and L. Duffin, eds., *Women and Work in Pre-industrial England* (1985), 1–23. Assesses changing thinking on the significance for women of transitions to capitalism and industrialisation.

3.332 **Fransson**, G., *Middle English Surnames of*

Occupation, Lund Studies in English, 3 (Lund, 1935).

3.333 **Goldberg**, P. J. P., 'Female labour, service and marriage in the late medieval North', *North. Hist.*, 22 (1986), 18–38.

3.334 — 'Women's work, women's role in the late medieval North', in M. Hicks, ed., *Profit, Piety and the Professions in Later Medieval England* (1990), 34–50.

3.335 — 'The public and the private: women in the pre-plague economy', in P. R. Coss and J. D. Lloyd, eds., *Thirteenth Century England* (1991), 75–89. Contains a critique of work by Hanawalt and Bennett; see nos. 3.88 and 3.100.

3.336 — *Women, Work and Life Cycle in a Medieval Economy, Women in York and Yorkshire, c. 1300–1520* (1992). Wide-ranging and important discussion of women's work in relation to life-cycle and marriage.

3.337 **Graham**, H., ' "A woman's work . . ." labour and gender in the late medieval countryside', in P. J. P. Goldberg, ed., *Woman is a Worthy Wight: Women in English society c. 1200–1500* (1992), 126–48. Discussion of women's work and critique of Bennett on women and brewing, 3.344.

3.338 **Hanawalt**, B., 'Peasant women's contribution to the home economy in late medieval England', in B. Hanawalt, ed., *Women and Work in Pre-industrial Europe* (Bloomington, Indiana, 1986), 3–19.

3.339 **Hutton**, D., 'Women in fourteenth-century Shrewsbury', in L. Charles and L. Duffin, eds., *Women and Work in Pre-industrial England* (1985), 83–99.

3.340 **Jordan**, W. C., 'Women and credit in the middle ages, problems and directions', *J. European Ec. Hist.*, 17.1 (1988), 33–61. Europe-wide.

3.341 **Kowaleski**, M., 'Women's work in a market town: Exeter in the late fourteenth century', in B. Hanawalt, ed., *Women and Work in Pre-industrial Europe* (Bloomington, Indiana, 1986), 145–64.

3.342 **Lacey**, K., 'Women and work in fourteenth – and fifteenth-century London', in L. Charles and L. Duffin, eds., *Women and Work in Pre-industrial England* (1985), 24–82. Includes material on the legal situation of women under common, canon and borough law.

3.343 **Middleton**, C., 'The sexual division of labour in feudal England', *New Left R.*,

113–14 (1979), 147–68. A Marxist interpretation of medieval peasant labour.
See also: 2.7; 2.120; 3.10; 3.16; 3.141; 3.155; 3.176; 3.177; 3.248; 3.275; 4.355.

(ii) Industrial

3.344 **Bennett**, J., 'The village ale wife: women and brewing in fourteenth-century England', in B. Hanawalt, ed., *Women and Work in Pre-industrial Europe* (Bloomington, Indiana, 1986), 20–36.

3.345 — 'Misogyny, popular culture and women's work', *History Workshop J.*, 31 (1991), 166–88. On the brewing industry.

3.346 **Blair**, J. and **Ramsay**, N., *English Medieval Industries. Craftsmen, Techniques, Products* (1991). Some information on women as blacksmiths, glovers, potters, tilers and in the textile industry.

3.347 **Dale**, M. K., 'The London silkwomen of the fifteenth century', *Ec. H. R.*, 4 (1933), 324–35. A classic article reprinted with an introduction comparing recent work on women and guilds elsewhere in Europe by M. Kowaleski and J. Bennett in *Signs*, 14.2 (1989), 474–501.

3.348 **Lacey**, K., 'The production of "narrow ware" by silkwomen in fourteenth- and fifteenth-century England', *Textile Hist.*, 18.2 (1987), 187–204. Appendix lists known silkwomen in London, 1300–1500.

3.349 **Robertson**, W. D., ' "And for my land thus hastow mordred me?" Land tenure, the cloth industry, and the Wife of Bath', *Chaucer Rev.*, 14 (1980), 403–20.

3.350 **Sutton**, A., 'Alice Claver, silkwoman of London and maker of mantle laces for Richard III and Queen Anne', *Ricardian*, 3.70 (1980), 243–7.
See also: 3.265; 3.337.

(iii) Agricultural and horticultural

3.351 **Ault**, W. O., *Open-Field Farming in Medieval England* (1972). A classic study with information on women.

3.352 **Beveridge**, W., 'Wages in the Winchester manors', *Ec. H. R.*, 7 (1936), 22–43. Still an important collection of statistics.

3.353 — 'Westminster wages in the manorial era', *Ec. H. R*, sec. ser., 8 (1955), 18–35.

3.354 **Middleton**, C., 'Peasants, patriarchy and the feudal mode of production in England,

a Marxist appraisal. Part 1 – property and patriarchal relations within the peasantry. Part 2 – feudal lords and the subordination of peasant women', *Sociological R.*, new ser., 29 (1981), 137–54.

3.355 **Penn**, S. A. C., 'Female wage earners in late fourteenth-century England', *Agric. H. R.*, 35 (1987), 1–14. Women in the rural labour force; contains warnings of possible gender bias in presentations under the Statute of Labourers.

3.356 **Roberts**, M., 'Sickles and scythes: women's work and men's work at harvest time', *Hist. Workshop J.*, 7 (1979), 3–28. The period following the Black Death.
See also: 3.88; 3.100.

(iv) Commercial

3.357 **Abram**, A., 'Women traders in medieval London', *Ec. J.*, 26 (1916), 276–85. A classic article.

3.358 **Hilton**, R. H., 'Lords, Burgesses and hucksters', *P. P.*, 97 (1982), 3–15, repr. in R. H. Hilton, *Class Conflict and the Crisis of Feudalism, Essays in Medieval Social History*, (1985), 194–204.

3.359 — 'Women traders in medieval England', in R. H. Hilton, ed., *Class Conflict and the Crisis of Feudalism, Essays in Medieval Social History* (1985), 205–15.
See also: 3.88; 3.341; 3.342.

(v) Professional

3.360 **Power**, E., 'Some women practitioners of medicine in the middle ages', *Pcdgs. Royal Scy. Medicine*, 14 (December, 1921), 21–3.
See also: 3.297; 3.562.

(h) WOMEN AND THE WIDER WORLD

3.361 **Luttrell**, A. T., 'Englishwomen as pilgrims to Jerusalem, Isolda Parewastell, 1365', in J. B. Holloway, C. S. Wright and J. Bechtold, eds., *Equally in God's Image: Women in the Middle Ages* (New York, 1990), 184–97.

3.362 **Weissman**, H. P., 'Margery Kempe in Jerusalem, *hysterica compassio* in the late middle ages', in M. J. Carruthers and E. D.

Kirk, eds., *Acts of Interpretation, the Text in its Context, 700–1600, Essays on Medieval and Renaissance Literature in Honor of E. Talbot Donaldson* (Norman, Oklahoma, 1982), 201–17.
See also: 3.141; 3.155; 3.336; 3.359; 3.540.

(i) WOMEN, POLITICS AND POWER

3.363 **Bagley**, J. J., *Margaret of Anjou* (no date).

3.364 **Baker**, D., 'A nursery of saints: St Margaret of Scotland reconsidered', in D. Baker, ed., *Medieval Women*, Studs. in Church History, Subsidia 1 (1978), 119–41.

3.365 **Barrow**, G. W. S., 'A kingdom in crisis: Scotland and the Maid of Norway', *Scot. H. R.*, 69 (1990), 120–41. Role of the Maid and active involvement of several other Scottish women in thirteenth-century politics.

3.366 **Bennett**, J. M., 'Public power and authority in the medieval English countryside', in M. Erler and M. Kowaleski, eds., *Women and Power in the Middle Ages* (Athens, Georgia, 1989), 18–36.

3.367 **Biles**, M., 'The indomitable belle, Eleanor of Provence, queen of England', in R. H. Bowers, ed., *Seven Studies in Medieval and English History and Other Historical Essays Presented to H. S. Snellgrove* (Jackson, Mississippi, 1983), 113–31 and 195–6.

3.368 **Blackley**, F. D., 'Queen Isabella and the Bishop of Exeter', in T. A. Sandquist and M. R. Powicke, eds., *Essays in Medieval History Presented to Bertie Wilkinson* (Toronto, 1968), 220–35.

3.369 **Boyle**, J. R., 'Who was Eddeva?', *Trans. East Riding Antiq. Soc.*, 4 (1896), 11–22. Discussion of the identity and landholding of a powerful eleventh-century woman.

3.370 **Brown**, E. A. R., 'Eleanor of Aquitaine, parent, queen and duchess', in W. W. Kibler, ed., *Eleanor of Aquitaine, Patron and Politician* (Austin, Texas, and London, 1976), 9–34.

3.371 — 'The political importance of family ties in the early fourteenth century: the marriage of Edward II of England and Isabelle of France', *Speculum*, 63.3 (1988), 573–95.

3.372 **Campbell**, M. W., 'Queen Emma and Ælfgifu of Northampton: Canute the Great's women', *Med. Scandinavia*, 4 (1971), 66–79.

3.373 **Carey**, J., 'Notes on the Irish war-goddess', *Éigse* 19.2 (1983), 263–75.

3.374 **Chandler**, V., 'Ada de Warenne, Queen mother of Scotland (c. 1123–1178)', *Scot. H. R.*, 60 (1981), 119–39.

3.375 — 'Intimations of authority: notes on three Anglo-Norman countesses', *Indiana Social Studs Q.*, 31 (1978), 5–17. Mabel of Bellême, Lucy of Bolingbroke and Elizabeth of Vermandois.

3.376 **Chibnall**, M., 'The Empress Mathilda and church reform', *T.R.H.S.* ser. 5, 38 (1988), 107–30. Also contains an important discussion of the chroniclers' picture of Mathilda.

3.377 — 'The Empress Mathilda and Bec-Hellouin', in R. A. Brown, ed., *Anglo-Norman Studies*, 10, 1987 (1988), 35–48. A dispute over the question of her burial place.

3.378 — *The Empress Mathilda, Queen Consort, Queen Mother and Lady of the English* (1991).

3.379 **Cutler**, K., 'Edith, queen of England 1045–66', *Med. Studs.*, 35 (1973), 222–31.

3.380 **Ellis Davidson**, H. R., 'The legend of Lady Godiva', *Folklore* 80 (1969), 107–21.

3.381 **Erlanger**, P., *Margaret of Anjou, Queen of England*, E. Hyams, trans. (1970).

3.382 **Ferrante**, J. M., 'Public postures and private maneuvers: roles medieval women play', in M. Erler and M. Kowaleski, eds., *Women and Power in the Middle Ages* (Athens, Georgia, 1988), 213–29.

3.383 **Freeman**, E. F., 'The identity of Ælfgyva in the Bayeux Tapestry', *Annales de Normandie*, 41 (1991), 117–34. Argues she is Queen Emma. *See* 3.394.

3.384 **Hanson**, E. T., 'The powers of silence: the case of the Clerk's Griselda', in M. Erler and M. Kowaleski, eds., *Women and Power in the Middle Ages* (Athens, Georgia, 1988), 230–49.

3.385 **Herbert**, M., 'Goddess and king: the sacred marriage in early Ireland', *Women and Sovereignty, Cosmos, the Yearbook of the Traditional Cosmological Society*, Vol. 7 (1992), 264–75.

3.386 **Hunter**, J., 'Journal of the mission of

Queen Isabella for the court of France and of her long residence in that country', *Archaeologia*, 36 (1855), 242–57.

3.387   **Jones**, M., and Underwood, M., 'Lady Margaret Beaufort, 1443–1509', *Hist. Today*, 35.8 (1985), 23–30.

3.388   **Jones**, M. K. and **Underwood**, M. G., *The King's Mother. Lady Margaret Beaufort, Countess of Richmond and Derby* (1992).

3.389   **Kelly**, A. R., *Eleanor of Aquitaine and the Four Kings* (Cambridge, Mass., 1950, London, 1952).

3.390   **Lee**, P. A., 'Reflections of Power, Margaret of Anjou and the dark side of queenship', *Renaissance Q.*, 39.2 (1986), 183–217.

3.391   **Lifshitz**, F., 'The *Encomium Emmae Reginae*, a political pamphlet of the eleventh century?', *Haskins Soc. J.*, 1 (1989), 39–50. A queen's apologia.

3.392   **Loprete**, K. A., 'The Anglo-Norman card of Adela of Blois', *Albion*, 22 (1990), 269–89.

3.393   **MacGibbon**, D., *Elizabeth Woodville* (1938). Still the only full biography of this queen.

3.394   **McNulty**, J. B., 'The Lady Aelfgyva in the Bayeux tapestry', *Speculum*, 55 (1980), 659–68. On the mysterious identity of a woman in this highly political work. See 3.383.

3.395   **Menache**, S., 'Isabella of France, queen of England – a reconsideration', *J. Med. Hist.*, 10 (1984), 106–24.

3.396   **Menzies**, L., *St Margaret, Queen of Scotland* (1925).

3.397   **Meyer**, M. A., 'Women's estates in later Anglo-Saxon England: the politics of possession', *Haskins Soc. J.*, 3 (1991), 111–29.

3.398   **Monro**, C., *Letters of Queen Margaret of Anjou and Bishop Beckington and Others, Written in the Reigns of Henry V and Henry VI*, Camden Society, first ser., vol 86 (1863).

3.399   **Parsons**, D., ed., *Eleanor of Castile, 1290–1990, Essays to Commemorate the 700th Anniversary of her Death* (1991). Contains essays on the legend and reality, Eleanor crosses, burial customs and European context.

3.400   **Parsons**, J. C., 'Ritual and symbol in English medieval Queenship to 1500', in L. A. Fradenburg, ed., *Women and Sovereignty, Cosmos, the Yearbook of the Traditional Cosmological Society*, Vol. 7 (1992), 60–77.

3.401   — ed., *The Court and Household of Eleanor of Castile in 1290* (Toronto, Pontifical Institute of Medieval Studies, 1977).

3.402   **Prestwich**, M., 'Isabella de Vescy and the custody of Bamburgh castle', *Bull. Instit. Hist. Res.*, 44 (1971), 148–52.

3.403   **Reid**, N., 'Margaret "Maid of Norway" and Scottish queenship', *University of Reading Medieval Studs.*, 8 (1982), 75–96. The accession of a female minor.

3.404   **Searle**, E., 'Emma the Conqueror', in C. Harper-Bill, C. J. Holdsworth and J. L. Nelson, eds., *Studies in Medieval History Presented to R. Allen Brown* (1989), 281–8. Argues for the military interests of an eleventh-century queen.

3.405   **Smith**, G., *The Coronation of Elizabeth Woodville* (1935).

3.406   **Stafford**, P., *Queens, Concubines and Dowagers. The King's Wife in the Early Middle Ages* (London and Athens, Georgia, 1983). Europe-wide.

3.407   — 'Sons and mothers: family politics in the early Middle Ages', in D. Baker, ed., *Medieval Women*, Studs. in Church History, Subsidia 1 (1978), 79–100. Analysis of dynastic politics in early Middle Ages and their impact on women.

3.408   — 'The king's wife in Wessex, 800–1066', *P. P.*, 91 (1981), 3–27, repr. in H. Damico and A. Olsen, eds., *New Readings on Women in Old English literature* (Bloomington and Indianapolis, Indiana, 1991).

3.409   **Wainwright**, F. T., 'AEthelflaed, Lady of the Mercians', in P. Clemoes, ed., *The Anglo-Saxons, Studies Presented to Bruce Dickins* (1959), 53–69. Study of one of the few early medieval women to rule a kingdom.

3.410   **Wood**, C. T., 'The first two queens Elizabeth, 1464–1503', in L. O. Fradenburg, eds., *Women and sovereignty, Cosmos, the Yearbook of the Traditional Cosmological Society*, Vol. 7 (1992), 121–31.

See also: 3.10; 3.49; 3.50; 3.51; 3.76; 3.134; 3.148; 3.154; 3.195; 3.199; 3.206; 3.252; 3.253; 3.285; 3.477.

(j) WOMEN AND PROSTITUTION

3.411 **Karras**, R. M., 'The regulation of brothels in later medieval England', *Signs*, 14.2 (1989), 399–433.

3.412 **Post**, J. B., 'A fifteenth-century customary of the Southwark stews', *J. of Scy. of Archivists*, 5 (1977), 418–28.

See also: 3.10; 3.89; 3.317; 3.318; 3.336; 3.341.

(k) WOMEN AND CRIME

(i) Women as criminals

3.413 **Given**, J. B., *Society and Homicide in Thirteenth-century England* (Stanford, Conn., 1977). Chapter 3 on homicide and the medieval household and Chapter 7 for violence and sexual identity.

3.414 **Griffiths**, R. A., 'The trial of Eleanor Cobham: an episode in the fall of Duke Humphrey of Gloucester', *Bull. J. Ryl. Lib.*, 51 (1969), 381–99.

3.415 **Hanawalt**, B. A., 'The female felon in fourteenth-century England', *Viator*, 5 (1974), 253–68, reprinted in S. M. Stuard, ed., *Women in Medieval Society* (Philadelphia, 1976).

3.416 — 'The peasant family and crime in fourteenth-century England', *J. Brit. Studs.*, 13 (1974), 1–18.

See also: 2.120; 3.89; 3.275; 3.317.

(ii) Violence against women

3.417 **Carter**, J. M., 'Rape in medieval English society, the evidence of Yorkshire, Wiltshire and London, 1218–76', *Comitatus, a J. of Medieval and Renaissance Studs.*, 13 (1982), 33–63.

3.418 **Gransden**, A., 'The alleged rape by Edward III of the countess of Salisbury', *Eng. H. R.*, 87 (1972), 333–44. Rape used as a smear in war propaganda.

3.419 **Hawkes**, S. C. and **Wells**, C., 'Crime and punishment in an Anglo-Saxon cemetery', *Antiquity*, 49.194 (1975), 118–22. Argues

for evidence of rape and its punishment by death in a sixth-century cemetery. But see the response by N. Reynolds, 'The rape of the Anglo-Saxon women', *Antiquity*, 62.237 (1988), 715–18.

3.420 **Post**, J. B. 'Ravishment of women and the statute of Westminster', in J. H. Baker, ed., *Legal Records and the Historian* (1978), 150–64.

3.421 **Toner**, B., *The Facts of Rape* (1977). Survey of medieval common law of rape, 89–94.

3.422 **Walker**, S. S., 'Punishing convicted ravishers: statutory strictures and actual practice in thirteenth – and fourteenth-century England', *J. Med. Hist.*, 13.3 (1987), 237–50.

See also: 2.120; 3.110; 3.275; 3.413.

(l) WITCHCRAFT

3.423 **Crawford**, J., 'Evidences for witchcraft in Anglo-Saxon England', *Medium Aevum*, 32 (1963), 99–116.

3.424 **Harley**, D., 'Historians as demonologists: the myth of the midwife-witch', *Soc. Hist. Medicine*, 3.1 (1990), 1–26. Not specifically English but important.

3.425 **Kieckhefer**, R., *Late Medieval Witch Trials: their Foundations in Popular and Learned Culture 1300–1500* (Berkeley, California, 1976). Europe-wide.

3.426 **Kittel**, E. E., 'Toward a perspective on women, sex and witches in the later middle ages', in I. Matschinegg, B. Rath and B. Schuch, eds., *Von Menschen und ihren Zeichen, Sozialhistorische Untersuchungen zum Spätmittelalter und zur Neuzeit* (Bielefeld, 1990), 13–40. Growing hostility to women leading to greater significance of gender in identification of witches. Europe-wide.

3.427 **Meaney**, A. L., 'Women, witchcraft and magic in Anglo-Saxon England', in D. Scragg, ed., *Superstition and popular medicine in Anglo-Saxon England* (1989), 9–40.

3.428 **Neary**, A., 'The origins and character of the Kilkenny witchcraft case of 1324', *Pcdgs. of the Royal Irish Academy, Section*

C., 83.13 (1983), 333–50. Dame Alice Kyteler's case.

3.429 **Ross**, A., 'The divine hag of the pagan Celts', in V. Newall, ed., *The Witch Figure* (1973), 139–64.

3.430 **Russell**, J. B., *Witchcraft in the Middle Ages* (New York, 1972). Europe-wide.

3.431 **Wright**, T., *A Contemporary Narrative of the Proceedings Against Dame Alice Kyteler, Prosecuted for Sorcery in 1324, by Richard Ledrede, Bishop of Ossory* (1843).

See also: 3.296; 3.300; 3.414.

(m) WOMEN AND RELIGION

(i) General

3.432 **Aston**, M., 'Segregation in church', in W. J. Sheils and D. Wood, eds., *Women in the Church* (1990), 237–94. Geographically and chronologically wide-ranging article.

3.433 **Bynum**, C. W., *Fragmentation and Redemption, Essays on Gender and the Human Body in Medieval Religion* (New York, 1991). Not specifically British but an important collection of essays on female symbolism, asceticism, mysticism.

3.434 **Donahue**, C., 'The Valkyries and the Irish war goddesses', *Pubs. Mod. Lang. Assoc.*, 36 (1941), 1–12.

3.435 **Helbig**, A. K. 'Women in Ireland: three heroic figures', *University of Michigan Papers in Women's Studs.*, 1 (1974), 73–88.

3.436 **Hennessy**, W. M., 'The ancient Irish goddesses of war', *Revue Celtique*, 1 (1870), 32–55.

3.437 **MacCana**, P., 'Aspects of the theme of king and goddess in Irish literature', *Études Celtiques*, 7 (1955–6), 76–114 and 356–413; 8 (1958–9), 59–65.

3.438 — 'Women in Irish mythology', *The Crane Bag* 4.1 (1980), 7–11.

See also: 3.373; 3.499.

(ii) Saints and sanctity

3.439 **Baring Gould**, S. and **King**, M., 'The *Life of Brigid of Kildare*', *Vox Benedictina*, 3.1 (1986), 6–19. English translation reprinted from *Lives of the Saints* with a new introduction.

3.440 **Bethell**, D. L. T., 'The Lives of St Osyth of Essex and St Osyth of Aylesbury', *Analecta Bollandiana*, 88 (1970), 75–127.

3.441 **Bowen**, E. G., 'The cult of St Brigit', *Studia Celtica*, 8–9 (1973–4), 33–47.

3.442 **Boyle**, A., 'St Ninian and St Monenna', *Innes Review*, 18 (1967), 147–51.

3.443 **Braswell**, L., 'St. Edburga of Winchester: a study of her cult, A.D. 950 to 1300, with an edition of the fourteenth-century middle English and Latin lives', *Med. Studs.*, 33 (1971), 292–333.

3.444 **Clayton**, M., *The Cult of the Virgin Mary in Anglo-Saxon England* (1990).

3.445 **Delany**, S., trans., *A Legend of Holy Women, by Osbern Bokenham*, Medieval Studies, Sources and Appraisals, Vol. 1 (Notre Dame, 1992) A modern translation of the first all-female hagiography. Earlier edition ed. M. J. Serjeantson, *Legendys of Hooly Wummen*, Early English Text Scy (1938).

3.446 **Duffy**, E., 'Holy maydens, holy wyfes: the cult of women saints in fifteenth- and sixteenth-century England', in W. J. Sheils and D. Wood, eds., *Women in the Church* (1990), 175–96.

3.447 **Elkins**, S., *Holy Women of Twelfth Century England* (Chapel Hill, North Carolina, 1988). Good bibliography on nunneries.

3.448 **Millinger**, S., 'Humility and power: Anglo-Saxon nuns in Anglo-Norman hagiography', in J. A. Nichols and L. T. Shank, eds., *Distant Echoes, Medieval Religious Women*, Cistercian Studies, ser. no. 71 (Kalamazoo, Michigan, 1984), 5–28.

3.449 **Price**, J., 'La vie sainte Modwenne, a neglected Anglo-Norman Hagiographic text', *Medium Aevum*, 47 (1988), 172–89.

3.450 **Ridyard**, S. J., *The Royal Saints of Anglo-Saxon England, a Study of West Saxon and East Anglian Cults* (1989).

3.451 **Robertson**, E., 'The corporeality of female sanctity in *The Life of Saint Margaret*', in R. Blumenfeld-Kosinski and T. Szell, eds., *Images of Sainthood in Medieval Europe* (Ithaca, New York, 1991), 268–87.

3.452 **Sellner**, E. C., 'Brigit of Kildare, golden sparkling flame: a study in the liminality of women's spiritual power', *Vox Benedictina*, 8 (1991), 265–96.

3.453 **Sharpe**, R., '*Vitae S Brigitae*: the oldest texts', *Peritia*, 1 (1982), 81–106.

3.454 **Stenton**, F. M., 'St Frideswide and her times', in D. M. Stenton, ed., *Preparatory* to Anglo-Saxon England, collected papers of F. M. Stenton (1970), 224–33.

3.455 **Todd**, J. M., 'St Bega, cult, fact and legend', *Trans. Cumb. West. Antiq. Arch. Soc.*, 80 (1980), 23–35.

3.456 **Withycombe**, S. M., ' "O mihti meiden! O witti wummon!": the early English Katherine group as a model of sanctity', *Parergon, Bull. of the Australian and New Zealand Assoc. for Medieval and Renaissance Studies*, new ser., 9 (1991), 103–15.

3.457 **Wogan-Browne**, J., 'Saints' lives and the female reader', *Forum for Modern Language Studies*, 27 (1991), 314–32. Twelfth and thirteenth centuries.

3.458 — 'Queens, Virgins and mothers: Hagiographic representations of the abbess and her powers in twelfth- and thirteenth-century Britain', in L. O. Fradenburg, ed., *Women and sovereignty, Cosmos, the Yearbook of the Traditional Cosmological Society*, Vol. 7 (1992), 14–35.
See also: 3.63; 3.84; 3.364; 3.466.

(iii) Heresy

3.459 **Aston**, M., 'Lollard women priests?', in *Lollards and Reformers, Collected Papers of M. Aston* (1984), 49–70, first published *J. Ecc. Hist.*, 31 (1980), 441–61.

3.460 — 'William White's Lollard followers', in *Lollards and Reformers, Collected Papers of M. Aston* (1984), 71–99, first published *Catholic H. R.*, 68 (1982), 489–97. Includes discussion of trials of several women Lollards.

3.461 **Cross**, C., ' "Great reasoners in scripture", the activities of women Lollards 1380–1530, in D. Baker, ed., *Medieval Women*, Studies in Church History, Subsidia 1 (1978), 359–80.

3.462 **McSheffrey**, S., 'Women and lollardy, a reassessment', *Canadian J. of History*, 26 (1991), 199–223.
See also: 3.583.

(iv) Religious orders, nuns and anchoresses

3.463 **Ackerman**, R. W., 'The liturgical day in *Ancrene Riwle*', *Speculum*, 53 (1978), 734–44.

3.464 **André**, J. L., 'Widows and vowesses',

Royal Arch. Inst. G. B. and Ireland, 49 (1892), 69–82.

3.465 **Bateson**, M., 'Origins and early history of double monasteries', *T.R.H.S.*, new ser., 13 (1899), 137–198.

3.466 **Bitel**, L. M., 'Women's monastic enclosures in early Ireland: a study of female spirituality and male monastic mentalities', *J. Med. Hist.*, 12.1 (1986), 15–36.

3.467 **Bourdillon**, A. F. C., *The Order of Minoresses in England* (1926).

3.468 **Boyle**, A., 'The list of abbesses in Conchubranus' Life of St Monenna', *Ulster J. Arch.*, 34 (1971), 84–6.

3.469 **Burton**, J. E., *The Yorkshire Nunneries in the Twelfth and Thirteenth Centuries*, Borthwick Papers, 56 (1979).

3.470 **Clutterbuck**, R. H., 'The story of Wherwell abbey', *Hampshire Notes and Queries*, 4 (1889), 85–96.

3.471 **Constable**, G., *Medieval Monasticism, a Select Bibliography* (Toronto, 1976). Useful on women in religious orders, also on virginity.

3.472 — 'Aelred of Rievaulx and the nun of Watton. an episode in the early history of the Gilbertine order', in D. Baker, ed., *Medieval Women*, Ecclesiastical History Society, Subsidia 1 (1978), 205–26. A notorious sexual scandal.

3.473 **Cooke**, K., 'Donors and daughters: Shaftesbury abbey's benefactors, endowments and nuns *c.* 1086–1130', in M. Chibnall, ed., *Anglo-Norman Studies*, 12, 1989 (1990), 29–45. On the Normanisation of the nunnery.

3.474 **Cross**, J. E., 'A lost life of Hilda of Whitby: the evidence of the Old English martyrology', in *The Early Middle Ages*, *Acta* 6, 1972 (Binghampton, New York, 1982), 21–43.

3.475 **Dobson**, E. J., *The Origins of Ancrene Wisse* (1976).

3.476 **Eckenstein**, L., *Women under Monasticism* (1896). Still useful.

3.477 **Fell**, C. E., 'Hild, abbess of Streoneshalch', in H. Bekker-Nielsen et al., eds., *Hagiography and Medieval Literature, a Symposium* (ODense, 1981), 76–99. Hild(a) of Whitby.

3.478 **Frost**, C., 'The attitude to women and the adaptation to a female audience in the *Ancrene Wisse*', *AUMLA, J. Australasian Univ. Lang. and Lit. Assoc.*, 50 (1978), 235–50.

3.479 **Gilchrist**, R., *Gender and Material Culture: The Archaeology of Religious Women* (1993).

3.480 — ' "Blessed art thou among women": the archaeology of female piety', in P. J. P. Goldberg, ed., *Woman is a Worthy Wight: Women in English Society* c. *1200–1500* (1992), 212–26. A study of nunneries as an exercise in gender archaeology.

3.481 **Godfrey**, J., *The Church in Anglo-Saxon England* (1962). For chapter 10 especially, 'Monks and nuns in early England', 150–66.

3.482 — 'The double monastery in early English history', *Ampleforth J.*, 79 (1974), 19–32.

3.483 — 'The place of the double monastery in the Anglo-Saxon minster system', in G. Bonner, ed., *Famulus Christi, essays in commemoration of the thirteenth centenary of the birth of the Venerable Bede* (1976), 344–50.

3.484 **Golding**, B., 'Hermits, monks and women in twelfth-century France and England; the experience of Oabazine and Sempringham', in J. Loades, ed., *Monastic Studs.*, I (1990), 127–45.

3.485 **Graham**, R., *St Gilbert of Sempringham and the Gilbertines. A History of the only English Monastic Order* (1901). An order for men and women.

3.486 **Graves**, C. V., 'English Cistercian nuns in Lincolnshire', *Speculum*, 54 (1979), 492–9. Concerning Stixwould and Nun Cotham.

3.487 — 'The organisation of an English Cistercian nunnery in Lincolnshire', *Cîteaux: Commentarii Cistercienses*, 33, 3–4 (1982), 333–50. Nunnery of Stixwould.

3.488 **Harris**, B. J., 'A new look at the Reformation: Aristocratic women and nunneries, 1450–1540', *J. of British Studies*, 32 (1993), 89–113. Argues for lack of choice in women's entry to nunneries.

3.489 **Hicks**, M., 'The English minoresses and their early benefactors, 1281–1367', in J. Loades, ed., *Monastic Studs.*, I, (1990), 158–70.

3.490 **Holdsworth**, C. J., 'Christina of Markyate', in D. Baker, ed., *Medieval Women*, Studies in Church History, Subsidia 1 (1978), 185–204.

3.491 **Holloway**, J. B., 'Convents, courts and colleges: the Prioress and the second Nun', in J. B. Holloway, C. S. Wright and J. Bechtold, eds., *Equally in God's Image: Women in the Middle Ages* (New York, 1990), 198–215.

3.492 **Hugo**, T., *The Medieval Nunneries of the County of Somerset and the Diocese of Bath and Wells, together with the annals of their impropriated benefices, from the earliest times to the death of queen Mary* (1867).

3.493 **Hunt**, N., 'Notes on the history of Benedictine and Cistercian nuns in Britain', *Cistercian Studs.*, 8 (1973), 157–77.

3.494 **Jefferies Collins**, A., ed., *The Bridgettine Breviary of Syon Abbey*, Henry Bradshaw Society 96 for 1963 (1969).

3.495 **Kelly**, E., 'English Cistercian nunneries; dissolution or disintegration?', *Tjurunga: Australasian Benedictine R.*, 38 (1990), 51–72. Argues for healthy state on the eve of the Dissolution.

3.496 **Lapidge**, M., and Herren, M., *Aldhelm, the prose works* (1979). The earliest English treatise on virginity addressed to nuns.

3.497 **Luecke**, J., 'The unique experience of Anglo-Saxon nuns', in L. T. Shanks and J. A. Nicholl, eds., *Medieval Religious Women, Vol. 2 Peaceweavers* (Kalamazoo, Michigan, 1987), 55–65.

3.498 **McLaughlin**, M. M., 'Looking for medieval women: an interim report on the project "Women's religious life and communities 500–1500" ', in J. Loades, ed., *Monastic Studs.*, II (Bangor, 1991), 273–85.

3.499 **Meyer**, M. A., 'Women and the tenth-century English monastic reform', *Revue Benedictine*, 87 (1977), 34–61.

3.500 **Mountain**, J., 'Nunnery finances in the early fifteenth century', in J. Loades, ed., *Monastic Studs.*, II (Bangor, 1991), 263–72.

3.501 **Nichols**, J. A., 'The internal organisation of English Cistercian nunneries', *Cîteaux: Commentarii Cistercienses*, 30, 1 (1979), 23–40.

3.502 — 'Why found a medieval Cistercian nunnery?', *Medieval Prosopography*, 12 (1991), 1–28. Foundation of Marham Abbey, Norfolk by Isabel de Aubigny.

3.503 **Oliva**, M., 'Aristocracy or meritocracy? Office-holding patterns in late medieval nunneries', in W. J. Sheils and D. Wood, eds., *Women in the Church* (1990), 197–208.

3.504 **Peers**, C. R. and **Radford**, C. A. R., 'The Saxon monastery at Whitby', *Archaeologia*, 89 (1943), 27–88.

3.505 **Power**, E., *Medieval English Nunneries* c. *1275–1535* (1922). Still the important introduction, although many of its conclusions could now be questioned.

3.506 **Powicke**, F. M., 'Loretta, countess of Leicester', in J. G. Edwards, V. H. Galbraith and E. F. Jacob, eds., *Historical Essays in Honour of J. Tait* (1933), 247–72. A woman's inheritance and its loss, early life, religious seclusion.

3.507 **Reynolds**, R. E., '*Virgines subintroductae* in Celtic Christianity', *Harvard Theological R.*, 61 (1968), 547–66. Male and female religious living together.

3.508 **Robertson**, E., 'An anchorhold of her own: female anchoritic literature in thirteenth-century England', in J. B. Holloway, C. S. Wright and J. Bechtold, eds., *Equally in God's Image. Women in the Middle Ages* (New York, 1990), 170–83.

3.509 **Rosof**, P. J. F., 'The anchoritic base of the Gilbertine rule', *American Benedictine R.*, 33.2 (1982), 182–94.

3.510 **Salu**, M. B., trans., *The Ancrene Riwle* (1955). A rule of life for anchoresses.

3.511 **Schulenberg**, J. T., 'Women's monastic communities 500–1100: patterns of expansion and decline', *Signs*, 14.2 (1989), 261–92. An overview of France and England in particular.

3.512 **Sims-Williams**, P., 'Cuthswith, seventh-century abbess of Inkberrow, near Worcester, and the Würzburg MS of Jerome on Ecclesiastes', in P. Clemoes et al., eds., *Anglo-Saxon England*, 5 (1976), 1–21.

3.513 **Sumner**, N., 'The Countess Lucy's priory? The early history of Spalding priory and its estates', *University of Reading Medieval Studs.*, 13 (1987), 81–105.

3.514 **Talbot**, C. H., ed. and trans., *The Life of Christina of Markyate* (1959). Important contemporary life of a twelfth-century English anchoress. See M. Winterbottom, 'The Life of Christina of Markyate', *Analecta Bollandiana*, 105: 3–4 (1987), 281–7 for emendations to Talbot's text.

3.515 **Thompson**, S., 'The problem of the Cistercian nuns in the twelfth and early thirteenth centuries', in D. Baker, ed., *Medieval Women*, Studies in Church history, Subsidia 1 (1978), 227–52.

3.516 — 'Why English nunneries had no history: a study of the English nunneries founded after the Conquest', in J. A. Nichols and L. T. Shank, eds., *Distant Echoes, Medieval Religious Women*, 1, Cistercian Studies, ser. 71 (Kalamazoo, Michigan, 1984), 131–49.

3.517 — *Women religious, the Founding of English Nunneries after the Norman Conquest* (1991).

3.518 **Tillotson**, J. H., *Marrick Priory: a Nunnery in Late Medieval Yorkshire*, Borthwick Papers, 75 (1989).

3.519 **Tolhurst**, J. B. L., ed., *The Ordinale and Customary of the Benedictine Nuns of Barking Abbey*, 2 vols., Henry Bradshaw Society 65 and 66 (1927–28).

3.520 **Tolkien**, J. R. R., ed., *Ancrene Wisse edited from MS Corpus Christi College Cambridge 402*, Early English Text Scy, 249 (1962). Addressed to anchoresses.

3.521 **Warren**, A. K., *Anchorites and their Patrons in Medieval England* (Berkeley, California, 1985). Especially thirteenth to fifteenth centuries.

3.522 **Williams**, D. H., 'Cistercian nunneries in medieval Wales', *Cîteaux: Commentarii Cistercienses*, 29, 3 (1975), 155–74.

3.523 **Yorke**, B., ' "Sisters under the skin"? Anglo-saxon nuns and nunneries in southern England', in K. Bate et al., eds., *Medieval Women in Southern England*, Reading Medieval Studies, 15 (1989), 95–117.

See also: 3.12; 3.16; 3.35; 3.62; 3.63; 3.66; 3.447; 3.448; 3.458; 3.571; 3.573.

(v) **Religious experience, piety and philanthropy**

3.524 **Armstrong**, C. A. J., 'The piety of Cecily, duchess of York: a study in later medieval culture', in D. Woodruff, ed., *For Hilaire Belloc* (1942), 68–91.

3.525 **Bennett**, A., 'A book designed for a noble woman: an illuminated *Manuel des péchés* of the thirteenth century', in L. L. Brownrigg, ed., *Medieval Book Production, Assessing the Evidence* (Los Altos Hills, California, 1990), 163–81. Penitential treatise composed for Joan Tateshal, ob. 1310.

3.526 **Bitel**, L., 'Women's donations to churches in early Ireland', *J. Royal Soc. Antiq. Ireland*, 114 (1984), 5–23.

3.527 **Blackley**, F. D. and **Hermansen**, G., 'Isabella of France, Queen of England 1308–1358, and the late medieval cult of the dead', *Canadian J. Hist.*, 15 (1980), 23–47.

3.528 **Caspar**, R., ' "All shall be well": prototypical symbols of hope', *J. Hist. Ideas*, 42 (1981), 139–50. On Julian of Norwich.

3.529 **Crawford**, A., 'The piety of late medieval English queens', in C. Barron and C. Harper-Bill, eds., *The Church in Pre-Reformation Society, Essays in Honour of F. R. H. DuBoulay* (1985), 49–57.

3.530 **Cullum**, P.H., ' "And hir name was charite": charitable giving by and for women in late medieval Yorkshire', in P. J. P. Goldberg, ed., *Woman is a Worthy Wight: Women in English Society* c. *1200–1500* (1992), 182–211.

3.531 **Elliott**, D., 'Dress as mediator between inner and outer self: the pious matron of the high and later middle ages', *Med. Studs.* 53 (1991), 279–308. Includes discussion of Margery Kempe.

3.532 **Gibson**, G. M., 'Saint Anne and the religion of childbed. Some East Anglian texts and talismans', in K. Ashley and P. Sheingorn, eds., *Interpreting Cultural Symbols, Saint Anne in Late Medieval Society* (Athens, Georgia, 1990), 95–110.

3.533 **Goodman**, A. E., 'The piety of John Brunham's daughter of Lynn', in D. Baker, ed., *Medieval Women*, Studies in Church History, Subsidia 1 (1978), 347–58. About Margery Kempe.

3.534 **Hicks**, M., 'The piety of Margaret, Lady Hungerford (d.1478)', *J. Ecc. Hist.*, 38.1 (1987), 19–38.

3.535 **Hutchinson**, A. M., 'Devotional reading in the monastery and in the late medieval household', in M. G. Sargeant, ed., *De Cella in Seculum, Religious and Secular Life and Devotion in Late Medieval England* (1989), 215–27. Especially on the Brigittines of Syon.

3.536 **Robertson**, E., 'The rule of the body: the feminine spirituality of the *Ancrene Wisse*', in S. Fisher and J. E. Halley, eds., *Seeking the Woman in Late Medieval and Renaissance Writings: Essays in Feminist Contextual Criticism* (Knoxville, Tennessee, 1989), 109–34.

3.537 — *Early English Devotional Prose and the Female Audience* (Knoxville, Tennessee, 1990).

3.538 — 'Aspects of female piety in the *Prioress's Tale*', in C. D. Benson and E. Robertson, eds., *Chaucer's Religious Tales*, Chaucer Studies, 15 (1990), 145–60.

3.539 **Winstead**, K. A., 'Piety, politics and social commitment in Capgrave's *Life of Saint Katherine*', *Medievalia et Humanistica*, new ser., 17 (1991), 59–80.

See also: 2.120; 3.63; 3.206; 3.559; 3.571; 3.581; 3.584.

(vi) Mysticism

3.540 **Atkinson**, C. W., *Mystic and Pilgrim, the Book and the World of Margery Kempe* (Ithaca, New York, 1985).

3.541 **Barker**, P. S., 'The motherhood of God in Julian of Norwich's theology', *Downside R.*, 100:341 (1982), 290–304.

3.542 **Beckwith**, S., 'A very material mysticism: the medieval mysticism of Margery Kempe', in D. Aers, ed., *Medieval Literature, Criticism, Ideology and History* (1986), 34–57.

3.543 — 'Problems of authority in late medieval English mysticism: language, agency and authority in the Book of Margery Kempe', *Exemplaria*, 4.1 (1992), 171–99.

3.544 **Beer**, F., *Women and Mystical Experience in the Middle Ages* (1992). Includes Julian of Norwich and a chapter on Richard Rolle and the Yorkshire nuns.

3.545 **Bradley**, R., 'In the jaws of the bear: the journeys of transformation by women mystics', *Vox Benedictina*, 8 (1991), 116–75. Julian of Norwich and the *Ancrene Wisse*.

3.546 **Bynum**, C. W., *Holy Feast and Holy Fast, the Religious Significance of Food to Medieval Women* (Berkeley, California, 1987). Not specifically British but an important study of later medieval mysticism, female piety and asceticism.

3.547 **Colledge**, E. and **Walsh**, J., eds., *A Book of Showings to the Anchoress Julian of Norwich* (Toronto, 1978).

3.548 **Eberly**, S. S., 'Margery Kempe, St Mary Magdalene and patterns of contemplation', *Downside R.*, 107:368 (1989), 209–23.

3.549 **Gibson**, G. M., 'St Margery: *the Book of Margery Kempe*', in J. B. Holloway, C. S. Wright and J. Bechtold, eds., *Equally in God's Image: Women in the Middle Ages* (New York, 1990), 144–63. On her sufferings and 'martyrdom'.

3.550 **Harley**, M. P., 'A fifteenth-century revelation of a Cistercian nun', *Vox Benedictina*, 6.2 (1989), 120–7. Text and translation.

3.551 — 'The vision of Margaret Edward and

others at Canterbury, 29 July 1451', *Manuscripta*, 32.2 (1988), 146–51.

3.552 **Jones**, C., 'Julian of Norwich', in K. M. Wilson, ed., *Medieval Women writers* (1984), 269–96.

3.553 **Lagorio**, V. M. and **Bradley**, R., *The Fourteenth-century English Mystics: a Comprehensive Annotated Bibliography* (1981).

3.554 **Lang**, J., ' "The godly wylle" in Julian of Norwich', *Downside R.*, 102:348 (1984), 163–73.

3.555 **Molinari**, P., *Julian of Norwich, the Teachings of a Fourteenth-century Mystic* (1958).

3.556 **Reynolds**, F., 'Julian of Norwich', in J. Walsh, ed., *Pre-Reformation Spirituality* (New York, 1966), 198–209.

3.557 **Watkins**, R.N., 'Two women visionaries and death: Catherine of Siena and Julian of Norwich', *Numen* 30.2 (1983), 174–98.

3.558 **Watson**, N., 'The composition of Julian of Norwich's *Revelation of Love*', *Speculum*, 68 (1993), 637–83. Places the work in its historical setting.

See also: 3.362; 3.465; 3.505; 3.576; 3.584; 3.585.

(n) WOMEN AND EDUCATION

3.559 **Bell**, S. G., 'Medieval women book owners: arbiters of lay piety and ambassadors of culture', *Signs*, 7.4 (1982), 742–68. Argues for the importance of women in the formation and transmission of late medieval culture.

3.560 **Ferrante**, J. M., 'The education of women in the middle ages in theory, fact and fantasy', in P. Labalme, ed., *Beyond their Sex, Learned Women of the European Past* (New York, 1980), 9–42. Europe-wide.

3.561 **Schibanoff**, S., ' "Taking the gold out of Egypt"; the art of reading as a woman', in R. Evans and L. Johnson, eds., *Feminist Readings in Middle English Literature* (1994), 331–52. Discusses whether literacy was 'liberating' for women.

See also: 3.563.

(o) WOMEN AND THE ARTS

3.562 **Barratt**, A., 'Dame Eleanor Hull: a fifteenth-century translator', in R. Ellis et al., eds., *The Medieval Translator: the Theory and Practice of Translation in the Middle Ages* (1989), 87–101.

3.563 — ed., *Women's writing in Middle English* (1992). Medical, literary, mystical, spiritual and letter writing, introduction on women's education, authorship and a good bibliography.

3.564 **Bragg**, L., '*Wulf and Eadwacer*, *The wife's lament* and women's love lyrics of the Middle Ages', *Germanisch-Romanische Monatsschrift*, 70, new ser., 39 (1989), 257–68.

3.565 **Budny**, M., and **Tweddle**, D., 'The Maazeik embroideries' in P. Clemoes et al., eds., *Anglo-Saxon England*, 13 (1984), 65–96. Also contains general material on Old English women and embroidery.

3.566 **Christie**, A. G., *English Medieval Embroidery* (1938).

3.567 **Desmond**, M., 'The voice of exile: feminist literary history and the anonymous Anglo-Saxon elegy', *Critical Inquiry*, 16.3 (1990), 572–90. Considers 'Anon' authorship and suggests Anglo-Saxon literature be read for the 'female voice'.

3.568 **Dronke**, P., *Women Writers of the Middle Ages* (1984). Includes early medieval English nuns.

3.569 **Evans**, R. and **Johnson**, L., eds., *Feminist Readings in Middle English Literature* (1994). A collection of essays containing amongst other things much about women's readings of medieval English literature.

3.570 **Fulton**, H., 'Medieval Welsh poems to nuns', *Cambridge Medieval Celtic Studies*, 21 (1991), 87–112.

3.571 **Lochrie**, K., '*The Book of Margery Kempe*, the marginal woman's quest for literary authority', *J. Med. and Ren. Studs.*, 16.1 (1986), 33–55..

3.572 — *Margery Kempe and the Translations of the Flesh* (Philadelphia, 1991).

3.573 **MacBain**, W., ed., *The Life of St Catharine by Clemence of Barking*, Anglo-Norman Texts, 18 (1964). Clemence was a twelfth-century nun and hagiographer.

3.574 **Meale**, C. M., ed., *Women and Literature in Britain, 1150–1500* (1993). Women's access to written culture and their

3.575 **Parker**, R., *The Subversive Stitch; embroidery and the making of the feminine* (1984). A feminist reconsideration of the history of embroidery, Europe-wide.

3.576 **Provost**, W., 'Margery Kempe', in K. M. Wilson, ed., *Medieval Women Writers* (1984), 297–319.

3.577 **Robinson**, F. C., 'Old English poetry: the question of authorship', *ANQ, a Quarterly J. of Short Articles, Notes and Reviews*, new ser., 3.2 (1990), 59–64. Questions whether all authors of anonymous works were necessarily men.

3.578 **Sekules**, V., 'Women and art in England in the thirteenth and fourteenth centuries', in J. Alexander and P. Binski, eds., *Age of Chivalry, Art in Plantagenet England, 1200–1400* (1987), 41–8.

3.579 — 'Women's piety and patronage', in N. Saul, ed., *The Age of Chivalry, Court and Society in Late Medieval England* (1992), 120–31.

3.580 **Stone**, R. K., *Middle English Prose Style: Margery Kempe and Julian of Norwich* (The Hague, 1970).

3.581 **Tolley**, T., 'Eleanor of Castile and the "Spanish" style in England', in W. M. Ormrod, ed., *England in the Thirteenth Century*, Proceedings of the Harlaxton Symposium 1989 (1991). *See also:* 3.313; 3.540; 3.547; 3.552; 3.585.

3.583 **Johnson**, L. S., 'Margery Kempe, social critic', *J. of Med. and Ren. Studs.*, 22 (1992), 159–84.

3.584 **Mueller**, J. M., 'Autobiography of a new "creatur". Female spirituality, selfhood and authorship in *The book of Margery Kempe*', in M. B. Rose, ed., *Women in the Middle Ages and the Renaissance, Literary and Historical Perspectives* (Syracuse, New York, 1986), 155–71.

3.585 **Windeatt**, B. A., trans., *The Book of Margery Kempe* (1985). *See also:* 3.540; 3.571; 3.576.

(i) Diarists and letter writers

3.586 **Classen**, A., 'Emergence from the dark: female epistolary literature in the middle ages', *J. of the Rocky Mountains Med. and Ren. Assoc.*, 10 (1989), 1–15. Europe-wide.

3.587 **Fell**, C. E., 'Some implications of the Boniface correspondence', in H. Damico and A. H. Olsen, eds., *New Readings on Women in Old English Literature* (Bloomington and Indianapolis, Indiana, 1991), 29–43. Includes Boniface's women correspondents. *See also:* 3.87; 3.116; 3.144.

(p) AUTOBIOGRAPHY AND BIOGRAPHY

3.582 **Bradbury**, K. G., 'The world of Etheldreda Gardener: viewing a woman of the late fifteenth century through the lives of her husbands', *The Ricardian*, 9.115 (1991), 146–53.

(q) WOMEN AS HISTORIANS

3.588 **Stuard**, S. M., 'A new dimension? North American scholars contribute their perspective', in S. Mosher Stuard, ed., *Women in Medieval History and Historiography* (Philadelphia, 1987), 81–99. *See also:* 2.48; 2.86; 2.172.

4

EARLY MODERN
CIRCA 1500–1800

(a) GENERAL SURVEYS

4.1 **Amussen**, S., *An Ordered Society: Gender and Class in Early Modern England* (1988). Examines ideology and the interaction of class and gender in local communities.

4.2 — 'Gender, family and the social order, 1560–1725', in A. Fletcher and J. Stevenson, eds., *Order and Disorder in Early Modern England* (1985), 196–217.

4.3 **Cross**, C., 'Northern women in the early modern period: the female testators of Hull and Leeds., 1520–1650', *Yorks. Arch. J.*, 59 (1987), 83–94.

4.4 **Davis**, N. Z., and **Farge**, A., eds., *A History of Women in the West*; Vol. 3, *Renaissance and Enlightenment Paradoxes*, (Cambridge, Mass., 1993). Translated from the French, but of wide significance for British history also.

4.5 **Fraser**, A., *The Weaker Vessel: Women's Lot in Seventeenth Century England* (1984).

4.6 **Fritz**, P., and **Morton**, R., eds., *Woman in the Eighteenth Century and other Essays*, McMaster Uty. Assoc. for Eighteenth Century Studs., 4 (Toronto, 1976).

4.7 **George**, M., *Women in the first capitalist society: experiences in seventeenth century England* (1988). Anecdotal but lively.

4.8 **Hill**, B., *Women, work and sexual politics in the eighteenth century* (1990). A wide-ranging survey.

4.9 **Hogrefe**, P., *Tudor Women, Commoners and Queens* (Ames, Iowa, 1975).

4.10 — *Women of Action in Tudor England: Nine Biographical Sketches* (Ames, Iowa, 1977). A useful introduction, but details are sometimes unreliable.

4.11 **Houston**, R. A., 'Women in the economy and society of Scotland, 1500–1800', in R. A. Houston and I. D. Whyte, eds., *Scottish Society 1500–1800* (1989), 118–47.

4.12 **Hunt**, M., et al, eds., *Women and the Enlightenment* (New York, 1984). Also published as *Women and History*, 9, Spring (1984). Includes articles on Mary Astell; women and the London press; women and freemasonry.

4.13 **King**, M. L., *Women of the Renaissance* (Chicago, Illinois, 1991). Covers European debates on women but useful for Britain also.

4.14 **Latt**, D., 'Praising virtuous ladies: the literary image and historical reality of women in seventeenth century England', in M. Springer, ed., *What Manner of Woman: Essays on English and American Life and Literature* (New York, 1977), 39–64.

4.15 **MacCurtain**, M. and **O'Dowd**, M., eds., *Women in Early Modern Ireland* (1991). A wide-ranging and pioneering collection.

4.16 **Marshall**, R. K., *Women in Scotland 1660–1780* (1979). An exhibition catalogue.

4.17 **Mendelson**, S. H., *The Mental World of Stuart Women* (1987). Covers Aphra Behn, Mary (Boyle) Rich, countess of Warwick, and Margaret Cavendish, duchess of Newcastle.

4.18 **Mitchison**, R., *Life in Scotland* (1978).

4.19 **Notestein**, W., 'The English woman, 1580–1650', in J. H. Plumb, ed., *Studies in Social History: a Tribute to G. M. Trevelyan*

(1955, reprinted 1969), 69–107.

4.20 **Rowbotham**, S., *Women, Resistance and Revolution* (1974).

4.21 **Schwoerer**, L. G., 'Seventeenth century English women: engraven in stone', *Albion*, 16 (1984), 389–403. A review essay.

4.22 **Sharpe**, J. A., *Early Modern England: A Social History 1550–1760* (1987).

4.23 **Smout**, T. C., *A History of the Scottish People 1560–1830* (1969).

4.24 **Thompson**, R., *Women in Stuart England and America* (1974). Rather dated but comparative approach, stimulating and useful material.

4.25 **Travitsky**, B. S., 'Introduction: placing women in the English Renaissance', in A. M. Haselkorn and B. S. Travitsky, eds., *The Renaissance Englishwoman in Print: Counterbalancing the Canon* (Amherst, Mass, 1990), 3–41.

4.26 **Warnicke**, R. M., *Women of the English Renaissance and Reformation* (Westport, Conn., 1983).

4.27 **Whyte**, I. D., and **Whyte**, K. A., 'The geographical mobility of women in early modern Scotland', in L. Leneman, ed., *Perspectives in Scottish Social History: Essays in Honour of Rosalind Mitchison* (1988), 83–106.

4.28 **Wrightson**, K., *English Society 1580–1680* (1982). Useful discussions of familial and gender relationships.

See also: 2.124; 4.660.

(b) VIEWS OF WOMEN

4.29 **Armstrong**, N., *Desire and Domestic Fiction: a Political History of the Novel* (1987).

4.30 **Backscheider**, P., 'Defoe's women: snares and prey', *Studs.Eighteenth Cent. Cult.*, 5 (1976), 103–20.

4.31 **Ballaster**, R., Beetham, M., Frazer, E., and Hebron, S., *Women's Worlds: Ideology, Feminity and the Women's Magazine* (1991).

4.32 **Bennett**, J., 'Misogyny, popular culture and women's work', *Hist. Workshop J.*, 31 (1991), 166–88.

4.33 **Bornstein**, D., ed., *Distaves and Dames: Renaissance Treatises for and about Women* (New York, 1978). Facsimile reprints.

4.34 **Camden**, C., *The Elizabethan Woman* (New York, 1952).

4.35 **Chirelstein**, E., 'Lady Elizabeth Pope: the heraldic body', in L. Gent and N. Llewellyn, eds., *Renaissance Bodies: the Human Figure in English Culture*, c. *1540–1660* (1990), 36–59.

4.36 **Crandall**, C., *Swetnam the Woman-Hater: The Controversy and the Play* (Lafayette, Indiana, 1969).

4.37 **Davis**, N. Z., 'Woman on top', in N. Z. Davis, *Society and Culture in Early Modern France* (1975, reprinted 1987) 124–51. Relevant to early modern Britain also, and includes some English examples.

4.38 **Dugaw**, D., *Warrior Women and Popular Balladry 1650–1850* (1989).

4.39 **Dunn**, C. M., 'The changing image of women in Renaissance society and literature', in M. Springer, ed., *What Manner of Woman: Essays on English and American Life and Literature* (New York, 1977), 15–38.

4.40 **Dusinberre**, J., *Shakespeare and the Nature of Women* (1977). Compare 4.50.

4.41 **Ferguson**, M. W., **Quilligan**, M. and **Vickers**, N. J., eds., *Rewriting the Renaissance: The Discourses of Sexual Difference in Early Modern Europe* (Chicago, Illinois, 1986).

4.42 **Gagen**, J. E., *The New Woman: Her Emergence in English Drama, 1600–1730* (New York, 1954).

4.43 **George**, M., 'From goodwife to mistress: the transformation of the female in bourgeois culture', *Science and Soc.*, 37 (1973), 152–177.

4.44 **Gossett**, S., ' "Man-maid begone!": women in masques', *Eng. Lit. Ren.*, 18, (1988), 96–113.

4.45 **Henderson**, K. U., and **McManus**, B. F., *Half Humankind: Contexts and Texts of the Controversy about Women in England 1540–1640* (Urbana, Illinois, 1985).

4.46 **Hill**, C., 'Clarissa Harlowe and her times', in C. Hill, *Puritanism and Revolution* (1958, latest edn. 1986), 351–76.

4.47 **Honig**, E., 'In memory: Lady Dacre and Pairing by Hans Eworth', in L. Gent and N. Llewellyn, eds., *Renaissance Bodies: The Human Figure in English Culture* c. *1540–1660* (1990), 60–85.

4.48 **Hull**, S. W., *Chaste, Silent and Obedient: English Books for Women 1475–1640* (San Marino, California, 1982).

4.49 **Hunter**, J. E., 'The eighteenth century

English woman according to *The Gentleman's Magazine*', in P. Fritz and R. Morton, eds., *Woman in the Eighteenth Century and other Essays*, McMaster Uty. Assoc. for Eighteenth Century Studs., 4 (Toronto, 1976), 73–88.

4.50 **Jardine**, L., *'Still harping on Daughters': Women and Drama in the Age of Shakespeare* (1983). Compare 4.40.

4.51 **Jones**, A. R., 'Nets and bridles: early modern conduct books and sixteenth century women's lyrics', in N. Armstrong and L. Tennenhouse, eds., *The Ideology of Conduct: Essays on Literature and the History of Sexuality* (1987), 39–72.

4.52 — 'Counterattacks on "the Bayter of Women": three pamphleteers of the early seventeenth century', in A. M. Haselkorn and B. S. Travitsky, eds., *The Renaissance Englishwoman in Print* (Amherst, Mass., 1990), 45–62.

4.53 **Jones**, J. P., and **Seibel**, S.S., 'Thomas More's feminisms: to reform or re-form', in M. J. Moore, ed., *Quincentenial essays on St Thomas More*, special issue of *Albion* (1979), 67–77.

4.54 **Jones**, V., *Women in the Eighteenth Century: Constructions of Feminity* (1990). Extracts from a variety of sources.

4.55 **Jordanova**, L., *Sexual Visions: Images of Gender in Science and Medicine betweeen the Eighteenth and Twentieth Centuries* (1989).

4.56 **Khanna**, L. C., 'Images of women in Thomas More's poetry', in M. J. Moore, cd., *Quincentenial essays on St Thomas More*, special issue of *Albion* (1979), 78–88.

4.57 **Kusunoki**, A., ' "Their testament at their apron strings": the representation of Puritan women in early seventeenth century England', in S. P. Cerasano and M. Wynne-Davies, eds., *Gloriana's Face: Women, Public and Private, in the English Renaissance* (1992), 185–204.

4.58 **Lawless**, J. M., 'Images of "Poor" women in the writing of Irish men midwives', in M. MacCurtain and M. O'Dowd, eds., *Women in Early Modern Ireland* (1991), 291–303.

4.59 **Le Gates**, M., 'The cult of womanhood in eighteenth century thought,' *Eighteenth Cent. Studs.*, 10 (1976), 21–39.

4.60 **Leinward**, T. B., ' "This gulph of marriage": Jacobean citywives and Jacobean city comedy', *Women's Studs.*, 10, (1984), 245–60.

4.61 **Levin**, C., 'Women in the Book of Martyrs as Models of Behaviour in Tudor England', *Int. J. Women's Studs.*, 4 (1981), 196–207.

4.62 **Luria**, G. M. and **Tayler**, I., 'Gender and genre: women in the literature of the British Romantics', in M. Springer, ed., *What Manner of Woman: Essays in English and American Life and Literature* (New York, 1977).

4.63 **Maclean**, I. *The Renaissance Notion of Woman*, (1980). A vital introduction to medical and scientific ideas about women.

4.64 **Merchant**, C., *The Death of Nature: Women, Ecology and the Scientific Revolution* (New York, 1980, reprinted 1983 and 1990, with new preface). Influential, controversial overall argument.

4.65 **Newman**, K., *Fashioning Femininity and English RenaissanceDrama* (Chicago, Illinois, 1991).

4.66 **Nussbaum**, F., *The Brink of all we Hate: English Satires on Women, 1660–1750* (Lexington, Kentucky, 1984).

4.67 — ed., *Satires on Women*, Augustan Society reprints, 180 (Los Angeles, 1976). Facsimile reprints.

4.68 **O'Connor**, A., 'Images of the evil woman in Irish folklore: a preliminary survey', *Women's Studs. Int. For.*, 2 (1988), 281–5.

4.69 **O'Donnell**, S., 'Mr Locke and the ladies: the indelible words on the *tabula rasa*', *Studs. Eighteenth Cent. Cult.*, 8, (1979), 151–64.

4.70 **Purkiss**, D., 'Material Girls: The Seventeenth Century Woman Debate', in C. Brant and D. Purkiss, eds., *Women, Texts and Histories 1575–1760* (1992), 69–101.

4.71 **Richetti**, J. J., 'The portrayal of women in Restoration and Eighteenth century English literature', in M. Springer, ed., *What Manner of Woman: Essays on English and American Life and Literature* (New York, 1977), 65–97.

4.72 **Rogers**, K., *The Troublesome Helpmate: a History of Misogyny in Literature* (Seattle, 1966, reprint 1968).

4.73 **Rose**, M. B., *The Expense of Spirit: Love and Sexuality in English Renaissance Drama* (Ithaca, New York, 1988).

4.74 **Shepherd**, S., ed., *The Women's Sharp Revenge: Five Women's Pamphlets from the Renaissance* (1985).

4.75 **Shevelow**, K., *Women and Print Culture: The Construction of Femininity in the Early Periodical* (1989).

4.76 **Spufford**, M., *Small Books and Pleasant Histories. Popular Fiction and its Readership in Seventeenth Century England* (1981).

4.77 **Stallybrass**, P., 'Patriarchal territories: the body enclosed', in M. Ferguson, ed., *Rewriting the Renaissance* (1986), 123–42.

4.78 **Utley**, F. L., *The Crooked Rib: An Analytical Index to the Argument about Women in English and Scots Literature to the end of the year 1568* (1944, reprinted New York, 1970).

4.79 **Williford**, M., 'Bentham on the rights of women', *J. Hist. Ideas*, 36 (1975), 167–76.

4.80 **Wiltenburg**, J., *Disorderly Women and Female Power in the Street Literature of early modern England and Germany* (Charlottesville, Virginia, 1992).

4.81 **Woodbridge**, L., *Women and the English Renaissance: Literature and the Nature of Womankind* (1984).

4.82 **Wright**, L. B., *Middle-class culture in Elizabethan England* (Chapel Hill, North Carolina, 1935, reprinted Ithaca, New York, 1958). Still valuable.

4.83 **Yates**, L., 'The uses of women to a sixteenth century best-seller', *Hist. Studs.*, 18 (1979), 422–34.

See also: 4.117, 4.320; 4.448; 4.451; 4.587; 4.617; 4.660; 4.671; 4.737; 4.799; 4.877; 4.897.

(c) WOMEN AND FAMILY

(i) General

4.84 **Anderson**, M., *Approaches to the History of the Western Family* (1980).

4.85 **Blackman**, J., 'Women and men reproducing families: some comments', *J. Reg. Local Studs.*, 10 (1990), 60–75.

4.86 **Boulton**, J., *Neighbourhood and Society: A London Suburb in the Seventeenth Century* (1987). Useful for family structure and relationships.

4.87 **Collinson**, P., 'The Protestant family', in P. Collinson, *The Birthpangs of Protestant England: Religious and Cultural Change in the Sixteenth and Seventeenth Centuries* (1988), 60–93.

4.88 **Ezell**, M. J. M., *The Patriarch's Wife: Literary Evidence and the History of the Family* (Chapel Hill, North Carolina, 1987).

4.89 **Gottlieb**, B., *The Family in the Western World from the Black Death to the Industrial Age* (1993). Useful introductory survey.

4.90 **Hareven**, T. K., 'The history of the family and the complexity of social change', *American H. R.*, 96 (1991), 95–124.

4.91 **Hill**, C., 'The spiritualisation of the household', in C. Hill, *Society and Puritanism* (1964), 443–81.

4.92 **Houlbrooke**, R. A., *The English Family 1450–1700* (1984).

4.93 — *English Family Life 1560–1725, An Anthology of Diaries* (1988).

4.94 **Jordanova**, L., 'The representation of the family in the eighteenth century: a challenge for cultural history', in J. H. Pittock and A. A. Wear, eds., *Interpretation and Cultural History* (1991), 109–34.

4.95 **Larminie**, V., 'Settlement and sentiment: inheritance and personal relationships among two midland gentry families in the seventeenth century', *Mid. Hist.*, 12 (1987), 27–47.

4.96 **Laslett**, P., *The World We Have Lost Further Explored* (1983). The most recent version of a classic of demographic history.

4.97 — and **Wall**, R., eds., *Household and Family in Past Time* (1972).

4.98 **Levine**, D., *Family Formation in an Age of Nascent Capitalism* (1977). Demographic change linked to economic development.

4.99 — *Reproducing Families. The Political Economy of English Population History* (1987).

4.100 **Macfarlane**, A., *The Family Life of Ralph Josselin* (1970). A classic anthropologically informed study; could be more aware of inequalities of gender.

4.101 **Ozment**, S., *When Fathers Ruled: Family Life in Reformation Europe* (Cambridge, Mass., 1983). Continental European in the main but relevant for Britain also.

4.102 **Powell**, C. L., *English Domestic Relations 1487–1653* (New York, 1917). Outdated, but of some use for its discussion of source material.

4.103 **Rushton**, P., 'Property, power and family networks: The problem of disputed marriage in early modern England', *J. Fam. Hist.*, 11.3 (1986), 205–19.

4.104 **Stone**, L. *The Family, Sex and Marriage in England 1500–1800* (1977). See also reviews by Christopher Hill, *Ec. H. R.*, sec. ser., 31 (1978), 450–63; and Alan Macfarlane, *Hist. and Theory*, 18 (1979), 239–45. Of major influence although its arguments are widely contested.

4.105 **Tadmor**, N., ' "Family" and "friend" in *Pamela*: a case study in the history of the family in eighteenth century England', *Soc. Hist.*, 14 (1989), 290–306.

4.106 **Todd**, M., 'Humanists, Puritans and the Spiritualized Household', *Church Hist.*, 49 (1980), 18–34.

4.107 **Trumbach**, R., *The Rise of the Egalitarian Family. Aristocratic Kinship and Domestic Relations in Eighteenth Century England* (1978).

4.108 — ed., *Marriage, Sex and the Family in England 1660–1800* (New York, 1984–6). A series of facsimiles of contemporary pamphlets.

4.109 **Wrightson**, K., *English Society 1580–1680* (1982).

4.110 **Wrigley**, E. A., and **Schofield**, R. S., *The Population History of England 1541–1871: A Reconstruction* (1981).

See also: 4.440; 4.702.

(ii) Marriage

4.111 **Beckett**, J. V., 'The pattern of landownership in England and Wales, 1660–1880', *Ec. H. R.*, sec. ser., 37 (1984), 1–22. Useful for marriage settlements and the strategies of the landed elite.

4.112 **Bonfield**, L., *Marriage Settlements, 1601–1740: The adoption of the strict settlement* (1983). On property arrangements in elite families.

4.113 — 'Normative rules and property transmission: reflections on the link between marriage and inheritance in early modern England', in L. Bonfield, R. Smith and K. Wrightson, eds., *The World We Have Gained* (1986), 155–76.

4.114 **Boulton**, J., 'Itching after private marrying: marriage customs in seventeenth century London', *London J.*, 16 (1991), 15–34.

4.115 **Brodsky**, V., *Mobility and Marriage: The Family and Kinship in Early Modern London* (1989).

4.116 **Brodsky-Elliot**, V., 'Single Women in the London Marriage Market: Age, Status, Mobility, 1598–1619', in R. B. Outhwaite, ed., *Marriage and Society* (1981), 81–100.

4.117 **Brown**, I. Q., 'Domesticity, Feminism, and friendship: female aristocratic culture and marriage in England, 1660–1760', *J. Fam. Hist.*, 7 (1982), 406–24.

4.118 **Clay**, C., 'Marriage, inheritance and the rise of large estates in England, 1660–1815', *Ec. H. R.*, sec. ser., 21 (1968), 503–18.

4.119 — 'Property settlements, financial provision for the family and the sale of land', *J. Brit. Studs.*, 21 (1981), 18–38.

4.120 **Connolly**, S., 'Family, Love and Marriage: Some evidence from the early eighteenth century', in M. MacCurtain and M. O'Dowd, eds., *Women in Early Modern Ireland* (1991) 276–290.

4.121 **Corish**, P. J., 'Catholic Marriage under the Penal Code', in A. Cosgrove, ed., *Marriage in Ireland* (Dublin, 1985), 67–77.

4.122 **Davies**, K. M., 'Continuity and change in literary advice on marriage', in R. B. Outhwaite, ed., *Marriage and Society* (1981), 58–80.

4.123 — 'The sacred condition of equality – how original were Puritan doctrines of marriage?', *Soc. Hist.*, 1–2 (1977), 563–80.

4.124 **Dickson**, D., 'No Scythians Here: Women and Marriage in Seventeenth Century Ireland', in M. MacCurtain and M. O'Dowd, eds., *Women in Early Modern Ireland* (1991), 223–35.

4.125 **Durston**, C., ' "Unhallowed wedlocks": the regulation of marriage during the English Revolution', *Hist. J.*, 31 (1988), 45–59.

4.126 **Erickson**, A., 'Common law versus common practice: the use of marriage settlements in early modern England', *Ec. H. R.*, sec. ser., 43 (1990), 21–39.

4.127 **Fitzpatrick**, D., 'Divorce and Separation in Modern Irish History', *P. P.*, 114 (1986), 172–96.

4.128 **Friedman**, A., 'Portrait of a marriage: the Willoughby letters, 1585–6', *Signs*, 11 (1986), 542–56.

4.129 **Gillis**, J. R., *For Better, For Worse, British Marriages, 1600 to the Present* (1985).

4.130 **Habbakuk**, J. J., 'Marriage settlements in the eighteenth century', *T.R.H.S.*, 4th ser., 32 (1950), 15–30.

4.131 **Harris**, B. J., 'Marriage sixteenth-century style: Elizabeth Stafford and the third Duke of Norfolk', *J. Soc. Hist.*, 15 (1982), 371–82.

4.132 **Houlbrooke**, R., 'The making of marriage in mid-Tudor England: evidence from the records of matrimonial court litigation', *J. Fam. Hist.*, 10 (1985), 339–52.

4.133 **Ingram**, M., *The Church Courts, Sex and Marriage in England, 1570–1540* (1987). A thorough treatment of the ecclesiastical courts which attempted to regulate marriage and sexuality.

4.134 — 'The reform of popular culture? Sex and marriage in early modern England', in B. Reay, ed., *Popular Culture in Seventeenth Century England* (1985), 129–65.

4.135 **Jackson**, D., *Intermarriage in Ireland 1550–1650* (Montreal, 1970).

4.136 **Johnson**, J. T., *A Society Ordained by God: English Puritan Marriage Doctrine in the first half of the Seventeenth Century* (Nashville, Tennessee, and New York, 1970).

4.137 — 'English Puritan Thought on the ends of marriage', *Church Hist.*, 38 (1969), 429–36.

4.138 **Larminie**, V., 'Marriage and the family: the example of the seventeenth-century Newdigates', *Mid. Hist.*, 9 (1984), 1–22.

4.139 **MacCurtain**, M., 'Marriage in Tudor Ireland', in A. Cosgrove, ed., *Marriage in Ireland* (Dublin, 1985), 51–66.

4.140 **Malcolmson**, A., *Pursuit of the Heiress: Aristocratic Marriage in Ireland, 1750–1820* (1982).

4.141 **Mendelson**, S., 'Debate: "The weightiest business": marriage in an upper gentry family in seventeenth-century England', *P.P.*, 85 (1979), 128–35.

4.142 **Menefee**, S., *Wives for Sale. An Ethnographic Study of British Popular Divorce*, (1981).

4.143 **O'Hara**, D, ' "Ruled by my friends": aspects of marriage in the dioces of Canterbury *c*. 1540–1570', *Cont. and Change*, 6 (1991), 9–41.

4.144 — 'The language of tokens and the making of marriage', *Rural Hist.*, 3 (1992), 1–40.

4.145 **Outhwaite**, R. B., 'Marriage as business: opinions on the rise in aristocratic bridal portions on early modern England', in N. McKendrick and R. B. Outhwaite, eds., *Business Life and Public Policy* (1986), 21–37.

4.146 **Phillips**, R. R., *Putting Asunder. A History of Divorce in Western Society* (1988).

4.147 **Pollock**, L., ' "An action like a strategem": courtship and marriage from the Middle Ages to the twentieth century', *Hist. J.*, 30 (1987), 483–98.

4.148 **Prior**, M., 'Wives and wills, 1558–1700', in J. Chartres and D. Hey, eds., *English Rural Society 1500–1800: Essays in Honour of Joan Thirsk* (1990), 201–25.

4.149 — 'Conjugal love and the flight from marriage: poetry as a source for the history of women and the family', in V. Fildes,

ed., *Women as Mothers in Pre-industrial England: Essays in memory of Dorothy McClaren* (1990), 179–203.

4.150 **Rushton**, P., 'The broken marriage in early modern England, matrimonial cases from the Durham church courts, 1560–1630', *Archaeologia Aeliana*, 5th ser., 13 (1985), 187–96.

4.151 **Schofield**, R., 'English marriage patterns revisited', *J. Fam. Hist.*, 10 (1985), 2–20.

4.152 **Sharpe**, J. A., 'Plebeian Marriage in Stuart England: some evidence from popular literature', *T.R.H.S.*, 5th ser., 36 (1986)) 69–90.

4.153 **Sharpe**, P., 'Marital separation in the eighteenth and early nineteenth centuries', *Local Pop. Studs.*, 45 (1990), 66–70.

4.154 **Slater**, M., *Family Life in the Seventeenth Century. The Verneys of Claydon House* (1984).

4.155 — 'The weightiest business: marriage in an upper gentry family in seventeenth century England', *P. P.*, 72 (1976), 25–54.

4.156 — 'A Rejoinder', (to Mendelson: 4.141), *P. P.*, 85 (1979), 136–40.

4.157 **Stone**, L., *Road to Divorce. England 1530–1987* (1987).

4.158 — *Uncertain Unions. Marriage in England 1660–1753* (1992).

4.159 — *Broken Lives: Separation and Divorce in England, 1600–1857* (1993). 4.158 and 4.159 provide case study material as companions to 4.157, a general study.

4.160 **Wall**, A., 'Elizabethan precept and feminine practice: the Thynne family of Longleat', *Hist.*, 75 (1990), 23–38.

See also: 3.150; 4.181; 4.315.

(iii) Household structure and kinship

4.161 **Chaytor**, M., 'Household and kinship: Ryton in the 16th and early 17th centuries,' *Hist. Workshop J.*, 10 (1980), 25–60.

4.162 **Cressy**, D., 'Kinship and kin interactions in early modern England', *P.P.*, 113 (1986), 38–69.

4.163 **Goody**, J., **Thirsk**, J., and **Thompson**, E.P., eds., *Family and Inheritance: Rural Society in Western Europe, 1200–1800* (1976).

4.164 **Goose**, N., 'Household size and structure in early Stuart Cambridge', *Soc. Hist.*, 5 (1980), 347–85.

4.165 **Hajnal**, J., 'European Marriage Patterns in Perspective', in D. V. Glass and D. E. C. Eversley, eds., *Population in History* (1965), 101–43.

4.166 **Laslett**, P. 'Mean Household Size in England since the Sixteenth Century', in P. Laslett and R. Wall, eds., *Household and Family in Past Time* (1972), 123–58.

4.167 **McIntosh**, M. K., 'Servants and the household unit in an Elizabethan English community', *J. Fam. Hist.*, 9 (1984), 3–23.

4.168 **Seccombe**, W., 'The Western European Marriage Pattern in Historical Perspective', *J. Hist. Sociol.*, 3 (1990), 50–74.

4.169 **Wrightson**, K., 'Kinship in an English village: Terling, Essex 1500–1700', in R. M. Smith, ed., *Land, Kinship and Life-cycle* (1984), 313–32.

4.170 — and **Levine**, D., *Poverty and Piety in an English Village: Terling, 1525–1700* (1979). Useful for kinship links and family size.

(iv) Household management, home life, estate management, living standards

4.171 **Davidson**, C., *A Woman's Work is Never Done: A History of Housework in the British Isles, 1650–1950* (1982).

4.172 **Hole**, C., *The English Housewife in the Seventeenth Century* (1953).

4.173 **Lummis**, T. and **Marsh**, J., *The Woman's Domain: Women and the English Country House* (1990).

4.174 **Penny**, N., ed., *The Household Account Book of Sarah Fell of Swarthmore Hall* (1920).

4.175 **Scott-Moncrieff**, R., ed., *The Househould Account Book of Lady Grisell Baillie 1692–1733*, Scottish Historical Society (1911).

4.176 **Shammas**, C., 'The domestic environment in early modern England and America', *J. Soc. Hist.*, 14 (1981), 3–24.

4.177 — 'Food expenditure and economic well being in early modern England', *J. Ec. Hist.*, 43 (1983), 89–100.

See also: 4.358.

(v) Motherhood, child/parent relations

4.178 **Boucé**, P. G., 'Imagination, pregnant women and monsters in eighteenth century England and France', in G. S. Rousseau and R. Porter, eds., *Sexual Underworlds of the Enlightenment* (1987), 86–100.

4.179 **Charlton**, K., ' "Not publike onely but also private and domesticall": mothers and familial education in pre-industrial England', *Hist. Ed.*, 17 (1988), 1–20.

4.180 **Coster**, W., 'Purity, profanity and Puritanism: the churching of women, 1500–1700', in W. J. Sheils and D. Wood, eds., *Women in the Church*, Studies in Church History, 27 (1990), 377–87.

4.181 **Crawford**, P., 'Katharine and Philip Henry and their children: a case study in family ideology', *Trans. Hist. Scy. Lancs. Ches.*, 134 (1984), 39–73.

4.182 — 'Attitudes to pregnancy from a woman's spiritual diary, 1687–8', *Local Pop. Studs.*, 21 (1978), 43–5.

4.183 — ' "The sucking child": adult attitudes to childcare in the first year of life in seventeenth century England', *Cont. and Change*, 1 (1986), 23–54.

4.184 — 'The construction and experience of maternity in seventeenth century England', in V. Fildes, ed., *Women as Mothers in Pre-industrial England: Essays in memory of Dorothy McClaren* (1990) 3–38.

4.185 **Evenden**, D., 'Mothers and their midwives in seventeenth-century London', in H. Marland, ed., *The Art of Midwifery. Early Modern Midwives in Europe* (1993), 9–26.

4.186 **Fildes**, V., 'Maternal feelings re-assessed: child abandonment and neglect in London and Westminster, 1550–1800', in V. Fildes, ed., *Women as Mothers in Pre-industrial England: Essays in memory of Dorothy McClaren* (1990), 139–78.

4.187 — *Breasts, Bottles and Babies. A History of Infant Feeding* (1986).

4.188 — *Wet Nursing. A History from Antiquity to the Present* (1988).

4.189 — 'The English wet-nurse and her role in infant care, 1538–1800', *Medical Hist.*, 32 (1988), 142–73.

4.190 **Gelis**, J., *History of Childbirth* (1991).

4.191 **Hardyment**, C., *Dream Babies. Child care from Locke to Spock* (1983).

4.192 **Hughes**, M. J., 'Childrearing and social expectations in eighteenth century England: the case of the Colliers of Hastings,' *Studs. Eighteenth Cent. Cult.*, Vol. 13 (1984), 79–100.

4.193 **Illick**, J. E., 'Child-rearing in seventeenth century England and America', in L. De

43

Mause, ed., *The History of Childhood* (London and New York, 1976), 303–50. Once influential, now a much criticised approach. See 4.201–2.

4.194 **Lewis**, J. S., *In the Family Way: Childbearing in the British Aristocracy, 1760–1860* (New Brunswick, 1986).

4.195 **Marshall**, R. K., *Childhood in Seventeenth Century Scotland*, Scottish National Portrait Gallery, exhibition catalogue (1976).

4.196 **Mechling**, J., 'Advice to historians on advice to mothers,' *J. Soc. Hist.*, 9 (1975), 44–63.

4.197 **Newall**, F., 'Wet-nursing and childcare in Aldenham, Hertfordshire, 1595–1726: some evidence on the circumstances and effects of seventeenth century childrearing practices', in V. Fildes, ed., *Women as Mothers in Pre-industrial England: Essays in memory of Dorothy McClaren* (1990), 122–38.

4.198 **Pelling**, M., 'Child health as a social value in early modern England', *Soc. Hist. Medicine*, 1 (1988), 135–64.

4.199 **Pinchbeck**, I. and **Hewitt**, M., *Children in English Society*, 2 vols. (1969).

4.200 **Plumb**, J. H., 'The new world of children in eighteenth century England', *P. P.*, 67 (1975), 64–95.

4.201 **Pollock**, L., *Forgotten Children: Parent-child relations from 1500–1900* (1983). Opposes an 'evolutionary' approach.

4.202 — *A Lasting Relationship. Parents and Children over Three Centuries* (1987). Useful extracts from sources.

4.203 — 'Embarking on a rough passage: the experience of maternity in early modern society', in V. Fildes, ed., *Women as Mothers in Pre-industrial England: Essays in memory of Dorothy McClaren* (1990), 39–67.

4.204 **Rich**, A., *Of Women Born* (1977, reprinted 1979, 1981, 1984). Feminist literary account, very stimulating for historians.

4.205 **Sather**, K., 'Sixteenth- and seventeenth-century childrearing: a matter of discipline', *J. Soc. Hist.*, 22, (1988/9), 735–43.

4.206 **Schofield**, R. S. and **Wrigley**, E. A., 'Infant and child mortality in the late Tudor and early Stuart period', in C. Webster, ed., *Health, Medicine and Mortality in the Sixteenth Century* (1979), 61–95.

4.207 **Travitsky**, B. S., 'The new mother of the English Renaissance: her writings on motherhood', in C. N. Davidson and E. M. Broner, eds., *The Lost Tradition. Mothers and Daughters in Literature* (New York, 1980), 33–43.

4.208 **Tucker**, M. J., 'The child as beginning and end: fifteenth and sixteenth century English childhood', in L. De Mause, ed., *The History of Childhood* (London and New York, 1976), 229–57. Cf Illick: 4.193.

4.209 **Wilson**, A., 'Participant or patient? Seventeenth century childbirth from the mother's point of view', in R. Porter, ed., *Patients and Practitioners. Lay Perceptions of Medicine in Pre-industrial Society* (1985), 129–44.

4.210 — 'The ceremony of childbirth and its interpretations', in V. Fildes, ed., *Women as Mothers in Pre-industrial England: Essays in memory of Dorothy McClaren* (1990), 68–107.

4.211 **Wilson**, S., 'The myth of motherhood a myth: the historical view of European child-rearing', *Soc.Hist.*, 9, (1984), 181–98.

See also: 4.411.

(vi) Family size, family limitation, illegitimacy

4.212 **Connolly**, S. J., 'Illegitimacy and Pre-Nuptial Pregnancy in Ireland before 1864: the Evidence of some Catholic Parish Registers', *Irish Ec.Soc.Hist. J.*, 6 (1979), 5–23.

4.213 **Finlay**, R. A. P., *Population and Metropolis: The Demography of London, 1580–1650* (1981).

4.214 **Flinn**, M., et al, eds., *Scottish Population History* (1977).

4.215 **Hair**, P. E. H., 'Bridal pregnancy in earlier rural England further examined,' *Pop. Studs.*, 20 (1970), 59–70.

4.216 **Hill**, B., 'The marriage age of women and the demographers', *Hist.Workshop J.*, 28 (1989), 129–47.

4.217 **Laslett**, P., *Family Life and Illicit Love in Earlier Generations* (1977). Lively demographic study.

4.218 — and **Oosterveen**, K., 'Long-term trends in bastardy in England. A study of the illegitimacy figures in the parish registers and in the reports of the Register General, 1561–1960', *Pop. Studs.*, 27 (1975), 255–86.

4.219 — and **Smith**, R. M., eds., *Bastardy and its Comparative History. Studies in the History of Illegitimacy and Marital Nonconformism in Britain, France, Germany, Sweden, North America, Jamaica and Japan* (1980).

4.220 **Leneman**, L. and **Mitchison**, R., 'Scottish illegitimacy ratios in the early modern period', *Ec. H. R.*, sec. ser., 40 (1987), 41–63.

4.221 — 'Girls in trouble: the social and geographical setting of illegitimacy in early modern Scotland', *J. Soc. Hist.*, 21 (1987/8), 483–97.

4.222 **Mclaren**, A., *Reproductive Rituals: The Perception of Fertility in England from the Sixteenth to the Nineteenth Century* (1984).

4.223 — *A History of Contraception from Antiquity to the Present* (1991).

4.224 **Maclaren**, D., 'Marital fertility and lactation, 1570–1720', in M. Prior, ed., *Women in English Society* (1985), 22–53.

4.225 **Meteyard**, A., 'Illegitimacy and marriage in eighteenth century England', *J. Interdis. Hist.*, 10 (1980), 479–89.

4.226 **O'Connor**, A., 'Women in Irish Folklore: the testimony regarding illegitimacy, abortion and infanticide', in M. MacCurtain and M. O'Dowd, eds., *Women in Early Modern Ireland* (1991), 304–17.

4.227 **Rogers**, N., 'Carnal Knowledge: Illegitimacy in eighteenth century Westminster', *J. Soc. Hist.*, 23 (1989), 355–76.

4.228 **Schellekens**, J., 'The role of marital fertility in Irish population history, 1750–1840', *Ec. H. R.*, 46 (1993), 369–78.

4.229 **Schnucker**, R. B., 'Elizabethan birth control and Puritan attitudes', *J. Interdis. Hist.*, 4 (1975), 655–67.

4.230 **Wilson**, A., 'Illegitimacy and its implications in mid-eighteenth century London: the evidence of the Foundling Hospital', *Cont. and Change*, 4 (1989), 103–64.

4.231 **Wilson**, C., 'The proximate determinants of marital fertility in England, 1600–1789', in L. Bonfield, R. Smith and K. Wrightson, eds., *The World we have Gained* (1986), 203–30.

4.232 **Wrigley**, E. A., 'Family Limitation in preindustrial England,' *Ec. H. R.*, sec. ser., 19 (1966), 82–109. A classic article.

4.233 — 'Marriage, fertility and population growth in eighteenth century England', in R. B. Outhwaite, ed., *Marriage and Society* (1981), 137–85.

See also: 4.302; 4.326.

(vii) Single women

4.234 **Hill**, B., 'A refuge from men: the idea of a Protestant Nunnery', *P. P.*, 117 (1987), 107–30.

4.235 **Hufton**, O., 'Women without men: widows and spinsters in Britain and France in the eighteenth century', *J. Fam. Hist.* 9 (1984), 355–76.

4.236 **Sharpe**, P., 'Literally spinsters: a new interpretation of local economy and demography in the seventeenth and eighteenth centuries', *Ec. H. R.*, sec. ser., 44 (1991), 46–65.

4.237 **Wall**, R. 'Women alone in English society', *Annales de demographie historique* (1981), 303–17.

(viii) Widows

4.238 **Boulton**, J., 'London widowhood revisited: the decline of female remarriage in the seventeenth and early eighteenth centuries', *Cont. and Change*, 5 (1990), 323–55.

4.239 **Brodsky**, V., 'Widows in late Elizabethan London: remarriage, economic opportunity and family orientations', in L. Bonfield, R. Smith and K. Wrightson, eds., *The World we have Gained* (1986), 122–54.

4.240 **Carlton**, C., 'The widow's tale: male myths and female reality', *Albion*, 10 (1978), 118–29.

4.241 **Clarkson**, L., and **Crawford**, E. M., 'Life after death: widows in Carrick-on-Soir, 1799', in M. MacCurtain and M. O'Dowd, eds., *Women in Early Modern Ireland* (1991) 236–54.

4.242 **Holderness**, B. A., 'Widows in pre-industrial society: an essay upon their economic functions', in R. M. Smith, ed., *Land, Kinship and Life-Cycle* (1984), 423–42.

4.243 **Spufford**, M., *Contrasting Communities. English Villagers in the Sixteenth and Seventeenth Centuries* (1974). On Cambridge villages; the best local study covering treatment of widows.

4.244 **Todd**, B. J., 'The remarrying widow: a stereotype reconsidered', in M. Prior, ed., *Women in English Society* (1985), 54–92.

4.245 — 'Freebench and free enterprise: widows and their property in two Berkshire villages', in J. Chartres and D. Hey, eds., *English Rural Society 1500–1800: Essays in honour of Joan Thirsk*, (1990), 175–200.

4.246 **Wright**, S. J., 'The elderly and the bereaved in eighteenth century Ludlow', in M. Pelling and R. M. Smith, eds., *Life, Death and the Elderly: Historical Perspectives* (1991), 102–33.

See also: 4.399.

(d) LEGAL STATUS OF WOMEN

4.247 **Cioni**, M. L., *Women and Law in Elizabethan England* (New York, 1985).

4.248 — 'The Elizabethan chancery and women's rights', in D. L. Guth and J. W. McKenna, eds., *Tudor Rule and Revolution* (1982), 159–82.

4.249 **Doebler**, B. A. and **Warnicke**, R. M., 'Sex discrimination after death: a seventeenth century English study', *Omega*, 17 (1987), 309–20.

4.250 **Forbes**, T. R., 'A jury of matrons', *Medical Hist.*, 32 (1988), 23–33.

4.251 **Forte**, A. D. M., 'Some aspects of the law of marriage in Scotland: 1500–1700', in E. Craik, ed., *Marriage and Property*, (1981, sec. edn. 1991).

4.252 **Greenberg**, J., 'The legal status of English women in early eighteenth century common law and equity', *Studs. Eighteenth Cent. Cult.*, 4 (1975), 171–81.

4.253 **Harvey**, A., 'Burning women at the stake in eighteenth century England', *Crim. Justice Hist.*, 11 (1990), 193–5.

4.254 **Hogrefe**, P., 'Legal rights of Tudor women and their circumvention by men and women', *Sixteenth Cent. J.*, 3.1 (1972), 97–105.

4.255 **Nicholls**, K. W., 'Irishwomen and property in the sixteenth century', in M. MacCurtain and M. O'Dowd, eds., *Women in Early Modern Ireland*, (1991), 17–31.

4.256 **Normand**, Lord, ed., *An Introduction to Scottish Legal History*, Stair Society, Vol. 20 (1958). Contains several sections on the legal position of women, particularly in marriage.

4.257 **Okin**, S. M., 'Patriarchy and married women's property in England', *Eighteenth Cent. Studs.*, 17, (1983–4), 121–38.

4.258 **Oldham**, J. C., 'On pleading the belly: a history of the jury of matrons', *Crim. Justice Hist.*, 6 (1985), 1–64.

4.259 **Prest**, W. R., 'The law and woman's rights in early modern England', *Seventeenth Cent.*, 6 (1991), 169–87.

4.260 **Simms**, K., 'The Legal Position of Irishwomen in the later middle ages', *Irish Jurist*, 10 (1975), 96–111.

4.261 **Spring**, E., 'Law and the theory of the affective family', *Albion*, 16 (1984), 1–20.

4.262 — 'The heiress-at-law: English real property law from a new point of view', *Law H. R.* 8 (1990), 273–96.

4.263 **Staves**, S., *Married Women's Separate Property in England, 1660–1833* (Cambridge, Mass., 1990).

4.264 — 'British seduced maidens', *Eighteenth Cent. Studs.*, 14 (1980), 109–34.

4.265 — 'Pin money' (married women's property rights), *Studs. Eighteenth Cent. Cult.*, 14 (1985), 47–77.

See also: 4.126; 4.399.

(e) WOMEN AND HEALTH

4.266 **Atkinson**, C. B., and **Stoneman**, W. P., ' "These griping greefes and pinching pangs": attitudes to childbirth in Thomas Bentley's *The Monument of Matrones* (1582)', *Sixteenth Cent. J.*, 21, (1990), 193–203.

4.267 **Aveling**, J. H., *The Chamberlens and the Midwifery Forceps* (1882). Dated obviously, but still worth consulting.

4.268 **Beier**, L. M., 'In sickness and in health: a seventeenth century family's experience', in R. Porter, ed., *Patients and Practitioners. Lay Perceptions of Medicine in Pre-industrial England* (1985), 101–28.

4.269 — *Sufferers and Healers: the Experience of Illness in Seventeenth Century England* (1987).

4.270 **Carter**, J. and **Duriez**, T., *With Child. Birth Through the Ages* (1986).

4.271 **Crawford**, P., 'Attitudes to menstruation in seventeenth century England', *P. P.*, 91 (1981), 47–73.

4.272 **Eccles**, A., *Obstetrics and Gynaecology in Tudor and Stuart England* (1982).

4.273 **Erickson**, R. A., ' "The books of generation": some observations on the style of the English midwife books, 1671–1764', in P. G. Boucé, ed., *Sexuality in Eighteenth Century Britain* (1982), 74–94.

4.274 **Eshleman**, M. K., 'Diet during pregnancy in the sixteenth and seventeenth centuries', *J. Hist. Medicine*, 30 (1975), 23–39.

4.275 **Fissell**, M., *Patients, Power and the Poor in Eighteenth Century Bristol* (1991).

4.276 **Jordanova**, L., 'Gender, generation, health and science: William Hunter's obstetrical atlas', in W. Bynum and R. Porter, eds., *William Hunter and the Eighteenth Century Medical World* (1985), 385–412.

4.277 **Laurence**, A., 'Women's psychological disorders in seventeenth century Britain', in A. Angerman et al., eds., *Current Issues in Women's History* (1989), 203–20.

4.278 **Loudon**, I., *Obstetric Care and Maternal Mortality 1700–1900* (1991).

4.279 **Macdonald**, M., *Mystical Bedlam: Madness, Anxiety and Healing in Seventeenth Century England* (1981). Contains important discussions of the sources of anxiety for women.

4.280 **Malcolm**, E., 'Women and Madness in Ireland, 1600–1850', in M. MacCurtain and M. O'Dowd, eds., *Women in Early Modern Ireland* (1991), 318–34.

4.281 **Murphy-Lawless**, J., 'Male Texts and Female Bodies', in B. Torode, ed., *Text and Talk as Social Practice* (Dordrecht, 1989), 25–48.

4.282 **Oakley**, A., *The Captured Womb. A History of the Medical Care of Pregnant Women* (1984).

4.283 **Pollock**, L., *With Faith and Physic: the Diary of a Tudor Gentlewoman – Lady Grace Mildmay, 1552–1620* (1993).

4.284 **Porter**, R., *Disease, Medicine and Society in England 1550–1860* (2nd edn. 1993). The best general introduction to the history of medicine; some consideration of women's experiences.

4.285 **Radcliffe**, W., *The Secret Instrument* (1947). The Chamberlens' obstetric forceps.

4.286 **Ross**, I. C., ed., *Public Virtue, Private Love: the Early Years of the Rotunda Lying-in Hospital* (Dublin, 1986).

4.287 **Schofield**, R., 'Did the mothers really die? Three centuries of maternal mortality in "The world we have lost" ', in L. Bonfield, R. M. Smith and K. Wrightson, eds., *The World we have Gained* (1986), 231–60.

4.288 **Smith**, G., 'Thomas Tryon's regimen for women: sectarian health in the seventeenth century', in London Feminist History Group, *The Sexual Dynamics of History* (1983), 47–65.

4.289 **Smith**, H., 'Gynecology and Ideology in seventeenth century England', in B. A. Carroll, ed., *Liberating Women's History* (Urbana, Illinois, 1976), 97–114.

4.290 **Traister**, B. H., ' "Matrix and the pain thereof": a sixteenth century gynaecological essay', *Medical Hist.* 35 (1991), 436–51.

4.291 **Verluysen**, M. C., 'Midwives, medical men and "Poor women labouring of child": lying-in hospitals in eighteenth century London', in H. Roberts, ed., *Women, Health and Reproduction* (1981), 18–49.

4.292 **Wilson**, A., 'William Hunter and the varieties of man-midwifery', in W. Bynum and R. Porter, eds., *William Hunter and the Eighteenth century medical world* (1985), 343–70.

See also: 4.63; 4.108; 4.644 (for lying-in charities).

(f) WOMEN'S SEXUALITY

4.293 **Abelove**, H., 'Some speculations on the history of sexual intercourse during the long eighteenth century in England', *Genders*, 6 (1989), 125–30.

4.294 **Addy**, J., *Sin and Society in the Seventeenth Century* (1989). Anecdotal account based on church court records; cf 4.307; 4.326.

4.295 **Ballaster**, R., 'Manl(e)y forms: sex and the female satirist', in C. Brant and D. Purkiss, eds., *Women, Texts and Histories 1575–1760* (1992), 217–41.

4.296 **Barker**, F., *The Tremulous Private Body* (1984). A general literary account of attitudes to the self in seventeenth-century England.

4.297 **Boucé**, P. 'Some sexual beliefs and myths in eighteenth century Britain', in P. Boucé, ed., *Sexuality in Eighteenth Century Britain* (1982), 28–46.

4.298 — ed., *Sexuality in Eighteenth Century Britain* (1982).

4.299 **Brant**, C., 'Speaking of women: scandal and the law in the mid-eighteenth century', in C. Brant and D. Purkiss, eds., *Women, Texts and Histories 1575–1760* (1992), 242–70.

4.300 **Clark**, A., 'Whores and gossip: sexual reputation in London, 1770–1825', in A. Angerman et al., eds., *Current Issues in Women's History* (1989), 231–48.

4.301 **Dekker**, R. and **Van de Pol**, L., *The Tradition of Female Transvestism in Early Modern Europe* (1989).

4.302 **Emmison**, F. G., *Elizabethan Life: Volume Two: Morals and the Church Courts* (1973). Based on evidence from the church courts.

4.303 **Faderman**, L., *Surpassing the Love of Men: Romantic Friendship and Love between Women from the Renaissance to the Present* (New York, 1981).

4.304 **Frye**, R. M., 'The teachings of classical Puritanism on conjugal love', *Studs. in Ren.*, 2 (1955), 148–59.

4.305 **Gent**, L. and **Llewellyn**, N., eds., *Renaissance Bodies: the Human Figure in English Culture c. 1540–1660* (1990).

4.306 **Goreau**, A., 'Two English women in the seventeenth century: notes for an anatomy of female desire', in P. Ariès and A. Bejin, eds., *Western Sexuality: Practice and Precept in Past and Present Times*, A. Forster, trans. (1985), 103–13.

4.307 **Gowing**, L., 'Gender and the language of insult in early modern London', *Hist. Workshop J.*, 35 (1993), 1–21.

4.308 **Hair**, P., *Before the Bawdy Court: selections from church court and other records relating to the correction of moral offences in England, Scotland and New England* (1972).

4.309 **Haller**, W. and M., 'The Puritan Art of Love', *Hunt. Lib. Q.*, 5 (1942), 235–72.

4.310 **Horne**, W. C., ' "Between th' petticoat and the breeches": sexual warfare and the marriage debate in *Hudibras*', *Studs. Eighteenth Cent. Cult*, 11 (1982), 133–46.

4.311 **Howard**, J. E., 'Crossdressing, the Theatre and Gender Struggle in Early Modern England', *Shakespeare Q.*, 39 (1988), 418–40.

4.312 **Ingram**, M., 'Ridings, rough music and the "Reform of popular culture" in early modern England', *P. P.*, 105 (1985), 79–113.

4.313 **Laqueur**, T., *Making Sex: Body and Gender from the Greeks to Freud* (Cambridge, Mass., 1990).

4.314 — 'Orgasm, generation and the politics of reproductive biology', *Representations*, 14 (1986), 1–41. Reprinted in C. Gallagher, ed., *The Making of the Modern Body. Sexuality and Society in the Nineteenth Century* (1987), 1–41.

4.315 **Leites**, E., 'The duty to desire: love, friendship and sexuality in some Puritan theories of marriage', *J. Soc. Hist.*, 15 (1982), 383–408.

4.316 **Leneman**, L. and **Mitchison**, R., *Sexuality and Social Control: Scotland 1660–1780* (1989).

4.317 **Lucas**, R. V., 'Hic Mulier: the female transvestite in early modern England', *Ren. and Ref.*, new ser., 12.1 (1988), 65–84.

4.318 **Mclaren**, A., 'The pleasures of procreation: traditional and biomedical theories of conception', in W. Bynum and R. Porter, eds., *William Hunter and the Eighteenth-century Medical World* (1985), 323–41.

4.319 **Mavor**, E., *The Ladies of Llangollen, A Study of Romantic Friendship* (1971).

4.320 **Monter**, W., 'The pedestal and the stake: courtly love and witchcraft', in R. Bridenthal and C. Koonz, eds., *Becoming Visible. Women in European History* (first edn. Boston, Mass., 1977), 119–36.

4.321 **Orr**, B., 'Whore's rhetoric and the maps of love: constructing the feminine in Restoration erotica', in C. Brant and D. Purkiss, eds., *Women, Texts and Histories 1575–1760* (1992), 195–216.

4.322 **Perry**, R., 'Colonizing the breast: sexuality and maternity in eighteenth century England', *J. Hist. Sexuality*, 2 (1991–2), 204–34.

4.323 **Porter**, R., ' "The secrets of generation displayed": *Aristotle's Masterpiece* in eighteenth-century England', in R. P. Maccubbin, ed., *'Tis Nature's Fault. Unauthorised Sexuality during the Enlightenment* (1987), 7–21.

4.324 — 'Bodies of thought: thoughts about the body in eighteenth century England', in J. H. Pittock and A. A. Wear, eds., *Interpretation and Cultural History* (1991), 82–108.

4.325 — 'Mixed feelings: the Enlightenment and sexuality in eighteenth century Britain', in P. Boucé, ed., *Sexuality in Eighteenth Century Britain* (1982), 1–27.

4.326 **Quaife**, G. R., *Wanton Wenches and Wayward Wives. Peasants and Illicit Sex in Early Seventeenth Century England* (1979). Irritating interpretation, interesting material.

4.327 **Sharpe**, J. A., *Defamation and Sexual Slander in Early Modern England: The Church Courts at York*, Borthwick Papers, 58 (1980).

4.328 **Smith**, N., 'Sexual mores and attitudes in Enlightenment Scotland', in P. Boucé, ed., *Sexuality in Eighteenth Century Britain* (1982), 47–73.

4.329 **Thomas**, K. V., 'The Double Standard', *J. Hist. Ideas*, 20 (1959), 195–216.

4.330 **Thompson**, R., *Unfit for Modest Ears: A Study of Pornographic, Obscene and Bawdy Works written or published in England in the second half of the Seventeenth Century* (1979).

4.331 **Todd**, J., *Women's Friendship in Literature* (New York, 1980).

4.332 **Trumbach**, R., 'Sex, gender and sexual intent in modern culture: male sodomy and female prostitution in Enlightenment London', *J. Hist. Sexuality*, 2 (1991–2), 186–93.

4.333 **Turner**, J. G., *One flesh: Paradisal Marriage and Sexual Relations in the Age of Milton* (1987).

4.334 **Vaughan**, V. M., 'Daughters of the game: Troilus and Cressida and the sexual discourse of sixteenth century England', *Women's Studs. Int. For.*, 13 (1990), 209–20.

See also: 4.38; 4.77; 4.108; 4.227.

(g) POVERTY

4.335 **Beier**, A. L., *Masterless Men: The Vagrancy Problem in England, 1560–1640* (1985). Despite the title includes some material on women.

4.336 — 'Social problems in Elizabethan London', *J. Interdis.Hist.*, 9 (1978), 203–21.

4.337 — *The Problem of the Poor in Tudor and Stuart England* (1983).

4.338 **Brown**, W. N., 'The receipt of poor relief and family situation: Aldenham, Hertfordshire, 1630–90', in R. M. Smith, ed., *Land, Kinship and Life-cycle* (1984), 405–22.

4.339 **Leonard**, E. M., *The Early History of English Poor Relief* (1900). Still very useful.

4.340 **Marshall**, D., *The English Poor in the Eighteenth Century: A Study in Social and Administrative History* (1926).

4.341 **Pelling**, M., 'Old age, poverty and disability in early modern Norwich: work, remarriage and other expedients', in M. Pelling and R. M. Smith, eds., *Life, Death and the Elderly: Historical Perspectives* (1991), 74–101.

4.342 **Slack**, P., *Poverty and Policy in Tudor and Early Stuart England* (1988).

4.343 **Smith**, R. M., ed., *Land, Kinship and Life Cycle* (1984).

4.344 **Wales**, T., 'Poverty, poor relief and the life-cycle: some evidence from seventeenth century Norfolk', in R. M. Smith, ed., *Land, Kinship and Life Cycle* (1984), 351–404.

(h) WOMEN AND WORK

(i) General

4.345 **Bennett**, J., 'History that stands still: women's work in the European past', *Fem. Studs.*, 14 (1988), 269–83.

4.346 **Berg**, M., *The Age of Manufactures, 1700–1820* (1985, rev. edn. 1994).

4.347 **Brophy**, I., 'Women in the workforce', in D. Dickson, ed., *The Gorgeous Mask: Dublin 1700–1850* (Dublin, 1987), 51–63.

4.348 **Cahn**, S., *Industry of Devotion: the Transformation of Women's Work in England, 1500–1660* (New York, 1987). Based on printed sources only; her argument that women's position declined in this period is too simple and too sweeping.

4.349 **Charles**, L., and Duffin, L., eds., *Women and Work in Pre-industrial England* (1985) A very useful collection of detailed studies.

4.350 **Clark**, A., *The Working Life of Women in the Seventeenth Century* (1919, latest edn. ed. A. Erickson (1992). A pioneering study still of value.

4.351 **Collier**, M., *The Woman's Labour* (1739).

Augustan Society Reprint, 230 (Los Angeles, California, 1985).

4.352 **Earle**, P., 'The female labour market in London in the late seventeenth and early eighteenth centuries', *Ec. H. R.*, sec. ser., 42 (1989), 328–52.

4.353 **George**, D. M., *London Life in the Eighteenth Century* (1925, reprinted 1930).

4.354 **Honeyman**, K., and **Goodman**, J., 'Women's work, gender conflict and labour markets in Europe, 1500–1900', *Ec. H. R.*, sec. ser., 44 (1991), 608–28.

4.355 **Hudson**, P. and **Lee**, W. R., 'Women's work and the family economy in historical perspective', in P. Hudson and W. R. Lee, eds., *Women's Work and the Family Economy in Historical Perspective* (1990), 2–48.

4.356 **Laurence**, A., 'Women's work and the English civil war', *Hist Today*, 42 (June 1992), 20–5.

4.357 **McKendrick**, N., 'Home demand and economic growth: a new view of the role of women and children in the industrial revolution', in N. McKendrick, eds., *Historical Perspectives; Studies in English Thought and Society in Honour of J. H. Plumb* (1974), 152–210.

4.358 **Medick**, H., 'The proto-industrial family economy', in P. Kriedte, H. Medick and J. Schlumbohm, eds., *Industrialization before Industrialization* (1981), 38–73. Continental mainly but also useful for Britain.

4.359 **Middleton**, C., 'Women's Labour and the Transition to Pre-industrial Capitalism', in L. Charles and L. Duffin, eds., *Women and Work in Pre-industrial England* (1985), 181–206.

4.360 **Pinchbeck**, I., *Women workers and the Industrial Revolution, 1750–1850* (1930, reprinted 1981).

4.361 **Prior**, M., 'Women and the Urban Economy: Oxford 1500–1800', in M. Prior, ed., *Women in English Society 1500–1800* (1985), 93–117.

4.362 **Richards**, E., 'Women in the British economy since about 1700: an interpretation', *Hist.*, 69 (1974), 337–57.

4.363 **Roberts**, M., ' "Words they are Women, and Deeds. they are Men": Images of Work and Gender in Early Modern England', in L. Charles and L. Duffin, eds., *Women and Work in Pre-industrial England* (1985), 122–80.

4.364 — 'Women and Work in Sixteenth Century English Towns', in P. Corfield and D. Keene, eds., *Work in Towns 850–1850* (1990), 86–102.

4.365 **Shammas**, C., 'The world women knew: women workers in the north of England during the late seventeenth century', in R. S. Dunn and M. M. Dunn, eds., *The World of William Penn* (Philadelphia, Penn., 1986), 99–115.

4.366 **Tilly**, L. A. and **Scott**, J. W., *Women, Work and Family* (New York, 1978).

4.367 **Whyte**, I. D., 'Proto-industrialisation in Scotland', in P. Hudson, ed., *Regions and Industries: A perspective on the industrial revolution in Britain* (1989), 228–51.

4.368 **Wiesner**, M. E., 'Spinning out capital: women's work in the early modern economy', in R. Bridenthal, C. Koonz, S. Stuard, eds., *Becoming Visible. Women in European History* (sec. edn. Boston, Mass., 1987), 221–49.

4.369 **Wright**, S., 'Churmaids, Huswyfes and Hucksters: The Employment of Women in Tudor and Stuart Salisbury', in L. Charles and L. Duffin, eds., *Women and Work in Pre-industrial England* (1985), 100–21.

4.370 — ' "Holding Up Half the Sky": Women and their occupations in Eighteenth Century Ludlow', *Mid. Hist.*, 14 (1989), 53–74.

See also: 4.236.

(ii) Industrial

4.371 **Ben-Amos**, A. K., 'Women apprentices in the trades and crafts of early modern Bristol', *Cont. and Change*, 6 (1991), 227–54.

4.372 **Berg**, M., 'Women's work, mechanisation and the early phases of industrialisation in England', in P. Joyce, ed., *The Historical Meanings of Work* (1987), 64–98.

4.373 — 'What difference did women's work make to the industrial revolution?', *Hist. Workshop J.*, 35 (1993), 22–44.

4.374 **Crawford**, W. H., 'Women in the Domestic Linen Industry', in M. MacCurtian and M. O'Dowd, eds., *Women in Early Modern Ireland* (1991) 255–64.

4.375 **Labouchere**, R., *Abiah Darby, 1716–1793, of Coalbrookdale, Wife of Abraham Darby II* (1988).

4.376 **Lieb**, L. Y., ' "The works of women are symbolical": needlework in the eighteenth century', *Eighteenth Cent. Life*, 10 (1986), 28–46.

4.377 **Simonton**, D., 'Apprenticeship: training and gender in eighteenth century England' in M. Berg, ed., *Markets and Manufacture in Early Industrial Europe* (1991), 227–58.

4.378 **Willen**, D., 'Guildswomen in the city of York, 1560–1700', *The Historian*, 46 (1984), 204–18.

(iii) Agricultural

4.379 **Fussell**, G. E., and **Fussell**, K. R., *The English Countrywoman. Her Life in Farmhouse and Field from Tudor Times to the Victorian Age* (1953, reprinted 1981).

4.380 **Humphries**, J., 'Enclosures, common rights and women: the proletarianization of families in the late eighteenth and early nineteenth centuries', *J. Ec. Hist.*, 50 (1990), 17–42.

4.381 **King**, P., 'Customary rights and women's earnings: the importance of gleaning to the rural labouring poor, 1750–1850', *Ec. H. R.*, 44 (1991), 461–76.

4.382 **Kussmael**, A., *Servants in Husbandry in Early Modern England* (1981).

4.383 **Roberts**, M., 'Sickles and Scythes: women's work and men's work at harvest time', *Hist. Workshop J.*, 7 (1979), 3–28.

4.384 **Snell**, K. D. M., *Annals of the Labouring Poor: Social Change and Agrarian England, 1660–1900* (1985, reprinted 1987). Especially chapter entitled 'The apprenticeship of women', 270–319.

4.385 — 'Agricultural and seasonal unemployment, the standard of living, and women's work in the south and east, 1690–1860', *Ec. H. R.*, sec. ser., 34 (1981), 407–37.

4.386 **Valenze**, D., 'The art of women and the business of men: women's work and the dairy industry, *c.* 1740–1840', *P. P.*, 130 (1991), 142–69.

(iv) Commercial

4.387 **D'Cruze**, S., ' "To acquaint the ladies": women traders in Colchester, *c.* 1750–1800', *Local Histn.*, 17 (1986), 158–62.

4.388 **Elliott**, B., 'An eighteenth century Leicester business woman: the Countess Mary Migliorucci of Nevill Holt', *Leic. Arch. and Local Hist. Scy. Trans.*, 61 (1987), 77–82.

4.389 **Griffiths**, R. G., 'Joyce Jeffreys of Ham Castle: a seventeenth century business gentlewoman', *Trans. Arch. Scy. Worcs.*, 10 (1933), 1–32.

4.390 **Holderness**, B. A., 'Elizabeth Parkin and her investments, 1733–66: aspects of the Sheffield money market in the eighteenth century', *Trans. Hunter Arch. Scy.*, 10 (1973), 81–7.

4.391 **McNeill**, M., *The Life and Times of Mary Ann McCracken, 1770–1866* (Dublin, 1960, reprinted Belfast, 1988).

4.392 **Thwaites**, W., 'Women in the Market Place: Oxfordshire *c.* 1690–1800,' *Mid. Hist.*, 9 (1984), 23–35.

(v) Domestic

4.393 **Coutts**, W., 'Women, children and domestic servants in Dumfries in the seventeenth century', *Dumfriesshire and Galloway Nat. Hist. and Antiq. Scy. Trans.*, 61 (1986), 73–83.

4.394 **Cullen**, N., 'Women and the Preparation of Food in Eighteenth Century Ireland', in M. MacCurtain and M. O'Dowd, eds., *Women in Early Modern Ireland* (Edinburgh, 1991), 265–75.

4.395 **Hecht**, J. J., *The Domestic Servant Class in Eighteenth Century England* (1956, reprinted 1980). The best available treatment of a neglected topic.

4.396 **Kent**, D., 'Ubiquitous but Invisible: female domestic servants in mid-eighteenth century London', *Hist. Workshop J.*, 28 (1989), 111–29.

4.397 **Marshall**, D., 'The domestic servants of the eighteenth century', *Economica*, 9 (1929), 15–40.

4.398 — *The English Domestic Servant in History*, Historical Association. Pamphlet, General Ser., 13 (1949).

(vi) Women and consumption

4.399 **Erickson**, A. L., *Women and Property in Early Modern England* (1993). Important study based on probate records.

4.400 **Shammas**, C., *The Pre-industrial Consumer in England and America* (1990).

4.401 **Vickery**, A. J., 'Women and the world of goods: a Lancashire consumer and her possessions, 1751–81', in J. Brewer and R. Porter, eds., *Consumption and the World of*

Goods: Consumption and Society in the Seventeenth and Eighteenth Centuries (1993), 274–301.

4.402 **Weatherill**, L., 'A possession of one's own: women and consumer behaviour in England, 1660–1740', *J. Brit. Studs.*, 25 (1986), 131–56.

4.403 — *Consumer Behaviour and Material Culture in Britain*, 1600–1760 (1988). Thorough treatment, sensitive to gender, of a theme increasingly stressed in social history.

(vii) Professional

4.404 **Aveling**, J. H., *English Midwives: Their History and Prospects* (1872).

4.405 **Bell**, M., 'Mary Westwood, Quaker publisher', *Publishing Hist.*, 23 (1988), 5–66.

4.406 — 'Hannah Allen and the development of the puritan publishing business, 1646–1651', *Publishing Hist.*, 26 (1989), 5–56.

4.407 **Donnison**, J., *Midwives and Medical Men. A History of Inter-professional Rivalries and Women's Rights* (1977, 2nd ed., 1988).

4.408 **Forbes**, T. R., 'The regulation of English midwives in the eighteenth and nineteenth centuries', *Medical Hist.*, 15 (1971), 352–62.

4.409 **Harley**, D., 'Ignorant midwives–a persistent stereotype', *Bull. Soc. Hist. Medicine*, 28 (1981), 6–9. *See also* responses by B. Boss and J. Boss, Vol. 33 (1983), 71; and A. Wilson, Vol. 32 (1983), 46–9.

4.410 — 'Provincial midwives in England: Lancashire and Cheshire, 1660–1760', in H. Marland, ed., *The Art of Midwifery. Early Modern Midwives in Europe* (1993), 27–48.

4.411 **Hess**, A. G., 'Midwifery practice among the Quakers in southern rural England in the late seventeenth century', in H. Marland, ed., *The Art of Midwifery. Early Modern Midwives in Europe* (1993), 49–76.

4.412 **King**, H., 'The politick midwife: models of midwifery in the work of Elizabeth Cellier', in H. Marland, ed., *The Art of Midwifery. Early Modern Midwives in Europe* (1993), 115–30.

4.413 **Marland**, H., ed., *The Art of Midwifery: Early Modern Midwives in Europe* (1993).

4.414 **Schnorrenberg**, B. B., 'Is childbirth any place for a woman? The decline of midwifery in eighteenth century England', *Studs. Eighteenth Cent. Cult.*, 10 (1981), 393–408.

4.415 **Wyman**, A. L., 'The surgeoness: the female practitioner of surgery 1400–1800', *Medical Hist.*, 28 (1984), 22–41.

See also: 4.185.

(i) WOMEN AND THE WIDER WORLD

4.416 **Bailey**, S. F., *Women and the British Empire: An Annotated Guide to Sources* (New York and London, 1983).

4.417 **Brown**, L., 'The Romance of Empire: Oroonoko and the trade in slaves', in L. Brown and F. A. Nussbaum, eds., *The New Eighteenth Century* (1987), 41–61.

4.418 **Burnard**, T., 'Family continuity and female independence in Jamaica, 1665–1734', *Cont. and Change*, 7 (1992), 181–98.

4.419 **Casway**, J., 'Irish women overseas, 1500–1800', in M. MacCurtain and M. O'Dowd., eds., *Women in Early Modern Ireland* (1991), 112–32.

4.420 **Cressy**, D., *Coming Over: Migration and Communication between England and New England in the Seventeenth Century* (1984).

4.421 **Desai**, A., ed., *Turkish Embassy Letters by Lady Mary Wortley Montagu* (1993).

4.422 **Ferguson**, M., *Subject to Others: British Women and Colonial Slavery, 1670–1834* (1992).

4.423 — 'Mary Wollstonecraft and the problematic of slavery', *Fem. R.* 42, Autumn (1992), 82–102.

4.424 — *Colonial and Gender Relations from Mary Wollstonecraft to Jamaica Kincaid* (New York, 1992).

4.425 — 'British women writers and an emerging abolitionist discourse', *Eighteenth Century Theory and Interpretation*, 33 (1992), 3–23.

4.426 **Hendricks**, M. and **Parker**, P., eds., *Women, 'Race' and Writing in the Early Modern Period* (1993).

4.427 **Hutner**, H. 'Alphra Behn's *Oroonoko*: the politics of gender, race and class', in D. Spender, ed., *Living by the Pen: Early British Women Writers* (New York, 1992), 39–51.

4.428 **Melman**, B., *Women's Orients: English Women and the Middle East, 1718–1918: Sexuality, Religion and Work* (1991).

4.429 **Midgley**, C., *Women Against Slavery: the British Campaigns, 1780–1870* (1992).

4.430 **Walsh**, M., 'Some notes towards a history of the womenfolk of the wild geese', *Irish Sword*, 5 (1962), 98–106, 133–45.

4.431 **Walsh**, M. K., 'Irishwomen in exile, 1600–1800', *The O'Mahony Journal*, 11 (1981), 35–48.

(j) WOMEN, POLITICS AND POWER

(i) General

4.432 **Applewhite**, H. B. and **Levy**, D. G., eds., *Women and Politics in the Age of the Democratic Revolution* (Michigan, Ann Arbor, 1991). Mainly on Europe and America in the era of the French Revolution.

4.433 **Brady**, C., 'Political women and reform in Tudor Ireland', in M. MacCurtain and M. O'Dowd, eds., *Women in Early Modern Ireland* (1991), 69–90.

4.434 **Brennan**, T. and **Pateman**, C., ' "Mere auxiliaries to the commonwealth": women and the origins of liberalism', *Pol. Studs.* 27 (1979), 183–200.

4.435 **Cerasano**, S. P. and **Wynne-Davies**, M., eds., *Gloriana's Face: Women, Public and Private, in the English Renaissance* (1992). A collection by literary scholars.

4.436 **Clery**, E. J., 'Women, publicity and the coffee house myth', *Woman: A Cultural Review*, 2 (1991), 168–77.

4.437 **Colley**, L., *Britons: Forging the Nation, 1707–1837* (New Haven, Conn., 1992). Chapter 6.

4.438 **Crawford**, P., 'Public duty, conscience and women in early modern England', in J. Morrill, P. Slack and D. Woolf, eds., *Public Duty and Private Conscience in Seventeenth Century England* (1993), 57–76.

4.439 **Curtin**, N. J., 'Women and eighteenth-century Irish republicanism', in M. MacCurtain and M. O'Dowd, eds., *Women in Early Modern Ireland* (1991), 133–44.

4.440 **Durston**, C., *The Family in the English Revolution* (1988). Descriptive account of family disruption in the 1640s and 1650s.

4.441 **Houlbrooke**, R., 'Women's social life and common action in England from the 15th century to the eve of the Civil War', *Cont. and Change*, 1 (1986), 171–89.

4.442 **Laqueur**, T. W., 'The Queen Caroline affair: politics as art in the reign of George IV,' *J. Mod. Hist*, 54.3 (1982), 417–66.

4.443 **Needham**, G. B., 'Mary de la Rivière Manley, Tory Defender', *Hunt. Lib. Q.*, 12 (1948–9), 253–88.

4.444 **O'Dowd**, M., 'Women and war in Ireland in the 1640s', in M. MacCurtain and M. O'Dowd, eds., *Women in Early Modern Ireland* (1991), 91–111.

4.445 **Palmer**, W., 'Gender, violence and rebellion in Tudor and early Stuart Ireland', *Sixteenth Cent. J.*, 23 (1992), 699–712.

4.446 **Pateman**, C., *The Disorder of Women: Democracy, Feminism and Political Theory* (1989).

4.447 — *The Sexual Contract* (1988). Feminist political theory; important for early modern understandings of gender and power; cf 2.179.

4.448 **Schochet**, G. J., 'Patriarchalism, Politics, and Mass Attitudes in Stuart England', *Hist. J.*, 12 (1969), 413–41.

4.449 — *Patriarchalism in Political Thought: The Authoritarian Family and Political Speculation and Attitudes Especially in Seventeenth Century England* (New York, 1975).

4.450 **Schwoerer**, L. G., 'Women and the Glorious Revolution,' *Albion*, 18 (1986), 195–218.

4.451 **Shanley**, M., 'Marriage contract and social contract in seventeenth century English political thought', *Western Pol. Q.*, 32 (1979), 79–91.

4.452 **Shepherd**, A., 'Henry Howard and the lawful regiment of women', *Hist. Pol. Thought*, 12.4 (1991), 589–603.

4.453 **Wheelwright**, J., *Amazons and Military Maids* (1989).

4.454 **Zwicker**, S. N., 'Virgins and whores: the politics of sexual misconduct in the 1660's', in C. Condren and A. D. Cousins, eds., *The Political Identity of Andrew Marvell* (1990), 85–110.

See also: 2.179; 4.730; 4.877; 4.895; 4.896; 4.902.

(ii) Royal and aristocratic women

4.455 **Axtell**, M., *The Queen's Two Bodies: Drama and the Elizabethan Succession*

4.456 **Barroll**, L., 'The court of the first Stuart Queen', in L. L. Peck, ed., *The Mental World of the Jacobean Court* (1991), 191–208.

4.457 **Bassnett**, S., *Elizabeth I. A Feminist Perspective* (1988).

4.458 **Belsey**, A. and **Belsey**, C., 'Icons of divinity: portraits of Elizabeth I', in L. Gent and N. Llewellyn, eds., *Renaissance Bodies: the Human Figure in English Culture* c. *1540–1660* (1990), 11–35.

4.459 **Bernard**, G., 'The fall of Anne Boleyn', *Eng. H. R.*, 106 (1991), 584–610. For a contrary view, see Ives 4.505.

4.460 **Berry**, P., *Of Chastity and Power: Elizabethan Literature and the Unmarried Queen* (1989). Thought-provoking discussion of the connections between gender, power and representation.

4.461 **Bessborough**, Earl of, ed., *Georgiana: Extracts from the Correspondence of Georgiana, Duchess of Devonshire* (1955).

4.462 **Bucholz**, R. O., ' "Nothing but ceremony": Queen Anne and the limitations of royal ritual', *J. Brit. Studs.*, 30 (1991), 288–323.

4.463 **Carlton**, C., *Royal Mistresses* (1989).

4.464 **Chambers**, A., *Granuaille. The Life and times of Grace O'Malley* c. *1530–1603* (Dublin, 1979).

4.465 — *Eleanor, Countess of Desmond*, c. *1545–1638* (Dublin, 1986).

4.466 **Chapman**, H. W., *Mary II* (1953).

4.467 **Collinson**, P., 'The monarchical republic of Queen Elizabeth I', *Bull. J. Ry. Lib.*, 69 (1987), 394–424.

4.468 — *The English Captivity of Mary Queen of Scots* (1987).

4.469 **Cowan**, I. B., compiler, *The Enigma of Mary Stuart* (1971).

4.470 **Dawson**, J. E., 'Mary Queen of Scots, Lord Darnley and Anglo-Scottish relations in 1565', *Int. H. R.*, 8 (1986), 1–24.

4.471 **Donaldson**, G., *The First Trial of Mary Queen of Scots* (1969).

4.472 — *Mary Queen of Scots* (1974).

4.473 — *All the Queen's Men: Power and Politics in Mary Stewart's Scotland* (1983).

4.474 — 'Mary Stewart, governor of Scotland', *Uty. Edinburgh J.*, 33 (1987), 95–8.

4.475 **Doran**, S., 'Religion and politics at the court of Elizabeth I: the Habsburg marriage negotiations of 1559–1567', *Eng. H. R.*, 104 (1989), 908–26.

4.476 **Dowling**, M., 'Anne Boleyn and reform', *J. Ecc. Hist.*, 35 (1984), 30–46.

4.477 — 'Anne Boleyn as patron', in D. Starkey, ed., *Henry VIII: A European Court in England* (1991), 107–11.

4.478 **Erickson**, C., *The First Elizabeth* (New York, 1983).

4.479 **Fitzgerald**, B., ed, *The Correspondence of Emily, Duchess of Leinster*, 3 vols. (Dublin, 1949–55).

4.480 **Fleming**, D. H., *Mary Queen of Scots* (1897). Still useful.

4.481 **Fraser**, A., *Mary Queen of Scots* (1969).

4.482 — *The Six Wives of Henry VIII* (1992).

4.483 **Godber**, J., *The Marchioness Grey of Wrest Park*, Bedfordshire Historical Record Society, 47 (1968).

4.484 **Grant**, D., *Margaret the First* (1957). Still useful, on the Duchess of Newcastle.

4.485 **Gregg**, E., *Queen Anne* (1980).

4.486 **Haigh**, C., *Elizabeth I* (1988).

4.487 — ed., *The Reign of Elizabeth I* (1984).

4.488 **Hamilton**, E., *The Illustrious Lady: A Biography of Barbara Villiers, Countess of Castlemanine and Duchess of Cleveland* (1979).

4.489 **Harris**, B., 'Property, power and personal relations: elite mothers and sons in Yorkist and early Tudor England', *Signs*, 15.3 (1990), 606–32.

4.490 — 'Profit, power and passion: Mary Tudor, Charles Brandon and Arranged Marriage in early Tudor England,' *Fem. Studs.* 15 (1989), 59–88.

4.491 — 'Women and politics in early Tudor England,' *Hist. J.* 33, June 1990, 259–81.

4.492 **Harris**, F., *A Passion for Government: The Life of Sarah, Duchess of Marlborough* (1991).

4.493 — 'Accounts of the conduct of Sarah, Duchess of Marlborough, 1704–1742', *Brit. Lib. J.*, 8 (1982), 7–35.

4.494 — ' "The Honourable Sisterhood": Queen Anne's maids of honour', *Brit.Lib.J.*. 19.2 (1993), 181–98.

4.495 — and **Jones**, C., ' "A question . . . carried by bishops, pensioners, placemen and idiots": Sarah, Duchess of Marlborough and the Lords' Division over the Spanish Convention, 1 March 1739', *Parl. Hist.*, 11 (1992), 254–77.

4.496 **Haugaard**, W. P., 'Katherine Parr: the religious convictions of a Renaissance Queen', *Renaissance Q.*, 22 (1969), 346–59.

4.497 — 'Elizabeth Tudor's *Book of Devotions*: a neglected clue to the queen's life and character', *Sixteenth Cen. J.*, 12 (1981), 79–106.

4.498 **Heisch**, A., 'Queen Elizabeth I: parliamentary rhetoric and the exercise of power,' *Signs*, 1 (1975), 31–55.

4.499 — 'Queen Elizabeth I and the persistence of patriarchy', *Fem. R.*, 4 (1980), 45–56.

4.500 **Hibbard**, C. M., 'The role of a queen consort. The household and court of Henrietta Maria, 1625–1642', in R. G. Asch and A. M. Birke, eds., *Princes, Patronage and the Nobility. The Court at the Beginning of the Modern Age* (1991), 315–27.

4.501 **Holmes**, M., *Proud Northern Lady: Lady Anne Clifford, 1590–1676* (1976).

4.502 **Hopkins**, L., *Elizabeth I and her Court* (1990).

4.503 — *Women who would be Kings: Female Rulers of the Sixteenth Century* (New York, 1991).

4.504 **Ives**, E., *Anne Boleyn* (1986). The standard work. See also Warnicke 4.562.

4.505 — 'The fall of Anne Boleyn reconsidered', *Eng. H. R.*, 107 (1992), 651–64. A reply to Bernard: 4.459.

4.506 **Jones**, K., *A Glorious Fame, the Life of Margaret Cavendish, Duchess of Newcastle, 1623–1673* (1988).

4.507 **Jones**, N. L., 'Elizabeth, edification and the Latin prayer book of 1560', *Church Hist.*, 53 (1984), 174–86.

4.508 **Jordan**, C., 'Women's rule in sixteenth-century British political thought', *Renaissance Q.*, 40 (1987), 421–51.

4.509 — 'Representing political androgyny: More on the Siena portrait of Queen Elizabeth I', in A. M. Haselkorn and B. S. Travitsky, eds., *The Renaissance Englishwoman in Print* (Amherst, Mass., 1990), 157–76.

4.510 **King**, J. N., 'Patronage and piety: the influence of Catherine Parr', in M. P. Hanney, ed., *Silent but for the Word: Tudor Women as Patrons, Translators, and Writers of Religious Works* (Kent, Ohio, 1985) 43–60.

4.511 — 'Queen Elizabeth: representations of the Virgin Queen', *Renaissance Q.*, 43 (1990), 30–74.

4.512 **King**, W., ed., *Memoirs of Sarah, Duchess of Marlborough, together with her characters of contemporaries and her opinions* (1930, reprinted 1969).

4.513 **Lee**, M., 'The daughter of debate: Mary Queen of Scots after 400 years', *Scot.*

H.R., 68 (1989), 70–9. A useful review article.

4.514 **Lee**, P. A., ' "A bodye politique to governe": Aylmer, Knox and the debate on queenship', *The Historian*, 52 (1990), 242–61.

4.515 **Levin**, C., 'Lady Jane Grey: Protestant Queen and Martyr', in M. P. Hannay, ed., *Silent but for the Word: Tudor Women as Patrons, Translators, and Writers of Religious Works* (Kent, Ohio, 1985), 92–106.

4.516 — 'Queens and claimants: political insecurity in sixteenth century England', in J. Sharistanian, ed., *Gender, Ideology and Action: Historical Perspectives on Women's Public Lives* (Westport, Conn., 1986), 41–66.

4.517 — 'John Foxe and the responsibilities of Queenship', in M. B. Rose, ed., *Women in the Middle Ages and the Renaissance* (New York, 1986), 113–33.

4.518 — ' "Would I could give you help and succour": Elizabeth I and the politics of touch', *Albion*, 21 (1989), 191–205.

4.519 — 'Power, politics, and sexuality: images of Elizabeth I', in J. Brinks, A. Coubert and M. Horowitz, eds., *The Politics of Gender in Early Modern Europe* (Kirksville, Missouri, 1989), 95–110.

4.520 **Levine**, M., *The Early Elizabethan Succession Question 1558–1568*, (Stanford, California, 1965).

4.521 — 'The place of women in Tudor government', in D. J. Guth and J. McKenna, eds., *Tudor Rule and Revolution: Essays for G.R. Elton from his American Friends* (1982), 109–23.

4.522 **Lindley**, D., *The Trials of Frances Howard: Fact and Fiction at the Court of King James* (1993). Wide-ranging literary–historical analysis of the most serious scandal at the Jacobean court.

4.523 **Loades**, D., *The Reign of Mary Tudor: Politics, Government and Religion in England* (1979, 2nd edn. 1991).

4.524 — *Mary Tudor. A Life* (1989).

4.525 — 'The reign of Mary Tudor: historiography and research', *Albion*, 21 (1989), 547–58.

4.526 **Lynch**, M., ed., *Mary Stewart: Queen in Three Kingdoms* (1988). A very important collection of essays.

4.527 — 'Queen Mary's triumph: the baptismal celebrations at Stirling in December 1566', *Scot. H. R.*, 69 (1990), 1–20. A broad

4.528 **Macaffrey**, W., *Elizabeth I* (1993). The latest biography.

4.529 — *The Shaping of the Elizabethan Regime* (1968).

4.530 — *Queen Elizabeth and the Making of Policy 1572–1588* (1981).

4.531 — *Elizabeth I: War and Politics, 1588–1603* (Princeton, New Jersey, 1992).

4.532 **McClure**, P. and **Wells**, P. H., 'Elizabeth I as a second Virgin Mary', *Renaissance Studs.*, 4 (1990), 38–70.

4.533 **Marcus**, L. S., 'Shakespeare's comic heroines, Elizabeth I and the political uses of androgyny', in M. B. Rose, ed., *Women in the Middle Ages and the Renaissance: Literary and Historical Perspectives*, (New York, 1986), 133–53.

4.534 **Marshall**, R. K., *Elizabeth I* (1990).

4.535 — *Mary I* (1993).

4.536 **Mathew**, D., *Lady Jane Grey: the Setting of the Reign* (1972).

4.537 **Mattingly**, G., *Catherine of Aragon* (Boston, Mass., 1941).

4.538 **McConica**, J. K., *English Humanists and Reformation Politics under Henry VIII and Edward VI* (1965). Chapter 7, 200–34, is on the role of Catherine Parr.

4.539 **Marshall**, R. K., *Mary of Guise* (1977).

4.540 **Martienssen**, A. K., *Queen Katherine Parr* (1973).

4.541 **Mendelson**, S. H., *The Mental World of Stuart Women: Three Studies*, (1987).

4.542 **Montrose**, L., ' "Shaping Fantasies": figurations of gender and power in Elizabethan culture', *Representations* 2 (1983), 61–89. Reprinted as ' "A Midsummer Night's Dream" and the shaping fantasies of Elizabethan culture: Gender, Power, Form', in M. Ferguson et al., eds., *Rewriting the Renaissance* (Chicago and London, 1986), 65–87.

4.543 — ' "Eliza, Queene of shepheardes", and the pastoral of power', *Engl. Lit. Ren.*, 10 (1980), 153–82.

4.544 **Neale**, J. E., *Queen Elizabeth I: A Biography* (1934; many reprints, latest edn. 1979).

4.545 — *Elizabeth I and her Parliaments*, 2 vols. (1953, 1957).

4.546 **Ogilvy**, M. F. E., Countess of Airlie, *In Whig Society 1775–1818* (1921). Extracts from the correspondence of Viscountess Melbourne and Viscountess Palmerston.

4.547 **Perry**, M., *The Word of a Prince: the Life of Elizabeth I from Contemporary Documents* (1990).

4.548 **Phillips**, J. E., *Images of a Queen: Mary Stuart in Sixteenth Century Literature* (Los Angeles, California, 1964).

4.549 **Pollock**, L., ' "Teach her to live under obedience": the making of women in the upper ranks of early modern England', *Cont. and Change*, 4 (1989), 231–58.

4.550 **Scalingi**, P. L., 'The sceptre or the distaff: the question of female sovereignty, 1516–1607', *Historian*, 41 (1978), 59–75.

4.551 **Schwind**, M. L., 'Nurse to all rebellions: Grace O'Malley and sixteenth century Connacht', *Eire-Ireland*, 13 (1978), 40–61.

4.552 **Schwoerer**, L. *Lady Rachel Russell: 'One of the Best of Women'* (Baltimore, Md., and London, 1988).

4.553 — 'Images of Queen Mary II, 1689–1695', *Renaissance Q.*, 42 (1989), 717–48.

4.554 **Smailes**, H., and **Thomson**, D., *The Queen's Image*, Scottish National Portrait Gallery (1987). A catalogue of an exhibition to mark the four hundredth anniversary of the execution of Mary Queen of Scots.

4.555 **Smith**, A. G. R., ed., *The last years of Mary Queen of Scots* Roxburghe Club (1990).

4.556 **Smuts**, R. M., 'The Puritan followers of Henrietta Maria in the 1630s', *Eng. H. R.*, 93 (1978), 18–34.

4.557 **Strong**, R., *The Cult of Elizabeth: Elizabethan Portraiture and Pageantry* (1977).

4.558 — *Gloriana: the Portraits of Queen Elizabeth* (1987).

4.559 **Teague**, F., 'Queen Elizabeth in her speeches', in S. P. Cerasano and M. Wynne-Davies, eds., *Gloriana's Face: Women, Public and Private, in the English Renaissance* (1992), 63–78.

4.560 — 'Elizabeth I, Queen of England', in K. M. Wilson, ed., *Women Writers of the Renaissance and Reformation* (Athens, Georgia, 1987), 522–47.

4.561 **Veevers**, E., *Images of Love and Religion: Queen Henrietta Maria and Court Entertainments* (1989).

4.562 **Warnicke**, R. M., *The Rise and Fall of Anne Boleyn: Family Politics at the Court of Henry VIII* (1989). Controversial; see reviews by Ives, *Hist. J.* 34 (1991) and Wormald, *J. Ecc. Hist.*, 43 (1991).

4.563 — 'The eternal triangle and court politics: Henry VIII, Anne Boleyn and Sir Thomas Wyatt', *Albion*, 18 (1986), 565–79.

4.564 — 'Sexual Heresy at the court of Henry VIII', *Hist. J.*, 30 (1987), 247–68.

4.565 **Weil**, R. J., 'The politics of legitimacy: women and the warming pan scandal', in L. Schwoerer, ed., *The Revolution of 1688–9: Changing Perspectives* (1992), 65–82.

4.566 **White**, B., *The Cast of Ravens* (1965). Conventional analysis of the Howard–Overbury scandal. Now see Lindley 4.522.

4.567 **Wiesner**, M., 'Women's defence of their public role', in M. B. Rose, ed., *Women in the Middle Ages and the Renaissance: Literary and Historical Perspectves* (Syracuse, 1986), 1–27.

4.568 **Wilson**, J., 'The Harefield entertainment and the cult of Elizabeth I', *Antiquaries J.*, 66 (1986), 315–29.

4.569 **Woods**, S., 'Spenser and the problems of women's rule', *Hunt. Lib. Q.*, 48 (1985), 141–58.

4.570 **Wormald**, J., *Mary Queen of Scots: A Study in Failure* (1988). Includes a very useful bibliography.

4.571 **Wright**, P., 'A change in direction: the ramifications of a female household', in D. Starkey, ed., *The English Court from the Wars of the Roses to the Civil War* (1987), 147–72.

4.572 **Wynne-Davies**, M., 'The Queen's Masque: Renaissance women and the seventeenth century court masque', in S. P. Cerasano and M. Wynne-Davies, eds., *Gloriana's Face: Women, Public and Private, in the English Renaissance* (1992), 79–104.

4.573 **Yates**, F. A., 'Queen Elizabeth as Astraea', in F. A. Yates, *Astraea: the Imperial Theme in the Sixteenth Century* (1975), 29–87.

See also: 4.790; 4.922.

(iii) Women and protest

4.574 **Bohstedt**, J. 'The myth of the feminine food riot: women as proto-citizens in English community politics, 1790–1810', in H. B. Applewhite and D. G. Levy, eds., *Women and Politics in the Age of the Democratic Revolution* (Michigan, 1991), 21–60.

4.575 — 'Gender, household and community politics: women in English riots 1790–1810', *P. P.*, 120 (1990), 88–122.

4.576 **Crawford**, P., 'The challenges to Patriarchalism: how did the Revolution affect women?', in J. Morrill, ed.,

Revolution and Restoration: England in the 1650s (1992), 112–28.

4.577 **Higgins**, P., 'The reactions of women, with special reference to women petitioners', in B. Manning, ed., *Politics, Religion and the English Civil War* (1973), 179–222.

4.578 **McArthur**, E. A., 'Women petitioners and the Long Parliament', *Eng. H. R.*, 24 (1909), 698–709. Pioneering article. See Higgins 4.577.

4.579 **McEntee**, A. M., ' "The (un)civill susterhood of oranges and lemons": female petitioners and demonstrators, 1642–1653', *Prose Studs.*, 14 (1991), 92–111.

4.580 **Schnorrenberg**, B. B., 'The brood hen of faction: Mrs Macauley and radical politics, 1765–1775', *Albion*, 2 (1979), 33–43.

4.581 **Travitsky**, B., 'The Lady Doth Protest: protest in the popular writings of Renaissance Englishwomen', *Eng. Lit. Ren.*, 14 (1984), 255–83.

4.582 **Trubowitz**, R., 'Female preachers and male wives: gender and authority in Civil War England', *Prose Studs.*, 14 (1991), 112–33.

4.583 **Walter**, J., 'Grain riots and popular attitudes to the Law: Maldon and the Crisis of 1629', in J. Brewer and J. Styles, eds., *An Ungovernable People. The English and their Law in the Seventeenth and Eighteenth Centuries* (1980), 47–84.

See also: 4.37.

(iv) Feminism

4.584 **Barker-Benfield**, G. J., 'Mary Wollstonecraft: eighteenth century commonwealthwoman', *J. Hist. Ideas*, 50 (1989), 95–115.

4.585 **Bell**, S. G. and **Offen**, K. M., eds., *Women, the Family and Freedom* (Stanford, California, 1983). Extracts from sources (not just for Britain). Vol. 1 covers 1750–1880.

4.586 **Brody**, M., 'Mary Wollstonecraft: sexuality and women's rights', in D. Spender, ed., *Feminist Theorists. Three Centuries of Women's Intellectual Traditions* (1983), 40–59.

4.587 **Browne**, A., *The Eighteenth Century Feminist Mind* (1987). 'Feminist mind' is rather an abstraction, but there is useful material here.

4.588 **Ferguson**, M., *First Feminists : British Women Writers 1578–1799* (Bloomington, Indiana, 1985). Useful extracts from women's writing, with introductory material; the isolation of supposedly 'feminist' elements from the broader works of these writers may create distortions.

4.589 — and **Todd**, J., *Mary Wollstonecraft* (Boston, Mass., 1984).

4.590 **Fitz**, L. T., ' "What says the married woman?" Marriage theory and feminism in the English Renaissance', *Mosaic*, 13 (1980), 1–22.

4.591 **Gallagher**, C., 'Embracing the Absolute: the politics of the female subject in seventeenth century England', *Genders*, 1 (1988), 24–39.

4.592 **George**, M., *One Woman's "Situation": a study of Mary Wollstonecraft* (Urbana, Illinois, 1970).

4.593 **Halsband**, R., ' "Condemned to petticoats": Lady Mary Wortley Montague as Feminist and Writer', in R. B. White, ed., *The Dress of Words: Essays on Restoration and Eighteenth century Literature in Honour of Richmond F. Bond* (Manhattan, Kansas, 1978), 35–52.

4.594 **Hill**, B., ed., *The First English Feminist: Mary Astell* (1986). The most accessible edition of her writings.

4.595 **Horner**, J. M., 'The English women novelists and their connection with the feminist movement, 1688–1797', *Smith College Studies in Modern Languages, II* (Northampton, Mass., 1929–30). An early study, still of some value.

4.596 **Janes**, R., 'Mary, Mary, Quite Contrary, or Mary Astell and Mary Wollstonecraft compared', *Studs. Eighteenth Cent. Cult.*, 5 (1976), 121–39.

4.597 **Jordan**, C., *Renaissance Feminism. Literary Texts and Political Models* (Ithaca, New York, 1990).

4.598 — 'Feminism and the humanists: the case of Sir Thomas Elyot's *Defence of Good-Women*', *Renaissance Q.*, 36.2 (1983), 181–201. Also in M. Ferguson et al., eds., *Rewriting the Renaissance* (Chicago, Illinois, and London, 1986), 242–58.

4.599 **Kaplan**, C., 'Wild nights: pleasure/sexuality/feminism', in C. Kaplan, *Sea Changes: Essays on Culture and Feminism* (1986) 31–56. On Wollstonecraft.

4.600 **Kelly**, J., 'Early feminist theory and the *Querelle des Femmes*, 1400–1789', *Signs*, 8.1 (1982), 4–28. Reprinted in *Women, History and Theory: the Essays of Joan Kelly*, (Chicago, Illinois, 1984), 65–109.

4.601 **Kinnaird**, J., 'Mary Astell and the conservative contribution to English feminism', *J. Brit. Studs.*, 19 (1979), 53–75. A version of this is also included in D. Spender, ed., *Feminist Theorists. Three Centuries of Women's Intellectual Traditions* (1983), 28–39.

4.602 **Kramer**, A., ' "Thus by the Musick of a Ladyes Tongue": Margaret Cavendish's dramatic innovation in women's education', *Women's H. R.*, 2 (1993), 57–79.

4.603 **Lorch**, J. *Mary Wollstonecraft. The Making of a Radical Feminist* (1990).

4.604 **Luria**, G., ed., *The Feminist Controversy in England 1788–1810* (New York, 1974). A very useful reprinting of many eighteenth century texts, e.g. Mary Hays, *Appeal to the Men of Great Britain in Behalf of Women*, (1798), Priscilla Wakefield, *Reflections on the Present Conditions of the Female Sex* (1798), as well as Hannah More and Mary Wollstonecraft.

4.605 **McGuire**, M. A., 'Margaret Cavendish, Duchess of Newcastle, on the nature and status of women', *Int. J. Women's Studs.* 1 (1978), 193–205.

4.606 **Mitchell**, J., 'Women and Equality', in A. Oakley and J. Mitchell, eds., *The Rights and Wrongs of Women* (1976), 379–99.

4.607 **Nadelhaft**, J., 'The Englishwoman's sexual civil war: feminist attitudes towards men, women and marriage, 1650–1740', *J. Hist. Ideas*, 43 (1982), 555–79. To be used with caution.

4.608 **Offen**, K., 'Defining Feminism: a comparative historical approach', *Signs*, 14 (1988), 119–57.

4.609 **Perry**, R., *The Celebrated Mary Astell: An Early English Feminist* (Chicago, Illinois, 1986).

4.610 — 'The veil of chastity: Mary Astell's feminism', in P. Boucé, ed., *Sexuality in Eighteenth Century Britain* (1982), 141–58.

4.611 — 'Radical doubt and the liberation of women', *Eighteenth Cent. Studs.*, 18 (1985), 472–94.

4.612 **Reiss**, T. J., 'Revolution in bounds: Wollstonecraft, women and reason', in L. Kauffman, ed., *Gender and Theory. Dialogues on Feminist Criticism* (1989), 11–50.

4.613 **Riley**, D., *Am I that Name? Feminism and the Category of 'Women' in History* (1988).

4.614 **Roberts**, M. M. and **Mizuta**, T., eds., *Sources of British Feminism*, 6 vols. (1993). This reprints sources from Mary Astell (1701) to Emmeline Pankhurst (1914).

4.615 **Rogers**, K., *Feminism in Eighteenth-century England* (Brighton and Urbana, Illinois, 1982). Based on literary sources, perhaps too uncritical a notion of feminism.

4.616 **Sarahson**, L. T., 'A science turned upside down: feminism and the natural philosophy of Margaret Cavendish', *Hunt. Lib. Q.*, 47 (1984), 299–307.

4.617 **Shepherd**, S., *Amazons and Warrior Women: Varieties of Feminism in Seventeenth Century Drama* (1981).

4.618 — ed., *The Women's Sharp Revenge* (1985). A collection of five pamphlets (1580–1640) debating the nature of women.

4.619 **Smith**, H., *Reason's Disciples: Seventeenth Century English Feminists* (Urbana, Illinois, 1982).

4.620 **Spender**, D., ed., *Feminist Theorists. Three Centuries of Women's Intellectual Traditions* (1983).

4.621 **Taylor**, B., 'Mary Wollstonecraft and the wild wish of early feminism', *Hist. Workshop J.*, 33 (1992), 197–219.

4.622 **Todd**, J. M., 'The biographies of Mary Wollstonecraft: review essay', *Signs*, 1 (1976), 721–34.

4.623 — *A Wollstonecraft Anthology* (Bloomington, Indiana, 1973, reprinted Cambridge, 1989).

4.624 — *Mary Wollstonecraft. An Annotated Bibliography* (New York, 1976)..

4.625 — and **Butler**, M., eds., *The Works of Mary Wollstonecraft*, 7 vols. (1989).

4.626 **Tomalin**, C., *The Life and Death of Mary Wollstonecraft* (1974).

4.627 **Walters**, M., 'The rights and wrongs of women: Mary Wollstonecraft, Harriet Martineau, Simone de Beauvoir', in J. Mitchell and A. Oakley, eds., *The Rights and Wrongs of Women* (1976), 304–78.

4.628 **Williamson**, M. L., 'Who's afraid of Mrs Barbauld? The Bluestocking and Feminism', *Int. J. Women's Studs.*, 3 (1980), 89–102.

4.629 **Wollstonecraft**, M., *A Vindication of the Rights of Women* (1792). Most accessible current edition, M. B. Kramnick, ed. (1972).

See also: 4.117; 4.819.

(k) WOMEN, SOCIAL POLICY AND THE STATE

4.630 **Hopkins**, M. A., *Hannah More and her Circle* (New York, 1947).

4.631 **James**, M., *Social Problems and Policy during the Puritan Revolution* (1930). A classic study, although it could be more sensitive to gender.

4.632 **Jones**, M. G., *Hannah More* (Cambridge, 1952).

4.633 **Jordan**, W. K., *Philanthropy in England, 1480–1660* (1959).

4.634 — *The Charities of London 1480–1660* (1960). 4.633 and 4.634 are thorough surveys of charitable activity with much useful information about female philanthropy.

4.635 **Kunze**, B. Y., ' "Poore and in necessity": Margaret Fell and Quaker female philanthropy in northwest England in the late seventeenth century', *Albion*, 21 (1989), 559–80.

4.636 **Larson**, E. S., 'A measure of power: the personal charity of Elizabeth Montagu', *Studs. Eighteenth Cent. Cult.*, 16 (1986), 197–210.

4.637 **Meyers**, M., 'Reform or Ruin: "A revolution in female manners" ', *Studs. Eighteenth Cent. Cult.*, 11 (1982), 199–216.

4.638 **Pederson**, S., 'Hannah More meets Simple Simon: Tracts, chapbooks and popular culture in late eighteenth century England', *J. Brit. Studs.*, 25 (1986), 84–113.

4.639 **Roberts**, S., 'Fornication and bastardy in mid-seventeenth century Devon: how was the act of 1650 enforced?', in J. Rule, ed., *Outside the Law: Studies in Crime and Order, 1650–1850*, Exeter Papers in Economic History (1982), 1–20.

4.640 **Shoemaker**, R. B., 'Reforming the City: the Reformation of manners, campaigns in London, 1690–1738', in L. Davison et al., eds., *Stilling the Grumbling Hive: The Response to Social and Economic Problems in England, 1689–1750* (1992), 99–120.

4.641 **Snell**, K. D. M. and **Millar**, J., 'Lone-parent families and the welfare state', *Cont. and Change*, 2 (1987), 387–422.

4.642 **Thomas**, K., 'The Puritans and Adultery: the act of 1650 reconsidered', in K. Thomas and D. Pennington, eds., *Puritans and Revolutionaries: Essays in Seventeenth Century History Presented to Christopher Hill*

(1978), 257–82.

4.643 **Willen**, D., 'Women in the public sphere in early modern England: the case of the urban working poor', *Sixteenth Cent. J.*, 19 (1988), 559–75.
See also: 4.220; 4.326.

(l) PROSTITUTION

4.644 **Andrew**, D., *Philanthropy and Police: London Charity in the Eighteenth Century* (Princeton, New Jersey, 1989). Includes material on the Magdalen for 'penitential prostitutes'.

4.645 **Archer**, I., *The Pursuit of Stability: Social Relations in Elizabethan London* (1991). Chapter 6, 204–56.

4.646 **Griffiths**, P., 'The structure of prostitution in Elizabethan London', *Cont. and Change*, 8 (1993), 39–63.

4.647 **Harris**, T., 'The bawdy house riots of 1668', *Hist. J.*, 29 (1986), 143–52. More about the riots than the bawdy houses, but worth checking.

4.648 **Haselkorn**, A., *Prostitution in Elizabethan and Jacobean Comedy* (New York, 1983).

4.649 **Nash**, S., 'Prostitution and Charity: the Magdalen hospital, a case study', *J. Soc. Hist.*, 17 (1983/4), 617–28.

4.650 **Salgado**, G., *The Elizabethan Underworld* (1977).
See also: 4.108; 4.640.

(m) WOMEN AND CRIME

(i) Women as criminals

4.651 **Appleby**, J. C., 'Women and piracy in Ireland: from Grainne O'Malley to Anne Bonny' in M. MacCurtain and M. O'Dowd, eds., *Women in Early Modern Ireland* (1991), 53–68.

4.652 **Beattie**, J. M., 'The criminality of women in eighteenth-century England', *J. Soc. Hist.* 8:13 (1975), 80–116.

4.653 **Boose**, L. E., 'Scolding wives and bridling scolds: taming the woman's unruly member', *Shakespeare Q.*, 42 (1991), 179–213.

4.654 **Campbell**, R., 'Sentence of death by burning for women', *J. Legal Hist.*, 5 (1984), 44–59.

4.655 **Doody**, M. A., 'The law, the page and the body of women: murder and murderesses in the age of Johnson', *The Age of Johnson*, 1 (1987), 127–60.

4.656 **Gillespie**, R., 'Women and crime in seventeenth century Ireland', in M. MacCurtain and M. O'Dowd, eds., *Women in Early Modern Ireland* (1991), 43–52.

4.657 **Hoffer**, P. C. and **Hull**, N. E. H., *Murdering Mothers: Infanticide in England and New England 1558–1803* (New York, 1981).

4.658 **Malcolmson**, R. W., 'Infanticide in the eighteenth century', in J. Cockburn, ed., *Crime in England 1550–1800* (1977) 187–209.

4.659 **Sharpe**, J. A., 'Domestic homicide in early modern England', *Hist. J.*, 24 (1981), 29–48.

4.660 **Underdown**, D., 'The Taming of the Scold: the enforcement of patriarchal authority in early modern England', in A. J. Fletcher and J. Stevenson, eds., *Order and Disorder* (1985), 116–36.

4.661 **Weiner**, C. Z., 'Sex roles and crime in late Elizabethan Hertfordshire,' *J. Soc. Hist.*, 8.3 (1975), 38–60.

4.662 **Wrightson**, K., 'Infanticide in earlier seventeenth century England', *Local Pop. Studs.*, 15 (1975), 10–22.

(ii) Violence against women

4.663 **Bashar**, N., 'Rape in England between 1550 and 1700', in London Feminist History Group, *Sexual Dynamics of History* (1983), 28–46.

4.664 **Clark**, A., *Women's Silence, Men's Violence: Sexual Assault in England, 1770–1845* (1987).

4.665 **Hunt**, M., 'Wife beating, domesticity and women's independence in eighteenth century London', *Gend. and Hist.*, 4 (1992), pp 10–33.

4.666 **Ives**, E. W., ' "Agaynst taking awaye of women: the inception and operation of the abduction act of 1487', in E. W. Ives, R. J. Knecht and J. J. Scarisbrick, eds., *Wealth* and Power in Tudor England (1978), 21–44.

4.667 **Porter**, R., 'Rape – does it have a historical meaning?', in S. Tomaselli and R. Porter, eds., *Rape, an Historical and Cultural Enquiry* (1986), 216–36.

(n) WITCHCRAFT

4.668 **Anderson**, A., and **Gordon**, R., 'Witchcraft and the status of women', *Brit. J. Sociol.*, 29.2 (1978), 171–84.

4.669 **Black**, G. F., *Calendar of Cases of Witchcraft in Scotland 1570–1727* (New York, 1938).

4.670 **Clark**, S., 'Inversion, misrule and the meaning of witchcraft', *P. P.*, 87 (1980), 98–127.

4.671 **Easlea**, B., *Witch Hunting, Magic and the New Philosophy: an Introduction to Debates of the Scientific Revolution 1450–1750* (1980).

4.672 **Ewen**, C. L., *Witchhunting and Witch Trials* (1929).

4.673 — *Witchcraft and Demonianism* (1933). Both useful guides to legal and literary sources.

4.674 **Gregory**, A., 'Witchcraft, politics and "good neighbourhood" in early seventeenth century Rye', *P. P.*, 133 (1992), 31–66.

4.675 **Guskin**, P. J., 'The context of witchcraft: the case of Jane Wenham (1712)', *Eighteenth Cent. Studs.*, 15 (1981–2), 48–71.

4.676 **Harley**, D., 'Historians as Demonologists: The myth of the midwife-witch', *Soc. Hist. Medicine*, 3 (1990), 1–26.

4.677 **Hester**, M., *Lewd Women and Wicked Witches* (1992).

4.678 — 'The dynamics of male domination using the witch craze in sixteenth and seventeenth century England as a case study,' *Women's Studs. Int. For.*, 13 (1990), 9–19.

4.679 **Holmes**, C., 'Popular Culture? Witches, magistrates and divines in early modern England', in S. L. Kaplan, ed., *Understanding Popular Culture: Europe from the Middle Ages to the Nineteenth Century* (Berlin, 1984), 85–111.

4.680 — 'Women: Witnesses and witches', *P. P.*, 140 (1993), 45–78.

4.681 **Hufton**, O., 'Christine Larner and the Historiography of European Witchcraft', *Hist. Workshop J.*, 21 (1986), 166–70. Review article.

4.682 **Larner**, C., *Enemies of God: the Witchhunt in Scotland* (1981).

4.683 — 'Was witch-hunting woman hunting?', in C. Larner, *Witchcraft and Religion: the Politics of Popular Belief* (1984), 84–8.

4.684 — 'The crime of witchcraft in Scotland', in C. Larner, *Witchcraft and Religion: the Politics of Popular Belief* (1984), 23–34.

4.685 — 'Witchbeliefs and accusations in England and Scotland', in C. Larner, *Witchcraft and Religion: the Politics of Popular Belief* (1984) 69–78.

4.686 — **Lee**, C. H. and **McLachlan**, H. V., *A Source Book of Scottish Witchcraft* (1977).

4.687 **Levack**, B., *The Witch-hunt in Early Modern Europe* (1987).

4.688 — 'The Great Scottish Witchhunt of 1661–2', *J. Brit. Studs.*, 20 (1981), 90–108.

4.689 **Macdonald**, M., *Witchcraft and Hysteria in Elizabethan London* (1991).

4.690 **Macfarlane**, A., *Witchcraft in Tudor and Stuart England* (1970). A pioneering study, although challenged over treatment of women, and overall interpretation now controversial.

4.691 **Notestein**, W., *A History of Witchcraft in England* (Washington, 1911). Still of use.

4.692 **Rushton**, P., 'Women, witchcraft and slander in early modern England: cases from the church courts of Durham 1560–1675', *North. Hist.*, 18 (1982), 116–32.

4.693 **Sawyer**, R. C., ' "Strangely handled in all her lyms": witchcraft and healing in Jacobean England', *J. Soc. Hist.*, 22 (1988–9), 461–85.

4.694 **Seymour**, St John D., *Irish Witchcraft and Demonology* (Dublin, 1913).

4.695 **Sharpe**, J. A., 'Witchcraft and women in 17th century England: some Northern evidence', *Cont. and Change*, 6 (1991), 179–99.

4.696 — *Witchcraft in Seventeenth Century Yorkshire: Accusations and Counter Measures*, Borthwick Papers, 81 (1992).

4.697 **Stafford**, H., 'Notes on Scottish witchcraft cases 1590–91', in N. Downs, ed., *Essays in Honor of Conyers Read* (Chicago, Illinois, 1953), 96–118.

4.698 **Thomas**, K., *Religion and the Decline of Magic* (1971).

4.699 **Trevor-Roper**, H. R., *The European*

Witch-craze of the Sixteenth and Seventeenth Centuries (1969). Often reprinted.

4.700 **Unsworth**, C. R., 'Witchcraft beliefs and criminal procedure in early modern England', in T. G. Watkin, ed., *Legal Records and Historical Reality* (1989), 71–98.

See also: 4.320.

(o) WOMEN AND RELIGION

(i) General

4.701 **Bynum**, C. W., **Harrell**, S. and **Richman**, P., eds., *Gender and Religion: on the Complexity of Symbols* (Boston, Mass., 1986).

4.702 **Chrisman**, M., 'Family and religion in two noble families: French Catholic and English Puritan', *J. Fam. Hist.*, 8 (1983), 190–210.

4.703 **Crawford**, P., *Women and Religion in England, 1500–1720* (1993).

4.704 **Cross**, C., 'The religious life of women in sixteenth century Yorkshire', in W. J. Sheils and D. Wood, eds., *Women in the Church*, Studies in Church History, 27 (1990), 307–24.

4.705 **Greaves**, R. L., ed., *Triumph over Silence: Women in Protestant History* (Westport, Conn., 1985). Wide-ranging collection covering England, Europe and America.

4.706 **Malmgreen**, G., ed., *Religion in the Lives of English Women, 1760–1930*, (1986). Useful case-studies.

4.707 **Monter**, W., 'Protestant wives, Catholic saints and the devil's handmaid: women in the age of Reformations', in R. Bridenthal, C. Koonz and S. Stuard, eds., *Becoming Visible. Women in European History* (sec. edn. Boston, Mass., 1987), 203–19.

4.708 **Sheils**, W. J. and **Wood**, D., eds., *Women in the Church*, Studies in Church History, 27 (1990). Important collection; broader than British history.

4.709 **Willen**, D., 'Women and religion in Early Modern England', in S. Marshall, ed., *Women in Reformation and Counter-Reformation Europe* (Bloomington, Indiana, 1989), 140–65.

See also: 4.57; 4.180; 4.576; 4.577; 4.873; 4.927; 4.959; 4.965.

(ii) The Reformation

4.710 **Bainton**, R., *Women of the Reformation in France and England* (Minneapolis, Minn., 1973).

4.711 **Beilin**, E. V., 'Anne Askew's self-portrait in the *Examinations*' in M. P. Hannay, ed., *Silent but for the Word: Tudor Women as Patrons, Translators, and Writers of Religious Works* (Kent, Ohio, 1985), 77–91.

4.712 **Collinson**, P., 'The role of women in the English Reformation illustrated by the life and friendship of Anne Locke', in P. Collinson, *Godly People* (1983), 273–88. Originally published in G. J. Cuming, ed., *Studies in Church History*, 2 (1965), 258–72.

4.713 **Davis**, J. F., 'Joan of Kent, Lollardy and the English Reformation', *J.Ecc. Hist.*, 33 (1982), 225–33.

4.714 **Harris**, B. J., 'A new look at the Reformation: aristocratic women and nunneries, 1450–1540', *J. Brit. Studs.* 32.2 (1993), 89–113.

4.715 **Kilroy**, P., 'Women and the Reformation in seventeenth century Ireland', in M. MacCurtain and M. O'Dowd, eds., *Women in Early Modern Ireland* (1991), 179–96.

4.716 **Macek**, E., 'The emergence of a feminine spirituality in the *Book of Martyrs*', *Sixteenth Cent. J.*, 19 (1988), 63–80.

4.717 **Newman**, C. M., 'The Reformation and Elizabeth Bowes: a study of a sixteenth century northern gentlewoman', in W. J. Sheils and D. Wood, eds., *Women in the Church*, Studies in Church History, 27 (1990), 325–33.

4.718 **Wabuda**, S., 'Shunamites and nurses of the English Reformation: the activities of Mary Glover, niece of Hugh Latimer', in W. J. Sheil and D. Wood, eds., *Women in the Church*, Studies in Church History, 27 (1990), 335–44.

(iii) Catholic women

4.719 **Bossy**, J., *The English Catholic Community 1570–1850* (1978). Important argument about the attractions of Catholicism for women.

4.720 **Collett**, B., 'The civil servant and monastic reform: Richard Fox's translation of the Benedictine rule for women, 1517', in J. Loades, ed., *Monastic Studies: the Continuity of Tradition* (1990), 211–28.

4.721 **Corish**, P. J., 'Women and religious practice', in M. MacCurtain and M. O'Dowd, eds., *Women in Early Modern Ireland* (1991), 212–20.

4.722 **Greatrex**, J., 'On ministering to "certayne devoute and religiouse women": Bishop Fox and the Benedictine nuns of Winchester diocese on the eve of the dissolution', in W. J. Sheils and D. Wood, eds., *Women in the Church*, Studies in Church History, 27 (1990), 223–35.

4.723 **Hanlon**, J., 'These be but women', in C. H. Carter, ed., *From the Renaissance to the Counter-reformation* (New York, 1965), 371–400.

4.724 **Liebowitz**, R. P., 'Virgins in the service of Christ: the dispute over an active apostolate for women during the counter-reformation', in E. McLaughlin and R. Ruether, eds., *Women of Spirit* (New York, 1979), 131–52.

4.725 **O'Brien**, S., 'Women of the "English Catholic Community": nuns and pupils at the Bar Convent, York, 1680–1790', in J. Loades, ed., *Monastic Studies: the Continuity of Tradition* (1990), 267–82.

4.726 **Oliver**, M., *Mary Ward 1585–1645* (1960).

4.727 **Roberts**, A. F. B., 'The role of women in Scottish Catholic survival', *Scot. H. R.*, 70 (1991), 129–50.

4.728 **Rowlands**, M. B., 'Recusant women 1560–1640', in M. Prior, ed., *Women in English Society 1500–1800* (1985), 149–80.

(iv) Protestant women

4.729 **Coster**, W., 'Purity, profanity, and puritanism: the churching of women, 1500–1700', in W. J. Sheils and D. Wood, eds., *Women in the Church*, Studies in Church History, 27 (1990), 377–87.

4.730 **Eales**, J., *Puritans and Roundheads: the Harleys of Brampton Bryan and the Outbreak of the English Civil War* (1990). For Brilliana Harley.

4.731 — 'Samuel Clarke and the "lives" of godly women in seventeenth century England', in W. J. Sheils and D. Wood, eds., *Women in the Church*, Studies in Church History, 27 (1990), 364–76.

4.732 **King**, J. N., 'The Godly woman in Elizabethan iconography', *Renaissance Q.*, 28 (1985), 41–84.

4.733 **Lake**, P., 'Feminine piety and personal potency: the "Emancipation" of Mrs Jane Ratcliffe', *Seventeenth Century*, 2 (1987), 143–65.

4.734 **Lucas**, R. V., 'Puritan preaching and the politics of the family', in A. M. Haselkorn and B. S. Travitsky, eds., *The Renaissance Englishwoman in Print* (Amherst, Massachusetts, 1990), 224–40.

4.735 **Porterfield**, A., 'Women's attraction to Puritanism', *Church Hist.*, 60 (1991), 196–209.

4.736 **Shakespeare**, J. and **Dowling**, M., 'Religion and politics in mid-Tudor England: the recollections of Joan Hickman', *Bull. Inst. Hist. Res.*, 55 (1982), 94–102.

4.737 **Thickstun**, M. O., *Fictions of the Feminine: Puritan Doctrine and the Representation of Women* (Ithaca, New York, 1988).

4.738 **Willen**, D., 'Godly women in early modern England: puritanism and gender', *J. Ecc. Hist.*, 43 (1992), 561–80.

(v) Radical and non-conformist Protestant women

4.739 **Barbour**, H., 'Quaker prophetesses and Mothers in Israel', in J. W. Frost and J. M. Moore, eds., *Seeking the Light* (Wallingford and Haverford, Penn., 1986), 41–60.

4.740 **Berg**, C. and **Berry**, P., 'Spiritual whoredom: an essay on female prophets in the seventeenth century', in F. Barker, ed., *1642. Literature and Power in the Seventeenth Century* (1981), 37–54.

4.741 **Boulton**, D. J., 'Women and early Methodism', *Pcdgs. Wesley Hist. Scy.*, 43 (1981), 13–17.

4.742 **Brailsford**, M. R., *Quaker Women 1650–1690* (1915).

4.743 **Briggs**, J., 'She-preachers, widows and other women: the feminine dimension in Baptist life since 1600', *Baptist Q.*, 31 (1986), 337–52.

4.744 **Camden**, V. J., 'Domestic dissent in *The Narrative of the Persecution of Agnes Beaumont*', *Hist. European Ideas*, 11 (1989), 211–24.

4.745 **Capp**, B., *Fifth Monarchy Men: A Study in Seventeenth Century English Millenarianism* (1972). Deals also with women.

4.746 **Carre**, B., 'Early Quaker women in Lancaster and Lancashire', in M. Mullett, ed., *Early Lancaster Friends*, Centre for

4.747 **Carroll**, K. L., 'Martha Simmonds, a Quaker enigma', *J. Friends Hist. Scy.*, 53 (1972), 18–26.

4.748 **Cope**, E. S., 'Dame Eleanor Davies. Never soe mad a ladie?', *Hunt. Lib. Q.*, 50 (1987), 133–44.

4.749 — *Handmaid of the Holy Spirit: Dame Eleanor Davies, Never Soe Mad a Ladie* (Ann Arbor, Michigan, 1992).

4.750 **Crawford**, P., 'Historians, women and the civil war sects, 1640–1660', in S. M. Jack, ed., *Rulers, Religion and Rhetoric in Early Modern England: a Festschrift for Geoffrey Elton from his Australasian Friends*. Special issue of the Australian journal, *Parergon* (1988), 19–32.

4.751 **Cross**, C., ' "He-goats before the flocks": a note on the part played by women in the founding of some civil war churches', in G. Cuming and D. Baker, eds., *Popular Belief and Practice* (1972), 195–202.

4.752 **Dailey**, B. R., 'The visitation of Sarah Wight: Holy Carnival and the revolution of the Saints in civil war London', *Church Hist.*, 55 (1986), 438–55.

4.753 **Fell**, M., *Women's Speaking Justified* (1667). Augustan Society Reprint, D. Latt, ed., 194 (Los Angeles, California, 1979).

4.754 **Greaves**, R. L., 'Foundation builders: the role of women in early English nonconformity', in R. L. Greaves, ed., *Triumph over Silence: Women in Protestant History* (Westport, Conn., 1985), 75–92.

4.755 **Hempton**, D. and **Hill**, M., 'Women and protestant minorities in eighteenth century Ireland', in M. MacCurtain and M. O'Dowd, eds., *Women in Early Modern Ireland* (1991), 197–211.

4.756 **Hill**, C., *The World Turned Upside Down* (1972).

4.757 **Hinds**, H., ' "Who may binde where God hath loosed?": responses to sectarian women's writing in the second half of the seventeenth century', in S. P. Cerasano and M. Wynne-Davies, eds., *Gloriana's Face: Women, Public and Private in the English Renaissance* (1992), 205–27.

4.758 **Ingle**, H. L., 'A Quaker woman on women's roles: Mary Pennington to friends, 1678', *Signs*, 16 (1991), 587–96.

4.759 **Kohler**, C., *Meet we Must: a Life of Mary Pennington, 1623–1652* (1986).

4.760 **Kunze**, B. Y., 'Religious authority and social status in seventeenth century England: the friendship of Margaret Fell, George Fox and William Penn', *Church Hist*, 57 (1988), 170–88.

4.761 — *Margaret Fell and the Rise of Quakerism* (1993).

4.762 **Laurence**, A., 'A priesthood of she-believers: women and congregations in mid-seventeenth century England', in W. J. Sheils and D. Wood, eds., *Women in the Church*, Studies in Church History, 27 (1990), 345–63.

4.763 **Lord**, E., ' "A good archbishop": the countess of Huntingdon', *Archives*, 19 (1991), 423–32.

4.764 **Ludlow**, D., 'Shaking patriarchy's foundations: sectarian women in England, 1641–1700', in R. L. Greaves, ed., *Triumph over Silence: Women in Protestant History* (Westport, 1985), 93–123.

4.765 **Mack**, P., *Visionary Women: Ecstatic Prophecy in Seventeenth Century England* (Berkeley, California, 1992). Focuses on the Quakers but also deals with gender and spirituality generally.

4.766 — 'Women as prophets during the English Civil War', *Fem. Studs.*, 8 (1982), 19–45.

4.767 — 'Gender and spirituality in early English Quakerism, 1650–1665', in E. P. Brown and S. Stuard, eds., *Witnesses for Change: Quaker Women over Three Centuries* (New Brunswick, New Jersey, 1989), 31–68.

4.768 — 'The prophet and her audience: gender and knowledge in the *World Turned Upside Down*', in G. Eley and W. Hunt, eds., *Reviving the English Revolution: Reflections and Elaborations on the Work of Christopher Hill* (1988), 139–52.

4.769 **Malmgreen**, G., 'Domestic discords: women and the family in east Cheshire methodism, 1750–1830', in J. Obelkevich, L. Roper and R. Samuel, eds., *Disciplines of Faith: Studies in Religion, Politics, and Patriarchy* (1987), 55–70.

4.770 **Ross**, I., *Margaret Fell, Mother of Quakerism* (1949).

4.771 **Ruether**, R. R., 'Prophets and humanists: types of religious feminism in Stuart England', *J. Religions*, 70 (1990), 1–18.

4.772 **Smith**, C. F., 'Jane Lead: the feminine mind and art of a seventeenth century protestant mystic', in E. McLaughlin and R. Ruether, eds., *Women of Spirit* (New York, 1979), 183–203.

4.773 — 'Jane Lead: Mysticism and the Woman cloathed with the sun', in S. M. Gilbert and

North-west Regional studies (1978), 43–53.

S. Gubar, eds., *Shakespeare's Sisters: Feminist Essays on Women Poets* (Bloomington, Indiana, 1979), 3–18.

4.774 **Thomas**, K. V., 'Women and the Civil War Sects', in T. Aston, ed., *Crisis in Europe, 1560–1660* (1965), 317–40. First published in *P.P.*, 13 (1958), 42–62.

4.775 **Trevett**, C., *Women and Quakerism in the Seventeenth Century* (1991).

4.776 **Valenze**, D., *Prophetic Sons and Daughters: Female Preaching and Popular Religion in Industrial England* (Princeton, New Jersey, 1985).

4.777 **White**, E. M., ' "Little female lambs": women in the Methodist societies of Carmarthenshire, 1737–50', *Carmathenshire Antiquary*, 27 (1991), 31–6.

4.778 **Wright**, S., 'Quakerism and its implications for Quaker women: the women itinerant ministers of York meeting, 1780–1840', in W. J. Sheils and D. Wood, eds., *Women in the Church*, Studies in Church History, 27 (1990) 403–14.

See also: 4.411.

(vi) Piety and religious experience

4.779 **Bainton**, R. H., 'Feminine piety in Tudor England', in P. N. Brooks, ed., *Christianity and Spirituality: Essays in Honour of Gordon Rupp* (1975), 183–220.

4.780 **Mueller**, J., 'Devotion as difference: intertextuality in Queen Catherine Parr's *Prayers or Meditations*, (1545)', *Hun. Lib. Q.*, 53 (1990), 171–97.

4.781 — 'A Tudor Queen finds voice: Catherine Parr's *Lamentation of a Sinner*', in H. Dubrow and R. Strier, eds., *The Historical Renaissance: New Essays on Tudor and Stuart Literature and Culture* (Chicago, Illinois, 1988), 15–47.

4.782 **Parish**, D. L., 'The power of female pietism: women as spiritual authorities in seventeenth century England', *J. Religious Hist.*, 17 (1992), 33–46.

4.783 **Reynolds**, E. E., *Margaret Roper: Eldest Daughter of St Thomas More* (1960).

4.784 **Travitsky**, B. S., ' "His wife's prayers and meditations": Ms Egerton 607', in A. M. Haselkorn and B. S. Travitsky, eds., *The Renaissance Englishwoman in Print* (Amherst, Mass., 1990), 241–60. The writings of Elizabeth, Countess of Bridgewater.

4.785 **Verbrugge**, R. M., 'Margaret More Roper's personal expression in the *Devout Treatise Upon the Pater Noster*', in M. P. Hannay, ed., *Silent but for the Word: Tudor Women as Patrons, Translators, and Writers of Religious Work* (Kent, Ohio, 1985), 30–42.

(p) WOMEN AND EDUCATION

4.786 **Ballard**, G., *Memoirs of Several Ladies of Great Britain who have been Celebrated for their Writings or Skill in the Learned Languages, Arts and Sciences* (1752, reprinted Detroit, 1985).

4.787 **Brink**, J. R., 'Bathsua Makin: Educator and Linguist', in J. R. Brink, ed., *Female Scholars: A Tradition of Learned Women Before 1800* (Montreal, 1980), 86–100.

4.788 — 'Bathsua Reginald Makin: "most learned matron" ', *Hunt. Lib. Q*, 54 (1991), 313–26.

4.789 **Cressy**, D., *Literacy and the Social Order: Reading and Writing in Tudor and Stuart England* (1980).

4.790 **Dowling**, M., 'A woman's place? Learning and the wives of Henry VIII', *Hist. Today*, 41 (June 1991), 38–42.

4.791 **Fletcher**, J. M. and **Upton**, C. A., ' "Monastic enclave" or "open society"?: A consideration of the role of women in the life of an Oxford college community in the early Tudor period', *Hist. Ed.*, 16 (1987), 1–9.

4.792 **Friedman**, A. T., 'The influence of humanism on the education of girls and boys in Tudor England', *Hist. Ed. Q.*, 25 (1985), 57–70.

4.793 **Gardiner**, D., *English Girlhood at School* (1929).

4.794 **Green**, M. E., 'Elizabeth Elstob: the Saxon nymph', in J. R. Brink, ed., *Female Scholars: A Tradition of Learned Women Before 1800* (Montreal, 1980), 137–60.

4.795 **Holm**, J. B., 'The myth of a feminist humanism: Thomas Salter's *The Mirrhor of Modestie*', in C. Levin and J. Watson, eds., *Ambiguous Realities: Women in the Middle Ages and Renaissance* (Detroit, 1987), 197–218.

4.796 **Kamm**, J., *Hope Deferred: Girls' Education in English History* (1965).

4.797 **Kaufman**, G., 'Juan Luis Vives on the education of women', *Signs*, 3 (1978), 891–6.

4.798 **Kaufman**, P. I., 'Absolute Margaret: Margaret More Roper and "well-learned men" ', *Sixteenth Cent. J.*, 20 (1989), 443–56.

4.799 **Kelso**, R., *Doctrine for the Lady of the Renaissance* (Urbana, Illinois, 1956, reprinted 1978).

4.800 **Kowalski-Wallace**, B., 'Two Anomalous Women: Elizabeth Carter and Catherine Talbot', in F. M. Keener and S. E. Lorsch, eds., *Eighteenth Century Women and the Arts* (1988), 19–28.

4.801 **Lamb**, M. E., 'The Cooke sisters: attitudes toward learned women in the Renaissance', in M. P. Hannay, ed., *Silent but for the Word: Tudor Women as Patrons, Translators, and Writers of Religious Works* (Kent, Ohio, 1985), 107–25.

4.802 **Luria**, G., ed., *The Feminist Controversy in England 1788–1810* (New York, 1974). Includes reprints of Macauley, C., *Letters on Education* (1790), and More, H., *Strictures on the Modern System of Female Education* (1799).

4.803 **McAllister**, L. L., ed., *The History of Women in Philosophy*, Special issue of *Hypatia, A Journal of Feminist Philosophy*, 4 .1 (1989). Includes: Duran, J., 'Anne Viscountess Conway: A seventeenth century rationalist', 64–79, and Frankel, L., 'Damaris Cudworth Masham: A seventeenth century feminist philosopher', 80–90.

4.804 **MacCurtain**, M., 'Women, education and learning in early modern Ireland', in M. MacCurtain and M. O'Dowd, eds., *Women in Early Modern Ireland* (1991), 160–78.

4.805 **McCutcheon**, E., 'Margaret More Roper: the learned woman in Tudor England', in K. Wilson, ed., *Women Writers of the Renaissance and Reformation* (Athens, Georgia,1987), 449–80.

4.806 **McDermid**, J., 'Conservative feminism and female education in the eighteenth century', *Hist. Ed.*, 18 (1989), 309–22.

4.807 **McMullen**, N., 'The education of English gentlewomen 1540–1640', *Hist. Ed.*, 6 (1977), 87–101.

4.808 **Makin**, B., *An Essay to Revive the Antient Education of Gentelwomen* (1673). Augustan Society Reprint, 202 (1980).

4.809 **Meyer**, G. D., *The Scientific Lady in England, 1650–1760: An Account of her Rise, with Emphasis on the Major Roles of the Telescope and Microscope*, University of California Publications, English Studies., 12 (Berkeley, California, 1955).

4.810 **Miller**, P. J., 'Women's education, "self-improvement" and social mobility – a late eighteenth century debate', *Brit. J. Ed. Studs.* 20 (1972), 302–14.

4.811 **Myers**, M., 'Domesticating Minerva: Bathsua Makin's "curious" argument for women's education', *Studs. Eighteenth Cent. Cult.*, 14 (1985), 173–92.

4.812 **Myers**, S. H., *The Bluestocking Circle, Women, Friendship and the Life of the Mind in Eighteenth Century England* (1990).

4.813 **O'Day**, R., *Education and Society, 1500–1800: The Social Foundations of Education in Early Modern Britain* (1982).

4.814 **Perry**, R., 'George Ballard's biographies of learned ladies', in J. D. Browning, ed., *Biography in the Eighteenth Century*, Publications of the McMaster University Association for English Studies, 8 (New York, 1980), 85–111.

4.815 **Phillips**, P., *The Scientific Lady: a Social History of Women's Scientific Interests, 1520–1918* (1990).

4.816 **Reynolds**, M., *The Learned Lady in England, 1650–1750* (Boston, Mass., 1920, reprinted Gloucester, Mass., 1964).

4.817 **Schnorrenberg**, B. B., 'Education for women in eighteenth century England: an annotated bibliography', *Women and Lit.*, 4 (1976), 49–55.

4.818 **Spufford**, M., 'First steps in literacy: the reading and writing experiences of the humblest seventeenth century autobiographers', *Soc. Hist.*, 4 (1979), 407–35.

4.819 **Wallas**, A., *Before the Bluestockings* (1929). Important early work.

4.820 **Warnicke**, R. M., 'Women and humanism', in A. Rabil, ed., *Renaissance Humanism* (Philadelphia, 1988), 39–54.

4.821 **Watson**, F., *Vives and the Renaissance Education of Women* (1912).

4.822 **Wayne**, V., 'Some sad sentence: Vives' *Instruction of a Christian Woman*', in M. P. Hannay, ed., *Silent but for the Word: Tudor Women as Patrons, Translators, and Writers of Religious Works* (Kent, Ohio, 1985), 15–29.

See also: 4.108; 4.179; 4.377; 4.549; 4.587; 4.783.

(q) WOMEN AND THE ARTS

4.823 **Anstern**, L. P., ' "Sing againe syren": the female musician and sexual enchantment in Elizabethan life and literature', *Renaissance Q.*, 42 (1989), 420–48.

4.824 **Bergeron**, D. M., 'Women as patrons of English Renaissance Drama', in G. F. Lytle and S. Orgel, eds., *Patronage in the Renaissance* (Princeton, 1982), 274–90.

4.825 **Glanville**, P. and **Goldsborough**, J. F., eds., *Women Silversmiths, 1685–1845* (1990).

4.826 **Greer**, G., *The Obstacle Race* (1979).

4.827 **Harris**, A. S. and **Nochlin**, L., *Women Artists 1550–1950* (1976).

4.828 **Howe**, E., *Women and Drama: The First English Actresses* (1992). Most recent, thorough study of women as actresses after the Restoration.

4.829 **Jackson**, J. J., *Esther Inglis, Calligrapher, 1571–1624* (New York, 1937).

4.830 **Keener**, F. M. and **Lorsch**, S. E., eds., *Eighteenth Century Women and the Arts* (1988).

4.831 **Lamb**, M. E., 'The countess of Pembroke's patronage', *Eng. Lit. Ren.*, 12 (1982), 162–79.

4.832 **Lewalski**, B. K., 'Lucy Countess of Bedford: images of a Jacobean courtier and patroness', in K. Sharpe and S. N. Zwicker, eds., *Politics of Discourse* (Berkeley, California, 1987), 52–77.

4.833 **Mayer**, D. *Angelica Kauffman, R.A.* (1972).

4.834 **Richards**, S., *The Rise of the English Actress* (1993).

4.835 **Roberts**, D., *The Ladies. Female Patronage of Restoration Drama 1660–1700* (1989).

4.836 **Rosenthal**, A., 'Angelica Kauffman ma(s)king claims', *Art Hist.*, 15 (1992), 38–59.

4.837 **Roworth**, W. W., ed., *Angelica Kauffman: Continental Artist in Georgian England* (1992).

4.838 — 'Biography, criticism, art history: Anglica Kauffman in context', in F. M. Keener and S. E. Lorsch, eds., *Eighteenth Century Women and the Arts* (1988), 209–23.

4.839 **Schofield**, M. A., and **Macheski**, C., eds., *Curtain Calls: British and American Women and the Theater 1660–1820* (Athens, Ohio, 1991).

4.840 **Slatkin**, W., *Women Artists in History: From Antiquity to the Twentieth Century* (2nd edn. 1989).

4.841 **Wilson**, J. H., *All the King's Ladies: Actresses of the Restoration* (Chicago, Illinois, 1958).

See also: 4.376; 4.572.

(i) Women and writing

4.842 **Adburgham**, A., *Women in Print: Writing Women and Women's Magazines from the Restoration to the Accession of Victoria* (1972).

4.843 **Andreadis**, H., 'The sapphic-platonics of Katherine Philips, 1632–1664', *Signs*, 15 (1989), 34–60.

4.844 **Ballaster**, R., 'Seizing the means of seduction: fiction and feminine identity in Aphra Behn and Delarivier Manley', in I. Grundy and S. Wiseman, eds., *Women, Writing, History, 1640–1740* (1992), 93–108.

4.845 — ed., *New Atalantis*, by Delarivier Manley (1992).

4.846 **Barash**, C., 'Gender, authority and the "life" of an eighteenth century woman writer: Delarivier Manley's *Adventures of Rivella*,', *Women's Studs. Int. For.*, 10 (1987), 165–9.

4.847 **Beilin**, E., *Redeeming Eve: Women Writers of the English Renaissance* (Princeton, New Jersey, 1987).

4.848 **Bell**, M., **Parfitt**, G. and **Shepherd**, S., eds., *A Biographical Dictionary of English Women Writers, 1580–1720* (1990).

4.849 **Bowerbank**, S., 'The spider's delight: Margaret Cavendish and the 'female' imagination', *Eng. Lit. Ren.*, 14 (1984), 392–407.

4.850 **Brant**, C. and **Purkiss**, D., eds., *Women, Texts and Histories 1575–1760* (1992). Important collection covering both women's writing and writing about women. Feminist literary theory with crucial implications for historians.

4.851 **Brownley**, M. W., 'Samuel Johnson and the printing career of Hester Lynch Piozzi', *Bull. J. Ry. Lib.*, 67 (1985), 623–40.

4.852 **Cotton**, N., *Women Playwrights in England c. 1363–1750* (London and Toronto, 1980).

4.853 **Crawford**, P., 'Women's published writings, 1600–1700', in M. Prior, ed., *Women in English Society 1500–1800* (1985), 211–82.

4.854 **Cunningham**, B., 'Women and Gaelic literature, 1500–1800' in M. MacCurtain and M. O'Dowd, eds., *Women in Early Modern Ireland* (1991), 147–59.

4.855 **Ezell**, M. J. M., ' "To be your daughter in your pen": the social functions of literature in the writings of Lady Elizabeth Brackley and Lady Jane Cavendish', *Hunt. Lib. Q.*, 51 (1988), 281–96.

4.856 **Fischer**, S. K., 'Elizabeth Cary and tyranny, domestic and religious', in M. P. Hannay, ed., *Silent but for the Word: Tudor Women as Patrons, Translators, and Writers of Religious Works* (Kent, Ohio, 1985), 225–37.

4.857 **Freer**, C., 'Mary Sidney, Countess of Pembroke', in K. M. Wilson, ed., *Women Writers of the Renaissance and Reformation* (Athens, Georgia, 1987), 481–521.

4.858 **Gibson**, R. G., ' "My want of skill": Apologias of British women poets, 1660–1800', in F. M. Keener and S. E. Lorsch, eds., *Eighteenth Century Women and the Arts* (1988), 79–86.

4.859 **Goreau**, A., *Reconstructing Aphra: A Social Biography of Aphra Behn* (1980).

4.860 — *The Whole Duty of a Woman: Female Writers in Seventeenth Century England* (New York, 1985).

4.861 — 'Aphra Behn: a scandal to modesty', in D. Spender, ed., *Feminist Theorists* (1983), 8–27.

4.862 **Greer**, G., **Medoff**, J., **Sansome**, M. and **Hastings**, S., eds., *Kissing the Rod: an Anthology of Seventeenth Century Women's Verse* (1988). Includes much material not otherwise reprinted.

4.863 **Grundy**, I., 'The politics of female authorship: Lady Mary Wortley Montagu's reaction to the printing of her poems', *Book Collector*, 31 (1982), 19–37.

4.864 — and **Wiseman**, S., eds., *Women, Writing, History 1640–1740*, (1992). An important collection of essays.

4.865 **Hackett**, H., ' "Yet tell me some such fiction": Lady Mary Wroth's *Urania* and the "femininity" of Romance', in C. Brant and D. Purkiss, eds., *Women, Texts and Histories 1575–1760* (1992), 39–68.

4.866 **Hageman**, E. H., 'Katherine Philips: The matchless Orinda', in K. M. Wilson, ed., *Women Writers of the Renaissance and Reformation* (Athens, Georgia, 1987), 566–608.

4.867 — 'Recent studies in women writers of the English seventeenth century', *Eng. Lit.*

Ren. 18 (1988), 138–67.

4.868 — and **Roberts**, J. A., 'Recent studies in women writers of Tudor England', *Eng. Lit. Ren.* 14 (1984), 409–39.

4.869 **Halsband**, R., 'Women and literature in eighteenth-century England' in P. Fritz and R. Morton, eds., *Woman in the Eighteenth Century and other Essays* (Toronto, 1976), 55–72.

4.870 **Hannay**, M. P., *Philip's Phoenix: Mary Sidney, Countess of Pembroke* (1990).

4.871 — ' "Do what men may sing": Mary Sidney and the tradition of admonitory dedication', in M. P. Hannay, ed., *Silent but for the Word: Tudor Women as Patrons, Translators, and Writers of Religious Works*, (Kent, Ohio), 149–65.

4.872 — 'Mary Sidney: Lady Wroth', in K. M. Wilson, ed., *Women Writers of the Renaissance and Reformation* (Athens, Georgia 1987), 548–65.

4.873 — ed., *Silent but for the Word: Tudor Women as Patrons, Translators, and Writers of Religious Works* (Kent, Ohio, 1985).

4.874 **Haselkorn**, A. M. and **Travitsky**, B. S., eds., *The Renaissance Englishwoman in Print* (Amherst, Mass., 1990).

4.875 **Hobby**, E., *Virtue of Necessity: English Women's Writing 1649–88* (1988).

4.876 — ' "Discourse so unsavoury": women's published writings of the 1650's, in I. Grundy and S. Wiseman, eds., *Women, Writing, History 1640–1740* (1992), 16–32.

4.877 **Jones**, A. R., 'Counterattacks on "the Bayter of Women": three pamphleteers of the early seventeenth century', in A. M. Haselkorn and B. S. Travitsky, ed., *The Renaissance Englishwoman in Print* (Amherst, Mass., 1990), 45–62. Cf 4.170.

4.878 **Keeble**, N. H., ' "The colonel's shadow": Lucy Hutchinson, women's writing and the civil war', in T. Healy and J. Sawday, eds., *Literature and the English Civil War*, eds. Healy, T., and Sawday, J. (1990), 227–47.

4.879 **Krontiris**, T., *Oppositional Voices: Women as Writers and Translators of Literature in the English Renaissance* (1992).

4.880 **Kubek**, E. B., 'London as text: eighteenth century women writers and reading the city', *Women's Studs.*, 17 (1990), 303–39.

4.881 **Lewalski**, B. K., 'Of God and good women: the poems of Aemilia Lanyer', in M. P. Hannay, ed., *Silent but for the Word: Tudor Women as Patrons, Translators, and Writers of Religious Works* (Kent, Ohio,

1985), 203–24.

4.882 — *Writing Women in Jacobean England* (Cambridge, Mass., 1993).

4.883 **Lilley**, K., ed., *New Blazing World and Other Writings, by Margaret Cavendish, Duchess of Newcastle* (1992).

4.884 **Lock**, F. P., 'Astraea's "Vacant Throne": the successors of Aphra Behn', in P. Fritz and R. Morton, eds., *Woman in the Eighteenth Century and Other Essays*, McMaster Uty. Assoc. for Eighteenth Century Studs., 4 (Toronto, 1976), 25–36.

4.885 **Lonsdale**, R., ed., *Eighteenth Century Women Poets* (1989, reprinted in paperback 1990). A pioneering collection.

4.886 **Macarthy**, B. M., *Women Writers: their Contribution to the English Novel 1621–1744* (Cork, 1944).

4.887 **McCarthy**, W., *Hester Thrale Piozzi: Portrait of a Literary Woman* (Chapel Hill, North Carolina, 1985).

4.888 **Macheski**, C. and **Schofield**, M. A., eds., *Fetter'd or Free? British Women Novelists 1670–1815* (Athens, Ohio, 1985).

4.889 **Mahl**, M. R. and **Koon**, H., eds., *The Female Spectator: English Women Writers before 1800* (Bloomington, Indiana, 1977). Extracts from the writings of a range of authors from Catherine Parr to Hannah More.

4.890 **Manvell**, R., *Elizabeth Inchbald: England's Principal Woman Dramatist and Independent Woman of Letters in Eighteenth Century London: a Biographical Study* (Lanham and London, 1988).

4.891 **Medoff**, J., 'The daughters of Behn and the problem of reputation', in I. Grundy and S. Wiseman, eds., *Women, Writing, History 1640–1740* (1992), 33–54.

4.892 **Mendelson**, S. H., *The Mental World of Stuart Women* (1987). For Behn, Newcastle.

4.893 **Messenger**, A., 'Women poets and the pastoral trap: the case of Mary Whatley', in F. M. Keener and S. E. Lorsch, eds., *Eighteenth Century Women and the Arts* (1988), 93–105.

4.894 **Morgan**, F., ed., *The Female Wits: Women Playwrights of the Restoration*, (1981). Sources.

4.895 **Ollman**, N., 'The poet as mermaid: images of self in Margaret Cavendish and others', in F. M. Keener and S. E. Lorsch, eds., *Eighteenth Century Women and the Arts* (1988), 87–92.

4.896 **Paloma**, D., 'Margaret Cavendish:

defining the female self', *Women's Studs.* 7 (1980), 55–66.

4.897 **Pearson**, J., *The Prostituted Muse: Images of Women and Women Dramatists 1642–1737* (1988). Important study although conclusions are disputed.

4.898 **Perry**, R., *Women, Letters and the Novel* (New York, 1980).

4.899 **Purkiss**, D., ed., *Renaissance Women: the Plays of Elizabeth Cary and the Poems of Aemilia Lanyer* (1993).

4.900 **Roberts**, J., *The Poems of Lady Mary Wroth* (Baton Rouge, Louisiana, 1983).

4.901 **Rogers**, K., 'Anne Finch, Countess of Winchelsea: An Augustan Woman Poet', in S. M. Gilbert and S. Gubar, eds., *Shakespeare's Sisters: Feminist Essays on Women Poets* (Bloomington, Indiana, 1979), 32–46.

4.902 **Schnorrenberg**, B. B., 'Three eighteenth century English female utopias', *Women's Studs.*, 9 (1982), 262–73. Includes material on Astell.

4.903 **Simms**, K., 'The Poet as Chieftain's Widow: Bardic Elegies', in D. Ó'Corráin, L. Breatnach and K. McCone, eds., *Sages, Saints and Storytellers: Celtic Studies in Honour of Professor James Carney* (Maynooth, 1989), 400–11.

4.904 **Spencer**, J., *The Rise of the Woman Novelist from Aphra Behn to Jane Austen* (1986).

4.905 **Spender**, D., *Mothers of the Novel. 100 Good Women Writers before Jane Austen* (1986).

4.906 — *Women of Ideas and what Men have done to them from Aphra Behn to Adrienne Rich* (1982).

4.907 — ed., *Living by the Pen: Early British Women Writers* (New York, 1992).

4.908 **Stanton**, J. P., 'Statistical profile of women writing in English, from 1660–1800', in F. M. Keener and S. E. Lorsch, eds., *Eighteenth Century Women and the Arts* (1988), 247–54.

4.909 **Stecher**, H. F., *Elizabeth Singer Rowe, the poetess of Frome: a Study in Eighteenth Century Pietism* (Berne and Frankfurt, 1973).

4.910 **Swift**, C. R., 'Feminine Identity in Lady Mary Wroth's Romance Urania', *Eng. Lit. Ren.*, 14 (1984), 328–46.

4.911 **Thompson**, D., ed., *Selected Poems of Anne Finch, Countess of Winchelsea* (1987).

4.912 **Todd**, J., *The Sign of Angelica: Women, Writing and Fiction 1650–1800* (1992).

4.913 — ed., *A Dictionary of British and American Women Writers, 1660–1800* (1984).

4.914 — ed., *The poems of Aphra Behn: A Selection* (1993).

4.915 — ed., *The works of Aphra Behn*, 6 vols. (1992–4).

4.916 **Tomlinson**, S., ' "My brain the stage": Margaret Cavendish and the fantasy of female performance', in C. Brant and D. Purkiss, eds., *Women, Texts and Histories 1575–1760* (1992) 134–63.

4.917 **Travitsky**, B., ed., *The Paradise of Women: Writings by Englishwomen of the Renaissance* (Westport, Conn., 1981, revised edn. New York, 1989). Sources – includes a wide range of women's writings from Elizabeth I and Catherine Parr to Margaret Tyler and Jane Anger (pseudonym).

4.918 **Turner**, C., *Living by the Pen. Women Writers in the Eighteenth Century* (1992).

4.919 **Waller**, G., 'Struggling into discourse: the emergence of Renaissance women's writing', in M. P. Hannay, ed., *Silent but for the Word: Tudor Women as Patrons, Translators, and Writers of Religious Works* (Kent, Ohio, 1985), 238–56.

4.920 — *Mary Sidney, Countess of Pembroke: A Critical Study of her Writings and Literary Milieu* (Salzburg, 1979).

4.921 **Wilson**, K. M., ed, *Women Writers of the Renaissance and Reformation* (Athens, Georgia, 1987). A useful collection of modern studies.

4.922 **Wiseman**, S., 'Gender and status in dramatic discourse: Margaret Cavendish, Duchess of Newcastle', in I. Grundy and S. Wiseman, eds., *Women, Writing, History 1640–1740* (1992), 159–77.

4.923 **Woolf**, V., *Women and Writing*, M. Barrett, ed. (1979). Includes interesting comments on Aphra Behn and the Duchess of Newcastle.

See also: 4.295; 4.299; 4.581; 4.757.

(r) AUTOBIOGRAPHY AND BIOGRAPHY

(i) Methodology

4.924 **Bell**, P., *Regency Women: an Index to Biographies and Memoirs* (1991).

4.925 **Benstock**, S., 'The female self-engendered: autobiographical writing and theories of selfhood', *Women's Studs.*, 20 (1991), 5–14. Part of a special issue on autobiography.

4.926 — ed, *The Private Self: Theory and Practice of Women's Autobiographical Writing* (1988).

4.927 **Blecki**, C. L. C., 'Alice Hayes and Mary Pennington: personal identity within the traditions of Quaker spiritual autobiography', *Quaker Hist.*, 65 (1976), 19–31.

4.928 **Blodgett**, H., *Centuries of Female Days: English Women's Private Diaries* (1989).

4.929 **Chalmers**, H., ' "The person I am, or what they made me to be": the construction of the feminine subject in the autobiographies of Mary Carleton', in C. Brant and D. Purkiss, eds., *Women, Texts and Histories 1575–1760* (1992) 164–94.

4.930 **Delany**, P., *British Autobiography in the Seventeenth Century* (1969). Dated now, but an important introduction.

4.931 **Findley**, S. and **Hobby**, E., 'Seventeenth century women's autobiography', in F. Barker et al., eds., *1642: Literature and Power in the Seventeenth Century* (1981), 11–36.

4.932 **Fitzmaurice**, J., 'Fancy and the family: self characterizations of Margaret Cavendish', *Hunt. Lib. Q.*, 53 (1990), 198–209.

4.933 **Graham**, E., 'Authority, resistance and loss: gendered difference in the writings of John Bunyan and Hannah Allen', in A. Laurence, W. R. Owens and S. Sim, eds., *John Bunyan and his England, 1628–88* (1990), 115–30.

4.934 —, **Hinds**, H., **Hobby**, E. and **Wilcox**, H., eds., *Her Own Life: An Anthology of Autobiographical Writings by Seventeenth Century Women* (1989). A very useful collection.

4.935 **Jelinek**, E. C., *The Tradition of Women's Autobiography: From Antiquity to the Present* (Boston, Mass., 1986).

4.936 **Matthews**, W., *British Diaries: An Annotated Bibliography of British Diaries Written Between 1442 and 1942* (1950).

4.937 **Mendelson**, S. H., 'Stuart women's diaries and occasional memoirs', in M. Prior, ed., *Women in English Society 1500–1800* (1985), 181–210.

4.938 **Nussbaum**, F., *The Autobiographical Subject: Gender and Ideology in Eighteenth*

Century England (Baltimore, Maryland, and London, 1985).

4.939 **Rose**, M. B., 'Gender, genre and history: seventeenth century Englishwomen and the art of autobiography', in M. B. Rose, ed., *Women in the Middle Ages and the Renaissance: Literary and Historical Perspectives* (New York, 1986), 245–78.

4.940 **Spacks**, P. A., *Imagining a Self: Autobiography and Novel in Eighteenth century England* (1976).

4.941 — 'Scrapbook of a self: Mrs Piozzi's late journals', *Harvard Lib. Bull.*, 18 (1970), 221–47.

4.942 **Stanley**, L., *The Auto/biographical I: Theory and Practice of Feminist Autobiography* (1992). Mostly later modern but relevant for early modern scholars too.

4.943 **Stewart**, L. and **Wilcox**, H., 'Why hath this lady writ her own life?: studying early female autobiography', in A. Thompson and H. Wilcox, eds., *Teaching Women: Feminism and English Studies* (1989), 61–70.

4.944 **Warnicke**, R. M., 'Lady Mildmay's journal: a study in autobiography and meditation in Reformation England', *Sixteenth Cent. J.*, 20 (1989), 55–68.

See also: 4.875; 4.895; 4.896.

(ii) Autobiographies, diarists and letter writers

4.945 **Balderston**, K. C., ed., *Thraliana: the Diary of Mrs Hester Lynch Thrale (later Mrs Piozzi) 1776–1809*, 2 vols. (1942, 2nd edn. 1951).

4.946 **Brant**, C., ed., *The Letters of Mary Wortley Montagu* (1992). A selection; cf. Halsband 4.951.

4.947 **Byrne**, M. St Clare, ed., *The Lisle Letters*, 6 vols. (1981). A vast early Tudor collection; important for elite women.

4.948 **Clifford**, D. J. H., ed., *The Diaries of Lady Anne Clifford* (1990).

4.949 **Climenson**, E. J., ed., *Elizabeth Montagu, the Queen of the Blue Stockings: Her correspondence from 1720–1761*, 2 vols. (1906).

4.950 **Day**, A., ed., *Letters from Georgian Ireland: the Correspondence of Mary Delany, 1731–1768* (Belfast, 1991).

4.951 **Halsband**, R., ed., *Complete Letters of Lady Mary Wortley Montagu*, 3 vols. (1965–7).

4.952 **Henstock**, A., ed., *The Diary of Abigail Gawthorne of Nottingham, 1751–1810*, Thoroton Scy. Vol. 33 (1980).

4.953 **Hughey**, R., ed., *The Correspondence of Lady Katherine Paston 1603–1627* Norfolk Record Scy., 14 (1941).

4.954 **Jackson**, C., ed., *The Autobiography of Mrs Alice Thornton of East Newton, Co. York*, Surtees Scy., 62 (1873).

4.955 **Lewis**, T. T., ed., *Letters of the Lady Brilliana Harley*, Camden Scy., old series, Vol. 58 (1854); cf 4.730.

4.956 **Loftis**, J., ed., *The Memoirs of Anne, Lady Halkett and Ann, Lady Fanshawe* (1979).

4.957 **Luddy**, M., ed., *The Diary of Mary Matthew* (1991).

4.958 **Mavor**, E., ed., *Life with the Ladies of Llangollen* (1984).

4.959 **Meads**, D. M., ed., *Diary of Lady Margaret Hoby 1599–1605* (Boston, Mass., 1930).

4.960 **Morgan**, F., *A Woman of no Character: An Autobiography of Mrs Manley* (1986).

4.961 **Morris**, C., ed., *The Journeys of Celia Fiennes* (1949). Travels in Britain. Many editions.

4.962 **Newton**, E., ed., *Lyme Letters 1660–1760* (1925). Of the Legh family of Lyme, Disley, Cheshire; much useful material on gentry women.

4.963 **Nicholson**, M. H., ed., *The Correspondence of Anne, Viscountess Conway, Henry More and their friends* (New Haven, 1930, 2nd edn. with new editorial material by Sarah Hutton 1992).

4.964 **Osborne**, D., *Letters to Sir William Temple*, K. Parker, ed. (1987). The most accessible edition.

4.965 **Searle**, A., ed., *Barrington Family Letters 1628–32*, Camden Scy., 4th ser., Vol. 28 (1983). Includes useful material on women members of the family.

4.966 **Sutherland**, J., ed., *Memoirs of the Life of Colonel Hutchinson with the Fragment of an Autobiography of Mrs Hutchinson* (Oxford, 1973).

4.967 **Verney**, F. P. and Verney, M. M., *Memoirs of the Verney Family*, 4 vols. (1892–9, 2nd edn. in 2 vols. 1925). Covers the seventeenth century.

4.968 **Verney**, M. M., ed., *Verney Letters of the Eighteenth Century*, 2 vols. (1930).

4.969 **Wall**, A., ed., *Two Elizabethan Women: the Correspondence of Joan and Maria Thynne 1575–1611*, Wiltshire Record Scy., 38 (1982).

See also: 4.283.

(s) WOMEN AS HISTORIANS

4.970 **Boos**, F., and **Boos**, W., 'Catherine Macauley: historian and political reformer', *Int. J. Women's Studs.*, 3 (1980), 49–65.

4.971 **Davis**, N. Z., 'Gender and genre: women as historical writers, 1400–1820', in P. H. Labalme, ed., *Beyond their Sex: Learned Women of the European Past* (New York, 1980), 153–82.

4.972 **Donnelly**, L. M., 'The celebrated Mrs Macauley', *Wm. and Mary Q.*, 3rd ser., 6 (1949), 173–207.

4.973 **Hill**, B., *The Repulican Virago, The Life and Times of Catherine Macauley, Historian* (1992). Most comprehensive treatment of the republican historian.

4.974 **Withey**, L. E., 'Catherine Macauley and the uses of history: ancient rights, perfectionism and propaganda', *J. Brit. Studs.*, 16 (1976), 59–83.

See also 4.580.

5

MODERN
1800 TO PRESENT

(a) GENERAL SURVEYS

5.1 **Allen**, D. E., 'The women members of the Botanical Society of London, 1836–56', *Brit. J. Hist. Sc.*, 13.3 (1980), 240–54. Biographical details of women members. Suggests that women were allowed to join because the Society was not prestigious.

5.2 **Beddoe**, D., *Back to Home and Duty* (1989). Insightful account of women's experiences between the wars.

5.3 **Boston**, A., ed., *Wave Me Goodbye: Stories of the Second World War* (1988).

5.4 **Branca**, P., *Women in Europe since 1750* (1978). A study based on modernisation theory which concentrates on England and France. Inadequate evidence for sweeping generalisations.

5.5 **Chamberlain**, M., *Fenwomen: A Portrait of Women in an English Village* (1975). Social history, using oral evidence, covering all aspects of women's lives in an isolated village.

5.6 **Considine**, J., ed., *Missing Pieces: Women in Irish History* (Dublin, 1983).

5.7 **Crow**, D., *The Victorian Woman* (1971).

5.8 **Davidoff**, L., *The Best Circles: Society, Etiquette and the Season* (1973). Pioneering study into the functions and rituals of upper-class society.

5.9 **Delamont**, S. and **Duffin**, L., eds., *The Nineteenth-century Woman: Her Cultural and Physical World* (1978). Collection of articles using insights from social anthropology. Focus of the book is the relationship perceived between women's bodies and minds in nineteenth-century thought.

5.10 **Dunbar**, J., *The Early Victorian Woman* (1953).

5.11 **Glasgow Women's Studies Group**, *Uncharted Lives: Extracts from Scottish Women's Experience, 1850–1982* (1983).

5.12 **Higgonet**, M. R., et al, eds., *Behind the Lines: Gender and Two World Wars* (New Haven, Conn., 1987). Collection of essays arguing that war is a gendering activity. Calls into question the equation of war with liberation.

5.13 **John**, A. V., ed., *Our Mothers' Land: Chapters in Welsh Women's History, 1830–1939* (1991). Most recent collection of articles on varied aspects of women's history in Wales.

5.14 **Kitchen**, P., comp., *War, Peace and Rural Life as Seen Through the Pages of the W.I. Magazine, 1919–1959* (1990).

5.15 **Land**, H., 'The changing place of women in Europe', *Daedalus*, 108, Spring (1979), 73–94. Changes for European women since the 1960s.

5.16 **Lang**, C., *Keep Smiling Through: Women in the Second World War* (1989).

5.17 **Lewis**, J., *Women in England, 1870–1950: Sexual Divisions and Social Change* (1984). Excellent overview drawing together recent research.

5.18 — *Women in Britain since 1945: Women, Family, Work and the State in the Post-War Years* (1991).

5.19 **Luddy**, M. and **Murphy**, C., eds., *Women Surviving: Studies in Irish Women's History in the Nineteenth and Twentieth Centuries*

(Dublin, 1990).

5.20 **Lummis**, T. and **Marsh**, J., *The Woman's Domain: Women and the English Country House* (1990).

5.21 **Marwick**, A., *Women At War, 1914–18* (1977). Argues that war brought lasting changes for women.

5.22 **Minns**, R., *Bombers and Mash: The Domestic Front, 1939–45* (1980).

5.23 **Mooney**, M., 'Women in Ireland', *Labour Monthly*, 61.2 (1979), 75–81.

5.24 **Newton**, J. L., **Ryan**, M. P. and **Walkowitz**, J. R., eds., *Sex and Class in Women's History: Essays from Feminist Studies* (1983). Articles reprinted from *Feminist Studies* with an excellent introduction which surveys the literature on issues relating to sex and class in British and American women's history.

5.25 **Reynolds**, S., ed., *Women, State and Revolution: Essays on Power and Gender in Europe since 1789* (1986).

5.26 **Roberts**, E., *A Woman's Place: An Oral History of Working-Class Women, 1890–1940* (1984).

5.27 **Sheridan**, D., 'Ambivalent memories: women and the 1939–45 war in Britain', *Oral Hist.*, 18.1 (1990), 32–40.

5.28 **Summerfield**, P., 'Women in two world wars', *Historian*, 23, Summer (1989), 3–8.

5.29 **Thane**, P., 'Late Victorian women', in A. O'Day, ed., *Later Victorian Britain, 1867–1900* (1988), 175–208. Excellent discussion of women's lives and the realities behind the stereotypes.

5.30 — 'Towards equal opportunities? Women in Britain since 1945', in T. Gourvish and A. O'Day, eds., *Britain since 1945* (1991).

5.31 **Thomas**, G., *Life On All Fronts: Women in the First World War* (1989).

5.32 **Thompson**, P., *The Edwardians: The Remaking of British Society* (1975). Based on oral interviews with women and men who discuss work, family, childhood and community.

5.33 **Vicinus**, M., ed., *Suffer and Be Still: Women in the Victorian Age* (Bloomington, Indiana, 1972). Pioneering collection of essays surveying and analysing stereotypes of femininity which Victorian women fought against.

5.34 — *A Widening Sphere: Changing Roles of Victorian Women* (Bloomington, Indiana, 1977). Companion volume to above which examines the variety and complexity of some Victorian women's lives despite the social and legal constraints of the period.

5.35 **Whitelegg**, E., et al, eds., *The Changing Experience of Women* (1984). Articles on varied aspects of women's experience e.g. work, family, sexuality.

5.36 **Wilson**, E., *Only Halfway to Paradise: Women in Post-War Britain, 1945–1968* (1980).

5.37 **Winkler**, V., 'Women in post-war Wales', *Llafur*, 4.4 (1987), 69–77.

(b) VIEWS OF WOMEN

5.38 **Adams**, J. E., 'Woman red in tooth and claw: nature and the feminine in Tennyson and Darwin', *Vict. Studs.*, 33.1 (1989), 7–27.

5.39 **Alaya**, F., 'Victorian science and the "genius" of woman', *J. Hist. Ideas*, 38, April-June (1977), 261–80.

5.40 **Annas**, J. M., 'Mill and the *Subjection of Women*', *Philos.*, 52 (1977), 179–94.

5.41 **Bacchi**, C., 'Evolution, eugenics and women: the impact of scientific theories on attitudes towards women, 1870–1920', in E. Windshuttle, ed., *Women, Class and History* (Melbourne, 1980).

5.42 **Basch**, F., *Relative Creatures: Victorian Women in Society and the Novel, 1837–67* (1974). Juxtaposes representations of women in the Victorian novel against women's social position in order to explore 'the relationship of the novelist to his work and society'.

5.43 **Bratton**, J. S., *The Impact of Victorian Children's Fiction* (1981).

5.44 **Campbell**, E., 'Of mothers and merchants: female economics in Christina Rossetti's "Goblin Market" ', *Vict. Studs.*, 33.3 (1990), 393–410.

5.45 **Casteras**, S. P., 'Virgin vows: the early Victorian artists' portrayal of nuns and novices', *Vict. Studs.*, 24.2 (1981), 157–84.

5.46 — *The Substance and the Shadow: Images of Victorian Womanhood* (New Haven, Conn., 1982).

5.47 — *Images of Victorian Womanhood in English Art* (1987).

5.48 **Christ**, C., 'The feminine subject in Victorian poetry', *Eng. Lit. Hist.*, 54, Summer (1987), 385–402.

5.49 **Conway**, J., 'Stereotypes of femininity in a theory of sexual evolution', in M. Vicinus, ed., *Suffer and Be Still: Women in the Victorian Age* (Bloomington, Indiana, 1972), 140–54.

5.50 **Digby**, A., 'Women's biological straitjacket', in S. Mendus and J. Rendall, eds., *Sexuality and Subordination: Interdisciplinary Studies of Gender in the Nineteenth Century* (1989), 192–220. Analyses medical texts of Georgian and Victorian Britain, in particular gynaecological and psychiatric literature, for their depiction of women.

5.51 **Duffin**, L., 'Prisoners of progress: women and evolution', in S. Delamont and L. Duffin, eds., *The Nineteenth Century Woman: Her Cultural and Physical World* (1978), 57–91.

5.52 **Easlea**, B., *Science and Sexual Oppression: Patriarchy's Confrontation with Woman and Nature* (1981).

5.53 **Edelstein**, T. J., 'They sang "the song of the shirt": the visual iconology of the seamstress', *Vict. Studs.*, 23.2 (1980), 183–210. Image of the seamstress in Victorian painting.

5.54 **Elshtain**, J. B., *Public Man, Private Woman: Women in Social and Political Thought* (1981). On the dichotomy of nature/culture in enlightenment thought.

5.55 **Fee**, E., 'The sexual politics of Victorian social anthropology', in M. Hartman and L. W. Banner, eds., *Clio's Consciousness Raised: New Perspectives on the History of Women* (1974), 86–102. Examines work of six anthropologists to demonstrate how they provide an evolutionary justification for the role of women in their own society.

5.56 **Ferguson**, M., *Forever Feminine: Women's Magazines and the Cult of Femininity* (1983).

5.57 **Finch**, C., ' "Hooked and buttoned together": Victorian underwear and representation of the female body', *Vict. Studs.*, 34.3 (1991), 337–63.

5.58 **Grisewood**, H., ed., *Ideas and Beliefs of the Victorians* (New York, 1966). Collection of short articles on a wide range of Victorian ideas and beliefs.

5.59 **Hall**, C., 'The early formation of Victorian domestic ideology', in S. Burman, ed., *Fit Work for Women* (1979), 15–32. Seminal study of the importance of evangelicals in the identification of women with domesticity.

5.60 **Helsinger**, E. K., **Sheets**, R. L. and **Veeder**, W., *The Woman Question: Defining Voices, 1837–83. Society and Literature in Britain and America*, Vols. 1–3 (1983). Middle-class views of the 'woman question' expressed through fiction and non-fiction. Analysis mixed with document extracts.

5.61 **Hobsbawm**, E., 'Man and woman in socialist iconography', *Hist. Workshop J.*, 6 (1978), 121–38. Controversial article comparing images of men and women as expressed by the socialist movement with the social realities of the nineteenth and early twentieth centuries.

5.62 **Jordanova**, L., *Sexual Visions: Images of Gender in Science and Medicine between the Eighteenth and Twentieth Centuries* (1989). Discusses how scientific writing is permeated with the language of gender.

5.63 **Kaplan**, C., ' "Like a housemaid's fancies": the representation of working-class women in nineteenth-century writing', in S. Sheridan, ed., *Grafts: Feminist Cultural Criticism* (1988), 55–75.

5.64 **Light**, A., *Forever England. Femininity, Literature and Conservatism between the Wars* (1991).

5.65 **Marks**, P., *Bicycles, Bangs and Bloomers: The New Woman in the Popular Press* (1990).

5.66 **Marsh**, J., *Pre-Raphaelite Women: Images of Femininity* (1988).

5.67 **Mason**, T., 'The domestication of female socialist icons: a note in reply to Eric Hobsbawm', *Hist. Workshop J.*, 7 (1979), 170–5. Uses German examples to make a general critique of Hobsbawm's methodology.

5.68 **Maynard**, M., ' "A dream of fair women": revival dress and the formation of late Victorian images of femininity', *Art Hist.*, 12 (1989), 322–41.

5.69 **Michie**, H., *The Flesh Made Word: Female Figures and Women's Bodies* (1987). Examines coded Victorian representations of the female body.

5.70 **Migglestone**, L. C., 'Lady-like accents: female pronunciation and perceptions of prestige in nineteenth-century England', *Notes and Queries*, 37 (1990), 44–52.

5.71 **Millett**, K., 'The debate over women: Ruskin vs Mill', in M. Vicinus, ed., *Suffer and Be Still: Women in the Victorian Age* (Bloomington, Indiana, 1972), 121–39.

5.72 **Mitchell**, J., 'Women and equality', in

J. Mitchell and A. Oakley, eds., *The Rights and Wrongs of Women* (1976), 379–99. Wide ranging essay examining concepts of equality in different historical periods.

5.73 **Mosedale**, S. S., 'Science corrupted. Victorian biologists consider the "woman question" ', *J. Hist. Biol.*, 2, Spring (1978), 1–55.

5.74 **Mosucci**, O., *The Science of Woman: Gynaecology and Gender in England, 1800–1929* (1990).

5.75 **Nead**, L., 'The Magdalene in modern times: the mythology of fallen women in Pre-Raphaelite painting', in R. Betterton, ed., *Looking at Images of Femininity in the Visual Arts Media* (1987), 94–127.

5.76 — *Myths of Sexuality: Representations of Women in Victorian Britain* (1988).

5.77 **Nunokawa**, J., '*Tess*, tourism and the spectacle of the woman', in L. M. Shires, ed., *Rewriting the Victorians: Theory, History and the Politics of Gender* (1992), 70–86.

5.78 **Okin**, S. M., *Women in Western Political Thought* (Princeton, 1979).

5.79 **Ortner**, S. B., 'Is female to male as nature is to culture?', in M. Z. Rosaldo and L. Lamphere, eds., *Women, Culture and Society* (Stanford, 1974), 67–88.

5.80 **Pugh**, E. L., 'Florence Nightingale and John Stuart Mill debate women's rights', *J. Brit. Studs.*, 21.2 (1982), 118–38.

5.81 **Rendall**, J., 'Virtue and commerce: women in the making of Adam Smith's political economy', in E. Kennedy and S. Mendus, eds., *Women in Western Political Philosophy* (Brighton, 1987).

5.82 **Richards**, J., *Boys Will Be Girls: The Feminine Ethic and British Children's Fiction, 1857–1917* (1991).

5.83 **Roberts**, H. E., 'Marriage, redundancy and sin: the painter's view of women in the first twenty-five years of Victoria's reign', in M. Vicinus, ed., *Suffer and Be Still: Women in the Victorian Age* (Bloomington, Indiana, 1972), 45–76.

5.84 — ' "The exquisite slave": the role of clothes in the making of the Victorian woman', *Signs*, 2.3 (1977), 554–69.

5.85 **Rosenberg**, R., 'In search of woman's nature, 1850–1920', *Fem. Studs.*, 2 (1974–5).

5.86 **Russett**, C. E., *Sexual Science : The Victorian Construction of Womanhood* (Cambridge, Mass., 1990).

5.87 **Sacks**, K., 'Engels revisited: women, the organisation of production and private property', in M. Z. Rosaldo and L. Lamphere, eds., *Women, Culture and Society* (Stanford, California, 1974), 207–22.

5.88 **Shires**, L. M., 'Of Maenads, mothers and feminized males: Victorian readings of the French Revolution', in L. M. Shires, ed., *Rewriting the Victorians: Theory, History and the Politics of Gender* (1992), 147–65.

5.89 **Shuttleworth**, S., 'Demonic mothers: ideologies of bourgeois motherhood in the mid-Victorian era', in L. M. Shires, ed., *Rewriting the Victorians: Theory, History and the Politics of Gender* (1992), 31–51.

5.90 **Tinkler**, P., 'Learning through leisure: feminine ideology in girls' magazines, 1920–50', in F. Hunt, ed., *Lessons for Life: The Schooling of Girls and Women, 1850–1950* (1987), 60–79.

5.91 **Valverde**, M., 'The love of finery: fashion and the fallen woman in nineteenth-century social discourses', *Vict. Studs.*, 32.2 (1989), 169–88.

5.92 **Walsh**, L., 'Images of women in nineteenth-century schoolbooks', *Irish Ed. Studs.*, 4.1 (1984), 73–87.

5.93 **Walters**, M., 'The Rights and Wrongs of Women: Mary Wollstonecraft, Harriet Martineau, Simone de Beauvoir', in J. Mitchell and A. Oakley, eds., *The Rights and Wrongs of Women* (1976), 304–78.

5.94 **Weiner**, G., 'Harriet Martineau: A Reassessment', in D. Spender, ed., *Feminist Theorists: Three Centuries of Women's Intellectual Traditions* (1983), 60–74.

5.95 **Weintraub**, R., ed., *Fabian Feminist: Bernard Shaw and Women* (Philadelphia, Penn., 1977).

5.96 **Weissman**, J., *Half Savage and Hardy and Free: Women and Rural Radicalism in the Nineteenth-Century Novel* (Middletown, Conn., 1987). Argues that in the context of a rural community women had powerful roles which have been ignored by feminist critics.

5.97 **Williams**, S. R., 'The true "Cymraes": images of women in women's nineteenth-century Welsh periodicals', in A. V. John, ed., *Our Mothers' Land: Chapters in Welsh Women's History, 1830–1939* (1991), 69–91. Examines the first Welsh periodical intended for women, *Y Gymraes (The Welshwoman)*.

5.98 **Williford**, M., 'Bentham on the rights of women', *J. Hist. Ideas*, 36 (1975), 167–76.

5.99 **Wright**, E. M., 'The representation of women and girls in post-war secondary school English course books, parts 1 & 2', *Hist. Ed. Scy. Bull.*, 31, Spring (1983), 25–32, 33–42.

5.100 **Zaborsky**, D., 'Victorian feminism and Gissing's *The Odd Woman*: "Why are women redundant?" ', *Women's Studs. Int. For.*, 8.5 (1985), 489–96.

See also: 5.377; 5.454; 5.476; 5.516; 5.1355.

(c) WOMEN AND FAMILY

(i) General

5.101 **Anderson**, M., *Approaches to the History of the Western Family, 1500–1914* (1980). Useful overview of the literature.

5.102 — 'Sociological history and the working-class family: Smelser re-visited', *Soc. Hist.*, 1.3 (1976), 317–34. A critique of a structuralist-functionalist approach.

5.103 **Aries**, P., *Centuries of Childhood* (1962). Important study which inspired a new way of looking at family history.

5.104 **Branca**, P., 'Image and reality: the myth of the idle Victorian woman', in M. Hartman and L. Banner., eds., *Clio's Consciousness Raised: New Perspectives on the History of Women* (1974), 179–91. Notes the variety of middle-class incomes and households and contests the view that middle-class Victorian women were leisured.

5.105 **Buckley**, S., 'The family and the role of women', in A. O'Day, ed., *The Edwardian Age* (1979), 133–43.

5.106 **Caine**, B., 'Family history as women's history: the sisters of Beatrice Webb', *Fem. Studs*, 12.2 (1986), 295–319. Stimulating analysis of the importance of the ties between the Potter sisters.

5.107 **Davidoff**, L., 'The family in Britain', in F. M. L. Thompson, ed., *The Cambridge Social History of Britain, 1750–1950, vol. 2: People and their Environment* (1990), 71–129.

5.108 — and **Hall**, C., *Family Fortunes: Men and Women of the English Middle Class, 1780–1850* (1987). Important,

pathbreaking study of the development of the family, gender roles and class during early industrialisation which transforms our view of the making of the middle class. Based on detailed research into Birmingham.

5.109 **Flax**, J., 'The family in contemporary feminist thought: a critical review', in J. B. Elshtain, ed., *The Family in Political Thought* (1982), 223–339.

5.110 **Hareven**, T. K., 'Modernization and family history: perspectives on social change', *Signs*, 2.1 (1976), 190–206. Argues that modernisation theory can be useful if it is recognised that men and women modernise at different rates in the family.

5.111 — 'The history of the family and the complexity of social change', *Am. H. R.*, 96.1 (1991), 95–124. Surveys the state of the field of family history since the late 1950s, focusing on Europe and America.

5.112 — ed., *Transitions: The Family and the Life Course in Historical Perspective* (New York, 1978). Collection of articles exploring the relationship between family life-cycle and historical time, based largely on American data.

5.113 **Harris**, B., 'Recent work on the history of the family: a review article', *Fem. Studs.*, 3, 3/4 (1976), 159–72.

5.114 **Holley**, J., 'The two family economies of industrialism: factory workers in Victorian Scotland', *J. Fam. Hist.*, 6.1 (1981), 57–69.

5.115 **Humphries**, J., 'Working-class family, women's liberation and class struggle: the case of nineteenth-century British history', *R. Rad. Pol. Ec.*, 9.3 (1977), 25–41.

5.116 — 'Enclosures, common rights and women: the proletarianisation of families in the late eighteenth and early nineteenth centuries', *J. Ec. Hist.*, 50.1 (1990), 17–42.

5.117 **Lees**, L., 'Mid-Victorian migration and the Irish family economy', *Vict. Studs.*, 20.1 (1976), 25–43. Focuses on changes affecting women who migrated to cities and argues that wives became more dependent.

5.118 **Levine**, D., 'Industrialisation and the proletarian family in England', *P. P.*, 107 (1985), 168–203.

5.119 **Lewis**, J., ed., *Labour and Love: Women's Experience of Home and Family, 1850–1940* (1986). Important collection of articles representing the most recent approaches and research in this area.

5.120 **Mitchison**, R., *British Population Change since 1860* (1977). Summary of the literature with some material relating specifically to women.

5.121 **Nicholson**, L. J., *Gender and History: The Limits of Social Theory in the Age of the Family* (New York, 1986).

5.122 **Peterson**, M. J., *Family, Love and Work in the Lives of Victorian Gentlewomen* (Bloomington, Indiana, 1989). Reassessment of the stereotyping of nineteenth-century middle-class women.

5.123 **Rapp**, R., **Ross**, E. and **Bridenthal**, R., 'Examining family history', in J. L. Newton, M. P. Ryan and J. R. Walkowitz, eds., *Sex and Class in Women's History* (1983), 232–58. Suggest that the family as an analytical category has only a limited value for historical explanation. The concept of 'mode of social reproduction' would be more useful.

5.124 **Redlich**, P., 'Women and the family', in M. MacCurtain and D. Ó'Corráin, eds., *Women in Irish Society: The Historical Dimension* (Dublin, 1978), 82–91. Concentrates on the twentieth century.

5.125 **Ross**, E., ' "Not the sort that would sit on the doorstep": respectability in pre-World War 1 London neighbourhoods', *Int. Labor and Working-Class Hist.*, 27 (1985), 39–59.

5.126 **Scott**, J. and **Tilly**, L., 'Women's work and the family in nineteenth-century Europe', *Comp. Studs. Soc. and Hist.*, 17.1 (1975), 36–64. Seminal article discussing the family economy.

5.127 **Scott**, J. W., 'The history of the family as an affective unit', *Soc. Hist*, 4.3 (1979), 509–16. A review essay.

5.128 **Thompson**, P. and **Vigne**, T., 'On family life, work and the community before 1918: the Essex project', *Oral Hist*, 3, Spring (1975), 2–3.

5.129 **Titmuss**, R., *Essays on the Welfare State* (1963). Contains an interesting chapter on changes in women's lives since the nineteenth century, in particular the impact of a smaller family size.

5.130 **Wohl**, A. S., ed., *The Victorian Family* (1978).

See also: 2.183; 5.1371; 5.1372.

(ii) Marriage, divorce, concubinage, adultery

5.131 **Anderson**, M., 'Marriage patterns in Victorian Britain: an analysis based on registration district data for England and Wales, 1861', *J. Fam. Hist.*, 1.1 (1976), 55–78.

5.132 **Anderson**, N. F., 'Cousin marriage in Victorian England', *J. Fam. Hist.*, 11.3 (1986), 285–302.

5.133 **Anderson**, O., 'The incidence of civil marriage in Victorian England and Wales', *P. P.*, 69 (1975), 50–87.

5.134 — 'A rejoinder', *P. P.*, 84 (1979), 155–62. A reply to Floud and Thane, 5.144.

5.135 **Ayers**, P. and **Lambertz**, J., 'Marriage relations, money and domestic violence in working-class Liverpool', in J. Lewis, ed., *Labour and Love: Women's Experience of Home and Family, 1850–1940* (1986), 194–219.

5.136 **Bland**, L., 'Marriage laid bare: middle-class women and marital sex, *c.* 1880–1914', in J. Lewis, ed., *Labour and Love: Women's Experience of Home and Family, 1850–1914* (1986), 122–46.

5.137 **Brooks**, M., 'Love and possession in a Victorian household: the example of the Ruskins', in A. S. Wohl, ed., *The Victorian Family* (1978), 82–100.

5.138 **Caine**, B., *Destined to Be Wives: The Sisters of Beatrice Webb* (1986). Fascinating insight into marital relationships based on the letters of the sisters.

5.139 **Colwell**, S., 'The incidence of bigamy in eighteenth and nineteenth-century England', *Fam. Hist.*, 11, 75 (1980).

5.140 **Copelman**, D. M., ' "A new comradeship between men and women": family, marriage and London's women teachers, 1870–1914', in J. Lewis, ed., *Labour and Love: Women's Experience of Home and Family, 1850–1940* (1986), 174–93.

5.141 **Crafts**, N. F. R., 'Average age at first marriage for women in mid-nineteenth century England and Wales: a cross section study', *Pop. Studs.*, 32.1 (1978), 21–6. Suggests urbanisation had little impact on the lowered age of marriage or on population growth before 1850.

5.142 **Davies**, K. M., 'Continuity and change in literary advice on marriage', in R. B. Outhwaite, ed., *Marriage and Society: Studies in the Social History of Marriage*

(1981), 58–80.

5.143 **Fitzpatrick**, D., 'Divorce and separation in modern Irish history', *P. P.*, 114 (1987), 172–9.

5.144 **Floud**, R. and **Thane**, P., 'The incidence of civil marriage in Victorian England and Wales', *P. P.*, 84 (1979), 146–54. A critique of Olive Anderson's view that legal problems in Nonconformist chapel marriages were not significant in explaining an increase in civil marriage in England.

5.145 **Gaskin**, K., 'Age at first marriage in Europe before 1850: a summary of family reconstitution data', *J. Fam. Hist.*, 3.1 (1978), 23–36.

5.146 **Gillis**, J. R., *For Better, For Worse: British Marriages 1600 to the Present* (1986). Suggests that the history of marriage is varied and uneven.

5.147 **Glass**, D. V., 'Marriage frequency and economic fluctuations in England and Wales, 1851–1934', in L. Hogben, ed., *Political Arithmetic: A Symposium of Population Studies* (1938), 251–82.

5.148 **Hajnal**, J., 'European marriage patterns in perspective', in D. V. Glass and D. E. C. Eversley, eds., *Population in History* (1965), 101–43.

5.149 **Hammerton**, A. J., *Cruelty and Companionship: Conflict in Nineteenth-Century Married Life* (1992). Discusses politics of everyday life in middle- and working-class families.

5.150 **Himmelfarb**, G., *Marriage and Morals Among the Victorians: Essays* (1986).

5.151 **Hinde**, P. R. A., 'The marriage market in the nineteenth-century English countryside', *J. European Ec. Hist.*, 18.2 (1989), 383–92.

5.152 **Holtzman**, E., 'The pursuit of married love: women's attitudes towards sexuality and marriage in Great Britain, 1918–39', *J. Soc. Hist.*, 16, Winter (1982), 39–51.

5.153 **Horstman**, A., *Victorian Divorce* (1985).

5.154 **Jalland**, P., *Women, Marriage and Politics, 1860–1914* (1986). Explores the attitudes of female relatives of politicians to marriage and the family. Suggests their behaviour often differed from prescribed ideals of motherhood.

5.155 **Johansson**, S. R., 'Sex and death in Victorian England: an examination of age and sex specific death rates, 1840–1910', in M. Vicinus, ed., *A Widening Sphere: Changing Roles of Victorian Women*

(Bloomington, Indiana, 1977), 163–81.

5.156 **Laslett**, P., 'Age at menarche in Europe since the eighteenth century', in T. K. Rabb and R. I. Rotberg, eds., *The Family in History: Interdisciplinary Essays* (New York, 1973), 28–46.

5.157 **McGregor**, O. R., *Divorce in England: A Centenary Study* (1957).

5.158 **Machin**, G. I. T., 'Marriage and the churches in the 1930s: royal abdication and divorce reform, 1936–7', *J. Ecc. Hist.*, 42 (1991), 68–81.

5.159 **Mackenzie**, J., *A Victorian Courtship: The Story of Beatrice Potter and Sidney Webb* (1979).

5.160 **Menefee**, S. P., *Wives for Sale: An Ethnographic Study of British Popular Divorce* (1981).

5.161 **Outhwaite**, R. B., 'Problems and perspectives in the history of marriage', in R. B. Outhwaite, ed., *Marriage and Society: Studies in the Social History of Marriage* (1981).

5.162 **Perkin**, J., *Women and Marriage in Victorian England* (1989).

5.163 **Peterson**, M. J., 'No angels in the house: the Victorian myth and the Paget women', *Am. H. R.*, 89.3 (1984), 677–708.

5.164 **Phillips**, R., *Putting Asunder: A History of Divorce in Western Society* (1988). Focuses on the theory and practice of divorce in England, France and America from medieval times to the present.

5.165 **Roberts**, E., 'Working wives and their families', T. Barker and M. Drake, eds., in *Population and Society in Britain, 1850–1980* (1982), 140–71. Married Lancashire textile workers.

5.166 **Rose**, P., *Parallel Lives: Five Victorian Marriages* (1984).

5.167 **Ross**, E., ' "Fierce questions and taunts": married life in working-class London, 1870–1914', *Fem. Studs.*, 8.3 (1982), 575–602. Concentrates on male violence against women.

5.168 **Rowntree**, G. and **Carrier**, N. H., 'The resort to divorce in England and Wales, 1857–1957', *Pop.Studs.*, 11.3 (1958), 188–233.

5.169 **Savage**, G. L., 'The wilful communication of a loathsome disease: marital conflict and venereal disease in Victorian England', *Vict. Studs.*, 34.1 (1990), 35–54.

5.170 **Schoen**, R. and **Baj**, J., 'Twentieth century cohort marriage and divorce in England and Wales', *Pop. Studs.*, 38.3

(1984), 439–50.

5.171 **Schofield**, R., 'English marriage patterns revisited', *J. Fam. Hist.*, 10.1 (1985), 2–20.

5.172 **Showalter**, E., 'Family secrets and domestic subversion: rebellion in the novels of the 1860s', in A. S. Wohl, ed., *The Victorian Family* (1978), 101–16.

5.173 **Stone**, L., *Road to Divorce: England, 1530–1987* (1990).

5.174 **Strong**, B., 'Towards a history of the experiential family: sex and incest in the nineteenth-century family', *J. Marr. and Fam.*, 33.3 (1973), 457–66.

5.175 **Taylor**, S., 'The effect of marriage on job possibilities for women and the ideology of the home: Nottingham, 1890–1930', *Oral Hist*, 5.2 (1977), 46–61.

5.176 **Thomas**, D., 'The social origins of marriage partners of the British peerage in the eighteenth and nineteenth centuries', *Pop. Studs.*, 26.1 (1972), 91–112.

5.177 **Thompson**, D., 'Courtship and marriage in Preston between the wars', *Oral Hist*, 3.2 (1975) 39–44.

5.178 **Trustram**, M., *Women of the Regiment: Marriage and the Victorian Army* (1984).

5.179 **Vincent**, D., 'Love and death in the nineteenth-century working class', *Soc. Hist.*, 5.2 (1980), 223–47. Discusses autobiographies as a source for understanding family experiences.

5.180 **Weir**, D. R., 'Rather never than late: celibacy and age at marriage in English cohort fertility', *J. Fam. Hist.*, 9.4 (1984), 340–54.

5.181 **Wilcox**, P., 'Marriage, mobility and domestic service in Victorian Cambridge', *Local Pop. Studs.*, 29, Autumn (1982), 19–34.

5.182 **Wolfram**, S., *Inlaws and Outlaws: Kinship and Marriage in England, 1800–1980* (1986).

5.183 **Woods**, R. I. and **Hinde**, P. R. A., 'Nuptuality and age at marriage in nineteenth-century England', *J. Fam. Hist.*, 10.2 (1985), 119–44.

See also: 5.300.

(iii) Household structure

5.184 **Anderson**, M., *Family Structure in Nineteenth-Century Lancashire* (1970). Uses the census to suggest the persistence of family networks despite industrialisation.

Importance of economic exchange among family members. Useful chapter on women's work and family relations in textiles.

5.185 **Gittins**, D., 'Marital status, work and kinship, 1850–1930', in J. Lewis, ed., *Labour and Love: Women's Experience of Home and Family, 1850–1950* (1986), 248–67. On women's work and its relationship to family roles.

5.186 **Haslett**, J. and **Lowe**, W. J., 'Household structure and overcrowding among the Lancashire Irish during the mid-nineteenth century', *Histoire Sociale*, 10.19 (1977), 45–58.

5.187 **Hinde**, P. R. A., 'Household structure, marriage and the institution of service in nineteenth-century rural England', *Local Pop. Studs.*, 35, Autumn (1985), 43–51.

5.188 **Laslett**, P., 'Size and structure in the households of England over three centuries', *Pop. Studs.*, 23 (1969), 199–223.

5.189 **Lees**, L., 'Patterns of lower-class life: Irish slum communities in nineteenth-century London', in S. Thernstrom and R. Sennett, eds., *Nineteenth-Century Cities: Essays in the New Urban History* (New Haven, Conn., 1969), 359–85.

5.190 **Matras**, J., 'Social strategies of family formation: data for British female cohorts born 1831–1906', *Pop. Studs.*, 19 (1965–66), 167–81.

5.191 **Medick**, H., 'The proto-industrial family economy: the structural function of household and family during the transition from peasant to industrial capitalism', *Soc. Hist.*, 1.3 (1976), 291–315.

5.192 **Roberts**, E., 'The working-class extended family: functions and attitudes, 1890–1940', *Oral Hist.*, 12.1 (1984), 48–55.

5.193 **Smith**, R., 'Early Victorian household structure: a case study of Nottinghamshire', *Int. R. Soc. Hist.*, 15 (1970), 69–84.

See also: 5.482.

(iv) Household management, social conditions

5.194 **Ayers**, P., 'The hidden economy of dockland families: Liverpool in the 1930s', in P. Hudson and W. R. Lee, eds., *Women's Work and the Family Economy in*

Historical Perspective (1990), 271–90.

5.195 **Branca**, P., *Silent Sisterhood: Middle-Class Women in the Victorian Home* (1975). Uses household manuals to suggest middle-class women played an active role in household management and were not leisured.

5.196 **Buckley**, A., 'Neighbourliness: myth and history', *Oral Hist.*, 11.1 (1983), 44–51.

5.197 **Collier**, F., *The Family Economy of the Working Classes in the Cotton Industry, 1784–1833* (1921, reprinted 1965).

5.198 **Crook**, B., ' "Tidy women": women in the Rhondda between the wars', *Oral Hist.*, 10.2 (1982), 40–6.

5.199 **Cullen**, M., 'Breadwinners and providers: women in the household economy of labouring families, 1835–6', in M. Luddy and C. Murphy, eds., *Women Surviving: Studies in Irish Women's History in the Nineteenth and Twentieth Centuries* (Dublin, 1990), 85–116.

5.200 **Davidson**, C., *Woman's Work is Never Done: A History of Housework in the British Isles, 1650–1950* (1982).

5.201 **Davin**, A., 'Child labour, the working-class family and domestic ideology in nineteenth-century Britain', *Dev. and Change*, 13.4 (1982), 633–52.

5.202 **Hall**, C., 'Married women at home in Birmingham in the 1920s and 1930s', *Oral Hist.*, 5.2 (1977), 62–83.

5.203 **Hardyment**, C., *From Mangle to Microwave: The Mechanization of Household Work* (1988).

5.204 **Hopkins**, E., 'The decline of the family work unit in Black country nailing', *Int. R. Soc. Hist.*, 22.2 (1977), 184–97.

5.205 **Jones**, D., 'Counting the cost of coal: women's lives in the Rhondda, 1881–1911', in A. V. John, ed., *Our Mothers' Land: Chapters in Welsh Women's History, 1830–1939* (1991), 109–33.

5.206 **Mourby**, K., 'The wives and children of the Teesside unemployed., 1919–39', *Oral Hist.*, 11.2 (1983), 56–60.

5.207 **Oakley**, A., *Woman's Work: The Housewife Past and Present* (New York, 1974).

5.208 **Pugh**, M., 'Women, food and politics, 1880–1930', *Hist. Today*, 41.3 (1991), 14–20.

5.209 **Roberts**, E., 'Working-class standards of living in Barrow and Lancaster, 1890–1914', *Ec. H. R.*, sec. ser., 30.3 (1977), 306–21. Uses oral evidence to re-assess women's often hidden contribution to family living standards.

5.210 — 'Working-class standards of living in three Lancashire towns, 1890–1914', *Int. R. Soc. Hist.*, 27.1 (1982), 43–65. Introduces material from Preston.

5.211 — ' "Women's Strategies", 1890–1940', in J. Lewis, ed., *Labour and Love: Women's Experience of Home and Family, 1850–1940* (1986), 222–47.

5.212 — and **Liddington**, J., 'Working-class women in the North West, 1 & 2', *Oral Hist.*, 5.2 (1977), 7–45.

5.213 **Ross**, E., 'Survival networks: women's neighbourhood sharing in London before World War II', *Hist. Workshop J.*, 15 (1983), 4–27.

5.214 **Summerfield**, P., 'Women, work and welfare: a study of child care and shopping in Britain in the Second World War', *J. Soc. Hist.*, 17, December (1983), 249–70.

5.215 **Tibbott**, S. M., 'Laundering in the Welsh home', *Folklife*, 19 (1981), 36–57.

See also: 5.340; 5.343; 5.480; 5.481; 5.505; 5.507; 5.572; 5.601.

(v) Motherhood, child/parent relations

5.216 **Dyhouse**, C., 'Mothers and daughters in the middle-class home *c.* 1870–1914', in J. Lewis, ed., *Labour and Love: Women's Experience of Home and Family, 1850–1940* (1986), 27–47.

5.217 **Fildes**, V., *Wet Nursing: A History from Antiquity to the Present* (1988). A descriptive account looking at the universality of the practice of wet nursing throughout Europe and over time.

5.218 **Garrett**, E. M., 'The trials of labour: motherhood versus employment in a nineteenth-century textile centre', *Capital and Class*, 5.1 (1990), 121–54.

5.219 **Helterline**, M., 'The emergence of modern motherhood: motherhood in England, 1899 to 1959', *Int. J. Women's Studs.*, 3, November/December (1980), 45–56.

5.220 **Horn**, P., *The Victorian Country Child* (1985).

5.221 **Jamieson**, L., 'Limited resources and limiting conventions: working-class mothers and daughters in urban Scotland *c.* 1890–1925', in J. Lewis, ed., *Labour and Love: Women's Experience of Home and Family, 1850–1940* (1986), 48–69. Based on oral interviews.

5.222 **Peretz**, E., 'The costs of modern motherhood to low income families in inter-war Britain', in V. Fildes, L. Marks and H. Marland, eds., *Women and Children First: International Maternal and Infant Welfare, 1870–1945* (1992), 257–80.

5.223 **Pollock**, L. A., *Forgotten Children: Parent–Child Relations from 1500–1900* (1983).

5.224 **Ross**, E., 'Labour and love: rediscovering London's working-class mothers, 1870–1918', in J. Lewis, ed., *Labour and Love: Women's Experience of Home and Family, 1850–1940* (1986), 72–96.

5.225 **Scannell**, D., *Mother Knew Best: An East End Childhood, 1914–35* (1974).

5.226 **Vigne**, T., 'Parents and children, 1890–1918. Distance and dependence', *Oral Hist.*, 3, Fall (1975), 6–13.

5.227 **Wilson**, S., 'The myth of motherhood a myth: the historical view of European childrearing', *Soc. Hist.*, 9.2 (1984), 181–98. Wide-ranging review of the literature.

(vi) Socialisation of girls

5.228 **Burman**, R., ed., 'Growing up in Manchester Jewry: the story of Clara Weingard', *Oral Hist.*, 12.1 (1984), 56–63. Compiled from recordings.

5.229 **Dyhouse**, C., *Girls Growing Up in Late Victorian and Edwardian England* (1981). A key text which explores infant mortality and the socialisation of girls at home and at school.

5.230 **Gorham**, D., *The Victorian Girl and the Feminine Ideal* (1982). Girlhood in the middle-class family.

5.231 **Humphries**, S., *Hooligans or Rebels? An Oral History of Working-Class Childhood and Youth, 1889–1939* (1981). Useful for a study of motherhood as well as childhood.

5.232 **Pinchbeck**, I. and **Hewitt**, M., *Childhood in English Society. Vol. 11. From the Eighteenth Century to the Children's Act, 1948* (1973). An account of children's lives based on official documents.

5.233 **Roberts**, E., 'Learning and living – socialisation outside school', *Oral Hist.*, 3.2 (1975), 14–28.

5.234 — 'The Family', in J. Benson, ed., *The Working Class in England, 1850–1914* (1985), 1–29. Discusses the socialisation of children using oral evidence.

5.235 **Thompson**, T., *Edwardian Childhoods* (1981). Reminiscences of family life from oral interviews.

5.236 **Walvin**, J., *A Child's World. A Social History of English Childhood, 1800–1914* (1982).

(vii) Family size, family limitation, infant mortality, illegitimacy

5.237 **Askham**, J., *Fertility and Deprivation: A Study of Differential Fertility Amongst Working-Class Families in Aberdeen* (1976).

5.238 **Banks**, J. A., *Prosperity and Parenthood: A Study of Family Planning Among the Victorian Middle Class* (1954). A seminal study which emphasises the importance of the 'paraphenalia of gentility', in affecting family size.

5.239 — *Victorian Values: Secularism and the Size of Families* (1981). Stresses the power of the husband in relation to fertility control.

5.240 — and **Banks**, O., 'The Bradlaugh–Besant trial and the English newspapers', *Pop. Studs.*, 8 (1954–5), 22–34.

5.241 **Banks**, O. and **Banks**, J. A., *Feminism and Family Planning in Victorian England* (1964). Emphasises conservatism of feminist views on sexuality and the family. Contends that feminists played little part in the campaign for birth control.

5.242 **Behlmer**, G. K., 'Deadly motherhood: infanticide and medical opinion in Mid-Victorian England', *J. Hist. Medicine.*, 34 (1979), 403–27.

5.243 — *Child Abuse and Moral Reform in England, 1870–1908* (Stanford, California, 1982).

5.244 **Brookes**, B., 'Women and reproduction, *c.* 1860–1919', in J. Lewis, ed., *Labour and Love: Women's Experience of Home and Family, 1850–1940* (1986), 148–71.

5.245 — *Abortion in England, 1900–1967* (1988).

5.246 **Burr-Litchfield**, R., 'The family and the mill: cotton mill work, family work patterns and fertility in mid-Victorian Stockport', in A. S. Wohl, ed., *The Victorian Family* (1978), 180–96. Suggests that changes in the economic roles of family members affected the birth rate.

5.247 **Crafts**, N. F. R., 'Duration of marriage, fertility and women's employment opportunities in England and Wales in 1911', *Pop. Studs.*, 43 (1989), 325–35.

5.248 **Davey**, C., 'Birth control in Britain during the inter-war years: evidence from the Stopes correspondence', *J. Fam. Hist.*, 13.3 (1988), 329–46.

5.249 **Davies**, M., 'Corsets and conception: fashion and demographic trends in the nineteenth century', *Comp. Studs. Soc. and Hist.* 24, October (1982), 611–41.

5.250 **Dyhouse**, C., 'Working-class mothers and infant mortality in England, 1895–1914', *J. Soc. Hist.*, 12.2 (1978), 248–67. Argues that women's work had little effect on infant mortality rates.

5.251 **Fairchilds**, C., 'Female sexual attitudes and the rise of illegitimacy: a case study', *J. Interdis. Hist.*, 8.4 (1978), 627–67.

5.252 **Fryer**, P., *The Birth Controllers* (1965).

5.253 **Gillis**, J. R., 'Servants, sexual relations and the risks of illegitimacy in London, 1801–1900', *Fem. Studs.*, 5.1 (1979), 142–73.

5.254 **Gittins**, D., 'Married life and birth control between the wars', *Oral Hist.*, 3.2 (1975), 53–64.

5.255 — 'Women's work and family size between the Wars', *Oral Hist.*, 5.2 (1977), 84–100. Analyses the interrelationship between married women's work, the role of the family and wives' relationship with husbands.

5.256 — *Fair Sex: Family Size and Structure*, 1900–39 (1982). Examines interrelationship between husbands and wives and their relations to kin and the workplace in order to understand the process involved in family limitation. A key study for methodology and approach.

5.257 **Hall**, R., *Passionate Crusader: The Life of Marie Stopes* (1977).

5.258 **Henriques**, U. R. G., 'Bastardy and the New Poor Law', *P. P.*, 37 (1967), 103–29.

5.259 **Higginbotham**, A. R., 'Sin of the age: infanticide and illegitimacy in Victorian London', *Vict. Studs.*, 32, Spring (1989), 319–38.

5.260 **Knight**, P., 'Women and abortion in Victorian and Edwardian England', *Hist. Workshop J.*, 4 (1977), 57–69. Discusses abortion as an aspect of 'female sub-culture'.

5.261 **Langer**, W. M., 'The origins of the birth control movement in England in the early nineteenth century', *J. Interdis. Hist.*, 5.4 (1975), 669–86.

5.262 **Laslett**, P., *Family Life and Illicit Love in Early Generations* (1977). Useful data on illegitimacy.

5.263 **Lewis**, J., 'The ideology and politics of birth control in inter-war Britain', *Women's Studs. Int. Q.*, 2.1 (1979), 33–48.

5.264 **Love**, R., ' "Alice in Eugenics-Land": feminism and eugenics in the scientific careers of Alice Lee and Ethel Elderton', *Annals of Science*, 36 (1979), 145–58.

5.265 **McLaren**, A., 'Contraception and the working classes: the ideology of the English birth control movement in its early years', *Comp. Studs. Soc. and Hist.*, 18 (1976), 236–51.

5.266 — 'Abortion in England', *Vict. Studs.*, 20.4 (1977), 379–400.

5.267 — 'The early birth control movement: an example of medical self help', in J. Woodward and D. Richards, ed., *Health Care and Popular Medicine in Nineteenth-Century England: Essays in the Social History of Medicine* (1977), 89–104.

5.268 — 'Women's work and the regulation of family size', *Hist. Workshop J.* 4 (1977), 70–81. Interesting discussion of the relationship between women's employment and family size in the second half of the nineteenth century.

5.269 — *Birth Control in Nineteenth-Century England* (1978). Comprehensive study examining class differences. Gives weight to feminist involvement in birth control campaign.

5.270 — 'Contraception and its discontents: Sigmund Freud and birth control', *J. Soc. Hist.*, 12.4 (1979), 513–29.

5.271 — *A History of Contraception From Antiquity to the Present Day* (1990). Wide-ranging study of contraception across several countries.

5.272 **Robin**, A., 'Illegitimacy in Colyton, 1851–1881', *Cont. and Change*, 2.2 (1987), 307–42.

5.273 **Rose**, J., *Marie Stopes and the Sexual Revolution* (1992).

5.274 **Rose**, L., *Massacre of the Innocents: Infanticide in Britain, 1800–1939* (1986).

5.275 **Sauer**, R., 'Infanticide and abortion in nineteenth-century Britain', *Pop. Studs.*, 32.1 (1978), 81–93.

5.276 **Seccombe**, W., 'Starting to stop: working-class fertility decline in Britain', *P. P.*, 126 (1990), 151–88.

5.277 **Shorter**, E., 'Illegitimacy, sexual revolution and social change in modern Europe', *J. Interdis. Hist.*, 1 (1971), 231–72. Charts an increase in pre-marital

5.278 — 'Female emancipation, birth control and fertility in European history', *Am. H. R.*, 78.3 (1973), 605–40. Opens debate on Europe's high birth and illegitimacy rates in early industrialisation.

5.279 **Soloway**, R. A., 'Neo Malthusians, eugenists and the declining birth rate in England, 1900–18', *Albion*, 10.3 (1978), 264–86. Suggests that the agreement between eugenists and neo-Malthusians over opposition to indiscriminate breeding broke down as population declined after 1918.

5.280 — *Birth Control and the Population Question in England, 1877–1930* (Chapel Hill, North Carolina, 1982).

5.281 **Teitelbaum**, M. S., *The British Fertility Decline: Demographic Transition in the Crucible of the Industrial Revolution* (Princeton, New Jersey, 1984).

5.282 **Tilly**, L. A., **Scott**, J. W. and **Cohen**, M., 'Women's work and European fertility patterns', *J. Interdis. Hist.*, 6.3 (1976), 447–76. Suggest the migration of young women made them vulnerable to illegitimate pregnancies.

5.283 **Winter**, J. M., 'Aspects of the impact of the First World War on infant mortality in Britain', *J. European Ec. Hist.*, 11.3 (1982), 713–38. Suggests full employment and higher wages were most important in affecting infant mortality rates.

5.284 **Wohl**, A. S., 'Sex and the single room: incest among the Victorian working classes', in A. S. Wohl, ed., *The Victorian Family* (1978), 197–216.

5.285 **Woods**, R. I., **Watterson**, P. A. and **Woodward**, J. H., 'The causes of rapid infant mortality decline in England and Wales, 1861–1921, part 2', *Pop. Studs.*, 43.1 (1989), 113–32.

5.286 **Wrong**, D., 'Class fertility differentials before 1850', *Social Research*, 25 (1958), 70–86.

See also: 3.150; 5.304; 5.1147.

(viii) Spinsters and widows

5.287 **Anderson**, M., 'The social position of spinsters in mid-Victorian Britain', *J. Fam. Hist.*, 9.4 (1984), 377–93.

5.288 **Freeman**, R. and **Klaus**, P., 'Blessed or not? The new spinster in England and the United States in the late nineteenth and early twentieth centuries', *J. Fam. Hist.*, 9.4 (1984), 394–414.

5.289 **Hufton**, O., 'Women without men: widows and spinsters in Britain and France in the eighteenth century', *J. Fam. Hist.*, 9.4 (1984), 355–76.

5.290 **Winter**, J., 'Widowed mothers and mutual aid in early Victorian Britain', *J. Soc. Hist.* 17, Fall (1983), 115–25.

See also: 5.354.

(d) LEGAL STATUS OF WOMEN

5.291 **Acland**, A., *Caroline Norton* (1948). Biography of a woman who was instrumental in bringing about a change in the law on women's rights to infant custody.

5.292 **Anderson**, N. F., 'The "Marriage with a Deceased Wife's Sister Bill" controversy: incest, anxiety and the defence of family purity in Victorian England', *J. Brit. Studs.*, 21.2 (1982), 67–86.

5.293 **Anderson**, S., 'Legislative divorce-law for the aristocracy?', in G. R. Grubin and D. Sugarman, eds., *Law, Economy and Society, 1750–1914: Essays in the History of English Law* (1984), 412–44.

5.294 **Bailey**, V. and **Blackburn**, S., 'The Punishment of Incest Act, 1908: a case study of law creation', *Crim. Law R.* (1979), 708–18.

5.295 **Brophy**, J. and **Smart**, C., *Women in Law: Explorations in Law, Family and Sexuality* (1985).

5.296 **Clark**, A., 'Humanity or Justice? Wifebeating and the law in the eighteenth and nineteenth centuries', in C. Smart, ed., *Regulating Motherhood: Historical Essays on Marriage, Motherhood and Sexuality* (1992), 187–206.

5.297 **Craik**, E. M., *Marriage and Property* (1984). Collection of essays on marriage, women and property from Ancient Greece to nineteenth-century Britain and America.

5.298 **Edwards**, S. M., *Female Sexuality and the Law: A Study of Constructs of Female*

Sexuality as they Inform Statute and Legal Procedure (1981). Suggests family law has codified family relations in line with a norm of heterosexuality and reinforced views of 'proper' gendered behaviour.

5.299 **Gordon**, W. M., 'The right of women to graduate in medicine: Scottish judicial attitudes in the nineteenth century', *J. Legal Hist.*, 5.2 (1984), 136–51.

5.300 **Hammerton**, A. J., 'Victorian marriage and the law of matrimonial cruelty', *Vict. Studs.*, 33.2 (1990), 269–92.

5.301 **Harrison**, R. and **Mort**, F., 'Patriarchal aspects of nineteenth-century state formation: property relations, marriage and divorce and sexuality', in C. Smart, ed., *Capitalism, State Formation and Marxist Theory: Historical Investigations* (1980), 79–109.

5.302 **Holcombe**, L., 'Victorian wives and property: reform of the Married Women's Property Law, 1857–1882', in M. Vicinus, ed., *A Widening Sphere: Changing Roles of Victorian Women* (Bloomington, Indiana, 1977), 3–28.

5.303 — *Wives and Property: Reform of the Married Women's Property Law in Nineteenth-Century England* (1983).

5.304 **Keown**, J., *Abortion, Doctors and the Law: Some Aspects of the Legal Regulation of Abortion in England from 1803–1982* (1988).

5.305 **Minor**, I., 'Working-class women and matrimonial law reform, 1890–1914', in D. Martin and D. Rubenstein, eds., *Ideology and the Labour Movement: Essays Presented to John Saville* (1979), 103–24. On the position of working-class women and the law.

5.306 **O'Donovan**, K., 'The male appendage – legal definitions of women', in S. Burman, ed., *Fit Work for Women* (1979), 134–52.

5.307 **Poovey**, M., 'Covered but not bound: Caroline Norton and the 1857 Matrimonial Causes Act', *Fem. Studs.*, 14.3 (1988), 467–86.

5.308 **Reiss**, E., *The Rights and Duties of Englishwomen: A Study in Law and Public Opinion* (1934). A detailed discussion of the legal position of married women.

5.309 **Sachs**, A., 'The myth of male protectiveness and the legal subordination of women: an historical analysis', in C. Smart and B. Smart, eds., *Women, Sexuality and Social Control* (1974), 27–40.

5.310 — and **Wilson**, J., *Sexism and the Law:*

A Study of Male Beliefs and Judicial Bias (1978). Study of Britain and the United States.

5.311 **Savage**, G. L., 'Divorce and the Law in England and France prior to the First World War', *J. Soc. Hist.*, 22.3 (1988), 499–514.

5.312 — 'The divorce court and the Queen's Proctor: legal patriarchy and the sanctity of marriage in Victorian England', *Historical Papers/Communications Historiques*, (Ottawa, 1989), 210–27.

5.313 **Shanley**, M. L., ' "One must ride behind": married women's rights and the Divorce Act of 1857', *Vict. Studs.*, 25.3 (1982), 355–76. Examines controversies over divorce and the implications for women and the family.

5.314 — *Feminism, Marriage and the Law in Victorian England, 1850–1895* (Princeton, New Jersey, 1989). Important recent study.

5.315 **Staves**, S., *Married Women's Separate Property in England, 1660–1833* (Cambridge, Mass., 1990).

5.316 **Stetson**, D., *A Woman's Issue: The Politics of Family Law Reform in England* (Conn., 1982). Studies the history of divorce and the 1857 Matrimonial Causes Act.

5.317 **Stone**, O. W., 'The status of women in Great Britain', *Am. J. Comp. Law*, 20 (1972), 592–621. Deals with the legal status of women.

5.318 **Travers**, R. L., *Husband and Wife in English Law* (1956).

5.319 **Vogel**, V., 'Whose property? The double standard of adultery in nineteenth-century law', in C. Smart, ed., *Regulating Motherhood: Historical Essays on Marriage, Motherhood and Sexuality* (1992), 147–65.

See also: 5.153; 5.157; 5.158; 5.164; 5.173; 5.362; 5.406; 5.418; 5.482; 5.483; 5.546; 5.639; 5.648.

(e) WOMEN AND HEALTH

5.320 **Bullough**, V. and **Voght**, M., 'Women, menstruation and nineteenth-century medicine', *Bull. Hist. Medicine*, 47 (1973), 66–82.

5.321 **Clarke**, J. N., 'Sexism, feminism and medicalism: a decade review of literature on gender and illness', *Sociology of Health and Illness*, 5.1 (1983), 62–82.

5.322 **Dally**, A., *Women Under the Knife: A History of Surgery* (1991).

5.323 **Duffin**, L., 'The conspicuous consumptive: woman as an invalid', in S. Delamont and L. Duffin, eds., *The Nineteenth-Century Woman: Her Cultural and Physical World* (1978), 26–56. Relates women's illness to their social role in Victorian period.

5.324 **Ehrenreich**, B. and **English**, D., *Complaints and Disorders: The Sexual Politics of Sickness* (Old Westbury, New York, 1973). Use material from the US to discuss general issues relating to disease/ sex.

5.325 **Fee**, E., 'Nineteenth-century craniology: the study of the female skull', *Bull. Hist. Medicine*, 53.3 (1979), 415–33. How Victorians used craniology to demonstrate women's inferiority.

5.326 **Figlio**, K., 'Cholorosis and chronic disease in nineteenth-century Britain: the social constitution of somatic illness in a capitalist society', *Soc. Hist.*, 3.2 (1978), 167–97. Stimulating discussion of the relationship between medicine, capitalist development and the adolescent girl.

5.327 **Fox**, E., 'Powers of life and death: aspects of maternal welfare in England and Wales between the wars', *Medical Hist.*, 35.3 (1991), 328–52.

5.328 **Harrison**, Barbara H., ' "Some of them gets lead poisoned": occupational lead exposure in women, 1880–1914', *Soc. Hist. Medicine*, 2 (1989), 171–95.

5.329 — 'Suffer the working day: women in the "dangerous trades", 1880–1914', *Women's Studs. Int. For.*, 13, 1/2 (1990), 79–90. Health threats to women in selected industries and the consequences for women of state intervention.

5.330 **Harrison**, Brian, 'Women's health and the women's movement in Britain, 1840–1940', in C. Webster, ed., *Biology, Medicine and Society* (1980), 15–71. Discusses anti-feminism in the medical profession and feminist distrust of doctors.

5.331 **Hunter**, D., 'Hysteria, psychoanalysis and feminism: the case of Anna O', *Fem. Studs.*, 9.3 (1983), 465–88 .

5.332 **Jordan**, T. E., 'Linearity, gender and social class in economic influences on heights of Victorian youth', *Hist. Meths.*, 24.3 (1991), 116–23.

5.333 **Kenner**, C., *No Time for Women: Exploring Women's Health in the 1930s and Today* (1985).

5.334 **Lewis**, J. S., 'Maternal health in the English aristocracy: myths and realities, 1790–1840', *J. Soc. Hist.*, 17.1 (1983), 97–114.

5.335 — *In The Family Way: Childbearing in the British Aristocracy* (New Brunswick, New Jersey, 1986).

5.336 **Loudon**, I., 'Deaths in childbed from the eighteenth century to 1935', *Medical Hist.*, 30 (1986), 1–41.

5.337 — 'Maternal mortality, 1880–1950. Some regional and international comparisons', *Soc. Hist. Medicine*, 1.2 (1988), 183–228. Suggests place of delivery and skill of birth attendant were more important than socio-economic factors in explaining lower maternal mortality rates.

5.338 — *Death in Childbirth: An International Study of Maternal Care and Maternal Mortality, 1800–1950* (1992).

5.339 **Miller**, J. H., ' "Temple and sewer": childbirth, prudery and Victoria Regina', in A. S. Wohl, ed., *The Victorian Family* (1978), 23–43. Changing attitudes towards practices of childbirth.

5.340 **Mitchell**, M., 'The effect of unemployment on the social condition of women and children in the 1930s', *Hist. Workshop J.*, 19 (1985), 105–27.

5.341 **Oakley**, A., 'Wisewomen and medical men: changes in the management of childbirth', in J. Mitchell and A. Oakley, eds., *The Rights and Wrongs of Women* (1976), 17–58.

5.342 — *The Captured Womb: A History of the Medical Care of Pregnant Women* (1984).

5.343 **Oren**, L., 'The welfare of women in labouring families: England, 1860–1950', in M. Hartman and L. W. Banner, eds., *Clio's Consciousness Raised: New Perspectives on the History of Women* (1974), 226–44. Discusses the unequal division of resources in working-class families which led to poorer health, nutrition and clothing for women.

5.344 **Rubinstein**, A., 'Subtle poison: the puerperal fever controversy in Victorian Britain', *Hist. Studs.*, 20.80 (1983), 420–38.

5.345 **Shorter**, E., *A History of Women's Bodies* (1982). A very controversial general study.

5.346 **Showalter**, E., 'Victorian women and insanity', *Vict. Studs.*, 23.2 (1980), 157–81.

5.347 — *The Female Malady: Women, Madness and English Culture, 1830–1980* (New York, 1985). Stimulating study of the way in which ideas about femininity have shaped the definition and treatment of female insanity.

5.348 — and **Showalter**, E., 'Victorian women and menstruation', in M. Vicinus, ed., *Suffer and Be Still: Women in the Victorian Age* (Bloomington, Indiana, 1972), 38–44.

5.349 **Shuttleworth**, S., 'Female circulation: medical discourse and popular advertising in the mid-Victorian era', in M. Jacobus, E. Fox Keller and S. Shuttleworth, eds., *Body/Politic* (1990), 47–68.

5.350 **Smith**, F. B., 'Ethics and disease in the later nineteenth century: the Contagious Diseases Acts', *Hist. Studs.*, 15 (1971), 118–35.

5.351 **Vertinsky**, P. A., *The Eternally Wounded Woman: Women, Exercise and Doctors in the Late Nineteenth Century* (1990). Examines differing views about women and exercise in Britain and America and analyses the impact of these on the lifestyle of middle-class women.

5.352 **Webster**, C., 'Healthy or hungry thirties', *Hist. Workshop J.*, 13 (1982), 110–29. Examines health of men, women and children.

5.353 **Winter**, J. M., 'The impact of the First World War on civilian health in Britain', *Ec. H. R.*, sec. ser., 30.3 (1977), 487–502.

5.354 — 'Infant mortality, maternal mortality and public health in Britain in the 1930s', *J. European Hist.*, 8, Autumn (1979), 439–62.

(f) WOMEN AND SEXUALITY

5.355 **Auchmuty**, R., 'By their friends we shall know them: the lives and networks of some women in North Lambeth, 1880–1940', in Lesbian History Group, eds., *Not A Passing Phase: Reclaiming Lesbians in History, 1840–1985* (1989), 77–98.

5.356 **Bailey**, P., 'Parasexuality and glamour: the Victorian barmaid as cultural prototype', *Gend. and Hist.*, 2.2 (1990), 148–72.

5.357 **Barker-Benfield**, B., 'The spermatic economy: a nineteenth-century view of

sexuality', *Fem. Studs.*, 1 (1973), 45–56.

5.358 **Barret-Ducrocq**, F., *Love in the Time of Victoria: Sexuality, Class and Gender in Nineteenth-Century London* (1991).

5.359 **Beales**, H. L., 'Victorian ideas of sex', in H. Grisewood, ed., *Ideas and Beliefs of the Victorians* (New York, 1966), 351–8.

5.360 **Benenson**, H., 'Victorian sexual ideology and Marx's theory of the working class', *Int. Labor and Working-Class Hist.*, 25 (1984), 1–23.

5.361 **Bland**, L., 'Purity, motherhood, pleasure or threat? Definitions of female sexuality, 1900–1970s', in S. Cartledge and J. Ryan, ed., *Sex and Love* (1983), 8–29.

5.362 — ' "Guardians of the race" or "vampires upon the nation's health"? Female sexuality and its regulation in early twentieth-century Britain', in E. Whitelegg et al., eds., *The Changing Experience of Women* (1984), 373–88.

5.363 — ' "Cleansing the portals of life": the venereal disease campaign in the early twentieth century', in M. Langan and B. Schwarz, eds., *Crises in the British State, 1880–1930* (1985), 192–208. Argues that feminist definitions and solutions to the problem of venereal disease were marginalised during the First World War.

5.364 — 'In the name of protection: the policing of women in the First World War', in C. Smart and J. Brophy, eds., *Women in Law: Explorations in Law, Family and Sexuality* (1985), 23–49.

5.365 — 'Rational sex or spiritual love? The Men and Women's Club of the 1880s', *Women's Studs. Int. For.*, 13, 1/2 (1990), 33–48. Examines women's difficulties in putting masculinity on the agenda in discussions of sexuality.

5.366 **Boulmelha**, P., *Thomas Hardy and Women: Sexual Ideology and Narrative* (1982).

5.367 **Brandon**, R., *The New Women and the Old Men: Love, Sex and the Woman Question* (1990). Examines the marital and sexual relationships of late-Victorian intellectuals, including Havelock Ellis, Olive Schreiner, Eleanor Marx, the Webbs, Margaret Sanger and G. B. Shaw.

5.368 **Clark**, A., 'Rape or seduction? A controversy over sexual violence in the nineteenth century', in London Feminist History Group, *Men's Power, Women's Resistance: The Sexual Dynamics of History* (1983), 13–27. Uses a particular controversy to examine tensions over standards of sexual behaviour.

5.369 **Cominos**, P. T., 'Late Victorian sexual respectability and the social system', *Int. R. Soc. Hist.*, 8.1 and 8.2 (1963), 18–48 and 216–50.

5.370 — 'Innocent *femina sensualis* in unconscious conflict', in M. Vicinus, ed., *Suffer and Be Still: Women in the Victorian Age* (Bloomington, Indiana, 1972), 155–72. Discusses contradictions in belief women are naturally sexually innocent.

5.371 **Costello**, J., *Love, Sex and War: Changing Values, 1939–45* (1985). Description of wartime sexual activities between the Americans and the British.

5.372 **Cott**, N. F., 'Passionless: an interpretation of Victorian sexual ideology, 1790–1850', *Signs*, 4.2 (1978), 219–36.

5.373 **Coward**, R., *Patriarchal Precedents: Sexuality and Social Relations* (1983). Examines debates around patriarchy and matriarchy in the nineteenth century and how they underpinned social theories relating to the family, sexual relations and sexual characteristics.

5.374 **Davidoff**, L., 'Class and gender in Victorian England: the diaries of Arthur J Munby and Hannah Culwick', in J. L. Newton, M. P. Ryan and J. Walkowitz, eds., *Sex and Class in Women's History* (1983), 17–71. Explores sexual connotations of the diaries, and connections between class, gender and sexuality.

5.375 **Davies**, R., ' "In a broken dream": some aspects of sexual behaviour and the dilemmas of the unmarried mother in South-West Wales, 1887–1914', *Llafur*, 3.4 (1983), 24–33.

5.376 **DeGroot**, J., ' "Sex and race": the construction of language and image in the nineteenth century', in S. Mendus and J. Rendall, eds., *Sexuality and Subordination: Interdisciplinary Studies of Gender in the Nineteenth Century* (1989), 89–128.

5.377 **Digby**, A., 'Women's biological straitjacket', in S. Mendus and J. Rendall, eds., *Sexuality and Subordination: Interdisciplinary Studies of Gender in the Nineteenth-Century* (1989), 192–220. Analyses the way in which medical texts, in particular gynaecological and psychiatric literature, depicted women.

5.378 **DuBois**, E. C. and **Gordon**, L., 'Seeking ecstacy on the battlefield: danger and pleasure in nineteenth-century feminist

sexual thought', *Fem. Studs.*, 9.1 (1983), 7–25. Based on American literature but raises general questions about the importance of social purity politics for feminists.

5.379 **Faderman**, L., *Surpassing the Love of Men: Romantic Friendship and Love between Women from the Renaissance to the Present* (New York, 1981). Pioneering study of lesbian history.

5.380 **Faraday**, A., 'Lessoning lesbians: girls' schools, co-education and anti-lesbianism between the wars', in C. Jones and P. Mahoney, eds., *Learning Our Lines: Sexuality and Social Control in Education* (1989), 23–45.

5.381 **Foucault**, M., *History of Sexuality: Vol. 1. An Introduction* (1979). Key theoretical text which challenged received notions of sexuality and has influenced historians of the subject.

5.382 **Gilbert**, H., *A Woman's History of Sex* (1987).

5.383 **Giles**, J., ' "Playing hard to get": working-class women, sexuality and respectability in Britain, 1918–40', *Women's H. R.*, 1.2 (1992), 239–56.

5.384 **Gill**, D., *Illegitimacy, Sexuality and the Status of Women* (1972).

5.385 **Glover**, E., 'Victorian ideas of sex', in H. Grisewood, ed., *Ideas and Beliefs of the Victorians* (New York, 1966), 358–64. Examines psycho-sexual and unconscious influences on sexual attitudes and behaviour.

5.386 **Harrison**, B., 'Underneath the Victorians', *Vict. Studs.*, 10.3 (1967), 239–62. Review of Marcus (5.398) in which Harrison criticises the latter's use of evidence.

5.387 **Hooper**, C., 'Child sexual abuse and the regulation of women: variations on a theme', in C. Smart, ed., *Regulating Womanhood: Essays on Marriage, Motherhood and Sexuality* (1992), 53–77.

5.388 **Humphries**, S., *A Secret World of Sex: Forbidden Fruit: The British Experience, 1900–1950* (1988). Based on oral interviews.

5.389 **Jackson**, M., 'Sexual liberation or social control? Some aspects of the relationship between feminism and the social construction of sexual knowledge in the early twentieth century', *Women's Studs. Int. For.*, 6 (1983), 1–17.

5.390 **Jeffreys**, S., ' "Free from all uninvited

touch of man": women's campaigns around sexuality, 1880–1914', *Women's Studs. Int. For.*, 5.6 (1982), 629–45. Notes feminist involvement in social purity.

5.391 — 'Sex reform and anti-feminism in the 1920s', in London Feminist History Group, *Men's Power, Women's Resistance: The Sexual Dynamics of History* (1983), 177–202.

5.392 — *The Spinster and Her Enemies: Feminism and Sexuality* (1985). Critique of sexologists with their emphasis on heterosexuality and the 'repressed' spinster. Gives a positive view of social purity feminists and disputes the thesis that Victorian sexual puritanism gave way to a sexual revolution.

5.393 **Jordanova**, L. J., 'Natural facts: a historical perspective on science and sexuality', in C. P. MacCormack and M. Strathern, eds., *Nature, Culture and Gender* (1980), 42–69.

5.394 **Lansbury**, C., 'Gynaecology, pornography and the anti-vivisection movement', *Vict. Studs.*, 28.3 (1985), 413–38.

5.395 **Lesbian Oral History Group**, eds., *Inventing Ourselves: Lesbian Life Stories* (1989).

5.396 **L'Esperance**, J., 'Doctors and women in nineteenth-century society: sexuality and role', in J. Woodward and D. Richards, eds., *Health Care and Popular Medicine in Nineteenth-Century England: Essays in the Social History of Medicine* (1977), 105–27. Doctors' views of male and female sexuality and their role in preserving male dominance.

5.397 — 'Women's mission to women: explorations in the double standard and female sexuality in nineteenth-century England', *Social History-Histoire Sociale*, 12 (1979), 316–88.

5.398 **Marcus**, S., *The Other Victorians: A Study of Sexuality and Pornography in Mid-Nineteenth Century England* (1967). Explains pornography in terms of a conflict between demands of the sex drive and a social fabric disrupted by change.

5.399 **Mendus**, S. and **Rendall**, J., eds., *Sexuality and Subordination: Interdisciplinary Studies of Gender in the Nineteenth Century* (1989). Collection of essays arising from a women's studies course on Victorianism.

5.400 **Mennell**, J. E., 'The politics of frustration: "the maiden tribute of modern Babylon" and the morality movement of 1885', *North Dakota Quarterly*, 49 (1981), 68–80.

5.401 **Montgomery**, D., 'Response to Harold Benenson, "Victorian sexual ideology and Marx's theory of the working class" ', *Int. Labor and Working-Class Hist.*, 25, Spring (1984), 24–9. See 5.360.

5.402 **Mort**, F., 'Purity feminism and the state: sexuality and moral politics, 1880–1914', in M. Langan and B. Schwartz, eds., *Crises in the British State, 1880–1930* (1985), 209–25.

5.403 — *Dangerous Sexualities: Medico-Moral Politics in England since 1830* (1987). Discusses the interplay between public health issues and sexual politics, leading to demands for the regulation of sexual behaviour.

5.404 **Mosse**, G. L., 'Nationalism and respectability: normal and abnormal sexuality in the nineteenth century', *J. Contemp. Hist.*, 17.2 (1982), 221–46.

5.405 **Murphy-Lawless**, J., 'The silencing of women in childbirth or let's hear it for Bartholomew and the boys', *Women's Studs. Int. For.*, 11.4 (1988), 293–9. Examines approaches to women's sexuality in Ireland.

5.406 **Newburn**, T., *Permission and Regulation: Law and Morals in Post-War Britain* (1992). Guide to key legislative changes in 1960s on abortion, prostitution, obscenity and homosexuality.

5.407 **Nord**, D. E., ' "Neither pairs nor odd": Beatrice Webb, Margaret Harkness, Amy Levy and the promise of female community in late nineteenth-century London', *Signs*, 15.4 (1990), 733–54. Uses three female writers to explore female friendship, the search for sexual identity and the difficulties for women trying to live independently.

5.408 **Oram**, A., ' "Embittered, sexless or homosexual": attacks on spinster teachers, 1918–1939', in A. Angerman et al., eds., *Current Issues in Women's History* (1989), 183–202.

5.409 — 'Repressed and thwarted, or bearer of the new world? The spinster in inter-war feminist discourses', *Women's H. R.*, 1.3 (1992), 413–34. Argues against the view that sexologists silenced a feminist politics of spinsterhood between the wars.

5.410 **Padgug**, R. A., 'Sexual matters: on conceptualising sexuality in history', *Radical H. R.*, 20, Spring/Summer (1979),

3–24.

5.411 **Pearl**, C., *The Girl With the Swansdown Seat: An Informal Report on Some Aspects of Mid-Victorian Morality* (1955).

5.412 **Pearsall**, R., *The Worm in the Bud: The World of Victorian Sexuality* (New York, 1969).

5.413 **Peterson**, M. J., 'Dr Acton's enemy: medicine, sex and society in Victorian England', *Vict. Studs.*, 29.4 (1986), 569–90.

5.414 **Ross**, E., 'Response to Harold Benenson's "Victorian sexual ideology" ', *Int. Labor and Working-Class Hist.*, 25, Spring (1984), 30–6. See 5.360.

5.415 — and **Rapp**, R., 'Sex and society: a research note from social history and anthropology', in A. Snitow, C. Stansell and S. Thompson, eds., *Desire: The Politics of Sexuality* (1984), 105–26. Discuss varied forces shaping 'modern sexuality' at an individual and class level.

5.416 **Showalter**, E., *Sexual Anarchy: Gender and Culture at the Fin de Siecle* (1990).

5.417 **Smart**, C., 'Disruptive bodies and unruly sex: the regulation of reproduction and sexuality in the nineteenth century', in C. Smart, ed., *Regulating Womanhood: Essays on Marriage, Motherhood and Sexuality* (1992), 7–32.

5.418 — ed., *Regulating Womanhood: Essays on Marriage, Motherhood and Sexuality* (1992).

5.419 **Smith**, F. B., 'Sexuality in Britain, 1800–1900: some suggested revisions', in M. Vicinus, ed., *A Widening Sphere: Changing Roles of Victorian Women* (Bloomington, Indiana, 1977), 182–98.

5.420 **Smout**, T. C., 'Aspects of sexual behaviour in nineteenth-century Scotland', in A. A. MacLaren, ed., *Social Class in Scotland: Past and Present* (1976), 55–85.

5.421 **Stevens**, C., 'The history of sexuality in Britain and America, 1800–1975: course method and Bill of Rights', *Women's Studs. Q.*, 16, Spring/Summer (1988), 87–96.

5.422 **Summerfield**, P. and **Crockett**, N., ' "You weren't taught that with the welding: lessons in sexuality in the Second World War', *Women's H. R.*, 1.3 (1992), 435–54. Use oral interviews to explore what women themselves perceived to be the effects of war on sexual mores.

5.423 **Thomas**, K., 'The double standard', *J. Hist. Ideas*, 20 (1959), 195–216. Important early work exploring the double standard of morality and sexual behaviour.

5.424 **Trudgill**, E., *Madonnas and Magdalens: The Origins and Development of Victorian Sexual Attitudes* (1976). Discusses the forms and contradictions of Victorian sexual ideology and behaviour.

5.425 **Vicinus**, M., ' "One more life to stand beside me": emotional conflicts of first-generation college women in England', *Fem. Studs.*, 6.3 (1982), 603–28.

5.426 — 'Sexuality and power: a review of current work in the history of sexuality', *Fem. Studs.*, 8.1 (1982), 133–56.

5.427 — 'Distance and desire: English boarding school friendships', *Signs*, 9 (1984), 600–22.

5.428 **Walkowitz**, J., 'Science, feminism and romance : the Men and Women's Club, 1885–1889', *Hist. Workshop J.*, 21 (1986), 37–59. Examines the tensions between men and women in discussions around sexuality at the Club.

5.429 — *City of Dreadful Delight: Narratives of Sexual Danger in Late-Victorian London* (1992). An innovative study which examines the relationship between power, politics and sexuality through an analysis of the representation of sexual issues, including prostitution and the Jack the Ripper murders, in the press and in fiction.

5.430 **Weeks**, J., 'Movements of affirmation: sexual meanings and homosexual identities', *Radical H. R.*, 20, Spring/Summer (1979), 164–80.

5.431 — *Sex, Politics and Society: The Regulation of Sexuality since 1800* (1981). Comprehensive and now standard analysis of changing attitudes to sexuality in Britain.

5.432 — *Sexuality and Its Discontents. Meanings, Myths and Modern Sexualities* (1985). Relates present discontents to historical developments.

See also: 2.185; 5.152; 5.550; 5.1176; 5.1224.

(g) WOMEN AND WORK

(i) General

5.433 **Alexander**, S., **Davin**, A. and **Hostettler**, E., 'Labouring women: a reply to Eric Hobsbawm', *Hist. Workshop J.*, 8 (1979),

174–82. Suggest labour historians should view working-class women as workers in own right, not just as wives and daughters.

5.434 **Allen**, M., 'The domestic ideal and the mobilization of womanpower in World War II', *Women's Studs. Int. For.*, 6.4 (1983), 401–11. Labour policies to draw women into work were structured by domestic ideal.

5.435 **Amsden**, A., *The Economics of Woman and Work* (1980). Describes different theories of women's work.

5.436 **Anthias**, F., 'Women and the reserve army of labour: a critique of Veronica Beechey', *Capital and Class*, 10, Spring (1980), 50–63.

5.437 **Barron**, R. D. and **Norris**, G. M., 'Sexual divisions and the dual labour market', in D. L. Barker and S. Allen, eds., *Dependence and Exploitation in Work and Marriage* (1976), 47–69. Sociological model for examining the sex division of labour in paid employment.

5.438 **Beechey**, V., 'Women and production: a critical analysis of some sociological theories of women's work', in A. Kuhn and A. M. Wolpe, eds., *Feminism and Materialism: Women and Modes of Production* (1978), 155–97.

5.439 — 'The sexual division of labour and the labour process', in S. Wood, ed., *The Degradation of Work? Skill, Deskilling and the Labour Process* (1982), 54–73. Discusses the concept of socially constructed skill in relation to the sex division of labour.

5.440 **Benenson**, H., 'The "family wage" and working women's consciousness in Britain, 1880–1914', *Pol. and Scy.*, 19.1 (1991), 71–108.

5.441 **Benson**, J., *The Penny Capitalists: A Study of Nineteenth-Century Working-Class Entrepreneurs* (1983). Study of ways in which working-class men and women made a living independently of employers.

5.442 **Bertaux**, N. E., 'The roots of today's "women's jobs" and "men's jobs": using the index of dissimilarity to measure occupational segregation by gender', *Explorations in Economic Hist.*, 28 (1991), 433–59.

5.443 **Bradley**, H., *Men's Work, Women's Work: A History of the Sex-Typing of Jobs in Britain* (1987).

5.444 **Branca**, P., 'A new perspective on women's work: a comparative typology', *J.*

Soc. Hist., 9.2 (1975), 129–53. Attempts to produce a typology of women's work from the census.

5.445 **Braybon**, G. and **Summerfield**, P., *Out of the Cage: Women's Experiences in Two World Wars* (1987). Based on oral testimony.

5.446 **Brophy**, I., 'Women in the workforce', in D. Dickson, ed., *The Gorgeous Mask: Dublin, 1700–1850* (Dublin, 1987), 51–62.

5.447 **Bruegel**, I., 'Women as a reserve army of labour: a note on the recent British experience', *Fem. R.*, 3 (1979), 12–23.

5.448 — 'Women's employment, legislation and the labour market', in J. Lewis, ed., *Women's Welfare/Women's Rights* (1983), 130–69. A review of theories of women's position in the labour market.

5.449 **Burman**, R., 'The Jewish woman as breadwinner: the changing value of women's work in a Manchester immigrant community', *Oral Hist.*, 10.2 (1982), 27–39.

5.450 **Burman**, S., ed., *Fit Work for Women* (1979). Articles on women's work, both paid and unpaid.

5.451 **Campling**, J., 'Frances Chevalier and women's work in Ipswich, 1896–1919', *Suffolk R.*, 4.3 (1974), 111–13.

5.452 **Chinn**, C., *They Worked All Their Lives: Women of the Urban Poor in England, 1880–1939* (1988).

5.453 **Cliff**, S., 'Technical change and occupational sex-typing', in D. Knight and H. Wilmott, eds., *Gender and the Labour Process* (1986), 74–93.

5.454 **Condell**, D. and **Liddiard**, J., *Working for Victory? Images of Women in the First World War* (1987). Photographs with critical comments.

5.455 **Crew**, J., 'Women's wages in Britain and Australia during the First World War', *Labour Hist.*, 57, November (1989), 27–43.

5.456 **Crofts**, W., 'The Attlee Government's pursuit of women', *Hist. Today*, 36.8 (1986), 29–35. Discusses attempts by the government to increase female participation in the workforce.

5.457 **Crompton**, R., **Hantrais**, L. and **Walters**, P., 'Gender relations and employment', *Brit. J. Sociol.*, 41.3 (1990), 329–49.

5.458 **Custers**, P., *Women's Work: The History and Theory of the Sex Division of Labour* (1990).

5.459 **Daly**, M. E., 'Women in the Irish workforce from pre-industrial to modern times', *J. Irish Labour Hist. Scy.*, 7 (1981), 74–82.

5.460 **Davidoff**, L. and **Westover**, B., ' "From Queen Victoria to the Jazz Age". Women's World in England, 1880–1939', in L. Davidoff and B. Westover, eds., *Our Work, Our Lives, Our Words. Women's History and Women's Work* (Totowa, New Jersey, 1986), 1–35. Overview of changes in women's employment and relationship to the family.

5.461 — eds., *Our Work, Our Lives, Our Words. Women's History and Women's Work* (Totowa, New Jersey, 1986). Essays based on oral interviews/evidence.

5.462 **Davies**, R., *Women and Work* (1975). Chapter on changing position of women at work over 300 years.

5.463 **Dawes**, F., *A Woman's Place – Women at Work from 1830 to the Present* (1976).

5.464 **Dex**, S., *The Sexual Division of Work. Conceptual Revolutions in the Social Sciences* (1985). Considers way in which taking women's work seriously has revolutionised sociological theories of work.

5.465 — 'Issues of gender and employment', *Soc. Hist.*, 13.2 (1988), 141–50.

5.466 **Ferguson**, N., 'Women's work: employment opportunities and economic roles, 1918–1939', *Albion*, 7 (1975), 55–68.

5.467 **Frank**, P., 'Women's work in the Yorkshire inshore fishing industry', *Oral Hist.*, 4.1 (1976), 57–72.

5.468 **Gordon**, E. and Breitenbach, E., eds., *The World is Ill Divided: Women's Work in Scotland in the Nineteenth and Twentieth Centuries* (1990). Essays revealing the heterogeneity of Scottish women's experience of work.

5.469 **Gross**, E., 'Plus ca change . . .? The sexual structure of occupations over time', *Social Problems*, 16, Fall (1968), 198–206. Uses census data to show the persistence of the sex division of labour in the nineteenth and twentieth centuries.

5.470 **Guest**, R. and **John**, A. V., *Lady Charlotte: A Biography of the Nineteenth Century* (1989). Biography of an ironmaster's wife who not only ran the family business, but also had a varied life which included translating Welsh literature. Explores issues raised by writing biography.

5.471 **Hakim**, C., *Occupational Segregation: A Comparative Study of the Degree and Pattern of the Differentiation between Men's and Women's Work in Britain, the United States*

and Other Countries (1979). Stimulating discussion of how to use the census to examine work patterns, with detailed statistics for the twentieth century.

5.472 — 'Census reports as documentary evidence: the census commentaries, 1801–1951', *Sociolog. R.*, 28.3 (1980), 551–81.

5.473 **Hartmann**, H., 'Capitalism, patriarchy and the case for job segregation by sex', in Z. R. Eisenstein, ed., *Capitalist Patriarchy and the Case for Socialist Feminism* (New York, 1979), 211–30. Suggests patriarchal relations between the sexes explain why male workers chose to exclude women workers from certain types of employment rather than organise them.

5.474 **Hewitt**, M., *Victorian Working Wives and Mothers* (1958). Analyses contemporary views of the working mother.

5.475 **Higgs**, E., 'Women, occupations and work in the nineteenth-century censuses', *Hist. Workshop J.*, 23 (1987), 59–80. Stimulating discussion of the need to exercise caution in using the census to study gender divisions at work.

5.476 **Hiley**, M., *Victorian Working Women: Portraits from Life* (1979). Collection of photographs.

5.477 **Holcombe**, L., *Victorian Ladies at Work: Middle-Class Women in England and Wales, 1850–1914* (1973). Descriptive account of commercial and professional occupations.

5.478 **Hollis**, P., 'Working women', *Hist.*, 62.206 (1977), 439–45. Wide-ranging review article.

5.479 **Honeyman**, K. and **Goodman**, J., 'Women's work, gender conflicts and labour markets in Europe, 1500–1900', *Ec. Hist. R.*, sec. ser., 44 (1991), 608–28.

5.480 **Hudson**, P. and **Lee**, W. R., 'Women's work and the family economy in historical perspective', in P. Hudson and W. R. Lee, eds., *Women's Work and the Family Economy in Historical Perspective* (1990), 2–48. Useful historiographical survey.

5.481 — eds., *Women's Work and the Family Economy in Historical Perspective* (1990). Important collection of articles analysing women's work and contribution to the family economy in several European countries. Comparative and interdisciplinary.

5.482 **Humphries**, J., 'Class struggle and the persistence of the working-class family', *Cambridge J. Ec.*, 1.3 (1977), 241–55.

Argues women gained from protective legislation through the increased wages of male relatives. The family promoted mutual dependence and provided potential for class cohesion.

5.483 — 'Protective legislation, the capitalist state and working-class men', *Fem. R.*, 7 (1981), 1–33.

5.484 — ' "The most free from objection": the sexual division of labour and women's work in nineteenth-century England', *J. Ec. Hist.*, 47.4 (1987), 929–50.

5.485 **Hurstfield**, J., *Labouring Women: Female Workers in Twentieth-Century Britain* (1987).

5.486 **John**, A. V., 'Beyond paternalism: the ironmaster's wife in the industrial community', in A. V. John, ed., *Our Mothers' Land: Chapters in Welsh Women's History, 1830–1939* (1991), 43–68.

5.487 — *Unequal Opportunities: Women's Employment in England, 1800–1918* (1986). Essential reading. Articles representing the most recent research on women's work with an excellent introduction.

5.488 **Jones**, F. L., 'Occupational statistics revisited: the female labour force in early British and Australian censuses', *Australian Ec. H. R.*, 27.2 (1987), 56–76.

5.489 **Jordan**, E., 'Female unemployment in England and Wales, 1851–1911: an examination of the census figures for 15–19 year olds', *Soc. Hist.*, 13.2 (1988), 175–90.

5.490 **Knight**, D. and **Wilmott**, H., eds., *Gender and the Labour Process* (1986).

5.491 **Leneman**, L., 'Fit for heroes? Women and Scottish land settlement after World War One', *Oral Hist.*, 19.2 (1991), 55–8.

5.492 **Leser**, C. V., 'The supply of women for gainful work in Britain', *Pop. Studs.* 9.2 (1955), 142–58. Uses the census, 1851–1951, to show how the proportion of occupied women remained constant, but age/marital status changed.

5.493 **Lewenhak**, S., *Women and Work* (1980). Survey of women's work since the Stone Age, drawing on anthropological and historical evidence. Argues that only recently has women's status as workers declined.

5.494 — 'Women at work: subcontracting, craft unionism and women in England with special reference to the West Midlands, 1750–1914', in A. Wright and R. Shackleton, eds., *Worlds of Labour: Essays in Birmingham Labour History* (1983), 1–17.

5.495 **McLaughlin**, E., 'Women and work in Derry City: a survey', *J. Irish Labour Hist. Scy.*, 14 (1989), 35–46.

5.496 **Neff**, W., *Victorian Working Women, 1831–1850* (1929). Classic account of the working lives of Victorian women and society's attitude towards them, using historical and literary material.

5.497 **Owen**, R., *Women and Work* (1989).

5.498 **Phillips**, A. and **Taylor**, B., 'Sex and skill: notes towards a feminist economics', *Fem. R.*, 8 (1980), 79–88. Key article for an understanding of the way in which skill is gendered.

5.499 **Richards**, E., 'Women in the British economy since about 1700: an interpretation', *Hist.*, 59.197 (1974), 337–57. The participation of women in paid employment outside the home.

5.500 **Roberts**, E., *Women's Work, 1840–1940* (1988). Excellent synthesis of recent publications.

5.501 **Rose**, S. O., *Limited Livelihoods: Gender and Class in Nineteenth-Century England* (1992). Stimulating recent study on gender and work in the nineteenth century.

5.502 **Scott**, J. and **Tilly**, L., 'Women's work and the family in nineteenth-century Europe', in E. Whitelegg et al., eds., *The Changing Experience of Women* (1982), 45–70.

5.503 **Smith**, H. L., 'The issue of "equal pay for equal work" in Great Britain, 1914–1919', *Societas*, 8, Winter (1978), 39–52.

5.504 — 'The problem of "equal pay for equal work" in Great Britain during World War II', *J. Mod. Hist.*, 53.4 (1981), 652–72.

5.505 **Tebbutt**, M., *Making Ends Meet: Pawnbroking and Working-Class Credit* (1983).

5.506 **Thompson**, P., 'Women in the fishing: the roots of power between the sexes', *Comp. Studs. Soc. and Hist.*, 27.1 (1985), 3–32.

5.507 **Tilly**, L. and **Scott**, J., *Women, Work and Family* (New York, 1975). Seminal study of the complex interrelationship between women's work and family life in France and England in the nineteenth and twentieth centuries.

5.508 **Treble**, J., 'The seasonal demand for adult labour in Glasgow, 1890–1914', *Soc. Hist.*, 3, 1 (1978), 43–60.

5.509 **Walby**, S., *Patriarchy at Work: Patriarchal and Capitalist Relations in Employment, 1800–1984* (1986).

5.510 **West**, J., ed., *Work, Women and the Labour*

Market (1982). Collection of articles exploring gender divisions and skill at the workplace in the twentieth century.

5.511 **Williams**, B., *Women and Work* (1991).

5.512 **Williams**, L. J. and **Jones**, D., 'Women at work in the nineteenth century', *Llafur*, 3.3 (1982), 20–32. Welsh women workers.

5.513 **Worsnop**, J., 'A re-evaluation of the "problem of surplus women" in nineteenth-century England: the case of the 1851 census', *Women's Studs. Int. For.*, 13, 1/2 (1990), 21–31. Argues that women involved in the debate were challenging definitions and formation of gender.

5.514 **Zeitlin**, J., 'Theories of women's work and occupational segregation', *Scy. Study Labour Hist., Bull.*, 54 (1989), 6–10.

See also: 5.185; 5.175; 5.1411.

(ii) Industry/mining

5.515 **Adams**, C., et al, *Under Control: Life in a Nineteenth-Century Silk Factory* (1983).

5.516 **Alexander**, L. M., 'Following the thread: Dickens and the seamstress', *Vict. News.*, 80, Fall (1991), 1–7.

5.517 **Alexander**, S., 'Women's work in nineteenth-century London: a study of the years 1820–1850', in J. Mitchell and A. Oakley, eds., *Rights and Wrongs of Women* (1976), 59–111. Important article drawing attention to the development of a specific sex division of labour in early industrialisation and the diversity of women's paid work . Focuses on homework and workshop employment.

5.518 **Beddoe**, D., 'Munitionettes, maids and mams: women in Wales, 1914–1939', in A. V. John, ed., *Our Mothers' Land: Chapters in Welsh Women's History, 1830–1939* (1991), 189–209.

5.519 **Berg**, M., *The Age of Manufactures, 1700–1820* (1985). Valuable discussion of domestic industry.

5.520 — 'Women's work, mechanisation and the early phases of industrialisation in England', in P. Joyce, ed., *The Historical Meanings of Work* (1986), 64–98.

5.521 **Boyle**, E., *The Irish Flowerers* (1971). Lacemaking trade.

5.522 **Braybon**, G., 'The need for women's labour in the First World War', in E. Whitelegg et al., eds., *The Changing Experience of Women* (1982), 90–104.

5.523 — *Women Workers in the First World War:*

The British Experience (1981). Discusses munitions workers and challenges the view that war brought lasting gains for women workers.

5.524 **Burke**, G., 'The decline of the Bal Maiden: the impact of change in the Cornish mining industry', in A. V. John, ed., *Unequal Opportunities: Women's Employment in England, 1800–1918* (1986), 178–204.

5.525 **Busfield**, D. F., 'Job definitions and inequality: the "unskilled" women workers of the West Riding textile industry', *Textile Hist.*, 19.1 (1989), 61–82.

5.526 **Bythell**, D., *The Sweated Trades: Outwork in Nineteenth-Century Britain* (1978).

5.527 **Carruthers**, S. L., ' "Manning the factories": propaganda and policy on the employment of women, 1939–47', *Hist.*, 75 (1990), 232–56.

5.528 **Cockburn**, C., *Brothers: Male Dominance and Technological Change* (1983). An account of women in printing from the Victorian period to the 1980s and the attitudes of male trade unionists.

5.529 **Collins**, B., 'Sewing and social structure: the flowerers of Scotland and Ireland', in R. Mitchison and P. Roebuck, eds., *Economy and Society in Scotland and Ireland, 1500–1939* (1988), 242–54.

5.530 — 'The organisation of sewing outwork in late nineteenth-century Ulster', in M. Berg, ed., *Markets and Manufacturers in Early Industrial Europe* (1991), 139–56.

5.531 **Coyle**, A., 'Sex and skill in the organisation of the clothing industry', in J. West, ed., *Work, Women and the Labour Market* (1982), 10–26. Relationship of women's low-skilled, low-paid work in clothing to the organisation of the work process.

5.532 **Culleton**, C. A., 'Gender charged munitions: the language of World War 1 munitions reports', *Women's Studs. Int. For.*, 11.2 (1988), 109–16. WWI writers of both sexes suggested women were drawn to munitions work because it was linked with sexuality and maternity.

5.533 **Dewar**, E., 'Women's work on the waterfront, 1916–1987', *N.W. Gp. Study Labour Hist.*, Bull. 14 (1989), 30–8.

5.534 **Evans**, C., 'Unemployment and the making of the feminine during the Lancashire cotton famine', in P. Hudson and W. R. Lee, eds., *Women's Work and the Family Economy in Historical Perspective* (1990), 248–70.

5.535 **Fredeman**, W. E., 'Emily Faithfull and the Victoria Press: an experiment in sociological bibliography', *The Library*, 29.2 (1974), 139–64.

5.536 **Freifeld**, M., 'Technological change and the "self acting" mule: a study of skill and the sexual division of labour', *Soc. Hist.*, 11.3 (1986), 319–43. Illuminating study of the interrelationship between skill, training and the sexual division of labour.

5.537 **Garrett**, E. M., 'The trials of labour: motherhood versus employment in a nineteenth-century textile centre', *Capital and Class*, 5.1 (1990), 121–54.

5.538 **Glucksmann**, M., *Women Assemble: Women Workers and the New Industries in Inter-War Britain* (1990).

5.539 **Grant**, L., 'Women in a car town: Coventry, 1920–45', in P. Hudson and W. R. Lee, eds., *Women's Work and the Family Economy in Historical Perspective* (1990), 220–46.

5.540 **Hall**, C., 'The world turned upside down? The working-class family in cotton textiles, 1780–1850', in E. Whitelegg et al., eds., *The Changing Experience of Women* (1982), 17–29.

5.541 **Holden**, P., 'True story of a Lancashire pit brow lass', *N.W. Gp. Study Labour Hist.*, Bull. 11 (1985), 1–7.

5.542 **Hudson**, P., 'Proto-industrialisation: the case of the West Riding wool textile industry in the eighteenth and early nineteenth centuries', *Hist. Workshop J.*, 12 (1981), 34–61.

5.543 **Hunt**, F., 'The London trade in the printing and binding of books: an experience in exclusion, dilution and de-skilling for women workers', *Women's Studs. Int. For.*, 6.5 (1983), 517–24.

5.544 — 'Opportunities lost and gained: mechanisation and women's work in the London bookbinding and printing trades', in A. V. John, ed., *Unequal Opportunities: Women's Employment in England, 1800–1918* (1986), 71–94.

5.545 **John**, A. V., 'The Lancashire pit brow lasses', *N.W. Gp. Study Labour Hist.*, Bull. 3 (1976), 1–5.

5.546 — 'Colliery legislation and its consequences: 1842 and the women miners of Lancashire', *Bull. J. Ry. Lib.*, 61.1 (1978–9), 98–114.

5.547 — *By the Sweat of Their Brow: Women Workers at Victorian Coal Mines* (1980).

5.548 — 'Scratching the surface: women, work and coalmining in England and Wales', *Oral Hist.*, 10.2 (1982), 13–26.

5.549 **Jordan**, E., 'The exclusion of women from industry in nineteenth-century Britain', *Comp. Studs. Soc. and Hist.*, 31.2 (1989), 309–26. Complex view of role of trade unionists.

5.550 **Lambertz**, J., 'Sexual harassment in the nineteenth-century cotton industry', *Hist. Workshop J.*, 19 (1985), 29–61.

5.551 **Lazonick**, W., 'Industrial relations and technological change: the case of the self acting mule', *Cambridge J. Ec.*, 3.3 (1979), 231–62. Stimulating discussion of the importance of gender divisions and hierarchies in textiles for skill definitions and management strategies.

5.552 **Lown**, J., 'Not so much a factory, more a form of patriarchy: gender and class during industrialisation', in E. Gamarnikow, et al., eds., *Gender, Class and Work* (1983), 28–45. Case study of Courtauld silk weavers, Essex, to illustrate argument that 'the relignment of patriarchal interests' marginalised women's status at work.

5.553 — *Women and Industrialization: Gender at Work in Nineteenth-Century England* (Minneapolis, Minn., 1990). Uses the employment of factory workers at the Courtauld silk mill to examine the relationship between work and community and the importance of patriarchal relationships in shaping men's and women's experience of work.

5.554 **McBride**, T. M., 'The long road home: women's work and industrialisation', in R. Bridenthal and C. Koonz, eds., *Becoming Visible: Women in European History* (Boston, Mass., 1977), 280–95.

5.555 **McDougall**, M. L., 'Working-class women during the Industrial Revolution, 1780–1914', in R. Bridenthal and C. Koonz, eds., *Becoming Visible: Women in European History* (Boston, Mass., 1977), 257–79. Compares Britain and France.

5.556 **McKendrick**, N., 'Home demand and economic growth: a new view of the role of women and children in the Industrial Revolution', in N. McKendrick, ed., *Historical Perspectives: Studies in English Thought and Society* (1974), 152–201.

5.557 **Mark-Lawson**, J. and **Witz**, A., 'From "family labour" to "family wage"? The case of women's labour in nineteenth-century coal mining', *Soc. Hist.*, 13.2 (1988), 151–74.

5.558 **Messenger**, B., *Picking Up the Linen Threads: Life in Ulster's Mills* (Austin, Texas, 1978).

5.559 **Morris**, J., 'The characteristics of sweating: the late nineteenth century London and Leeds tailoring trade', in A. V. John, ed., *Unequal Opportunities: Women's Employment in England, 1800–1918* (1986), 94–121.

5.560 — *Women Workers and the Sweated Trades: The Origins of Minimum Wage Legislation* (1986).

5.561 **Osterud**, N. G., 'Gender divisions and the organisation of work in the Leicester hosiery industry', in A. V. John, ed., *Unequal Opportunities: Women's Employment in England, 1800–1918* (1986), 45–70.

5.562 — 'Gender relations and the process of capitalist industrialization', *Scy. Study of Labour Hist.*, Bull. 54 (1989), 10–12.

5.563 **Owen-Jones**, S., 'Women in the tinplate industry, Llanelli, 1930–1950', *Oral Hist.*, 15.1 (1987), 42–9.

5.564 **Parr**, J., 'Disaggregating the sexual division of labour: a transatlantic case study', *Comp. Studs. Soc. and Hist.*, 30.3 (1988), 511–33. Hosiery industry in East Midlands and S.W. Ontario.

5.565 **Pennington**, S. and **Westover**, B., *A Hidden Workforce. Homeworkers in England, 1850–1985* (1989). The authors use a wide variety of sources to explore this often 'invisible' and neglected work group.

5.566 **Pinchbeck**, I., *Women Workers in the Industrial Revolution* (1930). Classic early study. Suggests women's emancipation was linked to their occupational role.

5.567 **Powell**, C., ' "Widows and others" on Bristol building sites: some women in nineteenth-century construction', *Local Histn.*, 20.2 (1990), 84–7.

5.568 **Price**, K., 'What did you do in the war, mam? Women steelworkers at the Consett Iron Company during the Second World War', *N. E. Gp. Study Labour Hist.*, Bull. 20 (1986), 14–29.

5.569 **Reynolds**, S., *Britannica's Typesetters: Women Compositors in Edwardian Edinburgh* (1989).

5.570 **Riley**, D., 'The free mothers: pronatalism and working mothers in industry at the end of the last war in Britain', *Hist. Workshop J.*, 11 (1981), 59–118. Interesting discussion of the way in which war reinforced the marginality of married women's work rather than challenging it.

5.571 **Rose**, S. O., 'Gender segregation in the transition to the factory: the English hosiery industry, 1850–1910', *Fem. Studs.*, 13.1 (1987), 163–84.

5.572 — 'Proto industry, women's work and the household economy in the transition to industrial capitalism', *J. Fam. Hist.*, 13.2 (1988), 181–93. Study of a Nottingham-shire village, 1851–81.

5.573 **Sarsby**, J., *Missuses and Mouldrunners: An Oral History of Women Pottery Workers at Work and at Home* (1988).

5.574 **Savage**, M., 'Trade unionism, sex segregation and the state: women's employment in "new industries" in inter-war Britain', *Soc. Hist.*, 13.2 (1988), 209–30.

5.575 **Schmiechen**, J., *Sweated Industries and Sweated Labour* (1984).

5.576 **Smith**, H., 'The womanpower problem in Britain during the Second World War', *Hist. J.*, 27.4 (1984), 925–46.

5.577 **Summerfield**, P., 'Women workers in Britain in the Second World War', *Capital and Class*, 1, Spring (1977), 242–67.

5.578 — *Women Workers in the Second World War* (1984). Discusses the ambivalence of government policies towards the recruitment of female industrial workers and argues that by the end of the war women were still identified with the family.

5.579 **Thom**, D., 'Women at the Woolwich Arsenal, 1915–1919', *Oral Hist.*, 6.2 (1978), 58–74.

5.580 — 'Tommy's sister: women at Woolwich in World War I', in R. Samuel, ed., *Patriotism: The Making and Unmaking of a National Identity: Vol. 2. Minorities and Outsiders* (1989), 144–57.

5.581 **Thomas**, J., *A History of the Leeds Clothing Trade* (1955). Contains useful information on employment conditions of tailoresses.

5.582 **Tolley**, R. S., 'Female employment and local industrial development: a case study of the Coalbrookdale coalfield', *N. Staffs. J. Field Studs.*, 13 (1973), 67–82.

5.583 **Treble**, J. H., 'The characteristics of the female unskilled labour market and the formation of the female casual labour market in Glasgow, 1891–1914', *Scot. Ec. Soc. Hist.*, 6 (1986), 33–46.

5.584 **Walker**, W. M., *Juteopolis: Dundee and its Textile Workers, 1885–1923* (1979).

5.585 **Westover**, B., ' "To fill the kids' tummies": the life and work of Colchester tailoresses, 1880–1918', in L. Davidoff and B. Westover, eds., *Our Work, Our Lives, Our Words. Women's History and Women's Work* (Totowa, New Jersey, 1986), 54–75.

5.586 **Whipp**, R., 'Women and the social organisation of work in the Staffordshire pottery industry, 1900–1930', *Mid. Hist.*, 12 (1987), 103–21.

5.587 — 'Kinship, labour and enterprise: the Staffordshire pottery industry, 1890–1920', in P. Hudson and W. R. Lee, eds., *Women's Work and the Family Economy in Historical Perspective* (1990), 184–203.

5.588 — *Patterns of Labour: Work and Social Change in the Pottery Industry* (1990). Examines the relationship between work, family and home.

5.589 **Wightman**, C., *Black Country Working Women*, (1991).
See also: 5.204; 5.1417.

(iii) Agriculture

5.590 **Bourke**, J., 'Women and poultry in Ireland, 1891–1914', *Irish Hist. Studs.*, 25.9 (1987), 293–310.

5.591 — ' "The health caravan". Domestic education and female labour in rural Ireland, 1890–1914', *Eire-Ireland*, 24, Winter (1989), 7–20.

5.592 — 'Dairywomen and affectionate wives: women in the Irish dairy industry, 1890–1914', *Agric. H. R.*, 38.2 (1990), 149–65.

5.593 — 'Working women: the domestic labour market in rural Ireland, 1890–1914', *J. Interdis. Hist.*, 21.3 (1991), 479–99.

5.594 **Davidoff**, L., 'The role of gender in the "First Industrial Nation": agriculture in England, 1780–1850', in R. Crompton and M. Mann, eds., *Gender and Stratification* (1986), 190–213.

5.595 **Fredericks**, A., 'The creation of "women's work" in agriculture: the women's Land Army during World War I', *Insurgent Sociologist*, 12, Summer (1984), 33–40.

5.596 **Horn**, P., *The Rural World, 1750–1850* (1980). Contains information on women's work.

5.597 — 'Child workers in the Victorian countryside: the case of Northamptonshire', *Northamptonshire P. P.*, 7 (1985–6), 173–85.

5.598 — *Victorian Countrywomen* (1991).

5.599 **Hostettler**, E., 'Women's work in the nineteenth-century countryside', *Scy. Study Labour Hist.*, Bull. 33 (1976), 9–12.

5.600 — 'Gourlay Steell and the sexual division of labour', *Hist. Workshop J.*, 4 (1977), 95–101. Effects on women's agricultural work of introduction of the scythe.

5.601 — ' "Making do": domestic life among East Anglian labourers, 1890–1910', in L. Davidoff and B. Westover, eds., *Our Work, Our Lives, Our Words. Women's History and Women's Work* (Totowa, New Jersey, 1986), 36–53.

5.602 **King**, P., 'Customary rights and women's earnings: the importance of gleaning to the rural labouring poor, 1750–1850', *Ec. H. R.*, sec. ser., 44.3 (1991), 461–76.

5.603 **Kitteringham**, J., 'Country work girls in nineteenth-century England', in R. Samuel, ed., *Village Life and Labour* (1975), 73–138.

5.604 **Miller**, C. 'The hidden workforce: female field workers in Gloucestershire, 1870–1901', *South. Hist.*, 6 (1984), 139–59.

5.605 **Roberts**, M., 'Sickles and scythes. Women's work and men's work at harvest time', *Hist. Workshop J.*, 7 (1979), 3–29.

5.606 **Snell**, K. D. M., 'Agricultural seasonal unemployment: the standard of living and women's work in the South and East, 1690–1860', *Ec. H. R.*, sec. ser., 24.3 (1981), 407–37.

5.607 **Valenze**, D., 'The art of women and the business of men: women's work and the dairy industry, c. 1740–1840', *P. P.*, 130 (1991), 142–69.

(iv) Commerce

5.608 **Anderson**, G., ed., *The White Blouse Revolution: Female Office Workers since 1870* (1988).

5.609 **Clinton**, A., *Post Office Workers: A Trade Union and Social History* (1984).

5.610 **Davin**, A., 'Telegraphists and clerks', *Scy. Study Labour Hist.*, Bull. 26 (1973), 7–9.

5.611 **Davy**, C., ' "A cissy job for a man: a nice job for girls": women shorthand typists in London, 1900–39', in L. Davidoff and B. Westover, eds., *Our Work, Our Lives, Our Words. Women's History and Women's Work* (Totowa, New Jersey, 1986), 124–44.

5.612 **Dohrn**, S., 'Pioneers in a dead-end profession: the first women clerks in bank and insurance companies', in G. Anderson, ed., *The White Blouse Revolution: Female Office Workers since 1870* (1988), 48–66.

5.613 **Gardiner**, M., *The Other Side of the Counter: The Life of the Shop Girl, 1925–1945* (1985).

5.614 **Grint**, K., 'Women and equality: the acquisition of equal pay in the Post Office, 1870–1961', *Sociology*, 22.1 (1987), 87–108.

5.615 **Hall**, C., 'The butcher, the baker, the candlestickmaker: the shop and the family in the Industrial Revolution', in E. Whitelegg et al., eds., *The Changing Experience of Women* (1982), 2–16.

5.616 — 'Strains in the "firm of wife, children and friends"? Middle-class women and employment in early nineteenth-century England', in P. Hudson and W. R. Lee, eds., *Women's Work and the Family Economy in Historical Perspective* (1990), 106–31.

5.617 **Lewis**, J., 'Women clerical workers in the late nineteenth and early twentieth centuries', in G. Anderson, ed., *The White Blouse Revolution: Female Office Workers since 1870* (1988).

5.618 **Silverstone**, R., 'Office work for women: an historical review', *Business Hist.*, 18 (1976), 98–110.

5.619 **Whitaker**, W. B., *Victorian and Edwardian Shopworkers: The Struggle to Obtain Better Conditions and a Half Holiday* (1973).

5.620 **Zimmeck**, M., 'Jobs for the girls: the expansion of clerical work for women, 1850–1914', in A. V. John, ed., *Unequal Opportunities: Women's Employment in England, 1800–1918* (1986), 152–77.

(v) Professional

5.621 **Abel-Smith**, B., *A History of the Nursing Profession* (1960). Standard text on the development of the profession.

5.622 **Allen**, P. and **Jolley**, M., eds., *Nursing, Midwifery and Health Visiting since 1900* (1982).

5.623 **Amies**, M., 'The Victorian governess and colonial ideas of womanhood', *Vict. Studs.*, 31.4 (1988), 537–66.

5.624 **Baly**, M., *Florence Nightingale and the Nursing Legacy* (1986).

5.625 — *A History of the Queen's Institute: 100 Years, 1887–1987* (1987). An organisation which provided nurses for rural areas.

5.626 **Black**, L., 'Attitudes towards the female Victorian schoolteacher – some empirical evidence from Wiltshire', *Bull. Hist. Ed. Scy.*, 25 (1980), 40–5.

5.627 **Blake**, C., *The Charge of the Parasols. Women's Entry to the Medical Profession* (1990).

5.628 **Carpenter**, M., 'Asylum nursing before 1914: a chapter in the history of labour', in C. Davies, ed., *Re-writing Nursing History* (1980), 123–46.

5.629 **Carrier**, J., 'The control of women by women: the women police', *Scy. Study Labour Hist.*, Bull. 26 (1973), 16–19.

5.630 **Corr**, H., 'The sexual division of labour in the Scottish teaching profession', in W. M. Humes and H. M. Paterson, eds., *Scottish Culture and Scottish Education, 1800–1980* (1983), 137–50.

5.631 **Cowell**, B. and **Wainwright**, D., *Behind the Blue Door: The History of the Royal College of Midwives, 1881–1981* (1981).

5.632 **Creese**, M. P. S., 'British women of the nineteenth and early twentieth centuries who contributed to research in the chemical sciences', *Brit. J. Hist. Sc.*, 24 (1991), 275–306.

5.633 **Crosthwait**, E., ' "The girl behind the man behind the gun": the Women's Army Auxiliary Corps, 1914–1918', in L. Davidoff and B. Westover, eds., *Our Work, Our Lives, Our Words. Women's History and Women's Work* (Totowa, New Jersey, 1986), 161–81.

5.634 **Davies**, C., 'Making sense of the census in Britain and the U.S.A.: the changing occupational classification and the position of nurses', *Sociolog. R.*, 28 (1980), 581–609.

5.635 — ed., *Re-Writing Nursing History* (1980). Collection of articles challenging conventional approaches to nursing history.

5.636 **Dingwall**, R., **Rafferty**, A. M. and **Webster**, C., *An Introduction to the Social History of Nursing* (1988). Wide-ranging account drawing together recent scholarship.

5.637 **Donnison**, J., *Midwives and Medical Men: A History of Inter-Professional Rivalries and Women's Rights* (1977). Detailed account of the struggle of midwives for professional status and recognition.

5.638 **Elston**, M. E., *Women in the Medical Profession* (1987).

5.639 **Forbes**, T. R., 'The regulation of English midwives in the eighteenth and nineteenth centuries', *Medical Hist.*, 15.4 (1971), 352–62.

5.640 **Gamarnikow**, E., 'The sexual division of labour: the case of nursing', in A. Kuhn and A. M. Wolpe, eds., *Feminism and Materialism: Women and Modes of Production* (1978), 96–123. Suggests that doctors, nurses and patients emulated the father, mother, child relation in the family and relates this to the patriarchal division of labour.

5.641 **Hector**, W., *The Work of Mrs Bedford Fenwick and the Rise of Professional Nursing* (1973).

5.642 **Horn**, P., 'Mid-Victorian elementary school teachers', *Local Histn.*, 12.3 & 4 (1976), 161–6.

5.643 — 'Oxfordshire village schoolteachers, 1800–1880', *Cake and Cockhorse*, Autumn (1976), 3–18.

5.644 — 'The recruitment, role and status of the Victorian country teacher', *Hist. Ed.* 9.2 (1980), 129–41.

5.645 — 'Mary Dew (1845–1936) of Lower Heyford: a model Victorian teacher', *Cake and Cockhorse*, 9.4 (1983), 112–25.

5.646 — 'Country teachers in Victorian Oxfordshire', *Cake and Cockhorse*, 10.8 (1988), 202–12.

5.647 — 'The Victorian governess', *Hist. Ed.* 18 (1989), 333–44.

5.648 **Howsam**, L., ' "Sound minded women": Eliza Orme and the study and practice of law in late-Victorian England', *Atlantis*, 15, Fall (1989), 44–55.

5.649 **Jones**, H., 'Women health workers: the case of the first women factory inspectors in Britain', *Soc. Hist. Medicine*, 1 (1988), 165–81.

5.650 **McFeely**, M. D., 'The lady inspectors: women at work, 1893–1921', *Hist. Today*, 36, November (1986), 47–53. Uncritical account of the achievements of the early women inspectors.

5.651 — *Lady Inspectors: The Campaign for a Better Workplace, 1893–1921* (1988).

5.652 **Mackenzie**, C., 'Women and psychiatric professionalization, 1780–1914', in London Feminist History Group, ed., *The Sexual Dynamics of History* (1983), 107–19.

5.653 **Maggs**, C. J., 'Nurse recruitment to four provincial hospitals, 1881–1921', in C. Davies, ed., *Re-writing Nursing History* (1980), 18–40.

5.654 — *The Origins of General Nursing* (1983). Examines the criteria for recruitment and

training of nurses. Discusses contemporary images of the nurse.

5.655 **Manton**, J., *Elizabeth Garrett Anderson* (1965). First woman doctor to qualify in England.

5.656 **Marrett**, C. B., 'On the evolution of women's medical societies', *Bull. Hist. Medicine*, 53.3 (1979), 434–48.

5.657 **Martindale**, H., *Women Servants of the State, 1870–1938: A History of Women in the Civil Service* (1938). A survey of the entry of women to the civil service by an eye witness.

5.658 **Moore**, J., *A Zeal for Responsibility: The Struggle for Professional Nursing in Victorian England, 1868–1883* (Athens, Georgia, 1988). Examines battles between nurses, doctors and administrators in two London hospitals over the professional status of nurses.

5.659 **Oram**, A., 'Serving two masters? The introduction of a marriage bar in teaching in the 1920's', in London Feminist History Group, ed., *The Sexual Dynamics of History* (1983), 134–48.

5.660 — ' "Sex antagonism" in the teaching profession: the equal pay issue, 1914–29', *Hist. Ed. R* (Australia and New Zealand), 14 (1985), 36–48.

5.661 — 'Inequalities in the teaching profession: the effect on teachers and pupils, 1910–39', in F. Hunt, ed., *Lessons for Life: The Schooling of Girls and Women, 1850–1950* (1987), 101–23. Examines gender-based professional rivalry and the resistance of the NUWT to gender stereotyping in schools.

5.662 — 'A master should not serve under a mistress: women and men teachers, 1900–1970', in S. Acker, ed., *Teachers, Gender and Careers* (New York, 1989), 21–34.

5.663 **Parkin**, D., 'Women in the armed services, 1940–5', in R. Samuel, ed., *Patriotism: The Making and Unmaking of a National Identity. Vol. 2: Minorities and Outsiders* (1989), 158–70.

5.664 **Partington**, G., *Women Teachers in the 20th Century in England and Wales* (1976). A very useful narrative.

5.665 **Pederson**, J. S., 'Schoolmistresses and headmistresses: elites and education in nineteenth-century England', *J. Brit. Studs.*, 15.1 (1975), 135–62. Examines extent to which professional status gave new powers to women teachers.

5.666 **Purvis**, J., 'Women and teaching in the nineteenth century', in R. Dale et al., eds., *Education and the State: Politics Patriarchy and Practice Vol. 2* (1981), 359–75.

5.667 **Sanderson**, K., 'A pension to look forward to? Women civil servants in London, 1925–1939', in L. Davidoff and B. Westover, eds., *Our Work, Our Lives, Our Words. Women's History and Women's Work* (Totowa, New Jersey, 1986), 145–60.

5.668 **Simnett**, A., 'The pursuit of respectability: women and the nursing profession', in R. White, ed., *Political Issues in Nursing: Past, Present and Future Vol. 2* (1986), 1–23.

5.669 **Summers**, A., 'Pride and prejudice: ladies and nurses in the Crimean War', *Hist. Workshop J.*, 16 (1983), 33–56.

5.670 — *Angels and Citizens: British Women as Military Nurses, 1854–1914* (1988).

5.671 — 'The mysterious demise of Sarah Gamp: the domiciliary nurse and her detractors, *c.* 1830–1860', *Vict. Studs.*, 32.3 (1989), 365–86.

5.672 **Towler**, J. and **Bramall**, J., *Midwives in History and Society* (1986).

5.673 **Tropp**, A., *The School Teachers* (1957).

5.674 **White**, R., *Social Change and the Development of the Nursing Profession: A Study of the Poor Law Nursing Service, 1848–1948* (1978).

5.675 **Widdowson**, F., *Going Up into the Next Class. Women and Elementary Teacher Training* (1983). Interesting discussion of training and social origins of women teachers.

5.676 — ' "Educating teacher": women and elementary teaching in London, 1900–1914', in L. Davidoff and B. Westover, eds., *Our Work, Our Lives Our Words. Women's History and Women's Work* (Totowa, New Jersey, 1986), 99–123.

5.677 **Zimmeck**, M., 'Strategies and strategems for the employment of women in the British Civil Service, 1919–1939', *Hist. J.* 27.4 (1984), 901–24 .

See also: 5.299; 5.1346; 5.1352; 5.1354; 5.1366; 5.1369; 5.1394.

(vi) Domestic

5.678 **Davidoff**, L., 'Domestic service and the working-class lifestyle', *Scy. Study Labour Hist.*, Bull. 26 (1973), 10–13.

5.679 — 'Mastered for life: servant and wife in Victorian and Edwardian England', *J. Soc. Hist.*, 7.4 (1974), 406–28.

5.680 — 'The separation of home and work: landladies and lodgers in nineteenth and twentieth-century England', in S. Burman, ed., *Fit Work for Women* (1979), 64–97. Interesting discussion of a neglected method of earning income.

5.681 **Ebery**, M. and **Preston**, B., *Domestic Service in Late Victorian and Edwardian England, 1871–1914* (1976). The authors share Horn's view (5.692) that domestic service declined as other work opportunities increased.

5.682 **Franklin**, J., 'Troops of servants: labour and planning in the country house, 1840–1914', *Vict. Studs.*, 19.2 (1975), 211–39.

5.683 **Gathorne-Hardy**, J., *The Rise and Fall of the Victorian Nanny* (1972).

5.684 **Green**, J. A. S., 'A survey of domestic services', *Lincs. Hist. Arch.*, 17 (1982), 65–9.

5.685 **Harrison**, M., 'Domestic service between the wars: the experience of two rural women', *Oral Hist.*, 16.1 (1988), 48–52.

5.686 **Hearn**, M., 'Life for domestic servants in Dublin, 1880–1920', in M. Luddy and C. Murphy, eds., *Women Surviving: Studies in Irish Women's History in the Nineteenth and Twentieth Centuries* (Dublin, 1990), 148–79.

5.687 **Higgs**, E., 'The tabulation of occupations in the nineteenth-century census with special reference to domestic servants', *Local Pop. Studs.*, 28 (1982), 58–66. Excellent discussion of the difficulties and rewards of using census data for women's work.

5.688 — *Domestic Servants and Households in Rochdale, 1851–1871* (New York, 1986).

5.689 — 'Domestic service and household production', in A. V. John, ed., *Unequal Opportunities: Women's Employment in England, 1800–1920* (1986), 124–50.

5.690 — 'Domestic servants and households in Victorian England', *Soc. Hist*, 8.2 (1983), 201–10.

5.691 **Horn**, P., 'Domestic service in Northamptonshire, 1830–1914', *Northamptonshire P. P.*, 5.3 (1975), 267–75.

5.692 — *The Rise and Fall of the Victorian Servant* (Dublin, 1975). Argues domestic service declined as other work opportunities increased.

5.693 **Huggett**, F. E., *Life Below Stairs: Domestic Servants in England from Victorian Times* (1977).

5.694 **Kushner**, T., 'Asylum or servitude? Refugee domestics in Britain, 1933–1945', *Scy. Study Labour Hist.*, Bull. 53 (1988), 19–27.

5.695 — 'Politics and race, gender and class: refugees, fascists and domestic service in Britain, 1933–1940', *Immigrants and Minorities*, 8, March (1989), 49–60.

5.696 **McBride**, T., *The Domestic Revolution: The Modernisation of Household Service in England and France, 1820–1920* (1976). Argues domestic service was a means by which rural female labour was modernised.

5.697 — ' "As the twig is bent": the Victorian nanny', in A. S. Wohl, ed., *The Victorian Family* (1978), 44–58. Argues that the experience of domestic service had an impact on subsequent marriages.

5.698 **Malcolmson**, P. E., 'Laundresses and the laundry trade in Victorian England', *Vict. Studs.*, 24, Summer (1981), 439–62.

5.699 — *English Laundresses: A Social History, 1850–1930* (Chicago, Illinois, 1986).

5.700 **Peterson**, M. J., 'The Victorian governess: status incongruence in family and society', in M. Vicinus, ed., *Suffer and Be Still: Women in the Victorian Age* (Bloomington, Indiana, 1972), 3–19. Social origins of governesses gave rise to their 'status ambiguity' in middle-class households.

5.701 **Taylor**, P., 'Mothers and daughters – maids and mistresses: domestic service between the wars', in J. Clarke, C. Critchens and R. Johnson, eds., *Working-Class Culture: Studies in History and Theory* (1979), 121–39.

See also: 5.1161.

(h) WOMEN AND THE WIDER WORLD

(i) Women travellers and emigrants

5.702 **Barber**, M., 'The "women Ontario welcomed": immigrant domestics for Ontario homes, 1870–1930', *Ontario Hist.*, 72.3 (1980), 148–72.

5.703 **Barr**, P., *A Curious Life for a Lady: The Story of Isabella Bird Bishop* (1970). Fellow of the Royal Geographical Society.

5.704 **Birkett**, D., *Spinsters Abroad: Victorian Lady Explorers* (1989). Uses collective biography to explore common patterns and meanings in the lives of women travellers.

5.705 — 'Mary Kingsley and West Africa', in G. Marsden, ed., *Victorian Values, Personalities and Perspectives in Nineteenth-Century Society* (1990), 171–86.

5.706 — *Mary Kingsley* (1992). Analyses complexities of a Victorian female traveller's ideas about women, race and politics.

5.707 **Blake**, S. L., 'A woman's trek: what difference does gender make?', *Women's Studs. Int. For.* 13.4 (1990), 347–55. Argues that representations of the relationship between traveller and Africans are tied to gender.

5.708 **Blakeley**, B. L., 'The Society for Oversea Settlement of British women and the problem of empire settlement, 1917–1936', *Albion*, 20.3 (1988), 421–44.

5.709 **Buckley**, S., 'British female emigration and imperial development: experiments in Canada, 1885–1931', *Hecate*, 3.2 (1977), 26–40.

5.710 **Diner**, H., *Erin's Daughters in America: Irish Immigrant Women in the Nineteenth Century* (1983).

5.711 **Erickson**, C., *English Women Immigrants in America in the Nineteenth Century: Expectations and Reality* (1983).

5.712 **Fitzpatrick**, D., 'A share of the honeycomb: education, emigration and Irishwomen', *Cont. and Change*, 1.2 (1986), 217–34.

5.713 **Flint**, J., 'Mary Kingsley – a re-assessment', *J. African Hist.*, 4 (1963), 95–104.

5.714 — 'Mary Kingsley', *African Affairs*, 64 (1965), 49–57.

5.715 **Frank**, K., 'Voyages out: nineteenth-century women travellers in Africa', in J. Sharistanian, ed., *Gender, Ideology and Action: Historical Perspectives on Women's Public Lives* (Westport, Conn., 1986), 67–93.

5.716 — *A Voyage Out: The Life of Mary Kingsley* (Boston, Mass., 1986). Sensitive biography of a woman who, through travel, became independent and involved in imperialist politics.

5.717 Hammerton, A. J., *Emigrant Gentlewomen: Genteel Poverty and Female Emigration, 1830–1919* (1979). A study of government and philanthropic emigration projects which suggests that middle-class women were adaptable to life in the colonies.

5.718 — ' "Without natural protectors": female immigration to Australia, 1832–1836', *Hist. Studs.*, 16.65 (1975), 539–66. Examines the origins of hostile attitudes to the emigration of single women.

5.719 Irwin, L., 'Women convicts from Dublin', in B. Reece, ed., *Irish Convicts: The Origins of Convicts Transported to Australia* (Dublin, 1989).

5.720 Jackson, P., 'Women in nineteenth-century Irish emigration', *Int. Migration R.*, 18.4 (1984), 1004–20.

5.721 Kneller, P., 'Welsh immigrant women as wage earners in Utica, New York, 1860–70', *Llafur*, 5.4 (1991), 71–8.

5.722 MacDonald, C., 'Ellen Silk and her sisters: female emigration to the New World', in London Feminist History Group, eds., *The Sexual Dynamics of History* (1983), 66–86.

5.723 Middleton, D., 'Some Victorian lady travellers', *Geographical J.*, 139 (1973), 65–75.

5.724 Mills, S., *Discourses of Difference: An Analysis of Women's Travel Writing and Colonialism* (1991).

5.725 Mooney, B., 'Women convicts from Wexford and Waterford', in B. Reece, ed., *Irish Convicts: The Origins of Convicts Transported to Australia* (Dublin, 1989).

5.726 Nolan, J., *Ourselves Alone: Women's Emigration from Ireland, 1885–1920* (Lexington, Virginia, 1989). Covers emigration to North America.

5.727 O'Carroll, I., *Models for Movers: Irish Women's Emigration to America* (Dublin, 1990).

5.728 Price, A. W., *The Ladies of Castlebrae: A Story of Nineteenth Century Travel and Research* (1985). A study of Agnes Lewis and Margaret Gibson, nineteenth-century biblical scholars.

5.729 Robinson, J., *Wayward Women: A Guide to Women Travellers* (1990).

5.730 Robinson, P., 'From Colleen to Matilda: Irish women convicts in Australia, 1788–1828', in C. Kiernan, ed., *Australia and Ireland: Bicentennial Essays* (Dublin, 1986), 96–111.

5.731 — *The Women of Botany Bay* (Macquarie, Australia, 1988). Irish female emigrants to Australia.

5.732 Rudd, J., 'Invisible exports: the emigration of Irish women this century', *Women's Studs. Int. For.*, 11.4 (1988), 307–12.

5.733 Russell, M., *The Blessings of a Good Thick Skirt: Women Travellers and Their World* (1986).

5.734 Stevenson, C., *Victorian Women Travel Writers in Africa* (Boston, Mass., 1982).

5.735 — 'Female anger and African politics: the case of two Victorian "lady travellers" ', *Turn of the Century Woman*, 2.1 (1985), 7–17.

5.736 Tinling, M., *Women in the Unknown: A Sourcebook on Women Explorers and Travellers* (New York, 1989). Includes material on Isabella Bird Bishop, 1831–1904, fellow of the Royal Geographical Society.

5.737 Tucker, J. E., 'Travelling with the ladies: women's travel literature from the nineteenth-century Middle East', *J. Women's Hist.*, 2 (1990), 245–50. On the writings of Lucy Duff Gordon and Mary Eliza Rogers.

5.738 Van Helton, J. J. and **Williams**, K., 'The crying need of South Africa: the emigration of single British women to the Transvaal, 1901–1910', *J. Southern African Studs.*, 10.1 (1983), 17–38.

5.739 Wheelwright, J., *Amazons and Military Maids: Women Who Dressed As Men in Pursuit of Life, Liberty and Happiness* (1989).

5.740 Williams, J., 'Irish female convicts and Tasmania', *Labour Hist.*, 44, May (1983), 1–17.

5.741 Winstone, H. V. F., *Gertrude Bell* (1980). Biography of a woman traveller (1868–1926) who was also a mountaineer, diplomat, historian and scholar.

See also: 5.1480; 5.1591.

(ii) Women and empire

5.742 Balhatchett, K., *Race, Sex and Class Under the Raj: Imperial Attitudes and Politics, 1793–1905* (1980). Suggests colonial women increased social distance between coloniser and colonised and worsened race relations.

5.743 **Barash**, C., 'Virile womanhood: Olive Schreiner's narratives of a master race', *Women's Studs. Int. For.*, 9.4 (1986), 333–40. Argues Schreiner used myths of transcultural motherhood to mediate between the conflicts arising from her affinities with both colonial rulers and the colonised in South Africa.

5.744 **Barr**, P., *The Memsahibs: The Women of Victorian India* (1976).

5.745 **Birkett**, D., 'The "white woman's burden" in the "white man's grave": the introduction of British nurses in colonial West Africa', in N. Chaudhuri and M. Strobel, eds., *Western Women and Imperialism: Complexity and Resistance* (Bloomington, Indiana, 1992), 176–88.

5.746 **Blakeley**, B. L., 'Women and imperialism: the Colonial Office and female emigration to South Africa, 1901–1910', *Albion*, 13, Summer (1981), 131–49.

5.747 **Boosquet**, B. and **Douglas**, C., *West Indian Women at War: British Racism in World War 2* (1991).

5.748 **Burton**, A. M., 'The white woman's burden: British feminists and the Indian woman, 1865–1915', *Women's Studs. Int. For.*, 13.4 (1990), 295–308. Reviews periodical literature and argues that British feminists constructed the image of a helpless Indian womanhood.

5.749 — 'The feminist quest for identity: British imperial suffragism and "global sisterhood", 1900–1915', *J. Women's Hist.*, 3.2 (1991), 46–81.

5.750 **Callaway**, H., *Gender, Culture and Empire: European Women in Colonial Nigeria* (1987).

5.751 — and **Helly**, D. O., 'Crusader for empire. Flora Shaw/Lady Lugard', in N. Chaudhuri and M. Strobel, eds., *Western Women and Imperialism: Complicity and Resistance* (Bloomington, Indiana, 1992), 79–97.

5.752 **Chaudhuri**, N., 'Memsahibs and motherhood in nineteenth-century colonial India', *Vict. Studs.*, 31.4 (1988), 517–36.

5.753 — 'Shawls, jewelry, curry and rice in Victorian Britain', in N. Chaudhuri and M. Strobel, eds., *Western Women and Imperialism: Complicity and Resistance* (Bloomington, Indiana, 1992), 232–46.

5.754 — and **Strobel**, M., *Western Women and Imperialism: Complicity and Resistance* (Bloomington, Indiana, 1992).

5.755 **Dagmar**, E., 'Age of Consent Act of 1891: colonial ideology in Bengal', *South Africa Research*, 3.2 (1983), 107–34.

5.756 **Davin**, D., 'British women missionaries in nineteenth-century China', *Women's H. R.*, 1.2 (1992), 257–72.

5.757 **Engels**, D., 'The limits of gender ideology, Bengali women, the colonial state and the private sphere, 1890–1920', *Women's Studs. Int. For.*, 12.4 (1989), 425–37.

5.758 **Ferguson**, M., *Subject to Others: British Women Writers and Colonial Slavery, 1670–1934* (1992).

5.759 **Forbes**, G. H., 'In search of the "pure heathen". Missionary women in nineteenth-century India', *Ec. Pol. Weekly*, 21, April (1986), ws2–ws8.

5.760 **Fowler**, M., *Below the Peacock Fan: First Ladies of the Raj* (1987). Portraits of four women and their complex reactions to representing Britain in India.

5.761 **Gertzel**, C., 'Margery Perham's image of Africa', *J. Imp. Commonwealth Hist.*, 19.3 (1981), 27–44.

5.762 **Haggis**, J., 'Gendering colonialism or colonising gender? Recent women's studies approaches to white women and the history of British colonialism', *Women's Studs. Int. For.*, 13, 1/2 (1990), 105–16.

5.763 **Hatem**, M., 'Through each other's eyes: the impact on the colonial encounter of the images of Egyptian, Levantine-Egyptian and European women, 1862–1920' in N. Chaudhuri and M. Strobel, eds., *Western Women and Imperialism: Complicity and Resistance* (Bloomington, Indiana, 1992), 35–58.

5.764 **Hyam**, R., 'Empire and sexual opportunity', *J. Imp. Commonwealth Hist.*, 1.2 (1986), 34–90.

5.765 — *Empire and Sexuality: The British Experience* (1990).

5.766 **Jacobs**, S. M., 'Give a thought to Africa: black women missionaries in Southern Africa', in N. Chaudhuri and M. Strobel, eds., *Women and Imperialism: Complicity and Resistance* (Bloomington, Indiana, 1992), 206–28.

5.767 **Jayaweera**, S., 'European women educators under the British colonial administration in Sri Lanka', *Women's Studs. Int. For.*, 13. 4 (1990), 323–32.

5.768 **Jolly**, M., ' "To save the girls for brighter and better lives": presbyterian missions and women in the south of Vanuatu, 1848–70', *J. Pacific Hist.*, 26 (1991), 27–48.

5.769 **Kirk-Greene**, A., 'Forging a relationship with the colonial administrative service, 1921–1939', *J. Imp. Commonwealth Hist.*, 19.3 (1981), 62–82. The subject is Margery Perham.

5.770 **Knapman**, C., *White Women in Fiji, 1835–1930. The Ruin of Empire?* (1986). Interesting analysis of the memsahib stereotype.

5.771 **Krebs**, P., ' "The last of the gentlemen's wars"? Women in the Boer War concentration camp controversy', *Hist. Workshop J.*, 33 (1992), 38–56.

5.772 **Krishna**, L, 'Mary Carpenter and the early crisis in teacher training for women in Calcutta', in R. L. Park, ed., *Patterns for Change in Modern Bengal* (East Lansing, Mich, 1979), 19–47.

5.773 **Lavin**, D., 'Margery Perham's initiation into African affairs', *J. Imp. Commonwealth Hist.*, 19.3 (1981), 45–61.

5.774 **Lind**, M. A., *The Compassionate Memsahibs. Welfare Activities of British Women in India, 1900–47* (Westport, Conn., 1988).

5.775 **MacMillan**, M., *Women of the Raj* (1988). Descriptive account of the experience of the memsahib.

5.776 **Maskiell**, M., 'Gender, kinship and rural work in colonial Punjab', *J. Women's Hist.*, 2 (1990), 35–71.

5.777 **Meyer**, S. L., 'Colonialism and the figurative strategy of *Jane Eyre*', *Vict. Studs.*, 33.2 (1990), 247–68.

5.778 **Mortimer**, J. S., 'Annie Besant and India, 1913–1917', *J. Contemp. Hist.*, 18.1 (1983), 61–78.

5.779 **Nair**, J., 'Uncovering the zenana: visions of Indian womanhood in English women's writings, 1813–1940', *J. Women's Hist.*, 2.1 (1990), 8–34.

5.780 **Oliver**, C., *Western Women in Colonial Africa* (Westport, Conn., 1982).

5.781 **Oliver**, R., 'Prologue: the two Miss Perhams', *J. Imp. Commonwealth Hist.*, 19.3 (1981), 21–6. Discusses the career of a woman who became the best-known figure in the study of colonial administration in Africa from the 1930s to the 1960s.

5.782 **Paxton**, N. L., 'Feminism under the Raj: complicity and resistance in the writings of Flora Annie Steel and Annie Besant', *Women's Studs. Int. For.*, 13.4 (1990), 333–46. Examines the autobiographical writings of two women to see how living in India under the Raj shaped their analysis of race, class, power and feminism.

5.783 **Porter**, A., 'Margery Perham, Christian missions and indirect rule', *J. Imp. Commonwealth Hist.*, 19.3 (1981), 83–100.

5.784 **Powell**, V., *Flora Annie Steel: Novelist of India* (1981).

5.785 **Ramusack**, B. N., 'Catalysts or helpers? British feminists, Indian women's rights and Indian independence', in G. Minault, ed., *The Extended family: Women and Political Participation in India and Pakistan* (Columbia, 1981), 109–50.

5.786 — 'Women's organisations and social change: the age of marriage issue in India', in N. Black and A. B. Cottrell, eds., *Women and World Change: Equity Issues in Development* (Beverley Hills, California, 1981), 198–216.

5.787 — 'Cultural missionaries, maternal imperialists, feminist allies: British woman activists in India, 1865–1945', *Women's Studs. Int. For.*, 13.4 (1990), 309–21. Discusses five women from outside the formal imperial establishment who had a concern for the conditions of Indian women and sought to promote social reforms.

5.788 **Rickard**, J., 'The anti-sweating movement in Britain and Victoria: the politics of empire and social reform', *Hist. Studs.*, 18.73 (1979), 582–97. Case study of the connections between radicalism, imperialism, social reform and women reformers.

5.789 **Roberts**, B., 'A work of empire: Canadian reformers and British female immigration', in L. Kealey, ed., *A Not Unreasonable Claim* (Toronto, 1979), 185–201.

5.790 **Robinson**, K., 'Margery Perham and the Colonial office', *J. Imp. Commonwealth Hist.*, 19.3 (1981), 185–96.

5.791 **Sinha**, M., 'Gender and imperialism: colonial policy and the ideology of moral imperialism in late nineteenth-century Bengal', in M. S. Kimmel, ed., *Changing Men: New Directions in Research on Men and Masculinity* (Beverly Hills, California, 1987).

5.792 — ' "Chathams, Pitts and Gladstones in petticoats": the politics of gender and race in the Ilbert Bill controversy, 1883–84', in N. Chaudhuri and M. Strobel, eds., *Western Women and Imperialism: Complicity and Resistance* (Bloomington, Indiana, 1992), 35–58.

5.793 **Spies**, S. B., 'Women and War', in P.

Warwick, ed., *The South African War: The Anglo Boer War, 1899–1902* (1980), 161–85.

5.794 **Strobel**, M., *European Women and the Second British Empire* (Bloomington, Indiana, 1991).

5.795 **Tranberg Hansen**, K., 'White women in a changing world. Employment, voluntary work and sex in post World War II Northern Rhodesia', in N. Chaudhuri and M. Strobel, eds., *Western Women and Imperialism: Complicity and Resistance* (Bloomington, Indiana, 1992), 247–68.
See also: 5.1028; 5.1062; 5.1063.

(i) WOMEN, POLITICS AND POWER

(i) General

5.796 **Arnstein**, W. L., 'Queen Victoria opens Parliament: the disinvention of tradition', *Hist. Res.*, 63 (1990), 178–94.

5.797 **Brennan**, T. and **Pateman**, C., ' "Mere auxiliaries to the commonwealth": women and the origins of Liberalism', *Pol. Studs.*, 27 (1979), 183–200.

5.798 **Brookes**, P., *Women at Westminster: An Account of Women in the British Parliament, 1918–1966* (1967).

5.799 **Campbell**, B., *The Iron Ladies: Why Do Women Vote Tory?* (1987).

5.800 **Clancy**, M., 'Aspects of women's contribution to the Oireachtas debate in the Free State, 1922–37', in M. Luddy and C. Murphy, eds., *Women Surviving: Studies in Irish Women's History in the Nineteenth and Twentieth Centuries* (Dublin, 1990), 206–32.

5.801 **Clark**, A., 'Queen Caroline and the sexual politics of popular culture in London, 1820', *Representations*, 31 (1990), 47–68.

5.802 **Currell**, M., *Political Woman* (1974). Early chapters discuss women's role in Parliament since 1918.

5.803 **Durham**, M., 'Women and the British Union of Fascists, 1932–1940', *Immigrants and Minorities*, 8 (1989), 3–18.

5.804 **Frow**, E. and **Frow**, R., eds., *Political*

Women, 1800–1850 (1989).

5.805 **Harrison**, B. H., 'Women in a men's house: the women MPs, 1919–1945', *Hist. J.*, 29.3 (1986), 623–54.

5.806 **Hirshfield**, C., 'Liberal women's organisations and the war against the Boers, 1899–1902', *Albion*, 14.1 (1982), 27–49.

5.807 **Hollis**, P., *Ladies Elect: Women in English Local Government, 1865–1914* (1987). Thorough analysis of a neglected sphere of women's involvement in politics.

5.808 — 'Women in council: separate spheres, public space', in J. Rendall, ed., *Equal or Different? Women's Politics, 1800–1914* (1987), 192–213. Suggests that the ideology of separate spheres could be used in both conservative and radical ways by women involved in local government.

5.809 **Kent**, S. S., 'Interrogating women's politics', *Gend. and Hist.*, 4, 2 (1992), 248–55.

5.810 **Laqueur**, T. W., 'The Queen Caroline affair: politics as art in the reign of George IV', *J. Mod. Hist.*, 54.3 (1982), 417–66.

5.811 **Longford**, E., *Victoria R.I.* (1965). Best one-volume biography.

5.812 **McCrone**, K., 'The National Association for the Promotion of Social Science and the advancement of Victorian women', *Atlantis*, 8 (1982), 44–66.

5.813 **MacCurtain**, M., 'Women, the vote and revolution', in M. MacCurtain and D. Ó'Corráin, eds., *Women in Irish Society: The Historical Dimension* (Dublin, 1978), 46–57. Politicisation of Irish women from 1867. Nationalism tended to overshadow women's equal rights.

5.814 **Manning**, M., 'Women in Irish national and local politics, 1922–77', in M. MacCurtain and D. Ó'Corráin, eds., *Women in Irish Society: The Historical Dimension* (Dublin, 1978), 92–102.

5.815 **Norris**, P., 'Gender differences in political participation in Britain: traditional, radical and revisionist models', *Govern. and Opp.*, 26.1 (1991), 56–74.

5.816 **Pugh**, E. L., 'The first woman candidate for Parliament: Helen Taylor and the election of 1885', *Int. J. Women's Studs.*, 1 (1978), 378–90.

5.817 **Randall**, V., *Women and Politics* (1982). Covers the period 1850–1980.

5.818 **Rendall**, J., ed., *Equal or Different? Women's Politics, 1800–1914,* (1987). Collection of articles on different aspects of women's involvement in politics.

5.819 **Rowbotham**, S., *Women, Resistance and Revolution* (1972). Wide-ranging discussion of the relationship between feminism and revolutionary movements in the past.

5.820 — *Woman's Consciousness, Man's World* (1973). Examines the development of a feminist consciousness and the position of women within the capitalist state, showing how the family and sexuality reflect and influence other aspects of social and economic life.

5.821 **Schneer**, J., 'Politics and feminism in "Outcast London": George Lansbury and Jane Cobden's campaign for the first London County Council', *J. Brit. Studs.*, 30, January (1991), 63–82.

5.822 **Sheppard**, M., 'The effects of the franchise provisions on the social and sex composition of the municipal electorate, 1882–1914', *Scy. Study Labour Hist.*, Bull. 44 (1982), 19–25.

5.823 **Shiman**, L. L., *Women and Leadership in Nineteenth-Century England* (1992). Focuses on women evangelicals, temperance and political action.

5.824 **Turnbull**, A., ' "So extremely like Parliament": the work of the women members of the London School Board, 1870–1904', in London Feminist History Group, ed., *The Sexual Dynamics of History* (1983), 120–33.

5.825 **Van Arsdel**, R. T., 'Victorian periodicals yield their secrets: Florence Fenwick Miller's three campaigns for the London School Board', *Hist. Ed. Scy. Bull.*, 38, Autumn (1986), 26–42.

5.826 **Walker**, L., 'Party political women: a comparative study of Liberal women and the Primrose League, 1890–1914', in J. Rendall, ed., *Equal or Different? Women's Politics, 1800–1914* (1987), 165–91.

5.827 **Webb**, R. K., *Harriet Martineau: A Radical Victorian* (1960).

See also: 5.694; 5.695; 5.771; 5.793; 5.1332; 5.1406.

(ii) Women and protest

5.828 **Alexander**, S., 'Women, class and sexual difference', *Hist. Workshop J.*, 17 (1984), 125–49. Stimulating discussion of women and radical politics, using psychoanalytic theory.

5.829 **Billington**, L. and Billington, R., ' "A burning zeal for righteousness": women in the British anti-slavery movement, 1820–1860', in J. Rendall, ed., *Equal or Different? Women's Politics, 1800–1914* (1987), 82–111. Explore the complex relationship between women's involvement in anti-slavery campaigns and the development of a women's movement.

5.830 **Bohstedt**, J., 'Gender, household and community politics: women in English riots, 1790–1810', *P. P.*, 120 (1988), 88–122.

5.831 **Cook**, J., *Radical Women in History* (1985).

5.832 **Cote**, J. M., *Anna and Fanny Parnell: Ireland's Patriot Sisters* (Dublin, 1991). The Parnells were leading members of the Ladies' Land League.

5.833 **Haverty**, A., *Constance Markievicz: An Independent Life* (1988). Biography of an Irish nationalist, feminist and supporter of the labour movement.

5.834 **Jones**, M., *A Radical Life. The Biography of Megan Lloyd George, 1902–66* (1991). A Liberal MP who became a Labour MP.

5.835 **Jones**, R. A. N., 'Women, community and collective action: the Ceffyl Pren tradition', in A. V. John, ed., *Our Mothers' Land: Chapters in Welsh Women's History, 1830–1939* (1991), 17–41.

5.836 **Kennon**, D. R., ' "An apple of discord": the woman question at the World's Anti-Slavery Convention of 1840', *Slavery and Abolition*, 5.3 (1984), 244–66.

5.837 **Malmgreen**, G., 'Anne Knight and the radical sub-culture', *Quaker Hist.*, 71, Fall (1982), 100–13. Anti-slavery activist who wrote an early pamphlet in favour of women's suffrage.

5.838 **Midgley**, C., *Women Against Slavery: The British Campaigns, 1780–1870* (1992). Important new study which emphasises the gendered nature of the anti-slavery campaign and women's distinct approach to the issue. Detailed analysis of the relationship between anti-slavery and the development of a women's movement.

5.839 **Moody**, T. W., 'Anna Parnell and the Land League', *Hermathena*, 118, Summer (1974), 5–17.

5.840 **Norman**, D., *Terrible Beauty: A Life of Constance Markievicz* (1987).

5.841 **O'Neill**, M., 'The Ladies' Land League', *Dublin Hist. Rec.*, 25.4 (1982), 122–33.

5.842 **Sklar**, K. K., ' "Women who speak for an entire nation": American and British women compared at the World Anti-Slavery Convention, London 1840', *Pacific H. R.* (1990), 453–99.

5.843 **Taylor**, C., *British and American Abolitionists: An Episode in Transatlantic Understanding* (1974). Letters from abolitionists with an introduction which draws together the secondary literature.

5.844 **Tebrake**, J. K., 'Irish peasant women in revolt: the Land League years', *Irish Hist. Studs.*, 28.109 (1992), 63–80. Agrarian protest movement 1879–82. Participation of rural women as protestors against evictions.

5.845 **Thomis**, M. and **Grimmett**, J., *Women in Protest, 1800–1850* (1982). Cover a variety of early protest movements including Chartism.

5.846 **Thompson**, E. P., 'The moral economy of the English crowd in the eighteenth century', *P. P.*, 50 (1971), 71–136. An early attempt to view women as active in political protest. Suggests resistance must be seen as complex and that it contributed to a new definition of women's power.

5.847 **Tyrrell**, A., ' "Women's mission" and pressure group politics in Britain, 1825–60', *Bull. J. Ryl. Lib.*, 63 (1980), 194–230.

5.848 **Walvin**, J., ed., *Slavery and British Society, 1776–1846* (1982). One of the first studies to emphasise women's involvement in the British abolitionist movement.

5.849 **Ward**, M., 'The Ladies' Land League', *Irish Hist. Workshop*, 1 (1981), 27–35.

5.850 — *Maud Gonne, Ireland's Joan of Arc* (1990). Biography of a leading Irish nationalist and feminist.

5.851 **Young**, J., *Women and Popular Struggles: A History of British Working-Class Women, 1500–1927* (1985).

See also: 5.1280.

(iii) Feminism

5.852 **Black**, N., 'Virginia Woolf: the life of natural happiness, 1882–1941', in D. Spender, ed., *Feminist Theorists: Three Centuries of Women's Intellectual Traditions* (1983), 296–313. Examines Woolf's feminist ideas.

5.853 **Bock**, G. and **James**, S., eds., *Beyond Equality and Difference: Citizenship, Feminist Politics and Female Subjectivity* (1992).

5.854 **Caine**, B., 'Women's natural state: marriage and the nineteenth-century feminists', *Hecate*, 3.2 (1977).

5.855 — 'Beatrice Webb and the Woman Question', *Hist. Workshop J.*, 14 (1982), 23–43. A re-assessment of Webb's attitudes towards the women's movement.

5.856 **Copelman**, D. M., 'Masculine faculty, women's temperament: Victorian women's quest for work and personal fulfillment', *Fem. Studs.*, 13.1 (1987), 185–201.

5.857 **Cullen**, C., 'How radical was Irish feminism between 1860 and 1920?', in P. J. Corish, ed., *Radicals, Rebels and Establishments: Historical Studies, V* (1985), 185–206.

5.858 **Dyhouse**, C., *Feminism and the Family in England, 1880–1939* (1989). Examines feminist ideas about the family, emphasising class differences.

5.859 **Gorham**, D., ' "Have we really rounded seraglio point?" Vera Brittain and inter-war feminism', in H. L. Smith, ed., *British Feminism in the Twentieth Century* (1990), 84–103. Explores Brittain's feminist ideas.

5.860 **Grylls**, R. G., 'Emancipation of women', in H. Grisewood, ed., *Ideas and Beliefs of the Victorians* (New York, 1966), 254–60.

5.861 **Kent**, S. K., 'Gender reconstruction after the First World War', in H. L. Smith, ed., *British Feminism in the Twentieth Century* (1990), 66–83. Argues feminists abandoned pre-war radical critiques of gender and sexuality.

5.862 **Levine**, P., 'Love, friendship and feminism in later nineteenth-century England', *Women's Studs. Int. For.*, 13, 1/2 (1990), 63–78. Examines the importance of friendship networks for understanding how a feminist culture was created. Argues for the need to redefine the meaning of the word 'politics'.

5.863 — ' "The humanising influences of five o'clock tea": Victorian feminist periodicals', *Vict. Studs.*, 33.2 (1990), 293–306.

5.864 **Maynard**, M., 'Privilege and patriarchy: feminist thought in the nineteenth century', in S. Mendus and J. Rendall, eds., *Sexuality and Subordination: Interdisciplinary Studies of Gender in the Nineteenth Century* (1989), 221–47.

5.865 **McKillen**, B., 'Irish feminism and national separatism, 1914–23', *Eire-Ireland*, 18.3 (1981), 122–33.

5.866 **Mitchell**, J., 'Feminism and femininity at

the turn of the century', in J. Mitchell, ed., *Women: The Longest Revolution. Essays on Feminism, Literature and Psychoanalysis* (1984).

5.867 **Mullin**, M., 'Representations of history, Irish feminism and the politics of difference', *Fem. Studs.*, 17.1 (1991), 29–50.

5.868 **Murray**, J. H., *Strong Minded Women and Other Lost Voices from Nineteenth-Century England* (New York, 1982).

5.869 **Rosenberg**, R., *Beyond Separate Spheres: The Intellectual Roots of Modern Feminism* (New Haven, Conn., 1982).

5.870 **Rossi**, A. S., *Essays on John Stuart Mill and Harriet Taylor Mill* (Chicago, Illinois, 1970).

5.871 — *The Feminist Papers: From Adams to De Beauvoir* (New York, 1974). Contains extracts from feminist writings with a commentary.

5.872 **Rover**, C., *Love, Morals and the Feminists* (1970). Emphasises the conservatism of feminist ideas about the family and sexuality.

5.873 **Spender**, D., 'Modern feminist theorists: reinventing rebellion', in D. Spender, ed., *Feminist Theorists: Three Centuries of Women's Intellectual Traditions* (1983), 366–80.

5.874 — *Time and Tide Wait for No Man* (1984). Contains biographical material on women who wrote for *Time and Tide* with extracts from the periodical in the 1920s.

5.875 — ed., *Feminist Theorists: Three Centuries of Women's Intellectual Traditions* (1983). Articles offering a fresh interpretation of the work and ideas of leading feminist thinkers.

5.876 **Stanley**, L., 'Olive Schreiner: new women, free women, all women, 1855–1920', in D. Spender, ed., *Feminist Theorists: Three Centuries of Women's Intellectual Traditions* (1983), 229–43. A fresh interpretation of Schreiner's life, raising methodological questions about the writing of feminist biography.

5.877 **Strauss**, S., '*Traitors to the Masculine Cause': The Men's Campaigns for Women's Rights* (Westport, Conn., 1982).

See also: 5.1272; 5.1300; 5.1339.

(iv) The women's movement

5.878 **Alberti**, J., *Beyond Suffrage: Feminists in War and Peace, 1914–28* (1989). A study of fourteen feminists active in politics in the 1920s and their different perspectives.

5.879 — 'Inside out: Elizabeth Haldane as a women's survivor in the 1920s and 1930s', *Women's Studs. Int. For.*, 13, 1/2 (1990), 117–25.

5.880 **Alexander**, S., ed., *Studies in the History of Feminism, 1850s-1930s* (1984).

5.881 **Anderson**, N. F., *Women Against Women in Victorian England: A Life of Eliza Lynn Linton* (Chicago, Illinois, 1987).

5.882 **Bailey**, H., *Vera Brittain* (1987). Biography of the feminist pacifist writer and activist, 1893–1970.

5.883 **Banks**, O., *Faces of Feminism: Study of Feminism as a Social Movement* (1981). Suggests that feminism encompassed three different ideologies and traces links with other social movements.

5.884 — *The Biographical Dictionary of British Feminists, Vol 1, 1800–1930* (1985).

5.885 — *Becoming A Feminist: The Social Origins of 'First Wave' Feminism* (1986). Analysis of the personal backgrounds and convictions of ninety-eight men and women active in the women's movement.

5.886 — *The Biographical Dictionary of British Feminists, Vol 2, A Supplement, 1900–45* (1990).

5.887 **Bell**, E. M., *Storming the Citadel: The Rise of the Woman Doctor* (1953). Thorough, descriptive account of the campaign to gain access to the medical profession.

5.888 **Bennett**, D., *Emily Davies and the Liberation of Women, 1830–1921* (1990). Most recent biography of the campaigner for women's education.

5.889 **Billington**, R., 'Ideology and feminism: why the suffragettes were "wild women" ', *Women's Studs. Int. For.*, 5.6 (1982), 663–74.

5.890 — 'Women, politics and local liberalism: from "female suffrage" to "votes for women" ', *J. Reg. Local Studs.*, 5.1 (1985), 1–14.

5.891 **Black**, N., 'Virginia Woolf and the women's movement', in J. Marcus, ed., *New Feminist Essays on Virginia Woolf II* (1981).

5.892 **Blackman**, J., 'The first women's liberation movement', in D. Rubinstein, ed., *People for the People* (1969), 179–85. Emphasises the importance of the Pankhursts in the struggle for the vote.

5.893 **Bostick**, T. P., 'The press and the launching of the women's suffrage movement, 1866–1867', *Vict. Period. R* , 13.4 (1980), 125–31. How a small group of early feminists used the press to publicise their cause.

5.894 — 'Women's suffrage, the press and the Reform Bill of 1867', *Int. J. Women's Studs.*, 3.4 (1980), 373–90. Analyses the treatment given to women's suffrage in nearly fifty newspapers.

5.895 **Brewer**, R. W., ' "She was part of it": Emily Lawless, 1845–1913', *Eire-Ireland*, 18, Winter (1983), 119–31.

5.896 **Bullock**, I. and **Pankhurst**, R., eds., *Sylvia Pankhurst: From Artist to Anti-Fascist* (1991).

5.897 **Burton**, H., *Barbara Bodichon, 1827–1891* (1949). One of the first women's rights campaigners, involved with the *English Women's Journal*, women's employment and the suffrage movement. Co-founder, with Emily Davies, of Girton College, Cambridge.

5.898 **Caine**, B., 'John Stuart Mill and the English women's movement', *Hist. Studs.*, 18.70 (1978), 52–67.

5.899 — 'Feminism, suffrage and the nineteenth-century English women's movement', *Women's Studs. Int. For.*, 5.6 (1982), 537–50. Notes the wide range of concerns of the nineteenth-century movement.

5.900 — *Victorian Feminists* (1992). A study of four leading feminists: Emily Davies, Millicent Fawcett, Frances Power Cobbe and Josephine Butler. Examines the relationship between personal experience and feminist commitment.

5.901 **Cook**, K. and **Evans**, N., ' "The petty antics of the bell-ringing boisterous band"? The women's suffrage movement in Wales, 1890–1918', in A. V. John, ed., *Our Mothers' Land: Chapters in Welsh Women's History, 1830–1939* (1991), 159–188.

5.902 **Doughan**, D., *Lobbying for Liberation: British Feminism, 1918–1968* (1980).

5.903 **Durham**, M., 'Suffrage and after: feminism in the early twentieth century', in M. Langan and B. Schwarz, eds., *Crises in the British State, 1880–1930* (1985), 179–91.

5.904 **Elston**, M. A., 'Women and anti-vivisection in Victorian England, 1870–1900', in N. A. Rupke, ed., *Vivisection in Historical Perspective* (1987), 259–94. Examines the complex relationship between the women's movement and the anti-vivisection campaign.

5.905 **Evans**, R. J., *The Feminists : Women's Emancipation Movements in Europe, America and Australasia, 1840–1920* (1977).

5.906 **Fair**, J. D., 'The policitial aspects of women's suffrage during the First World War', *Albion*, 8.3 (1976), 274–95.

5.907 **Fawcett**, M. G. F., *The Women's Victory and After: Personal Reminiscences, 1911–1918* (1920). Interesting account of the final years of the suffrage movement by the President of the NUWSS.

5.908 **First**, R. and **Scott**, A., *Olive Schreiner* (1980).

5.909 **Fletcher**, S., *Maude Royden: A Life* (1989). Biography of a suffragist, a member of the peace movement and a campaigner for women to be ordained.

5.910 **Forster**, M., *Significant Sisters: The Grassroots of Active Feminism, 1839–1939* (1986). Short biographies of feminists illustrating different aspects of the women's movement.

5.911 **Fulford**, R., *Votes for Women* (1957). Narrative account, emphasising role of militants.

5.912 **Garner**, L., *Stepping Stones to Women's Liberty: Feminist Ideas in the Women's Suffrage Movement, 1900–1918* (1984). Examines ideas of both militant and non-militant suffragists. Shows links between socialism, radicalism and feminist politics.

5.913 — *A Brave and Beautiful Spirit: Dora Marsden, 1882–1960* (1990). Biography of a suffragette and Founder of the *Freewoman*.

5.914 **Grant**, I., *The National Council of Women: The First Sixty Years, 1895–1955* (1955).

5.915 **Hale**, T. F., 'F. W. Pethwick Lawrence and the suffragettes', *Contemporary R.*, 225 (1974), 83–9.

5.916 **Hammond**, J. L. and **Hammond**, B., *James Stansfield: A Victorian Champion of Sex Equality* (1932). An MP very active in the campaign to repeal the Contagious Diseases Acts.

5.917 **Harrison**, B., *Separate Spheres: The Opposition to Women's Suffrage* (1978). Suggests separate spheres was at the heart of anti-suffragist arguments.

5.918 — 'The act of militancy: violence and the suffragettes, 1904–1914', in B. Harrison, ed., *Peaceable Kingdom: Stability and Change in Modern Britain* (1982), 26–81.

5.919 — 'Women's suffrage at Westminster, 1866–1928', in M. Bentley and J. Stevenson, eds., *High and Low Politics in Modern Britain: Ten Studies* (1983), 80–122.

5.920 — *Prudent Revolutionaries: Portraits of British Feminists between the Wars* (Oxford, 1988). Scholarly account but one which begs the question of who is a feminist and why the sixteen people in the book were selected.

5.921 **Hays Harper**, P., 'Votes for women: a graphic episode in the battle of the sexes', in A. H. Milton and L. Nochlin, eds., *Art and Architecture in the Service of Politics* (1978), 150–61. Examines British and American suffrage posters.

5.922 **Herstein**, S., *A Mid-Victorian Feminist: Barbara Leigh Smith Bodichon* (New Haven, Conn., 1983).

5.923 **Hirshfield**, C., 'A fractured faith: Liberal Party women and the suffrage issue in Britain, 1892–1914', *Gend. and Hist.*, 2.2 (1980), 173–97.

5.924 **Holton**, S. S., *Feminism and Democracy: Women's Suffrage and Reform Politics in Britain, 1900–1918* (1986). Important study which examines the building of an alliance between suffragists and the labour movement. New insights into the role played by women's suffrage in the development of reform politics.

5.925 — 'In sorrowful wrath: suffrage militancy and the romantic feminism of Emmeline Pankhurst', in H. L. Smith, ed., *British Feminism in the Twentieth Century* (1990), 7–24.

5.926 — 'The suffragist and the "average woman" ', *Women's H. R.*, 1.1 (1992), 9–24.

5.927 **Hume**, L. P., *The National Union of Women's Suffrage Societies, 1897–1914* (New York, 1982). The first recent study to examine the NUWSS and to re-assess its contribution to the suffrage movement.

5.928 **Jones**, E. W., 'A citadel stormed: the saga of three Welsh pioneers', *Hon. Scy. Cymmrodorion Trans.* (1984), 337–73. Discusses Emily Davies, George Edward Day and Elizabeth Hoggan.

5.929 **Kamm**, J., *Rapiers and Battleaxes: The Women's Movement and Its Aftermath* (1966). Useful narrative account.

5.930 **Kean**, H., *Deeds Not Words: The Lives of Suffragette Teachers* (1990).

5.931 **Kent**, S. K., 'The politics of sexual difference: World War 1 and the demise of British feminism', *J. Brit. Studs.*, 27.3 (1988), 232–53.

5.932 **King**, E., *The Scottish Women's Suffrage Movement* (1978).

5.933 **Klein**, V., 'The emancipation of women: its motives and achievements', in H. Grisewood, ed., *Ideas and Beliefs of the Victorians* (New York, 1966), 261–7.

5.934 **Lance**, K. C., 'Strategy choices of the Women's Social and Political Union, 1903–1918', *Soc. Sci. Q.*, 60, June (1979), 51–61.

5.935 **Leneman**, L., *A Guid Cause: Women's Suffrage in Scotland* (1991).

5.936 — 'Northern men and votes for women', *Hist. Today*, 41. 12 (1991), 35–41.

5.937 **Levenson**, L. and **Natterstad**, J. H., *Hanna Sheehy-Skeffington: A Pioneering Irish Feminist* (Syracuse, New York, 1986).

5.938 **Levine**, P., *Victorian Feminism, 1850–1900* (1987). Readable synthesis of the latest research/approaches in this area.

5.939 — *Feminist Lives in Victorian England* (1990). Studies the connections between women's public and private lives, emphasising the importance of friendship networks for understanding the nineteenth-century women's movement. Fresh, new approach.

5.940 **Lewis**, G., *Eva Gore Booth and Esther Roper: A Biography* (1988). They were active in the North of England Society for Women's Suffrage and worked closely with textile workers.

5.941 **Lewis**, J., 'Beyond suffrage: English feminism in the 1920s', *Maryland Historian*, 6 (1975), 1–17.

5.942 — 'In search of a real equality: women between the wars', in F. Gloversmith, ed., *Class, Culture and Social Change: A New View of the 1930s* (1980), 208–39.

5.943 **Liddington**, J., 'Re-discovering suffrage history', *Hist. Workshop J.*, 4 (1978), 192–202.

5.944 — 'Women cotton workers and the suffrage campaign: the radical suffragists in Lancashire, 1893–1914', in S. Burman, ed., *Fit Work for Women* (1979), 98–111.

5.945 — and **Norris**, J., *One Hand Tied Behind Us: The Rise of the Women's Suffrage Movement* (1978). Pioneering study, drawing attention to the involvement of Lancashire working women in the suffrage movement and the links between socialism

5.946 **Lloyd-Morgan**, C., 'From temperance to suffrage?', in A. V. John, ed., *Our Mothers' Land: Chapters in Welsh Women's History, 1830–1939* (1991), 135–158.

5.947 **Mackenzie**, M., *Shoulder to Shoulder* (1975). Illustrated history of the suffrage movement.

5.948 **McKillen**, B., 'Irish feminism and nationalist separatism, 1914–23, parts 1 & 2', *Eire-Ireland*, 17, Fall (1982), 52–67 and 17, Winter (1982), 72–90.

5.949 **Malmgreen**, G., *Women's Suffrage in England: Origins and Alternatives, 1792–1851* (1978).

5.950 **Marcus**, J., 'Transatlantic sisterhood: labor and suffrage links in the letters of Elizabeth Robbins and Emmeline Pankhurst', *Signs*, 3.3 (1978), 744–55.

5.951 **Markow**, A. B., 'George Gissing: advocate or provocateur of the women's movement', *Eng. Lit. in Trans.*, 25 (1982), 58–73.

5.952 **Mason**, F. M., 'The newer Eve: the Catholic Women's Suffrage Society in England, 1911–1923', *Catholic H. R.*, 72.4 (1986), 620–38.

5.953 **Matthews**, J., 'Barbara Bodichon: integrity in diversity, 1827–1891', in D. Spender, ed., *Feminist Theorists: Three Centuries of Women's Intellectual Traditions* (1983), 90–123.

5.954 **Mellown**, M., 'Vera Brittain: feminist in a new age, 1896–1970', in D. Spender, ed., *Feminist Theorists: Three Centuries of Women's Intellectual Traditions* (1983), 314–34.

5.955 **Mitchell**, D., *Women on the Warpath: The Story of the Women of the First World War* (1966).

5.956 — *The Fighting Pankhursts: A Study in Tenacity* (1967). Narrative account of the militant movement.

5.957 — *Queen Christabel: A Biography of Christabel Pankhurst* (1977). Biography written in the 'great woman' tradition which presents a negative view of its subject.

5.958 **Moore**, L., 'Feminists and femininity: a case study of WSPU propaganda and local response at a Scottish by-election', *Women's Studs. Int. For.*, 5.6 (1982), 675–84.

5.959 **Morgan**, D., *Suffragists and Liberals: The Politics of Women's Suffrage in Britain* (1975).

5.960 **Morrell**, C., '*Black Friday' and Violence Against Women in the Suffragette Movement* (1981).

5.961 **Mulford**, W., 'Socialist feminist criticism: a case study, women's suffrage and literature, 1906–14', in P. Widdowson, ed., *Re-Reading English* (1982), 179–92.

5.962 **Murphy**, C., *The Women's Suffrage Movement and Irish Society in the Early Twentieth Century* (1989).

5.963 — 'The time of the stars and stripes: the American influence on the Irish suffrage movement', in M. Luddy and C. Murphy, eds., *Women Surviving: Studies in Irish Women's History in the Nineteenth and Twentieth Centuries* (Dublin, 1990), 180–205.

5.964 **Neale**, R. S., 'Working-class women and women's suffrage', in R. S. Neale, *Class and Ideology in the Nineteenth Century* (1972), 143–68.

5.965 **Nestor**, P. A., 'A new departure in women's publishing: the *Englishwomen's Journal* and the *Victoria Magazine*', *Vict. Period. R.*, 15 (1982), 93–106.

5.966 **Neville**, D., 'Gan on hinnies, I like yer fine: suffragettes in the North East', *N. E. Gp. Study Labour Hist.*, Bull. 20 (1986), 1–8.

5.967 **Newsome**, S., *The Women's Freedom League, 1907–1957* (1957). A useful account of the activities of the less well known militant suffrage group.

5.968 **Oakley**, A., 'Millicent Garrett Fawcett: duty and determination, 1847–1929', in D. Spender, ed., *Feminist Theorists: Three Centuries of Women's Intellectual Traditions* (1983), 184–202.

5.969 **O'Neill**, M., 'The Dublin Women's Suffrage Society and its successors', *Dublin Hist. Rec.*, 38 (1984–5), 126–40.

5.970 **O'Neill**, W. L., *The Woman Movement: Feminism in the United States and England* (1969).

5.971 **Owens**, R. C., ' "Votes for ladies, votes for women": organised labour and the suffrage movement, 1876–1922', *J. Irish Labour Hist. Scy.*, 9 (1983), 32–47.

5.972 — *Smashing Times: A History of the Irish Women's Suffrage Movement, 1889–1922* (Dublin, 1984).

5.973 **Pankhurst**, C., *Unshackled: Or How We Won the Vote* (1959). Account of the militant suffrage movement, and its importance, by one of its leaders.

5.974 **Pankhurst**, E. S., *The Suffragette Movement: An Intimate Account of Persons* and *Ideals* (1931). Fascinating account of the suffrage movement by a famous participant which must be used with care.

5.975 **Park**, J., 'The British suffrage activists of 1913: an analysis', *P. P.*, 120, August (1988), 147–62.

5.976 **Pethwick-Lawrence**, E., *My Part in a Changing World* (1938). Account of the suffrage struggle by a former leader of the WSPU who split with the Pankhursts.

5.977 **Pugh**, M., 'Politicians and the women's vote, 1914–1918', *History*, 59.197 (1974), 358–74.

5.978 — *Women's Suffrage in Britain, 1867–1929* (1980).

5.979 — 'Domesticity and the decline of feminism, 1930–1950', in H. L. Smith, ed., *British Feminism in the Twentieth Century* (1990), 144–64.

5.980 — *Women and the Women's Movement in Britain, 1914–1959* (1992). Wide-ranging account of the relationship between the organised women's movement, the majority of women and the 'male political establishment', in a neglected period.

5.981 **Raeburn**, A., *The Militant Suffragettes* (1973).

5.982 **Ramelson**, M., *A Century of Struggle for Women's Rights* (1967). Lively narrative account of the struggle for the vote.

5.983 **Rendall**, J., *The Origins of Modern Feminism: Women in Britain, France and the United States, 1780–1860* (1985). Wide-ranging and stimulating study of the social, economic, political and cultural factors which affected women's social status and led to the development of a women's movement.

5.984 — ' "A moral engine"? Feminism, Liberalism and the *Englishwomen's Journal*', in J. Rendall, ed., *Equal or Different? Women's Politics, 1800–1914* (1987), 112–40.

5.985 — 'Friendship and politics: Barbara Leigh Smith Bodichon (1827–91) and Bessie Rayner Parkes (1829–1925)', in S. Mendus and J. Rendall, eds., *Sexuality and Subordination: Interdisciplinary Studies of Gender in the Nineteenth Century* (1989), 136–70.

5.986 **Rendel**, M., 'The contribution of the Women's Labour League to the winning of the franchise', in L. Middleton, ed., *Women in the Labour Movement: the British Experience* (1977), 57–83.

5.987 **Robson**, A. P. W., 'The founding of the

National Society for Women's Suffrage, 1866–1867', *Canadian J. Hist.*, 8 (1973), 1–22.

5.988 **Romero**, P. E., *Sylvia Pankhurst: Portrait of a Radical* (New Haven, Conn., 1987). A re-assessment of Sylvia Pankhurst which challenges the view that she was a feminist socialist.

5.989 **Rosen**, A., *Rise Up Women! The Militant Campaign of the Women's Social and Political Union, 1903–1914* (1974). Detailed account of the politics of the militant suffrage movement.

5.990 — 'Emily Davies and the women's movement, 1862–1867', *J. Brit. Studs.*, 19.2 (1979), 102–21.

5.991 **Rover**, C., *Women's Suffrage and Party Politics in Britain, 1866–1914* (1967). Examines the struggle for the vote at Parliamentary level.

5.992 **Rowbotham**, S., *The Past Is Before Us: The Ideas of the Women's Movement* (1989).

5.993 **Rubinstein**, D., *Before the Suffragettes: Women's Emancipation in the 1890s* (1986). Wide ranging study of a neglected period.

5.994 — 'Millicent Garrett Fawcett and the meaning of women's emancipation, 1886–99', *Vict. Studs.*, 34.3 (1991), 365–80.

5.995 — *A Different World for Women: The Life of Millicent Garrett Fawcett* (1992).

5.996 **Sarah**, E., *Re-assessments of 'First Wave' Feminism* (1982).

5.997 — 'Towards a re-assessment of first wave feminism', *Women's Studs. Int. For.*, 5.6 (1982), 519–24 .

5.998 — 'Christabel Pankhurst: reclaiming her power, 1880–1958', in D. Spender, ed., *Feminist Theorists: Three Centuries of Women's Intellectual Traditions* (1983), 259–83. Re-assessment of Christabel Pankurst which is positive about her role and contribution to feminist ideas.

5.999 **Smith**, H. L., 'British feminism in the 1920s', in H. L. Smith, ed., *British Feminism in the Twentieth Century* (1990). An overview of the aims and objectives of the women's movement in the 1920s.

5.1000 — ed., *British Feminism in the Twentieth Century* (1990). Important collection of articles, largely on the under-researched period of the inter-war years.

5.1001 **Spender**, D., *There's Always Been a Women's Movement This Century* (1983).

5.1002 **Stanley**, L. with A. Morley, *The Life, Times, Friends and Death of Emily Wilding*

Davison (1988). Stimulating re-appraisal of Davison's life, challenging mainstream view that the WSPU was synonymous with the Pankhursts. Raises key issues about biography writing.

5.1003 **Strachey**, B., *Remarkable Relations: The Story of the Pearsall Smith Family* (1980).

5.1004 **Strachey**, R., *The Cause: A Short History of the Women's Movement in Great Britain* (1928, reprinted 1978). Early general history of the women's movement by a former suffragist sympathetic to the constitutional groups.

5.1005 — *Millicent Garrett Fawcett* (1931). Sympathetic biography by a fellow member of the NUWSS.

5.1006 **Swanwick**, H. M., *I Too Have Been Young* (1935). Personal reminiscences by a leading member of the NUWSS and a peace campaigner.

5.1007 **Tickner**, L., *The Spectacle of Women: Imagery of the Suffrage Campaign, 1907–1914* (1987). Beautifully illustrated analysis of suffragist use of spectacle.

5.1008 **Ward**, M., ' "Suffrage first–above all else": an account of the Irish suffrage movement', *Fem. R*, 10 (1982), 21–36.

5.1009 **Widgery**, D., 'Sylvia Pankhurst', *Radical America*, 13.3 (1979), 23–38.

See also: 5.378; 5.402; 5.403; 5.409; 5.748; 5.749; 5.785; 5.786; 5.787; 5.1176; 5.1229; 5.1230; 5.1231; 5.1240; 5.1243; 5.1244; 5.1245; 5.1246; 5.1248; 5.1409; 5.1506; 5.1522.

(v) Women and the labour movement

5.1010 **Askwith**, B., *Lady Dilke: A Biography* (1969). Biography of the President of the Women's Trade Union League.

5.1011 **Barratt**, M. and **McIntosh**, M., 'The family wage: some problems for socialists and feminists', *Capital and Class*, 11 (1980), 71–87.

5.1012 **Beer**, R., *Matchgirls' Strike 1888: The Struggle Against Sweated Labour in London's East End* (1977).

5.1013 **Black**, N., *Social Feminism* (1989). Discusses three organisations, including the Women's Cooperative Guild.

5.1014 **Bondfield**, M., *A Life's Work* (1949). Autobiography of a trade union leader and first female Cabinet minister in a Labour government.

5.1015 **Boone**, G., *The Women's Trade Union Leagues in Great Britain and the United States of America* (New York, 1942).

5.1016 **Bornat**, J., 'Home and work: a new context for trade union history', *Oral Hist.*, 5.2 (1977), 101–23. Using oral interviews examines the interrelationship between home, work and women's trade unionism in Yorkshire textiles.

5.1017 — 'Lost leaders: women, trade unionism and the case of the General Union of Textile Workers, 1875–1914', in A. V. John, ed., *Unequal Opportunities: Women's Employment in England, 1800–1914* (1986), 206–33. Notes tensions between male union leaders' formal commitment to political equality and their underlying paternalism.

5.1018 — ' "What about that lass of yours being in a union?" Textile workers and their union in Yorkshire, 1888–1922', in L. Davidoff and B. Westover, eds., *Our Work, Our Lives, Our Words. Women's History and Women's Work* (Totowa, New Jersey, 1986), 76–98.

5.1019 **Boston**, S., 'The Rego strike', *Scy. Study Labour Hist.*, Bull. 38 (1979), 9–10.

5.1020 — *Women Workers and the Trade Unions* (1980).

5.1021 **Bruley**, S., *Feminism, Stalinism and the Women's Movement in Britain, 1920–1939* (New York, 1986).

5.1022 **Callcott**, M., 'The organisation of political support for Labour in the North of England: the work of Margaret Gibb, 1929–57', *N.E. Gp. Study Labour Hist.*, Bull. 11 (1977), 47–58.

5.1023 — 'Dr Marion Phillips: Labour MP, Sunderland, 1929–31', *N.E. Gp. Study Labour Hist.*, Bull. 20 (1986), 9–13.

5.1024 **Collette**, C., 'Socialism and scandal in 1900', *Hist. Workshop J.*, 23 (1987), 102–11. Examines labour movement attitudes to the relationship between Dora Montefiore and George Belt, a labour organiser.

5.1025 — *For Labour and For Women: The Women's Labour League, 1906–1918* (1989). First extended study of the League. Considers issue of separatism.

5.1026 **Daly**, M. E., 'Women, work and trade unionism', in M. MacCurtain and D. Ó'Corráin, eds., *Women in Irish Society: The Historical Dimension* (Dublin, 1978), 71–81.

5.1027 **Davis**, T., ' "What kind of woman is she?"

Women and Communist Party politics, 1941–55', in R. Brunt and C. Rowan, eds., *Feminism, Culture and Politics* (1982), 85–107.

5.1028 **Dinnage**, R., *Annie Besant* (1987).

5.1029 **Drake**, B., *Women in Trade Unions* (1921). Pioneering study providing a detailed description of the history of women's trade unionism and an analysis of its weaknesses.

5.1030 **Druker**, J., 'Women and trade unions', *Scy. Study Labour Hist.*, Bull. 37 (1978), 89–92. A review essay of the literature.

5.1031 **Ferguson**, S., 'Labour women and the social services', in L. Middleton, ed., *Women in the Labour Movement: The British Experience* (1977), 38–56.

5.1032 **Gaffin**, J., 'Women and co-operation', in L. Middleton, ed., *Women in the Labour Movement: The British Experience* (1977), 113–42.

5.1033 — and **Thoms**, D., *Caring and Sharing: The Centenary History of the Co-operative Women's Guild* (1983).

5.1034 **Godwin**, Dame A., 'Early years in the trade unions', in L. Middleton, ed., *Women in the Labour Movement: The British Experience* (1977), 94–112.

5.1035 **Goldman**, H., *Emma Paterson: Her Life and Times* (1974). Biography of the President of the Women's Protective and Provident League.

5.1036 **Gordon**, E., 'Women, work and collective action: Dundee jute workers, 1870–1906', *J. Soc. Hist.*, 21.1 (1987), 27–48.

5.1037 **Grant**, L., 'Women's work and trade unionism in Liverpool, 1890–1914', *Bull. N. W. Labour Hist. Scy.*, 7 (1980/1), 65–83.

5.1038 **Hamilton**, M. A., *Mary Macarthur* (1925). Biography of a leading female trade unionist by a close contemporary.

5.1039 **Hannam**, J., ' "In the comradeship of the sexes lies the hope of progress and social regeneration": women in the West Riding ILP, *c.* 1890–1914', in J. Rendall, ed., *Equal or Different? Women in Politics, 1800–1914* (1987), 214–38.

5.1040 — *Isabella Ford, 1855–1924* (1989). Biography of a leading suffragist, socialist and peace campaigner which emphasises the links between the three movements.

5.1041 — 'Women and the ILP, 1890–1914', in D. James, T. Jowitt and K. Laybourn, eds., *The Centennial History of the Independent Labour Party* (1992), 205–28.

5.1042 **Harris**, J., *Beatrice Webb: The Reluctant Feminist* (1984).

5.1043 **Hughes**, B., 'In defence of Ellen Wilkinson', *Hist. Workshop J.*, 7 (1979), 157–60.

5.1044 **Jacoby**, R. M., 'Feminism and class consciousness in the British and American Women's Trade Union Leagues, 1890–1925', in B. A. Carroll, ed., *Liberating Women's History* (Urbana, Illinois, 1976), 137–60.

5.1045 **John**, A. V., 'A miner struggle? Women's protests in Welsh mining history', *Llafur*, 4.1 (1984), 72–90.

5.1046 **Jones**, D., 'Women and Chartism', *History*, 68 (1983), 1–21.

5.1047 **Jones**, M., *Those Obstreperous Lassies: A History of the Irish Women Workers' Union* (Dublin, 1988).

5.1048 **Kapp**, Y., *Eleanor Marx, Vols. 1 & 2* (1972, 1976). Very thorough and detailed biography, but understates Marx's feminism.

5.1049 **King**, S., 'Feminists in teaching. The National Union of Women Teachers, 1920–1945', in A. Prentice and M. R. Theobald, eds., *Perspectives on the History of Women and Teaching* (1992), 182–201.

5.1050 **Kirk**, N., ed., 'Women and the labour movement', *N.W. Gp. Study Labour Hist.*, 7 (1980/1).

5.1051 **Land**, H., 'The family wage', *Fem. R.*, 6 (1980), 55–77. Discusses labour movement hostility to family allowances and support for a family wage.

5.1052 **Lewenhak**, S., 'The lesser trade union organisation of women than of men', *Scy. Study Labour Hist.*, Bull. 26 (1973), 19–22.

5.1053 — 'Women in the leadership of the Scottish Trades Union Congress, 1897–1970', *J. Scot. Labour Hist. Scy.*, 7, July (1973), 3–23.

5.1054 — *Women and the Trade Unions* (1977). Useful narrative.

5.1055 **Liddington**, J., *The Life and Times of a Respectable Rebel: Selina Cooper, 1864–1946* (1984). Biography of a working-class suffragist which sheds much light on the links between the women's movement and the labour movement.

5.1056 **Linklater**, A., *An Unhusbanded Life – Charlotte Despard: Suffragette, Socialist and Sinn Feiner* (1980).

5.1057 **Malmgreen**, G., *Neither Bread Nor Roses: Utopian Feminists and the English Working Class* (1978).

5.1058 **Mappen**, E., *Helping Women at Work: The Women's Industrial Council, 1889–1914*

(1985).

5.1059 — 'Strategists for change: social feminist approaches to the problems of women's work', in A. V. John, ed., *Unequal Opportunities: Women's Employment in England, 1800–1918* (1986), 234–59.

5.1060 **Middleton**, L., ed., *Women in the Labour Movement: The British Experience* (1977). Collection of essays on different aspects of women's involvement in the labour movement.

5.1061 **Mulvihill**, M., *Charlotte Despard: A Biography* (1989).

5.1062 **Nethercot**, A. H., *The First Five Lives of Annie Besant* (1961).

5.1063 — *The Second Four Lives of Annie Besant* (1963).

5.1064 **Nield Chew**, D., *The Life and Writings of Ada Nield Chew* (1982). Biography of a working-class woman who became active in trade unionism and socialist politics in the 1900s.

5.1065 **O'Brien**, J., *Women's Liberation in Labour History: A Case Study from Nottingham* (no date). Collective actions of women workers in Nottingham.

5.1066 **Olcott**, T., 'Dead centre: the women's trade union movement in London', *London J.*, 2.1 (1976), 33–50.

5.1067 **Oppenheim**, J., 'The odyssey of Annie Besant', *Hist. Today*, 39.9 (1990), 12–18.

5.1068 **Pankhurst**, R., 'Anna Wheeler: A pioneer socialist', *Political Q.*, 25 (1954), 132–43.

5.1069 **Phillips**, A., *Divided Loyalties: Dilemmas of Sex and Class* (1987). Readable introduction to the complex tensions between 'sisterhood' and 'class solidarity' viewed over time.

5.1070 **Pierotti**, A. M., *The Story of the National Union of Women Teachers* (1963).

5.1071 **Pretty**, D. A., 'Women and trade unionism in Welsh rural society', *Llafur*, 5.3 (1990), 5–13.

5.1072 **Price**, M. and **Glenday**, N., *Reluctant Revolutionaries: A Century of Headmistresses, 1874–1974* (1974). Official history of the Association of Headmistresses.

5.1073 **Purcell**, K., 'Militancy and acquiescence amongst women workers', in S. Burman, ed., *Fit Work for Women* (1979), 112–33. Analyses specific features of women's militancy.

5.1074 **Rose**, S. O., 'Gender antagonism and class conflict: exclusionary strategies of male trade unionists in nineteenth-century Britain', *Soc. Hist.*, 13.2 (1988), 191–208.

5.1075 — 'Gender at work: sex, class and industrial capitalism', *Hist. Workshop J.*, 21 (1986), 113–31. Discusses connections between the skilled male worker at work and his role in the family as a way to understand gender antagonism and exclusionary union practices.

5.1076 **Rowan**, C., 'Women in the Labour Party, 1906–1920', *Fem. R.*, 12 (1982), 74–91.

5.1077 **Rowbotham**, S., *A New World for Women: Stella Browne, Socialist Feminist* (1977). Discusses the campaign for birth control and abortion between the wars and tension within the labour movement.

5.1078 — 'Women and radical politics in Britain, 1830–1914', *Radical H. R.*, 19, Winter (1978/9), 149–59.

5.1079 — and **Weeks**, J., *Socialism and the New Life: The Personal and Sexual Politics of Edward Carpenter and Havelock Ellis* (1977). Illuminating discussion of the interconnections between personal and sexual life and socialist politics in the 1880s and 1890s.

5.1080 **Rubinstein**, D., 'Annie Besant', in D. Rubinstein, ed., *People for the People* (1969), 145–53.

5.1081 — 'Ellen Wilkinson re-considered', *Hist. Workshop J.*, 7 (1979), 161–9. Examines Wilkinson's opposition to comprehensive education.

5.1082 **Satre**, L. J., 'After the Match Girls' Strike: Bryant and May in the 1880s', *Vict. Studs.*, 26.1 (1982), 7–31.

5.1083 **Savage**, M., *The Dynamics of Working-Class Politics: The Labour Movement in Preston, 1880–1940* (1988). Holistic approach to understanding working-class politics which includes the role of gender relations.

5.1084 **Schwarzkopf**, J., 'The sexual division in the Chartist family', *Scy. Study Labour Hist.*, Bull. 54 (1989), 12–14.

5.1085 — *Women in the Chartist Movement* (1991).

5.1086 **Seccombe**, W., 'Patriarchy stabilized: the construction of the male breadwinner wage norm in nineteenth-century Britain', *Soc. Hist.*, 11.1 (1986), 53–76.

5.1087 **Smith**, H. L., 'Sex vs class: British feminists and the labour movement, 1919–29', *Historian*, 47, November (1984), 19–37.

5.1088 **Soldon**, N., *Women in British Trade Unions, 1874–1976* (Dublin, 1978). Narrative account.

5.1089 Stafford, A., *A Match to Fire the Thames* (1961). Colourful account of the Match Girls' Strike of 1888.

5.1090 Stewart, M. and **Hunter**, L., *The Needle is Threaded* (1964). Official history of the National Union of Tailors and Garment Workers. Little attention paid to gender divisions.

5.1091 Taylor, B., 'Religious heresy and feminism in early English socialism', in S. Lipshitz, ed., *Tearing the Veil: Essays on Femininity* (1978), 119–44.

5.1092 — 'Socialist feminism: utopian or scientific?', in R. Samuel, ed., *People's History, Socialist Theory* (1981), 158–63. Explores socialist feminist aspects of Owenism.

5.1093 — *Eve and the New Jerusalem: Socialism and Feminism in the Nineteenth Century* (1983). Key text which demonstrates how a recognition of gender issues can shed a new perspective on Owenism and early trade union struggles.

5.1094 — ' "The men are as bad as their masters" . . . Socialism, feminism and sexual antagonism in the London tailoring trade in the 1830s', in J. Newton et al., eds., *Sex and Class in Women's History* (1983), 187–220. Seminal article on the role of gender divisions within tailoring disputes.

5.1095 Thane, P., 'The women of the British Labour Party and feminism, 1906–45', in H. L. Smith, ed., *British Feminism in the Twentieth Century* (1990), 124–43.

5.1096 Thom, D., 'The bundle of sticks: women trade unionists and collective organisation before 1918', in A. V. John, ed., *Unequal Opportunities: Women's Employment in England, 1800–1918* (1986), 260–89.

5.1097 — *Feminism and the Labour Movement in Britain, 1850–1975* (1987).

5.1098 Thompson, D., 'Women and nineteenth-century radical politics: a lost dimension', in J. Mitchell and A. Oakley, eds., *The Rights and Wrongs of Women* (1976), 112–38. Argues working-class women were less involved in struggles for political rights after 1850.

5.1099 — *The Chartists: Popular Politics in the Industrial Revolution* (1986). Analyses women's role.

5.1100 — 'Women, work and politics in nineteenth-century England: the problem of authority', in J. Rendall, ed., *Equal or Different? Women's Politics, 1800–1914* (1987), 57–81.

5.1101 Todd, N., 'Labour women: the Bexley branch of the British Labour Party, 1945–50', *J. Contemp. Hist.*, 8 (1973), 159–73.

5.1102 Tolliday, S., 'Militance and organisation: women workers and trade unions in the motor trades in the 1930s', *Oral Hist*, 11.2 (1983), 42–55.

5.1103 Tsuzuki, C., *The Life of Eleanor Marx, 1855–98: A Socialist Tragedy* (1967).

5.1104 Vaux, J., 'Women workers and trade unions in nineteenth-century Britain', *Hecate*, 4 (1978).

5.1105 Vernon, B. D., *Ellen Wilkinson, 1891–1947* (1982). Biography of the Labour MP for Middlesborough.

5.1106 — *Margaret Cole, 1893–1980* (1986).

5.1107 Whipp, R., ' "Plenty of excuses, no money". The social bases of trade unionism as illustrated by the potters', *Scy. Study Labour Hist.*, Bull. 49 (1984), 29–37. Women's role in the National Union of Pottery Workers.

5.1108 Yeo, S., 'A new life: the religion of socialism in Britain, 1883–1896', *Hist. Workshop J.*, 4 (1977), 5–56. Discusses the involvement of women in the socialist 'revival'.

See also: 5.494; 5.528; 5.944; 5.945; 5.950; 5.971; 5.986; 5.1219; 5.1325; 5.1379.

(vi) Women and peace

5.1109 Bennett, Y. A., *Vera Brittain: Women and Peace* (1987).

5.1110 — 'Vera Brittain: feminism, pacifism and the problem of class, 1900–1953', *Atlantis*, 12.2 (1987), 18–23.

5.1111 Black, N., 'The mother's international: the Women's Co-operative Guild and feminist pacifism', *Women's Studs. Int. For.*, 7.6 (1984), 467–76.

5.1112 Brooks, M., 'Passive in war? Women internees in the Far East, 1942–5', in S. MacDonald, P. Holden and S. Ardener, eds., *Images of Women in Peace and War: Cross Cultural and Historical Perspectives* (1987), 166–78. Based on personal reminiscences of internees.

5.1113 Bussey, G. and **Tims**, M., *Pioneers for Peace: Women's International League for Peace and Freedom, 1915–1965* (1965). Solid, organisational history.

5.1114 Byles, J. M., 'Women's experience of World War One: suffragists, pacifists and poets', *Women's Studs. Int. For.*, 8.5 (1985), 473–87. Suggests suffrage movement and war transformed women's image of themselves as expressed through their poetry.

5.1115 **Costin**, L. B., 'Feminism, pacifism, internationalism and the 1915 International Congress of Women', *Women's Studs. Int. For.*, 5.5 (1982), 301–15.

5.1116 **Di Leonardo**, M., 'Morals, mothers and militarism: anti-militarism and feminist theory', *Fem. Studs.*, 11.3 (1985), 599–617. Review essay.

5.1117 **Eglin**, J., 'Women and peace: from the suffragists to the Greenham women', in R. Taylor and N. Young, eds., *Campaigns for Peace: British Peace Movements in the Twentieth Century* (1987), 221–59.

5.1118 **Evans**, R., *Comrades and Sisters: Feminism, Socialism and Pacifism in Europe, 1870–1945* (1987).

5.1119 **Foster**, C., *Women For All Seasons. The Story of the Women's International League for Peace and Freedom* (Athens, Georgia, 1989).

5.1120 **Liddington**, J., 'The Women's Peace Crusade: the history of a forgotten campaign', in D. Thompson, ed., *Over Our Dead Bodies: Women Against the Bomb* (1983), 180–244.

5.1121 — *The Long Road to Greenham: Feminism and Anti-Militarism in Britain since 1820* (1989). Readable and wide-ranging account of feminist analyses of militarism and the development of the women's peace movement.

5.1122 **MacDonald**, S., **Holden**, P. and **Ardener**, S., eds., *Images of Women in Peace and War: Cross Cultural and Historical Perspectives* (1987). Essays covering a variety of cultures and chronological periods.

5.1123 **Newbury**, J. V., 'Anti-war suffragists', *History*, 62.206 (1977), 411–25. Reinterpretation of the role of suffragists during WWI.

5.1124 **Oldfield**, S., *Spinsters of this Parish: The Life and Times of F. M. Mayor and Mary Sheepshanks* (1984). Contains interesting material on the women's peace movement of WWI.

5.1125 — *Women Against the Iron Fist: Alternatives to Militarism, 1900–1939* (1989).

5.1126 **Pierson**, R. R., ' "Did your mother wear army boots?": feminist theory and women's relation to war, peace and revolution', in S. MacDonald, P. Holden and S. Ardener, eds., *Images of Women in Peace and War: Cross Cultural and Historical Perspectives* (1987), 205–227.

5.1127 — ed., *Women and Peace: Theoretical, Historical and Practical Perspectives* (1987).

5.1128 **Reilly**, C. W., ed., *Scars Upon My Heart: Women's Poetry and Verse of the First World War* (1981).

5.1129 **Rowbotham**, S., *Friends of Alice Wheeldon* (1986). Introduction examines relationship between the socialist and feminist movements in WWI, followed by a play concerning characters from the movements.

5.1130 **Sager**, E. W., 'The social origins of Victorian pacifism', *Vict. Studs.*, 23.2 (1980), 211–36. Contains information on women members and supporters of the Peace Society.

5.1131 **Tylee**, C. M., ' "Maleness run riot" – the Great War and women's resistance to militarism', *Women's Studs. Int. For.*, 11.3 (1988), 199–210. Examines views of women themselves about the use of force and its dehumanising effects.

5.1132 **Vellacott**, J., 'Feminist Consciousness and the First World War', *Hist. Workshop J.*, 23 (1987), 81–101. Explores the impact of WWI on the ideas of suffragists.

5.1133 — ' "Women, peace and internationalism, 1914–1920": finding new words and creating new methods', in C. Chatfield and P. Van den Dungen, eds., *Peace Movements and Political Cultures* (Knoxville, Tenn., 1988).

5.1134 **Walker**, M., 'Labour women and internationalism', in L. Middleton, ed., *Women in the Labour Movement: The British Experience* (1977), 84–93. Covers the period before WWI to the 1950s.

5.1135 **Ward**, H., *A Venture in Goodwill: Being the Story of the Women's International League, 1915–1929* (1929).

5.1136 **Wiltsher**, A., *Most Dangerous Women: Feminist Peace Campaigners of the Great War* (1985). Lively narrative account of the international women's movement for peace which draws attention to a neglected group. Emphasises links between suffrage and peace.

(j) WOMEN AND WELFARE

(i) Women and philanthropy

5.1137 **Bell**, E. M., *Octavia Hill: A Biography* (1942). Early biography of the housing reformer.

5.1138 **Boyd**, N., *Josephine Butler, Octavia Hill and Florence Nightingale* (1982).

5.1139 **Darley**, G., *Octavia Hill: A Life* (1990).

5.1140 **Fido**, J., 'The Charity Organisation Society and social casework in London, 1869–1900', in A. P. Donajgrodzki, ed., *Social Control in Nineteenth-Century Britain* (1977), 207–30. Contains material on the role of women in the COS.

5.1141 **Gerard**, J., 'Lady bountiful: women of the landed class and rural philanthropy', *Vict. Studs.*, 30.2 (1987), 183–211.

5.1142 **Gorham**, D., 'Victorian reform as a family business: the Hill family', in A. S. Wohl, ed., *The Victorian Family* (1978), 119–47.

5.1143 **Harrison**, B., 'Philanthropy and the Victorians', *Vict. Studs.*, 9.4 (1966), 353–74.

5.1144 — 'For church, Queen and family: the Girls' Friendly Society', *P. P*, 61 (1973), 107–38. Interesting study of a Conservative organisation for girls.

5.1145 — 'State intervention and moral reform in nineteenth-century England', in P. Hollis, ed., *Pressure from Without in Early Victorian England* (1974), 289–322.

5.1146 **Hunt**, G., **Mellor**, J. and **Turner**, J., 'Wretched, hatless and miserably clad: women and Inebriate Reformatories from 1900–1913', *Brit. J. Sociol.*, 40 (1989), 244–70.

5.1147 **Jones**, G., 'Marie Stopes in Ireland: the Mothers' Clinic in Belfast', *Soc. Hist. Medicine*, 5.2 (1992), 255–78.

5.1148 **Jones**, J., *Eileen Younghusband: A Biography* (1984). Pioneer of social work.

5.1149 **Leonard**, J., 'Lady Bell and Edwardian Middlesborough', *N.E. Gp. Study Labour Hist.*, Bull. 8 (1974), 5–9. Critical assessment of Lady Bell's work as a social investigator.

5.1150 **Lewis**, J., *Women and Social Action in Victorian and Edwardian England* (1991). Stimulating analysis of the gendered nature of 'social action' and the tensions between social duty and family responsibilities through a study of prominent women 'philanthropists' and reformers.

5.1151 **Luddy**, M., 'Women and charitable organisation in nineteenth-century Ireland', *Women's Studs. Int. For.*, 11.4 (1988), 301–6. Argues that through charity work women broadened work horizons and promoted the right of women to be active in Irish society.

5.1152 **Malpass**, P., 'Octavia Hill', in P. Barker, ed., *Founders of the Welfare State* (1984), 31–6.

5.1153 **Manton**, J., *Mary Carpenter and the Children of the Streets* (1976). A biography of the Bristol Unitarian social reformer which focuses on her work with juvenile delinquents.

5.1154 **Metscher**, P., 'Mary Anne McCracken: a critical Ulsterwoman within the context of her times', *Eire*, 14.2 (1989), 143–58. Philanthropist, 1770–1866.

5.1155 **Moore**, M. J., 'Social work and social welfare: the organisation of philanthropic resources in Britain, 1900–1914', *J. Brit. Studs.*, 16.2 (1977), 85–104. Describes the foundation of the COS, Guild of Help movement and Social Welfare movement and discusses women's role.

5.1156 **Norman-Butler**, B., *Victorian Aspirations: The Life and Labour of Charles and Mary Booth* (1972).

5.1157 **Parker**, O., *For the Family's Sake: A History of the Mothers' Union, 1876–1976* (1975).

5.1158 **Pope**, B. C., 'Angels in the devil's workshop: leisured and charitable women in nineteenth-century England and France', in R. Bridenthal and C. Koonz, eds., *Becoming Visible: Women in European History* (Boston, Mass., 1977), 296–324.

5.1159 **Prochaska**, F., 'Women in English philanthropy, 1790–1830', *Int. R. Soc. Hist.*, 19.3 (1974), 426–45. Discusses relationship between women's philanthropy and social control in the period of the Napoleonic Wars.

5.1160 — *Women and Philanthropy in Nineteenth-Century England* (1980). Standard, detailed study of women's involvement in philanthropy.

5.1161 — 'Female philanthropy and domestic service in Victorian England', *Bull. Inst. Hist. Res.*, 59.129 (1981), 79–85. Argues that the employment of servants did not necessarily indicate middle-class status.

5.1162 — 'Body and soul: bible nurses and the poor in Victorian London', *Hist. Res.*, 60, October (1987), 336–48.

5.1163 — 'A mother's country: mothers' meetings and family welfare in Britain', *History*, 74.242 (1989), 379–99.

5.1164 **Rose**, J., *Elizabeth Fry* (1980). Biography of the Quaker penal reformer.

5.1165 **Ross**, E., 'Hungry children: housewives and London charity', in P. Mandler, ed., *The Uses of Charity* (Philadelphia, Penn., 1990), 161–96.

5.1166 **Schupf**, H. W., 'Single women and social reform in mid-nineteenth century England: the case of Mary Carpenter', *Vict. Studs.*, 17.3 (1974), 301–17.

5.1167 **Selleck**, R. J. W., 'Mary Carpenter: a confident and contradictory reformer', *Hist. Ed.*, 14.2 (1985), 101–16.

5.1168 **Shiman**, L. L., ' "Changes are dangerous!" Women and temperance in Victorian England', in G. Malmgreen, ed., *Religion in the Lives of English Women* (1986), 193–215.

5.1169 **Summers**, A., 'A Home from home – women's philanthropic work in the nineteenth century', in S. Burman, ed., *Fit Work for Women* (1979), 33–63. Argues that philanthropic work could lead women to challenge their social role as well as reinforcing it.

5.1170 **Tyrrell**, A., ' "Woman's mission" and pressure group politics in Britain, 1825–1860', *Bull. J. Ry. Lib.*, 63 (1980), 194–230.

5.1171 **Watts**, A. S., 'Octavia Hill and the influence of Dickens', *Hist. Today*, 24 (1974), 348–53.

5.1172 **Winter**, J., 'Widowed mothers and mutual aid in early Victorian Britain', *J. Soc. Hist.*, 17.1 (1983), 115–26.

5.1173 **Wohl**, A. S., 'Octavia Hill and the homes of the London poor', *J. Brit. Studs.*, 10.2 (1971), 105–31. Re-evaluation of Hill's work, emphasising its seriousness of purpose.

5.1174 **Yeo**, E., 'Social motherhood and the sexual communion of labour in British social science, 1850–1950', *Women's H. R.*, 1.1 (1992), 63–87.

See also: 5.774.

(ii) Women, social policy and the state

5.1175 **Blackburn**, S., 'Working-class attitudes to social reform: Black Country chain makers and anti-sweating legislation, 1880–1930', *Int. R. Soc. Hist.*, 33 (1989), 42–69.

5.1176 **Bland**, L., 'Feminist vigilantes of late Victorian England', in C. Smart, ed., *Regulating Motherhood: Historical Essays on Marriage, Motherhood and Sexuality* (1992), 33–52. Involvement of feminists in social purity campaigns.

5.1177 **Bock**, G. and **Thane**, P., eds., *Maternity and Gender Policies: Women and the Rise of European Welfare States, 1880–1950* (1991).

5.1178 **Cohen**, M. and **Hanagan**, M., 'The politics of gender and the making of the welfare state, 1900–1940: a comparative perspective', *J. Soc. Hist.*, 24.3 (1991), 469–84.

5.1179 **Cooter**, M., ed., *In the Name of the Child: Health and Welfare, 1880–1940* (1992).

5.1180 **Cosslett**, T., 'Childbirth on the National Health: issues of class, race and gender in two post-war British novels', *Women's Studs.*, 19.1 (1991), 99–119.

5.1181 **Crowther**, M. A., 'Family responsibility and state responsibility in Britain before the welfare state', *Hist. J.*, 25, March (1982), 131–45.

5.1182 **Davies**, C., 'The health visitor as mothers' friend: a woman's place in public health, 1900–1914', *Soc. Hist. Medicine*, 1 (1988), 39–60.

5.1183 **Davin**, A., 'Imperialism and motherhood', *Hist. Workshop J.*, 5 (1978), 9–65. Essential reading. Excellent discussion of how state policy can shape definitions of motherhood.

5.1184 **Deacon**, D., *Managing Gender: The State, the New Middle Class and Women Workers, 1830–1930* (1989).

5.1185 **Dingwall**, R. J., 'Collectivism, regionalism and feminism: health visiting and British social policy, 1850–1975', *J. Soc. Pol.*, 6.3 (1977), 291–315.

5.1186 **Dwork**, D., 'The milk option: an aspect of the history of the infant welfare movement in England, 1898–1908', *Medical Hist.*, 31, January (1987), 51–69.

5.1187 **Fildes**, V., **Marks**, L. and **Marland**, H., *Women and Children First: International Maternal and Infant Welfare, 1870–1945* (1992).

5.1188 **Garcia**, J., **Kilpatrick**, R. and **Richards**, M., eds., *The Politics of Maternity Care Services for Childbearing Women in Twentieth-Century Britain* (1990).

5.1189 **Harrison**, B., 'Women's health or social control? The role of the medical profession in relation to factory legislation in late-nineteenth-century Britain', *Sociology of Health and Illness*, 13.4 (1991), 409–91.

5.1190 **Holton**, S. S., 'Feminine authority and social order: Florence Nightingale's conception of nursing and health care', *Social Analysis*, 15 (1984), 59–72.

5.1191 **Land**, H., 'Eleanor Rathbone and the economy of the family', in H. L. Smith, ed., *British Feminism in the Twentieth Century* (1990), 104–23. Campaign for family allowances.

5.1192 **Lewis**, J., 'The English movement for family allowances, 1917–45', *Histoire Sociale*, 1.22 (1978), 441–59.

5.1193 — 'Dealing with dependency: state practices and social realities', in J. Lewis, ed., *Women's Welfare/Women's Rights* (1983), 17–37.

5.1194 — *The Politics of Motherhood: Maternal and Child Welfare in England, 1900–1939* (1980). Stimulating discussion of the development of child and maternal welfare policy, examining the views of professionals and of mothers.

5.1195 — 'The social history of social policy: infant welfare in Edwardian England', *J. Soc.Pol.*, 9.4 (1980), 463–86.

5.1196 — 'Eleanor Rathbone', in P. Barker, ed., *Founders of the Welfare State* (1984), 83–89.

5.1197 — 'The working-class wife and mother and state intervention, 1870–1918', in J. Lewis, ed., *Labour and Love: Women's Experience of Home and Family, 1850–1940* (1986), 98–120.

5.1198 — 'Models of equality for women: the case of state support for children in twentieth-century Britain', in G. Bock and P. Thane, eds., *Maternity and Gender Policies: Women and the Rise of European Welfare States, 1880–1950 (1991)*, 73–92.

5.1199 — and **Davies**, C., 'Protective legislation in Britain, 1870–1990: equality, difference and their implications for women', *Policy and Politics*, 19.1 (1990), 13–25.

5.1200 **Mark-Lawson**, J., et al, 'Gender and local politics: struggles over welfare, 1918–1939', in L. Murgatroyd et al., eds., *Localities, Class and Gender* (1985).

5.1201 **Marks**, L., 'Mother, babies and hospitals: "The London" and the provision of maternity care in East London, 1870–1939', in V. Fildes, L. Marks and H. Marland, eds., *Women and Children First: International Maternal and Infant Welfare, 1870–1945* (1992).

5.1202 **McKee**, E., 'Church-state relations and the development of Irish health policy: the mother-and-child scheme, 1944–53', *Irish Hist. Studs.*, 25, November (1986), 159–94.

5.1203 **McLoughlin**, D., 'Workhouses and Irish female paupers, 1840–70', in M. Luddy and C. Murphy, eds., *Women Surviving: Studies in Irish Women's History in the Nineteenth and Twentieth Centuries* (Dublin, 1990), 117–47.

5.1204 **Parker**, J., *Women and Welfare: Ten Victorian Women in Public Social Service* (1988). Seeks to explain why some middle-class Victorian women became involved in public service, by examining the lives of ten reformers.

5.1205 **Pedersen**, S., 'The failure of feminism in the making of the British welfare state', *Radical H. R.* 43, Winter (1989), 86–114.

5.1206 — 'Gender, welfare and citizenship in Britain during the Great War', *Am. H. R.*, 95.4 (1990), 983–1006.

5.1207 **Perkins**, J. A., 'Unmarried mothers and the Poor Law in Lincolnshire, 1800–1850', *Lincs. Hist. Arch.*, 20 (1985), 21–33.

5.1208 **Riley**, D., *War in the Nursery. Theories of the Child and the Mother* (1983). Explores advice literature for middle-class mothers.

5.1209 **Roebuck**, J. and **Slaughter**, J., 'Ladies and pensioners: stereotypes and public policy affecting old women in England, 1880–1940', *J. Soc. Hist.*, 13.1 (1979), 105–14.

5.1210 **Rowan**, C., ' "Mothers vote Labour!" The state, the labour movement and working-class mothers, 1900–1918', in R. Brunt and C. Rowan, eds., *Feminism, Culture and Politics* (1982), 59–84. Looks at attitudes of the WLL and the Women's Co-operative Guild to questions of state intervention and women's role in the family.

5.1211 **Smith**, F. B., *Florence Nightingale: Reputation and Power* (1982). A highly critical assessment of Nightingale as a reformer.

5.1212 **Sonya**, M. and **Koven**, S., 'Womanly duties: maternalist politics and the origins of welfare states in France, Germany, Great Britain and the United States, 1880–1920', *Am. H. R.* 95.4 (1990), 1076–1108.

5.1213 **Spensky**, M., 'Producers of legitimacy: homes for unmarried mothers in the 1950s', in C. Smart, ed., *Regulating Motherhood: Historical Essays on Marriage,*

Motherhood and Sexuality (1992), 100–18.

5.1214 **Spring**, E. and **Spring**, D., 'The real Florence Nightingale?', *Bull.Hist. Medicine*, 57 (1983), 285–90.

5.1215 **Steedman**, C., 'Bodies, figures and physiology: Margaret McMillan and the late nineteenth-century remaking of working-class childhood', in R. Cooter, ed., *In the name of the Child: Health and Welfare, 1880–1940* (1992), 19–44.

5.1216 **Stocks**, M. D., *Eleanor Rathbone* (1949). Biography by a sister activist which emphasises Rathbone's role in the campaign for family allowances.

5.1217 **Thane**, P., 'Women and the Poor Law in Victorian and Edwardian England', *Hist. Workshop J.*, 6 (1978), 29–51.

5.1218 — 'The debate on the declining birth rate in Britain: the "menace" of an ageing population, 1920s-50s', *Cont. and Change*, 5.2 (1990), 283–306.

5.1219 — 'Visions of gender in the making of the British welfare state: the case of women in the British Labour Party and social policy, 1906–1945', in G. Bock and P. Thane, eds., *Maternity and Gender Policies: Women and the Rise of the European Welfare States, 1880–1950* (1991), 93–118.

5.1220 **Walton**, R. G., *Women in Social Work* (1975). Explores relationship between women and social work and women's emancipation in the past as well as in contemporary society.

5.1221 **Whittaker**, F. W. and **Oleson**, V. L., 'The faces of Florence Nightingale: functions of the heroine legend in an occupational sub-culture', *Human Organisation*, 23 (1964), 123–30.

5.1222 **Wilson**, E., *Women and the Welfare State* (1977).

5.1223 **Woodham-Smith**, C., *Florence Nightingale, 1820–1910* (1950).

See also: 5.337; 5.354; 5.402; 5.788.

(k) WOMEN AND PROSTITUTION

5.1224 **Bristow**, R., *Vice and Vigilance: Purity Movements in Britain since 1700* (Dublin, 1977).

5.1225 **Davis**, T. C., 'Actresses and prostitutes in Victorian London', *Theatre R*. 13 (1988), 221–34.

5.1226 **Engel**, A., 'Immoral intentions: the University of Oxford and the problem of prostitution, 1827–1914', *Vict. Studs.*, 23.1 (1979), 79–107. Social origins of prostitutes.

5.1227 **Finnegan**, F., *Poverty and Prostitution: A Study of Victorian Prostitutes in York* (1979). Detailed analysis of social and geographical origins of prostitutes and their clients. Challenges the view that prostitutes were healthy and abandoned their profession with ease.

5.1228 **Gorham**, D., 'The "maiden tribute of modern Babylon" re-examined. Child prostitution and the idea of childhood in late Victorian England', *Vict. Studs.*, 21.3 (1978), 353–79.

5.1229 **Hamilton**, M., 'Opposition to the Contagious Diseases Acts, 1864–1886', *Albion*, 10.1 (1978), 14–27.

5.1230 **Harrison**, B., 'Josephine Butler', in J. F. G. Harrison et al., eds., *Eminently Victorian* (1974), 85–94.

5.1231 **L'Esperance**, J., 'The work of the Ladies' National Association for the repeal of the Contagious Diseases' Acts', *Scy. Study Labour Hist.*, Bull. 26 (1973), 13–16.

5.1232 **Littlewood**, B. and **Mahood**, L., 'Prostitutes, magdalenes and wayward girls: dangerous sexualities of working-class women in Victorian Scotland', *Gend. and Hist.*, 3.2 (1991), 160–75.

5.1233 **Luddy**, M., 'Prostitution and rescue work in nineteenth-century Ireland', in M. Luddy and C. Murphy, eds., *Women Surviving: Studies in Irish Women's History in the Nineteenth and Twentieth Centuries* (Dublin, 1990), 51–84.

5.1234 **McHugh**, P., *Prostitution and Victorian Social Reform* (1980).

5.1235 **Mahood**, L., 'The domestication of fallen women: the Glasgow Magdalene Institution, 1860–1890', in D. McCrone, S. Kendrick and P. Straw, eds., *The Making of Scotland: Nation, Culture and Social Change* (1989), 143–60.

5.1236 — 'The magdalene's friend: prostitution and social control in Glasgow, 1869–1890', *Women's Studs. Int. For.*, 13, 1/2 (1990), 49–62.

5.1237 — *The Magdalenes: Prostitution in the Nineteenth Century* (1990).

5.1238 **Marks**, L., 'Jewish women and Jewish

prostitution in the East End of London',
Jewish Q., 34.2 (1987), 6–10.

5.1239 **Pearson**, M., *The Age of Consent: Victorian Prostitution and Its Enemies* (1972).

5.1240 **Petrie**, G., *A Singular Iniquity: The Campaigns of Josephine Butler* (1971).

5.1241 **Post**, J. B., 'A Foreign Office survey of venereal disease and prostitution control, 1869–70', *Medical Hist.*, 22.3 (1978), 327–34.

5.1242 **Sigsworth**, E. M. and **Wyke**, T. J., 'A study of Victorian prostitution and venereal disease', in M. Vicinus, ed., *Suffer and Be Still: Women in the Victorian Age* (Bloomington, Indiana, 1972), 77–99.

5.1243 **Thane**, P., 'Josephine Butler', in P. Barker, ed., *Founders of the Welfare State* (1984), 17–23.

5.1244 **Uglow**, J., 'Josephine Butler: from sympathy to theory, 1828–1906', in D. Spender, ed., *Feminist Theorists: Three Centuries of Women's Intellectual Traditions* (1983), 146–64.

5.1245 **Walkowitz**, J. R., *Prostitution and Victorian Society: Women, Class and the State* (1980). Now-standard text on the LNA campaign to repeal the Contagious Diseases Acts. Analyses the feminist ideas of the LNA and the social origins of the leadership.

5.1246 — 'Male vice and feminist virtue: feminism and the politics of prostitution in nineteenth-century Britain', *Hist. Workshop J.*, 13 (1982), 79–93. Thought-provoking article on the implications of feminist involvement in campaigns to control male sexuality.

5.1247 — and **Walkowitz**, D. J., ' "We are not beasts of the field": prostitution and the poor in Plymouth and Southampton under the Contagious Diseases Acts', *Fem. Studs.*, 1, 3–4 (1973), 73–106.

5.1248 **Wood**, N., 'Prostitution and feminism in nineteenth-century Britain', *M/F: A Feminist Journal*, 7 (1982), 61–77.

See also: 5.350.

(l) WOMEN AND CRIME

(i) Women as criminals

5.1249 **Carlen**, P., et al, *Criminal Women: Some Autobiographical Accounts* (1985).

5.1249 **Conley**, C. A., *The Unwritten Law: Criminal Justice in Victorian Kent* (1991). Looks at lawbreakers and their sentencing according to class, gender and community status.

5.1251 **Davies**, R., ' "Do not go gentle into that good night"? Women and suicide in Carmarthenshire, *c*. 1860–1920', in A. V. John, ed., *Our Mothers' Land: Chapters in Welsh Women's History, 1830–1939* (1991), 93–108.

5.1252 **Dobash**, R. P., **Dobash**, R. E. and **Gutteridge**, S., *The Imprisonment of Women* (1986). Trace penal ideas and practices 1600–1900, before discussing the modern problems of women in prison.

5.1253 **Gribble**, L., *Such Lethal Ladies* (1985). An account of women murderers, 1800–1970.

5.1254 **Hartman**, M., *Victorian Murderesses: A True History of Thirteen Respectable French and English Women Accused of Unspeakable Crimes* (New York, 1977).

5.1255 **Huggett**, R. and **Berry**, P., *Daughters of Cain: The Story of Nine Women Executed since Edith Thompson in 1923* (1990).

5.1256 **Mannheimer**, J., 'Murderous mothers: the problem of parenting in the Victorian novel', *Fem. Studs.*, 5.3 (1979), 530–46.

5.1257 **Naish**, C., *Death Comes to the Maiden: Sex and Execution, 1431–1933* (1991).

5.1258 **Weis**, R., *Criminal Justice: the Story of Edith Thompson* (1990).

5.1259 **Zedner**, L., *Women, Crime and Custody in Victorian England* (1991).

(ii) Crimes against women

5.1260 **Bauer**, C. and **Ritt**, L., ' "A husband is a beating animal" – Frances Power Cobbe confronts the wife abuse problem in Victorian England', *Int. J. Women's Studs.*, 6 (1983), 99–118.

5.1261 **Clark**, A., *Women's Silence, Men's Violence: Sexual Assault in England, 1770–1845* (1987).

5.1262 **Conley**, A., 'Rape and justice in Victorian England', *Vict. Studs.*, 29.4 (1986), 519–36. Evidence from Kentish rape cases shows judicial procedures were very irregular and convictions were related to popular male attitudes rather than legal codes.

5.1263 **Hammerton**, A. J., 'The targets of "rough music": respectability and domestic violence in Victorian England', *Gend. and Hist.*, 3.1 (1991), 23–44.

5.1264 **Lambertz**, J., 'Feminists and the politics of wifebeating', in H. L. Smith, ed., *British Feminism in the Twentieth Century* (1990), 25–43.

5.1265 **May**, M., 'Violence in the family: an historical perspective', in J. P. Marton, ed., *Violence in the Family* (1978), 362–82.

5.1266 **Tomes**, N., ' "A torrent of abuse": crimes of violence between working-class men and women, 1849–1875', *J. Soc. Hist.*, 11 (1978), 328–45.

5.1267 **Walkowitz**, J. R., 'Jack the Ripper and the myth of male violence', *Fem. Studs*, 8.3 (1982), 542–74. Argues against the view that male violence and female victimisation had a single root cause or effect. Neither was universal.

See also: 5.429.

(m) WOMEN AND RELIGION

5.1268 **Anderson**, O., 'Women preachers in mid-Victorian England: some reflections on feminism, popular religion and social change', *Hist. J.*, 12 (1969), 467–84.

5.1269 **Arnstein**, W. L., 'Queen Victoria and Religion', in G. Malmgreen, ed., *Religion in the Lives of English Women, 1760–1930* (1986), 88–128. Examines the complexities of the Queen's religious views/beliefs.

5.1270 **Batchelor**, M., *Catherine Bramwell Booth, 1884–1987: The Story of Her Life* (1987). Biography of a leader of the Salvation Army.

5.1271 **Briggs**, J., 'She-preachers, widows and other women: the feminine dimension in Baptist life since 1600', *Baptist Q.*, 31.7 (1986), 337–51.

5.1272 **Burfield**, D., 'Theosophy and feminism: some explorations in nineteenth-century biography', in P. Holden, ed., *Women's Religious Experience* (1983), 27–53. Explores the appeal of theosophy for

feminists through the lives of more rank and file members.

5.1273 **Burman**, R., ' "She looketh well to the ways of her household": the changing role of Jewish women in religious life, *c.* 1880–1930', in G. Malmgreen, ed., *Religion in the Lives of English Women, 1760–1930* (1986), 234–59. Suggests women had an increasingly central role in Jewish religion in Manchester as compared with Eastern Europe, but argues that this did not lead to an increase in communal stature or authority.

5.1274 — 'Women in Jewish religious life: Manchester, 1880–1930', in J. Obelkevich, L. Roper and R. Samuel, eds., *Disciplines of Faith: Studies in Religion, Politics and Patriarchy* (1987), 37–55.

5.1275 **Clark**, A., 'The sexual crisis and popular religion in London, 1770–1820', *Int. Labor and Working-Class Hist.*, 34, Fall (1988), 56–69.

5.1276 **Clear**, C., *Nuns in Nineteenth-Century Ireland* (Dublin, 1987).

5.1277 — 'Walls within walls: nuns in nineteenth-century Ireland', in C. Curtain, P. Jackson and B. O'Connor, eds., *Gender in Irish Society* (Galway, 1987).

5.1278 — 'The limits of female autonomy: nuns in nineteenth-century Ireland', in M. Luddy and C. Murphy, eds., *Women Surviving: Studies in Irish Women's History in the Nineteenth and Twentieth Centuries* (Dublin, 1990).

5.1279 **Cooter**, R. J., 'Lady Londonderry and the Irish catholics of Seaham Harbour: "no popery" out of context', *Recusant Hist.*, 13.4 (1976), 288–98.

5.1280 **Corfield**, K., 'Elizabeth Heyrick: radical Quaker', in G. Malmgreen, ed., *Religion in the Lives of English Women, 1760–1930* (1986), 41–67. Examines the involvement of an active Quaker in the movement for the abolition of slavery.

5.1281 **Deacon**, A. and **Hill**, M., 'The problem of "surplus women" in the nineteenth century: secular and religious alternatives', *Sociological Yearbook of Religion in Britain*, 5 (1972), 87–102.

5.1282 **Dews**, D. C., 'Ann Carr and the female revivalists of Leeds', in G. Malmgreen, ed., *Religion in the Lives of English Women, 1760–1930* (1986), 68–87. A Primitive Methodist preacher (1783–1841) who was popular with the working class in Leeds.

5.1283 **Fahey**, T., 'Nuns in the Catholic church in

Ireland in the nineteenth century', in M. Cullen, ed., *Girls Don't Do Honours: Irish Women in Education in the Nineteenth and Twentieth Centuries* (Dublin, 1987), 7–30.

5.1284 **Greaves**, R. L., 'The role of women in early English Nonconformity', *Church Hist.*, 52.3 (1983), 299–311.

5.1285 **Heeney**, B., 'The beginnings of church feminism: women and the councils of the Church of England, 1897–1919', *J. Ecc. Hist.*, 33 (1982), 86–109.

5.1286 — 'Women's struggle for professional work and status in the Church of England, 1900–1930', *Hist. J.*, 26.2 (1983), 329–47.

5.1287 — *The Women's Movement in the Church of England, 1850–1930* (1988). Standard account.

5.1288 **Higginbotham**, A. R., 'Respectable sinners: Salvation Army rescue work with unmarried mothers, 1884–1914', in G. Malmgreen, ed., *Religion in the Lives of English Women, 1760–1930* (1986), 216–33.

5.1289 **Holden**, P., ed., *Women's Religious Experience* (1983).

5.1290 **Hopkins**, J. K., *A Woman to Deliver Her People: Joanna Southcott and English Millenarianism in an Era of Revolution* (Austin, Texas, 1982). Early nineteenth-century prophetess, the daughter of a Devon farmer, who had considerable popular appeal.

5.1291 **Isichei**, E., *Victorian Quakers* (1970). Contains material on women.

5.1292 **Johnson**, D., *Women in English Religion, 1700–1925* (New York, 1983).

5.1293 **Kane**, P. M., ' "The willing captive of home?": the English Catholic Women's League, 1906–20', *Church Hist.*, 60 (1991), 331–55.

5.1294 **Kowalski-Wallace**, B., 'Hannah and her sister: women and evangelism in early nineteenth-century England', *Nineteenth-Century Contexts*, 12.2 (1988), 29–52.

5.1295 **Lee**, J. J., 'Women and the church since the famine', in M. MacCurtain and D. Ó'Corráin, eds., *Women in Irish Society: The Historical Dimension* (Dublin, 1978), 37–45. Examines how the famine weakened women's economic position and the church reinforced rural conservatism, especially over sex/marriage.

5.1296 **MacCurtain**, M., 'Fulness of life: defining female spirituality in twentieth-century Ireland', in M. Luddy and C. Murphy, eds., *Women Surviving: Studies in Irish Women's History in the Nineteenth and Twentieth Centuries* (Dublin, 1990), 233–63. Discusses the experiences of laywomen.

5.1297 **Maison**, M., ' "Thine, only thine!" Women hymn writers in Britain, 1760–1835', in G. Malmgreen, ed., *Religion in the Lives of English Women, 1760–1930* (1986), 11–40.

5.1298 **Malmgreen**, G., 'Domestic discords: women and the family in East Cheshire Methodism, 1750–1830', in J. Obelkevich, L. Roper and R. Samuel, eds., *Disciplines of Faith: Studies in Religion, Politics and Patriarchy* (1987), 55–70.

5.1299 — ed., *Religion in the Lives of English Women, 1760–1930* (1986). Important collection of essays on varied topics relating to women and religion.

5.1300 **Millbank**, A., 'Josephine Butler: Christianity, feminism and social action', in J. Obelkevich, L. Roper and R. Samuel, eds., *Disciplines of Faith: Studies in Religion, Politics and Patriarchy* (1987), 154–64.

5.1301 **Murdoch**, N. H., 'Female ministry in the thought of Catherine Booth', *Church Hist.*, 53.3 (1984), 34–62.

5.1302 **Obelkevich**, J., **Roper**, L. and **Samuel**, R., eds., *Disciplines of Faith: Studies in Religion, Politics and Patriarchy* (1987). Collection of essays examining the interrelationship between religion, family, sexuality and culture.

5.1303 **O'Brien**, S., 'Terra incognita: the nun in nineteenth-century England', *P. P.*, 121 (1988), 110–40. Pioneering study of a neglected group.

5.1304 **O'Dowd**, L., 'The church, state and women: the aftermath of partition', in C. Curtain, P. Jackson and B. O'Connor, eds., *Gender in Irish Society* (Galway, 1987), 233–63. An analysis of the influence of the Catholic church on the lives of Irish women.

5.1305 **Owen**, A., 'The other voice: women, children and nineteenth-century spiritualism', in C. Steedman et al., eds., *Language, Gender and Childhood* (1985), 34–73.

5.1306 — 'Women and nineteenth-century spiritualism: strategies in the subversion of femininity', in J. Obelkevich, L. Roper and R. Samuel, eds., *Disciplines of Faith: Studies in Religion* (1987), 130–53.

5.1307 — *The Darkened Room. Women, Power and*

Spiritualism in Late Victorian England (1989).

5.1308 **Prelinger**, C. M., 'The female deaconate in the Anglican church: what kind of ministry for women?', in G. Malmgreen, ed., *Religion in the Lives of English Women, 1760–1930* (1986), 161–92.

5.1309 **Reed**, J. S., ' "A female movement": the feminization of nineteenth-century Anglo-Catholicism', *Anglican and Ecumenical Hist.*, 31 (1988), 199–238.

5.1310 **Roxburgh**, M. J., *Women's Work in the Church of England* (1958).

5.1311 **Smith**, K. E., 'Beyond public and private spheres: another look at women in Baptist history and historiography', *Baptist Q.*, 34 (1991), 79–87.

5.1312 **Valenze**, D., *Prophetic Sons and Daughters: Female Preaching and Popular Religion in Industrial England* (Princeton, New Jersey, 1985).

5.1313 **Wessinger**, C. L., *Annie Besant and Progressive Messianism (1847–1933)* (Lewiston/Queenston, 1988). Descriptive account of Besant's involvement in theosophy.

(n) WOMEN AND EDUCATION

5.1314 **Aldrich**, R. E., 'Educating our mistresses', *Hist. Ed*, 12.2 (1983), 93–102. Girls' secondary schooling in the 1860s and 1870s.

5.1315 **Anderson**, K., 'Frances Mary Buss: the founder as headmistress, 1850–1950', in R. M. Scrimgeour, ed., *The North London Collegiate School, 1850–1950* (1950).

5.1316 **Atkinson**, P., 'Fitness, feminism and schooling', in S. Delamont and L. Duffin, eds., *The Nineteenth-Century Woman: Her Cultural and Physical World* (1978), 92–133. The role of physical education in nineteenth-century feminist institutions.

5.1317 — 'Strong minds and weak bodies: sports, gymnastics and the medicalization of women's education', *Brit. J. Sports Hist.*, 2.1 (1985), 62–71.

5.1318 — 'The feminist physique: physical education and the medicalization of women's education', in J. A. Mangan and R. J. Park, eds., *From 'Fair Sex' to Feminism: Sport and Socialization of Women in the Industrial and Post-Industrial Eras* (1987), 38–57.

5.1319 **Avery**, G., *The Best Type of Girl: A History of Girls' Independent Schools* (1991).

5.1320 **Bailey**, K., ' "Plain and nothing fancy": Her Majesty's Inspectors and school needlework in the 1870s', *J. Ed. Admin. and Hist.*, 18.1 (1986), 34–45.

5.1321 **Binfield**, C., *Belmont's Portias: Victorian Nonconformists and Middle-Class Education for Girls* (1980).

5.1322 **Bingham**, C., ' "Doing something for women": Matthew Vassar and Thomas Holloway', *Hist. Today*, 36.6 (1986), 46–51. Philanthropic founders of women's colleges in nineteenth-century America and Britain.

5.1323 **Borer**, M. C., *Willingly to School: A History of Women's Education* (1976).

5.1324 **Bradbrook**, M. C., *That Infidel Place: A Short History of Girton College, 1869–1969* (1969).

5.1325 **Bradburn**, E., *Margaret McMillan: Portrait of a Pioneer* (1988). Biography of the socialist educational reformer.

5.1326 **Breathnach**, E., 'Charting new waters: women's experiences in higher education, 1879–1908', in M. Cullen, ed., *Girls Don't Do Honours: Irish Women in Education in the Nineteenth and Twentieth Centuries* (Dublin, 1987), 55–78.

5.1327 **Bryant**, M., *The Unexpected Revolution: A Study in the History of the Education of Women and Girls in the Nineteenth Century* (1979). Includes material on the development of a feminist network during the early campaigns.

5.1328 **Burstall**, S., *Retrospect and Prospect: Sixty Years of Women's Education* (1933).

5.1329 **Burstyn**, J. N., 'Education and sex: the medical case against higher education for women in England, 1870–1900', *Pcdgs. Am. Philos. Scy.*, 117.2 (1973), 79–89.

5.1330 — 'Women's education in England during the nineteenth century: a review of the literature, 1970–76', *Hist. Ed.*, 6.1 (1977), 11–19.

5.1331 — *Victorian Education and the Ideal of Womanhood* (1980). Analysis of the ideological role of education in defining femininity.

5.1332 **Carver**, R. N., 'The work of Kate Ryley on the Birkdale School Board, 1889–1902', *Hist. Ed. Scy. Bull.*, 38, Autumn (1986), 43–50.

5.1333 **Clarke**, A. K., *A History of the Cheltenham Ladies' College, 1853–1953* (1953).

5.1334 **Cookingham**, M. E., 'Blue stockings, spinsters and pedagogues: women college graduates, 1865–1910', *Pop. Studs.*, 38.3 (1984), 349–64.

5.1335 **Coombs**, M., *Charlotte Mason and the Parents' National Education Union: The Challenge of Victorian Spinsterhood* (1987).

5.1336 **Cullen**, M., ed., *Girls Don't Do Honours: Irish Women in Education in the Nineteenth and Twentieth Centuries* (Dublin, 1987).

5.1337 **David**, M., *The State, the Family and Education* (1980). Sociological analysis of the links between women's role in teaching, girls' education and ideas concerning women's social role.

5.1338 **Davin**, A., ' "Mind that you do as you are told": reading books for Board School girls', *Fem. R.*, 3 (1979), 89–98.

5.1339 **Delamont**, S., 'The contradictions in ladies' education', in S. Delamont and L. Duffin, eds., *The Nineteenth-Century Woman: Her Cultural and Physical World* (1978), 134–63. Examines the complexities of feminist and anti-feminist ideas about education.

5.1340 — 'The domestic ideology and women's education', in S. Delamont and L. Duffin, eds., *The Nineteenth-Century Woman: Her Cultural and Physical World* (1978), 164–87.

5.1341 **Dyhouse**, C., 'Social Darwinistic ideas and the development of women's education in England, 1880–1920', *Hist. Ed.*, 5.1 (1976), 41–58.

5.1342 — 'Good wives and little mothers: social anxieties and the schoolgirl's curriculum, 1890–1920', *Oxford R. Ed.*, 3.1 (1977), 21–35.

5.1343 — 'Towards a "feminine" curriculum for English schoolgirls; the demands of ideology, 1870–1963', *Women's Studs. Int. Q.*, 1.4 (1978), 297–311.

5.1344 — 'Miss Buss and Miss Beale: gender and authority in the history of education', in F. Hunt, ed., *Lessons for Life: The Schooling of Girls and Women, 1850–1950* (1987), 22–38.

5.1345 **Edwards**, E., 'Educational institutions or extended families? The reconstruction of gender in women's colleges in the late nineteenth and early twentieth centuries', *Gend. and Ed.*, 2.1 (1990), 17–35.

5.1346 — 'Alice Havergal Skillicorn: principal of Homerton College, Cambridge, 1935–60: a study of gender and power', *Women's H. R.*, 1.1 (1992), 109–29.

5.1347 **Evans**, W. G., *Education and Female Emancipation: the Welsh Experience, 1847–1914* (1990). The struggle for women's education in Wales.

5.1348 **Fitzpatrick**, D., 'A share of the honeycomb: education, emigration and Irishwomen', in M. Daly and D. Dickson, eds., *The Origins of Popular Literacy in Ireland* (Dublin, 1990), 167–87.

5.1349 **Fletcher**, S., *Women First: The Female Tradition in English Secondary Education, 1880–1940* (1984).

5.1350 — 'The making and breaking of a female tradition: women's physical education in England, 1880–1980', *Brit. J. Sports Hist.*, 2.1 (1985), 29–39.

5.1351 — *Feminists and Bureaucrats: A Study in the Development of Girls' Education in the Nineteenth Century* (1990). Analyses the founding of sixty secondary schools for girls.

5.1352 **Freeman**, C. B., *Mary Simpson of Boynton Vicarage: Teacher of Ploughboys and Critic of Methodism* (1972).

5.1353 **Gomersall**, M., 'Ideals and realities: the education of working-class girls, 1800–1870', *Hist. Ed.*, 17 (1988), 37–53.

5.1354 **Gordon**, P., 'Katherine Bathurst: a controversial woman inspector', *Hist. Ed.*, 17.3 (1988), 193–208.

5.1355 **Gorham**, D., 'The ideology of femininity and reading for girls, 1850–1914', in F. Hunt, ed., *Lessons for Life: The Schooling of Girls and Women, 1850–1950* (1987), 39–59.

5.1356 **Hamilton**, S., 'Interviewing the middle class: women graduates of the Scottish universities', *Oral Hist*, 10.2 (1982), 58–67.

5.1357 **Hargreaves**, J. A., ' "Playing like gentlemen while behaving like ladies": contradictory features of the formative years of women's sport', *Brit. J. Sports Hist.*, 2.1 (1985), 40–52.

5.1358 **Horn**, P., 'The education and employment of working-class girls, 1870–1914', *Hist. Ed.*, 17 (1988), 71–82.

5.1359 **Howarth**, J., 'Public schools, safety nets and educational ladders: the classification of girls' secondary schools, 1880–1914', *Oxford R. Ed.*, 11.1 (1985), 59–71.

5.1360 — and **Curthoys**, M., 'The political economy of women's higher education in late nineteenth and early twentieth –

century Britain', *Hist. Res.*, 60 (1987), 208–31.

5.1361 **Hunt**, F., 'Social class and the grading of schools: realities in girls' secondary education, 1880–1940', in J. Purvis, ed., *The Education of Girls and Women* (1985), 27–46.

5.1362 — 'Divided aims: the educational implications of opposing ideologies in girls' secondary schooling, 1850–1940', in F. Hunt, ed., *Lessons for Life: The Schooling of Girls and Women, 1850–1950* (1987), 3–21.

5.1363 — *Gender and Policy in English Education, 1902–44* (1991). Considers the impact of organisational policy on girls' schooling.

5.1364 — ed., *Lessons for Life: The Schooling of Girls and Women, 1850–1950* (1987). Important collection of articles exploring gender issues in education. Examines how ideologies of femininity dictated educational theory and practice.

5.1365 **Hurt**, J. S., *Elementary Schooling and the Working Classes, 1860–1918* (1979). Contains some information on girls.

5.1366 **Kamm**, J., *How Different From Us: A Biography of Miss Buss and Miss Beale* (1958).

5.1367 — *Hope Deferred: Girls' Education in English History* (1965). Detailed survey of girls' education.

5.1368 — *Indicative Past: A Hundred Years of the Girls' Public Day School Trust* (1971).

5.1369 **Kendall**, C. M., 'Higher education and the emergence of the professional woman in Glasgow, *c.* 1890–1914', *Hist. Universities*, 10 (1991), 199–223.

5.1370 **Leinster-Mackay**, D. P., 'Dame schools: a need for review', *Brit. J. Ed. Studs.*, 24.1 (1976), 33–48.

5.1371 **Levine**, D., 'Education and family life in early industrial England', *J. Fam. Hist.*, 4.4 (1979), 368–80.

5.1372 — 'Illiteracy and family life during the first Industrial Revolution', *J. Soc. Hist.*, 14.1 (1980), 25–44.

5.1373 **Lewis**, J., 'Parents, children, school fees and the London School Board, 1870–1890', *Hist. Ed.*, 11.4 (1982), 291–312.

5.1374 **McCrone**, K. E., ' "Play up! Play up! and play the game!" Sport at the late-Victorian girls' public schools', in J. A. Mangan and R. J. Park, eds., *From 'Fair Sex' to Feminism: Sport and the Socialization of Women in the Industrial and Post Industrial Eras* (1987), 97–129.

5.1375 — 'The "lady blue": sport at the Oxbridge women's colleges from their foundation to 1914', *Brit. J. Sports Hist.*, 3. 2 (1986), 191–215.

5.1376 — *Playing the Game: Sport and the Physical Emancipation of English Women, 1870–1914* (Lexington, Virginia, 1988). Argues sport could be a step towards women's emancipation while at the same time reinforcing their subordination to men.

5.1377 **McWilliams-Tullberg**, R., *Women at Cambridge: A Men's University – Though of a Mixed Type* (1975).

5.1378 — 'Women and degrees at Cambridge University', in M. Vicinus, ed., *A Widening Sphere: Changing Roles of Victorian Women* (Bloomington, Indiana, 1977), 117–45.

5.1379 **Mansbridge**, A., *Margaret McMillan: Prophet and Pioneer: Her Life and Work* (1932).

5.1380 **Manthorpe**, C., 'Science or domestic science? The struggle to define an appropriate science education for girls in twentieth-century England', *Hist. Ed.*, 15.3 (1986), 195–213.

5.1381 **Marks**, P., 'Femininity in the classroom: an account of changing attitudes', in J. Mitchell and A. Oakley, eds., *The Rights and Wrongs of Women* (1976), 176–98.

5.1382 **Martin**, J., ' "Hard headed and large hearted": women and the industrial schools, 1870–1885', *Hist. Ed.*, 20.3 (1991), 187–201.

5.1383 **Miller**, P. J., 'Women's education, self improvement and social mobility: a late eighteenth-century debate', *Brit. J. Ed. Studs.*, 20.3 (1972), 302–14.

5.1384 **O'Connor**, A. V., 'Influences affecting girls' secondary education in Ireland, 1860–1910', *Archivum Hibernicum*, 41 (1986), 83–98.

5.1385 — 'The revolution in girls' secondary education, 1860–1910', in M. Cullen, ed., *Girls Don't Do Honours: Irish Women in Education in the Nineteenth and Twentieth Centuries* (Dublin, 1987), 31–54.

5.1386 — and **Parkes**, S. M., *Gladly Learn and Gladly Teach: A History of Alexandra College and School, Dublin, 1866–1966* (Tallaght, 1983).

5.1387 **Park**, R. J., 'Sport, gender and society in a transatlantic Victorian perspective', *Brit. J. Sports Hist.*, 2.1 (1985), 5–28.

5.1388 — 'Sport, dress reform and the

emancipation of women in Victorian England: a reappraisal', *International J. Hist. Sport*, 6.1 (1989), 10–30.

5.1389 **Pedersen**, J. S., 'The reform of women's secondary and higher education. Institutional change and social values in mid and late Victorian England', *Hist. Ed. Q.*, 19.1 (1979), 61–91. Considers extent to which female educationalists helped to promote or to reject dominant values.

5.1390 — 'Some Victorian headmistresses: a conservative tradition of social reform', *Vict. Studs.*, 24.4 (1981), 463–88. Sympathetic interpretation of the importance of the overbearing headmistress.

5.1391 — *The Reform of Girls' Secondary and Higher Education in Victorian England: A Study of Elites and Educational Change* (New York, 1988).

5.1392 **Pointon**, M., 'Factors influencing the participation of women and girls in physical education, physical recreation and sport in Great Britain during the period 1850–1920', *Hist. Ed. Scy. Bull.* 24, Autumn (1979), 46–56.

5.1393 **Prentice**, A. and **Theobald**, M. R., 'The historiography of women teachers: a retrospect', in A. S. Prentice and M. R. Theobald, eds., *Perspectives on the History of Women and Teaching* (Toronto, 1991), 3–33.

5.1394 — eds., *Perspectives on the History of Women and Teaching* (Toronto, 1991). Collection of articles covering different countries.

5.1395 **Purvis**, J., 'Working-class women and adult education in nineteenth-century Britain', *Hist. Ed.*, 9.3 (1980), 193–212.

5.1396 — 'Towards a history of women's education in nineteenth-century Britain: a sociological analysis', *Westminster Studs. Ed.*, 4 (1981), 45–79.

5.1397 — *Hard Lessons: The Lives and Education of Working-Class Women in Nineteenth-Century England* (1989).

5.1398 — *A History of Women's Education in England* (1991).

5.1399 — ed., *The Education of Girls and Women* (1985).

5.1400 **Rendel**, M., 'How many women academics, 1912–76', in R. Deem, ed., *Schooling for Women's Work* (1980), 142–61. Statistical analysis based on Commonwealth year books – includes number of female academics, subjects taught etc.

5.1401 **Ridler**, A., *Olive Willis and Downe House* (1967).

5.1402 **Riordan**, J., 'The social emancipation of women through sport', *Brit. J. Sports Hist.*, 2.1 (1985), 53–61.

5.1403 **Roach**, J., 'Boys and girls at school, 1800–70', *Hist. Ed.*, 15.3 (1986), 147–59.

5.1404 **Robertson**, A., 'Catherine I. Dodd and innovation in teacher training, 1892–1905', *Hist. Ed. Scy. Bull.*, 47, Spring (1991), 32–41.

5.1405 **Rogers**, A., *Degrees By Degrees: The Story of the Admission of Oxford Women Students to Membership of the University* (1938).

5.1406 **Rubinstein**, D., 'Annie Besant and Stewart Headlam: the London School Board election of 1888', *East London Papers*, 13.1 (1970), 3–24.

5.1407 **Silver**, H., *The Concept of Popular Education* (1965). Includes a discussion of women's education.

5.1408 **Steedman**, C., ' "The mother made conscious". The historical development of a primary school pedagogy', *Hist. Workshop J.*, 20 (1985), 149–63.

5.1409 **Stephen**, B., *Emily Davies and Girton College* (1927).

5.1410 **Summerfield**, P., 'Cultural reproduction in the education of girls: a study of girls' secondary schooling in two Lancashire towns, 1900–50', in F. Hunt, ed., *Lessons for Life: The Schooling of Girls and Women, 1850–1950* (1987), 149–70. Discusses ambiguities in intentions of single sex schools towards preparing girls for marriage.

5.1411 — *Women, Work and Education, 1920–1950* (1988).

5.1412 **Sutherland**, G., *Elementary Education in the Nineteenth Century* (1971). Explores implications for women's employment, political and marital status.

5.1413 — *Policy Making in Elementary Education, 1870–1895* (1973).

5.1414 — 'The movement for the higher education of women: its social and intellectual context in England, *c.* 1840–1880', in P. Waller, ed., *Political and Social Change in Modern Britain* (1987), 91–116.

5.1415 **Theobald**, M. R., 'The accomplished woman and the propriety of intellect: a new look at women's education in Britain and Australia, 1800–50', *Hist. Ed.*, 17 (1988), 21–35.

5.1416 **Thom**, D., 'Better a teacher than a

hairdresser? "A male passion for equality" or, keeping Molly and Betty down', in F. Hunt, ed., *Lessons for Life: The Schooling of Girls and Women, 1850–1950* (1987), 124–45. Discusses intelligence testing and gender differences.

5.1417 **Thorburn**, D., 'Gender, work and schooling in the plaiting villages', *Local Histn.*, 19.3 (1989), 107–13. On Hertfordshire.

5.1418 **Tranter**, N. L., 'Organised sport and the middle-class woman in nineteenth-century Scotland', *Int. J. Hist. Sport*, 6.1 (1989), 31–48.

5.1419 **Tuke**, M. J., *A History of Bedford College for Women, 1849–1937* (1939).

5.1420 **Turnbull**, A., 'Learning her womanly work: the elementary school curriculum, 1870–1914', in F. Hunt, ed., *Lessons for Life: The Schooling of Girls and Women, 1850–1950* (1987), 83–100.

5.1421 **Tylecote**, M., *The Education of Women at Manchester University, 1883–1933* (1941).

5.1422 **Whitbread**, N., *Evolution of the Nursery–Infant School: A History of Infant and Nursery Education in Britain, 1800–1970* (1972).

5.1423 **Williams**, P., 'Pioneer women students at Cambridge, 1869–81', in F. Hunt, ed., *Lessons for Life: The Schooling of Girls and Women, 1850–1950* (1987), 171–91. Explores the motivations of this small, privileged group and the opposition they faced.

5.1424 **Wright**, A., 'Margery Allen and the nursery school movement, 1935–45', *Hist. Ed. Scy. Bull.*, 31, Spring (1983), 49–51.
See also: 5.229; 5.380; 5.425; 5.427.

(o) WOMEN AND THE ARTS

5.1425 **Agress**, L., *The Feminine Irony: Women on Women in Early Nineteenth-Century Literature* (1978).

5.1426 **Andrews**, L., 'Charlotte Brontë: the woman and the feminist', *Brontë Scy. Trans.*, 12.5 (1955), 351–60.

5.1427 **Atkinson**, C. B. and **Atkinson**, J., 'Sydney Owenson, Lady Morgan: Irish patriot and

first professional woman writer', *Eire-Ireland*, 15.2 (1980), 60–90.

5.1428 **Auerbach**, N., *Woman and the Demon: The Life of a Victorian Myth* (Cambridge, Mass., 1982). Gives a counter-interpretation of nineteenth-century writing.

5.1429 — *Ellen Terry: Player in Her Time* (New York, 1987). Biography which adds to our understanding of the stage.

5.1430 **Avery**, G., *Childhood's Pattern: A Study of the Heroes and Heroines of Children's Fiction, 1770–1950* (1975). On children's literature.

5.1431 **Berkman**, J. A., *The Healing Imagination of Olive Schreiner: Beyond South African Colonialism* (Amherst, Mass., 1989). Concentrates on her writing rather than her life.

5.1432 **Bindslev**, A. M., *Mrs Humphrey Ward. A Study in Late Victorian Feminine Consciousness and Creative Expression* (Stockholm, 1985).

5.1433 **Bowman**, N., *Women's Utopias in British and American Fiction* (1988). Traces effects of social change on women's writing.

5.1434 **Broughton**, T., 'Margaret Oliphant: the unbroken self', *Women's Studs. Int. For.*, 10.1 (1987), 41–52. Scottish writer on domestic life.

5.1435 **Brown**, L. W., 'Jane Austen and the feminist tradition', *Nineteenth-Century Fiction*, 28 (1973), 321–8.

5.1436 **Buckley**, C., 'Women designers in the English pottery industry, 1919–1939', *Women's Art J.* 5, Fall (1984)/Winter (1985), 11–15.

5.1437 — *Potters and Paintresses: Women Designers in the Pottery Industry, 1870–1955* (1990).

5.1438 **Cadogan**, M. and **Craig**, P., *You're A Brick Angela! A New Look at Girls' Fiction from 1839 to 1975* (1976). Discusses literature for girls, focusing on schoolgirl papers.

5.1439 **Callen**, A., *Angel in the Studio: Women in the Arts and Crafts Movement, 1870–1914* (1979).

5.1440 **Campbell**, M., *Lady Morgan: The Life and Times of Sydney Owenson* (1988). Irish woman writer.

5.1441 **Casteras**, C. P., 'Excluding women: the cult of the male genius in Victorian painting', in L. Shires, ed., *Rewriting the Victorians: Theory, History and the Politics of Gender* (1992), 116–46.

5.1442 **Chitty**, S., *Gwen John, 1876–1939* (1981). Recent biography of a neglected woman artist.

5.1443 **Clarke**, N., *Ambitious Heights: Writing, Friendship, Love: the Jewsbury Sisters* (1990). Concerns relationship between literary sisters.

5.1444 **Cooper**, H., *Elizabeth Barrett Browning: Woman and Artist* (Chapel Hill, North Carolina, 1988). Examines tensions in her early writings between gendered public and private roles.

5.1445 **Cosslett**, T., *Woman to Woman: Female Friendship in Victorian Fiction* (1988). Discusses women writers.

5.1446 **Crosby**, C., 'Reading the Gothic revival: "history" and *Hints on Household Taste*', in L. M. Shires, ed., *Rewriting the Victorians: Theory, History and the Politics of Gender* (1992), 101–15.

5.1447 **Cunningham**, A. R., 'The "new woman" fiction of the 1890s', *Vict. Studs.*, 17.2 (1973), 177–86.

5.1448 **Cunningham**, G., *The New Woman and the Victorian Novel* (1978).

5.1449 **Daims**, D., 'A criticism of their own: turn of the century feminist writers', *Turn-Of-The-Century Women*, 2.2 (1985), 22–31.

5.1450 **David**, D., *Intellectual Women and Victorian Patriarchy: Harriet Martineau, Elizabeth Barrett Browning, George Eliot* (New York, 1987). Uses Gramscian cultural theory to disentangle the relationship of the above to the formation of Victorian culture.

5.1451 **Drotner**, K., 'Schoolgirls, madcaps and air aces: English girls and their magazine reading between the wars', *Fem. Studs.*, 9.1 (1983), 33–52. Analyses girls' popular reading. Suggests it reinforced women's oppression as well as providing the site of utopian desires.

5.1452 **Evans**, M., 'Jane Austen's feminism', *Women's Studs. Int. For.*, 9.4 (1986), 313–21. Argues that Austen was a radical writer who challenged patriarchal expectations about women.

5.1453 **Flint**, K., 'The woman reader and the opiate of fiction, 1855–1870', in J. Hawthorn, ed., *The Nineteenth-Century British Novel* (1986), 47–62.

5.1454 **Flynn**, E. A. and **Schweickart**, P. P., *Gender and Reading: Essays on Readers, Texts and Contexts* (Baltimore, Ohio, 1986). Contains an annotated bibliography.

5.1455 **Forrester**, W., *Great Grandmama's Weekly: A Celebration of the Girls' Own Paper, 1880–1901* (1980).

5.1456 **Foster**, S., *The Victorian Women Novelists* (1984).

5.1457 **Gilbert**, S. M., 'Soldier's heart: literary men, literary women and the Great War', *Signs*, 8.3 (1983), 422–50. Suggests women found the Great War sexually liberating.

5.1458 — and **Gubar**, S., *The Madwoman in the Attic: The Woman Writer and the Nineteenth-Century Literary Imagination* (New Haven, Conn., 1978). The relationship of nineteenth-century women writers to the literary imagination.

5.1459 — *No Man's Land: The Place of the Woman Writer in the Twentieth Century Vol. 1. The War of the Words* (1988). Looks at men and women, examining the reasons for, and the relationship between, the war of words between the sexes.

5.1460 **Goode**, J., ' "The affections clad with knowledge": woman's duty and the public life', *Lit. and Hist.*, 9.1 (1983), 38–51.

5.1461 **Gorsky**, S. R., 'Old maids and new women: alternatives to marriage in Englishwomen's novels, 1847–1915', *J. Pop. Cult.*, 7 (1973), 680–85.

5.1462 **Hamer**, M., 'Jobs for the girls: Arnold Bennett and Virginia Woolf', *Lit. and Hist.*, 2nd ser., 1.2 (1990), 48–61. Letters from Virginia Woolf re publishing and making income from books.

5.1463 **Hanscombe**, G. and **Smyers**, V., *Writing For Their Lives: The Modernist Women, 1910–1940* (1987). Network of women writers influenced by modernism.

5.1464 **Harris**, J., 'Not suffering and not still: women writers and the *Cornhill Magazine*, 1860–1900', *Mod. Lit. Q.*, 47 (1986), 382–92. Includes Eliot, Gaskell and Oliphant.

5.1465 **Hayter**, A., 'The sanitary idea and a Victorian novelist', *Hist. Today*, 19.12 (1969).

5.1466 **Hodder**, K., 'The Lady of Shalott in art and literature', in S. Mendus and J. Rendall, eds., *Sexuality and Subordination: Interdisciplinary Studies of Gender in the Nineteenth Century* (1989), 60–85.

5.1467 **Holcomb**, A. M., 'Anna Jameson: the first professional English art historian', *Art Hist.*, 6, June (1983), 171–87.

5.1468 **Holledge**, J., *Innocent Flowers: Women in the Edwardian Theatre* (1981).

5.1469 **Hopkinson**, A., *Julia Margaret Cameron* (1986). Feminist appraisal of the Victorian woman photographer.

5.1470 **Hunt**, L. C., *A Woman's Portion: Ideology, Culture and the British Female Novel Tradition* (New York, 1988). Examines novels of Brontë, Austen and Eliot in relation to ideologies of gender elaborated in conduct manuals, diaries and letters.

5.1471 **Hurst**, M., *Maria Edgeworth and the Public Scene* (Miami, Florida, 1969).

5.1472 **Jaffe**, P., *Women Engravers* (1990).

5.1473 **Johnson**, C. L., *Jane Austen: Women, Politics and the Novel* (Chicago, Illinois, 1988).

5.1474 **Jones**, E. H., *Mrs Humphrey Ward* (New York, 1973).

5.1475 **Jones**, M. G., *Hannah More* (1952).

5.1476 **Kestner**, J., *Protest and Reform: The British Social Narrative By Women, 1827–1867* (Madison, Wisconsin, 1985).

5.1477 **Kirkham**, M., *Jane Austen, Feminism and Fiction* (1983).

5.1478 **Klaus**, P. O., 'Women in the mirror: using novels to study Victorian women', in B. Kanner, ed., *The Women of England from Anglo Saxon Times to the Present: Interpretive Bibliographical Essays* (1980), 296–344.

5.1479 **Kohfeldt**, M. L., *Lady Gregory: The Lady behind the Irish Renaissance* (New York, 1985). Irish woman writer.

5.1480 **Kroller**, E. M., 'First impressions: rhetorical strategies in travel writing by Victorian women', *Ariel E*, 21.4 (1990), 87–99.

5.1481 **Langbauer**, L., *Women and Romance: The Consolidation of Gender in the English Novel* (Ithaca, New York, 1990).

5.1482 **McCurry**, J., ' "Our lady dispossessed": female Ulster poets and sexual politics', *Colby Q.*, 27, March (1991), 4–8.

5.1483 **McGuinn**, N., 'George Eliot and Mary Wollstonecraft', in S. Delamont and L. Duffin, eds., *The Nineteenth-Century Woman: Her Cultural and Physical World* (1978), 188–204.

5.1484 **Maconachie**, M., 'Women's work and domesticity in the *English Woman's Journal*, 1858–64', in S. Alexander, ed., *Studies in the History of Feminism* (1984).

5.1485 **Maitland**, S., *Vesta Tilley* (1986). Short biography of the male impersonator which explores general issues related to cross-dressing.

5.1486 **Marsh**, J., *The Pre-Raphaelite Sisterhood* (1985). Examines women painters.

5.1487 — *Jane and May Morris: A Biographical Story, 1838–1939* (1986). Attempts to re-interpret Jane Morris's life and to discover the real woman behind the face on the canvas. More interesting for material on May Morris.

5.1488 — and **Nunn**, P. G., *Women Artists and the Pre-Raphaelite Movement* (1989).

5.1489 **Melman**, B., *Women and the Popular Imagination in the 1920s* (1988).

5.1490 **Melville**, J., *Ellen and Edy: A Biography of Ellen Terry and Her Daughter Edith Craig* (1987).

5.1491 **Mitchell**, S., 'Sentiment and suffering: women's recreational reading in the 1860s', *Vict. Studs.*, 21.2 (1977), 29–45.

5.1492 **Moers**, E., *Literary Women* (Garden City, New York, 1976).

5.1493 **Mumm**, S. D., 'Writing for their lives: women applicants to the Royal Literary Fund, 1840–1880', *Publishing Hist.*, 27 (1990), 27–47.

5.1494 **Newton**, J. L., *Women, Power and Subversion. Social Strategies in British Fiction, 1778–1860* (Athens, Georgia, 1981).

5.1495 **Nochlin**, L., *Women, Art and Power* (1989). Key essays on women artists and women in art history by a pioneer in the field.

5.1496 **Nord**, D. E., *The Apprenticeship of Beatrice Webb* (Amherst, Mass., 1985). An original analysis of Beatrice Webb as an author and of the social context which shaped her creativity.

5.1497 **Nunn**, P. G., 'Ruskin's patronage of women artists', *Women's Art J.*, 2, Fall (1981)/Winter (1982), 8–13.

5.1498 — *Victorian Women Artists* (1987).

5.1499 — ed., *Canvassing: Recollections by Six Victorian Women Artists* (1986).

5.1500 **O'Rourke**, R., 'Were there no women? British working-class writing in the inter-war period', *Lit. and Hist.*, 14.1 (1988), 48–63.

5.1501 **Petersen**, K. and **Wilson**, J. J., *Women Artists: Recognition and Reappraisal from the Early Middle Ages to the Twentieth Century* (1978).

5.1502 **Poovey**, M., *The Proper Lady and the Woman Writer: Ideology as Style in the Works of Mary Wollstonecraft, Mary Shelley and Jane Austen* (Chicago, Illinois, 1984).

5.1503 **Reynolds**, K., *Girls Only? Gender and Popular Children's Fiction in Britain, 1880–1910* (1990).

5.1504 **Shaw**, M., ' "To tell the truth of sex": confessions and abjection in late Victorian writing', in L. Shires, ed., *Rewriting the Victorians: Theory, History and the Politics of Gender* (1992), 87–100.

5.1505 **Showalter**, E., *A Literature of Their Own: British Women Novelists from Brontë to Lessing* (1982).

5.1506 **Spender**, D. and **Hayman**, C., compilers, *How the Vote Was Won and Other Suffragette Plays* (1985).

5.1507 **Stedman**, J. W., 'From dame to woman: W. S. Gilbert and theatrical transvestism', in M. Vicinus, ed., *Suffer and Be Still: Women in the Victorian Age* (Bloomington, Indiana, 1972), 20–37.

5.1508 **Stokes**, J., **Booth**, M. R. and **Bassnett**, S., *Bernhardt, Terry, Duse: The Actress in Her Time* (1988).

5.1509 **Stone**, D, 'Victorian feminism in the nineteenth-century novel', *Women's Studs.*, 1 (1972).

5.1510 **Stubbs**, P., *Women and Fiction: Feminism and the Novel, 1880–1920* (1979). Discusses relation of literary images of women to social reality. Selection of male and female writers.

5.1511 **Sutton-Ramspeck**, B., 'The personal is political: feminist criticism and Mary Ward's reading of the Brontës', *Vict. Studs.*, 34.1 (1990), 55–76.

5.1512 **Swindells**, J., *Victorian Writing and Working Women* (Minneapolis, Minn., 1985).

5.1513 **Sydie**, R. A., 'Women painters in Britain, 1768–1848', *Atlantis*, 5, April (1980), 144–75.

5.1514 **Tankard**, J. B. and **Van Valkenbergh**, M. R., eds., *Gertrude Jekyll: A Vision of Garden and Wood* (1989). Study of the garden designer and amateur photographer, 1843–1932.

5.1515 **Taylor**, H., ' "If a young painter be not fierce and arrogant god . . . help him": some women art students at the Slade *c.* 1895–9', *Art Hist.*, 9, June (1986), 232–44.

5.1516 **Thesing**, W. B., 'Mrs Humphrey Ward's anti-suffrage campaign: from polemics to art', *Turn-Of-The-Century Women*, 1 (1984), 22–35.

5.1517 **Thomson**, P., *The Victorian Heroine: A Changing Ideal, 1837–1873* (1956). Assesses the effect of the feminist movement on the heroine of the novel.

5.1518 **Tuchman**, G. and **Fortin**, N. E., *Edging Women Out: Victorian Novelists, Publishers and Social Change* (New Haven, Conn., 1989). Analyses social and institutional conditions governing the production and reception of women's literature in the nineteenth century.

5.1519 **Van Arsdel**, R., 'Women's periodicals and the new journalism: the personal interview', in J. Weiner, ed., *Papers for the Millions* (1989), 243–56.

5.1520 **Wheelwright**, J., ' "Amazons and military maids": an examination of female military heroines in British literature and the changing construction of gender', *Women's Studs. Int. For.*, 10.5 (1987), 489–502. Examines changes in the way in which women's role in the military was portrayed in literature from the mid-eighteenth to nineteenth century.

5.1521 **White**, C. L., *Women's Magazines, 1693–1968* (1970).

5.1522 **Whitelaw**, L., *The Life and Rebellious Times of Cicely Hamilton: Actress, Writer, Suffragist* (1990).

5.1523 **Whitlock**, G., ' "Everything is out of place": Radclyffe Hall and the lesbian literary tradition', *Fem. Studs.*, 13.3 (1987), 555–82.

5.1524 **Williams**, M., *Women in the English Novel, 1800–1900* (1984).

5.1525 **Wolf**, T. L., 'Women jewelers of the British arts and crafts movement', *J. Decorative and Propaganda Arts*, 14, Fall (1989), 28–45.

5.1526 **Yeo**, E., 'Men and Women in Robert Tressell's world', *Scy. Study Labour Hist.*, Bull. 54 (1989), 14–16.

5.1527 **Zlotnick**, S., ' "A thousand times I'd be a factory girl". Dialect, domesticity and working-class women's poetry in Victorian Britain', *Vict. Studs.*, 35.1 (1991), 7–27. Examines how dialect poetry helped silence working-class women.

See also: 5.724; 5.737; 5.1114; 5.1128.

(p) AUTOBIOGRAPHY AND BIOGRAPHY

(i) Methodology

5.1528 **Alexander**, Z., 'Let it lie upon the table: the status of black women's biography in the U.K.', *Gend. and Hist.*, 2.1 (1990), 22–33.

5.1529 **Barry**, K., 'Biography and the search for women's subjectivity', *Women's Studs. Int. For.*, 12.6 (1989), 561–78.

5.1530 — 'The new historical synthesis: women's biography', *J. Women's Hist.*, 1, Winter (1990), 75–105.

5.1531 **Bassett**, M. T., 'Man-made tales: deconstructing biography as a feminist act', *Auto/Biog. Studs.*, 3, Fall (1987), 46–56.

5.1532 **Benstock**, S., ed., *The Private Self: Theory and Practice of Women's Autobiographical Writings* (1988).

5.1533 **Birkett**, D. and **Wheelwright**, J., ' "How could she?" Unpalatable facts and feminist heroines', *Gend. and Hist.*, 2.1 (1990), 49–57. Discuss how feminist biographers approach their subjects when the latter do not conform to 'received notions of feminist thought'.

5.1534 **Brodzski**, B. and **Schenck**, C., eds., *Life/Lives. Theorizing Women's Autobiography* (Ithaca, New York, 1988).

5.1535 **Bunkers**, S. L., 'Subjectivity and self-reflexivity in the study of women's diaries as autobiography', *Auto/Biog. Studs.*, 5, Fall (1990), 114–24.

5.1536 **Chevigny**, B. G., 'Daughters writing: towards a theory of a women's biography', *Fem. Studs.*, 9, Spring (1983), 79–102.

5.1537 **Corbett**, M. J., 'Feminine authorship and spiritual authority in Victorian women writers' autobiographies', *Women's Studs.*, 18 (1990), 13–29.

5.1538 **Davis**, T., et al, 'The public face of feminism: early twentieth century writings on women's suffrage', in Centre for Contemporary Cultural Studies, ed., *Making Histories: Studies in History-Writing and Politics* (1982), 302–24. Suggests new ways of approaching autobiographies as a historical source. Explores relationship between the public and the private.

5.1539 **Denith**, S. and **Dodd**, P., 'The uses of autobiography', *Lit. and Hist.*, 14.1 (1988), 4–22. General exploration of the ways historians use autobiography, with some reference to gender.

5.1540 **Gagnier**, R., 'Social atoms: working-class autobiography, subjectivity and gender', *Vict. Studs.*, 30.3 (1987), 335–63.

5.1541 **Greenleaf**, W. H., 'Biography and the "amateur" historian: Mrs Woodham-Smith's "Florence Nightingale" ', *Vict. Studs.*, II:2 (1959), 190–202.

5.1542 **Hamilton**, P., ' "Inventing the self": oral history as autobiography', *Hecate*, 16, 1/2 (1990), 128–33.

5.1543 **Hannam**, J., 'Usually neglected in standard histories: some issues in working on the life of Isabella Ford, 1855–1924', in D. Farran, S. Scott and L. Stanley, eds., *Writing Feminist Biography* (1986), 4–27.

5.1544 **Huff**, C., ' "That profoundly female and feminist genre": the diary as feminist practice', *Women's Studs. Q.*, 17.3 & 4 (1989), 6–14.

5.1545 **Israel**, K. A. K., 'Writing inside the kaleidoscope: re-representing Victorian women public figures', *Gend. and Hist.*, 2.1 (1990), 40–8. Uses the life of Lady Dilke to explore representations of women in the past.

5.1546 **Jelinek**, E., 'Introduction: women's autobiography and the male tradition', in E. Jelinek, ed., *Women's Autobiography: Essays in Criticism* (Bloomington, Indiana, 1980), 1–20.

5.1547 — *The Tradition of Women's Autobiography From Antiquity to the Present* (Boston, Mass., 1986). Wide-ranging study which argues that women's autobiographies are different in kind from those of men in their choice of subject matter, self image and style.

5.1548 — ed., *Women's Autobiography: Essays in Criticism* (Bloomington, Indiana, 1980). Essays examining the autobiographies of literary and politically active women in Britain and the United States. Discusses whether their writings are different from those of men.

5.1549 **Morgan**, D., 'Masculinity, autobiography and history', *Gend. and Hist.*, 2.1 (1990), 34–9.

5.1550 **Myers**, M., 'Harriet Martineau's autobiography: the making of a female philosopher', in E. Jelinek, ed., *Women's Autobiography: Essays in Criticism* (Bloomington, Indiana, 1980), 112–32.

5.1551 **Park**, J., 'Women of their time: the growing recognition of the second sex in Victorian and Edwardian England', *J. Soc. Hist.*, 21.1 (1987), 49–68. Examines criteria for recognising the eminence of women and whether such criteria are different for men through an analysis of Victorian biographical compendia.

5.1552 **Quilligan**, M., 'Rewriting history: the difference of feminist biography', *Yale R.*, 77, Winter (1988), 259–86.

5.1553 **Smith**, S., 'The impact of critical theory on

the study of autobiography: marginality, gender and autobiographical practice', *Auto/Biog. Studs.*, 3, Fall (1987), 1–12.

5.1554 **Spacks**, P. M., 'Selves in hiding', in E. Jelinek, ed., *Women's Autobiography: Essays in Criticism* (Bloomington, Indiana, 1980), 112–32. Compares the autobiographies of five women active in public life, including Emmeline Pankhurst.

5.1555 **Stanley**, L., *Feminism and Friendship: Two Essays on Olive Schreiner* (1985). Uses friendship networks to explore different approaches to the writing of feminist biography.

5.1556 — 'Biography as microscope or kaleidoscope? The case of "power" in Hannah Culwick's relationship with Arthur Munby', *Women's Studs. Int. For.*, 10.1 (1987), 19–32.

5.1557 — 'Moments of writing: is there a feminist auto/biography', *Gend. and Hist.*, 2.1 (1990), 58–67. Examines whether there is a distinct women's autobiography and whether a feminist auto/biography is possible.

5.1558 — 'Romantic friendship? Some issues in researching lesbian history and biography', *Women's H. R*, 1.2 (1992), 193–216.

5.1559 **Steedman**, C., *Past Tenses. Essays on Writing, Autobiography and History* (1992).

5.1560 **Walters**, A., 'Self image and style: a discussion based on Estelle Jelinek's *The Tradition of Women's Autobiography from Antiquity to the Present*', *Women's Studs. Int. For.*, 10.1 (1987), 85–93.

5.1561 **Winston**, E., 'The autobiographer and her readers: from apology to affirmation', in E. Jelinek, ed., *Women's Autobiography: Essays in Criticism* (Bloomington, Indiana, 1980), 93–111. Charts changes in the relationship between the autobiographer and her readers over time.

See also: 5.179; 5.374; 5.470; 5.876.

(ii) Diarists, letter writers and autobiographers

5.1562 **Abel**, T., 'The diary of a poor Quaker seamstress: needles and penury in nineteenth-century London', *Quaker Hist.*, 75.2 (1986), 102–14.

5.1563 **Alexander**, Z. and **Dewjee**, A., eds., *Mary Seacole: Wonderful Adventures of Mrs Seacole in Many Lands* (1984).

Autobiography of a black nurse in the Crimean War.

5.1564 **Bishop**, A., ed., *Chronicle of Youth: Vera Brittain's War Diary, 1913–1917* (1981).

5.1565 — *Chronicle of Friendship: Vera Brittain's Diary of the Thirties, 1932–1939* (1986).

5.1566 **Blodgett**, H., 'A woman writer's diary: Virginia Woolf re-visited', *Prose Studies: History, Theory, Criticism*, 12, May (1989), 57–71.

5.1567 — *Centuries of Female Days: Englishwomen's Private Diaries* (1989).

5.1568 **Britain**, I., ' "Two of the nicest people if ever there was one": the correspondence of Sidney and Beatrice Webb', *Hist. Studs.*, 19.75 (1980), 286–92.

5.1569 **Burman**, R., ed., 'Growing up in Manchester Jewry: the story of Clara Weingard', *Oral Hist.*, 12.1 (1984), 56–63.

5.1570 **Burnett**, J., ed., *Destiny Obscure: Autobiographies of Childhood, Education and the Family from the 1820s to the late 1920s* (1982). Includes some female autobiographies.

5.1571 **Caine**, B., 'Beatrice Webb and her diary', *Vict. Studs.*, 27.1 (1983), 81–9.

5.1572 **Clarke**, P., *The Governesses. Letters from the Colonies, 1862–1882* (1985).

5.1573 **Cobbe**, F. P., *The Life of Frances Power Cobbe, Vols. 1 & 2* (1894). Autobiography of the feminist and anti-vivisectionist.

5.1574 **Cole**, M., ed., *Beatrice Webb's Diaries, 1924–1932* (1956).

5.1575 **Colvin**, C., *Maria Edgeworth: Letters from England, 1813–44* (1971).

5.1576 **Cooper**, J. E., 'Shaping meaning: women's diaries, journals and letters – the old and the new', *Women's Studs. Int. For.*, 10.1 (1987), 95–9. Examines whether women's diaries form a discrete genre.

5.1577 **Cox**, J., ed., *A Singular Marriage: A Labour Love Story in Letters and Diaries* (1988). On the marriage of James Ramsay and Margaret MacDonald.

5.1578 **Davidoff**, L., 'On the diaries of A. J. Munby and Hannah Culwick', *Fem. Studs.*, 5.1 (1979), 87–141.

5.1579 **Davies**, M. L., ed., *Life As We Have Known It By Co-operative Working Women* (1931). Brief autobiographies written by working women.

5.1580 **Davis**, G. and **Joyce**, B. A., eds., *Personal Writings by Women to 1900: A Bibliography of American and British Writers* (1989).

5.1581 **Dawkins**, H., 'The diaries and photographs of Hannah Culwick', *Art*

Hist., 10, June (1987), 154–87.

5.1582 **Eden-Green**, W. and **Eden-Green**, A., eds., *Testament of a Peace Lover: Letters from Vera Brittain* (1988). Weekly pacifist broadsheets published in World War Two.

5.1583 **Foley**, W., *A Child of the Forest* (1974). Personal account of a miner's daughter from the Forest of Dean and her life in domestic service.

5.1584 **Forrester**, H., *Twopence to Cross the Mersey* (1981). First of several personal accounts of a girl's poverty stricken childhood in Liverpool in the 1930s.

5.1585 **Gawthorpe**, M., *Up Hill to Holloway* (Prebscot, Maine, 1962). Interesting personal account by a suffragette and socialist.

5.1586 **Heinzelman**, K., ' "Household laws": Dorothy Wordsworth's *Grasmere Journal*', *Auto/Biog. Studs.*, 2, Winter (1986–1987), 21–6.

5.1587 **Heron**, L., *Truth, Dare or Promise: Girls Growing Up in the Fifties* (1985).

5.1588 **Huff**, C., *British Women's Diaries* (New York, 1985).

5.1589 — 'Chronicles of confinement: reactions to childbirth in British women's diaries', *Women's Studs. Int. For.*, 10.1 (1987), 63–8. Based on nineteenth-century writings.

5.1590 — 'Private domains: Queen Victoria and women's diaries', *Auto/Biog. Studs.*, 4, Fall (1988), 46–52.

5.1591 — 'Writer at large: culture and self in Victorian women's travel diaries', *Auto/Biog. Studs.*, 4, Winter (1988), 118–29.

5.1592 **Hughes**, A., *The Diary of a Farmer's Wife, 1796–1797* (1980).

5.1593 **Hughes**, A. V., *A London Child of the 1870s* (1934).

5.1594 **Huxley**, L., ed., *Elizabeth Barrett Browning: Letters to Her Sisters* (1932).

5.1595 **Jelinek**, E., 'Disguise autobiographies: women masquerading as men', *Women's Studs. Int. For.*, 10.1 (1987), 53–62.

5.1596 **Jewish Women in London Group**, *Generations of Memories: Voices of Jewish Women* (1989).

5.1597 **Kenney**, A., *Memoirs of a Militant* (1924). Personal account by a working-class leader of the WSPU and friend of the Pankhursts.

5.1598 **Lensink**, J. N., 'Expanding the boundaries of criticism: the diary as female autobiography', *Women's Studs.*, 14.1 (1987), 39–53.

5.1599 **Lewis**, J., 'Re-reading Beatrice Webb's

Diary', *Hist. Workshop J.*, 16 (1983), 143–6.

5.1600 **McCrindle**, J. and **Rowbotham**, S., eds., *Dutiful Daughters* (1977). Reminiscences of working-class women.

5.1601 **MacKenzie**, N. ed., *The Letters of Sidney and Beatrice Webb, Vols. 1–3* (1978).

5.1602 **and MacKenzie**, J., eds., *The Diary of Beatrice Webb. Vols 1–3* (1982–4).

5.1603 **Mayall**, D., 'Rescued from the shadows of exile: Nellie Driver, autobiography and the British Union of Fascists', *Immigrants and Minorities*, 8, March (1989), 19–39.

5.1604 **Meier**, O., *The Daughters of Karl Marx: Family Correspondence, 1866–98* (1982).

5.1605 **Mitchell**, H., *The Hard Way Up: Autobiography of Hannah Mitchell, Suffragette and Rebel* (1968). Personal, now classic, account of a working-class socialist and suffrage campaigner.

5.1606 **Montefiore**, D., *From a Victorian to a Modern* (1927). Member of the Social Democratic Federation and the Women's Social and Political Union.

5.1607 **Pankhurst**, E., *My Own Story* (1914). Leader of the Women's Social and Political Union.

5.1608 **Payne**, K., ed., *Between Ourselves: Letters Between Mothers and Daughters, 1750–1982* (1984).

5.1609 **Pethwick-Lawrence**, E., *My Part in a Changing World* (1938). Socialist member of the Women's Social and Political Union who was expelled in 1912. Peace campaigner in WWI who continued feminist activities between the wars.

5.1610 **Richmond**, E., *The Earlier Letters of Gertrude Bell* (1937).

5.1611 **Rive**, R., ed., *Olive Schreiner: The Olive Schreiner Letters, Vol. 1, 1871–1899* (1988).

5.1612 **Sanders**, V., *The Private Lives of Victorian Women: Autobiographies in Nineteenth-Century England* (New York, 1989).

5.1613 — ed., *Harriet Martineau: Selected Letters* (1990).

5.1614 **Simons**, J., *Diaries and Journals of Literary Women from Fanny Burney to Virginia Woolf* (1990).

5.1615 **Stanley**, L., ed., *The Diaries of Hannah Culwick: Victorian Maidservant* (1984).

5.1616 **Thompson**, F., *Lark Rise to Candleford* (1945). Sensitive account of rural life in the late nineteenth century.

5.1617 **Thompson**, T., ed., *Dear Girl: The Diaries and Letters of Two Working Women, 1897–1917* (1987). Fascinating glimpse of the feminist movement and socialism through the eyes of two working women.

5.1618 **Tristan**, F., *Flora Tristan's London Journal, 1840* (1980).

5.1619 **Vincent**, D., *Bread, Knowledge and Freedom: A Study of Nineteenth-Century Working-Class Autobiography* (1981). A study of working-class autobiographies, male and female, which sheds light on family life.

5.1620 **Webb**, B., *My Apprenticeship* (1926). Wide-ranging autobiography which explores the influences on Beatrice Webb's choice of social investigation as a career.

5.1621 — *Our Partnership* (1948). An account of the Webbs' life, working together as investigators, writers and Fabians.

5.1622 **Whitbread**, H., ed., *I Know My Own Heart: The Diaries of Anne Lister, 1791–1840* (1988). Intellectual from Shibden Hall, Halifax, who reveals her love for other women.

5.1623 **White**, D. V., *D for Doris, V for Victory* (1981). Account of a woman's experiences in World War Two.

5.1624 **Whitehead**, J., ed., ' "A grain of sand": Ellen Terry's letters to Amey Stansfield', *Theatre R.*, 13 (1988), 191–220.

See also: 5.1014.

(q) WOMEN AS HISTORIANS

5.1625 **Berg**, M., 'The first women economic historians', *Ec. H. R.*, 45.2 (1992), 308–29.

5.1626 **Carroll**, B. A., 'Mary Beard's *Woman As A Force in History*: a critique', in B. A. Carroll, ed., *Liberating Women's History* (Urbana, Illinois, 1976), 26–41.

5.1627 **Chibnall**, M., 'Eleonora Mary Carus-Wilson, 1899–1977', *Pcdgs. Brit. Acad.*, 18 (1982), 503–20.

5.1628 **Davis**, N. Z., 'Gender and genre: women as historical writers, 1400–1820', in P. H. Labalme, *Beyond Their Sex: Learned Women of the European Past* (New York, 1980), 153–82.

5.1629 **Dodd**, K., 'Cultural politics and women's historical writing: the case of Ray Strachey's *The Cause*', *Women's Studs. Int. For.*, 13, 1/2 (1990), 127–37. Analyses *The Cause* within the context of liberal and feminist politics of the 1920s to explain why Strachey marginalises working-class women and militants.

5.1630 **Krueger**, C. L., 'The "female paternalist" as historian: Elizabeth Gaskell's *My Lady Ludlow*', in L. M. Shires, ed., *Re-writing the Victorians: Theory, History and the Politics of Gender* (1992), 166–83.

5.1631 **Sklar**, K. K., 'American female historians in context, 1770–1930', *Fem. Studs.*, 3, 1/2 (1975), 171–84.

5.1632 **Smith**, B. G., 'Seeing Mary Beard', *Fem. Studs.*, 10.3 (1984), 399–416.

AUTHOR INDEX